LAST ORDERS

AT THE

WALNUT TREE SHADES

By

Jude Gudgin

One or two names have been changed or omitted
so as not to cause any embarrassment or offence.

Although I have tried to tell the whole truth and
nothing but the truth, if I have made any small
factual errors – I apologise.

ISBN 978-0-9570806-0-7

Cover designed by Stephen Harper

Printed by Barnwell Print Ltd,
Dunkirk Industrial Estate, Aylsham,
Norfolk, NR11 6SU

Published by Jude Gudgin

WORLD
LAND
TRUST™

www.carbonbalancedpaper.com
CBP00010280311113908

By using Carbon Balanced Paper
through the World Land Trust on this
publication we have offset 1083kg of
Carbon & preserved 91sqm of
critically threatened tropical forests.

Carbon Balanced Paper. One of the most sustainable forms of communication that
will reduce your carbon foot print and promote CSR. www.carbonbalancepaper.com

CHAPTERS

CHAPTERS

PREFACE

I never had any intention of writing a book about our life in the pub, and after reading it you may wonder: should I have bothered?

Have I ever attempted anything like this before? No.

Am I any good at grammar? No.

Do I have an infinite range of vocabulary? No.

Wat is my speling like? Not very good - but thank God for spellcheck!

Throughout our 25 years as licensees, I kept every article and newspaper cutting published about us personally, and the Walnut Tree Shades in general. These were shoved in a box and left to gather dust. I sometimes wrote 'one liners' about various incidents, so if I ever looked back it would remind me of that particular story.

I compiled three enormous scrap books, inserting all the published articles, menus and photographs. It recalled all the memories and events - good and bad - and felt so significant, that I wanted to share the stories.

One day I sat down at my computer, surrounded by scraps of paper and thought I would type all the stories in detail, print them off and pass them onto our daughter Lucy. She could show them to her children when they were older, and share a little bit of history and an insight into their Grandad and Nana's life running The Walnut Tree Shades pub.

I started typing; I typed some more, then more, and couldn't stop. The memories came flooding back, so I continued typing. I decided to do some background research into regulations and laws, and, suddenly, my little project was escalating into a mammoth task.

As I typed, Chris began looking over my shoulder and read a chapter or two,

'Ooh Jude, there is an awful amount of swearing.'

'Yes there is, because you are the main culprit, and I'm telling the story exactly how it was.'

Eventually I finished typing. And the result is the story of our life, loves, hates, joys, sadness, exhaustion, exhilaration, fears and thrills at the Walnut Tree Shades.

If I haven't mentioned you I am very sorry, it's not because we didn't appreciate you and your custom.

We loved our years at the pub and have wonderful memories to treasure forever, but I have to say I'm enjoying retirement more. I am content with the simple things in life (and I should know being married to Chris) and don't need much to be happy.

Thinking about running a pub? What advice would I give? Would I suggest it was a good proposition? Well, read this first; then make up your own mind.

ONCE UPON A TIME

Firstly: for all those people who have never heard of Chris Gudgin: secondly for those who already know him, and wish they didn't, and finally: for the people who love him dearly, I will begin my tale with a short history of his life, so you have a general picture of the character and personality of the man who came to epitomise the Walnut Tree Shades itself.

Chris was born on 24th December 1946. His mother had a wicked sense of humour, so she called him Christopher Robin. (Good job my name's not Alice.)

He is an only child, but not a spoilt one. He says that Christmas morning was so exciting for him, waiting to see what Father Christmas had brought. Oh! it's an orange again - and a selection box if you were really lucky!

He has lived in Norwich, Norfolk all his life, going to the local school without getting into too much trouble during his school years, although on the last day of term, when he put a stink bomb under the teacher's chair and got caught, he did have an additional remark written on the bottom of his report in a different coloured ink stating: 'He tends to have lapses of irresponsibility.'

On leaving school at the age of 15, Chris went to work at Hubbard Bros., as a trainee fitter welder, learning the art of making cellar flaps, intricate iron stairways and a variety of metal work. It was a job he quite enjoyed and, after a few years, he was quite knowledgeable and extremely good at his job.

Unfortunately for me, even 30 years later, he still likes to point out gates he has made, and the complex ironwork involved. After at least 20 different references to the same gates, I really cannot pretend to be interested anymore.

As Chris reached the terrible teens in the 60's, the Mods and Rockers were in full swing. Chris was a Mod, wearing a Parka coat and riding his scooter, along with his mates, down to Yarmouth or Margate at weekends, to whichever place they thought the action might be.

The action to Chris meant having a fight somewhere. The weekend would be rather uneventful if they weren't thrown out of a club, or hadn't landed a few punches on someone, after having popped a few purple hearts and other assorted pills.

Chris always says the film Quadrophenia epitomises him and his life, (a shame, he doesn't look anything like Sting!) God, and he does love to reminisce over those days with his friends! Of all the trouble they used to get up to, of the time when............ yawn, yawn.

Chris was obnoxious in those days (or should I say, he was more obnoxious in those days). There was the time the police came to his work place to arrest him about a stolen bike wheel that just happened to be in his possession. Chris insisted he had found the wheel.

They decided to take him to the police station for questioning, firstly telling him to get the chewing gum out of his mouth, (Chris' idea was that chewing gum made you look really hard - sitting with one side of your mouth protruding up and down and your tongue trying to swirl the gum round so that it stays one side of your mouth making your head tilt and one eye sag down!)

1

Eventually, after some interrogation, they decided to let him off with a warning but only with instructions he must return to the station the next day to receive a reprimand from the Inspector, to which Chris answered,

'No way, I'm going to London tomorrow, I'll come the following day'.

However, Chris wouldn't leave it at that, making a point of telling the police as they had dragged him down to the police station, that they could drive him back to work.

'OK,' said the police, and put him in the car,

'But we won't take you back to work, we will escort you home, and while we are at it, we will have a word with your parents.'

So, Chris thinking he was being a smart arse with the police, ended up getting a terrible rollicking from both his parents, being banned from going away, and told to start growing up. This maybe was the turning point in his life.

Chris later started a part time job in a local pub in the evenings, and this was the start of his interest in the service industry.

He had many girlfriends and a fiancé at quite a young age, but by the time I met him he was 26 years old, had shagged many women (so he tells me!), and was beginning to be more responsible and settled, so after a two year courtship we were married on 5th September 1975.

Not long after Chris and I started dating, he had a bad car accident one Friday night out with the boys, and ended up with a broken arm in plaster for nearly six months, and so was unable to work.

During this time he got extremely lazy, and didn't want to do anything, or go anywhere. Luckily, a guy called Mike, who had just opened an American hamburger restaurant in Norwich asked Chris about his ideas and opinions about refurbishing a room above the restaurant to create a cocktail bar. He talked to Chris about him possibly running and managing the operation.

When Chris' arm had healed and the plaster removed, he returned to his old job as a fitter welder. However, his interest in making gates had long gone, so after several warnings from his boss, Chris was finally sacked for sitting on the toilet for 20 minutes reading the Sun newspaper.

In retrospect, this actually was the best thing that could have happened to him, as he went straight back to see Mike, and began working full time as manager of the Skid Row Cocktail bar, on the top floor above Captain America's Hamburger Heaven.

As the months went by, Chris became more experienced and knowledgeable with cocktails, constantly experimenting and creating new ones, attending exhibitions and setting up bars for various functions and exhibitions. Some of these were a total waste of time, involving driving a couple of hundred miles, creating a bar out of chipboard, with fancy material round the bottom to conceal the tables, only to find the stand sited at the wrong end of the exhibition where nobody bothered to venture. So, after unloading all the beer and spirits and setting up a masterpiece, taking about £30 all day, it all had to come down, loaded back into the van and driven 200 miles home!

As he was (still is!) such a popular character in Norwich, the Skid Row bar was always busy, and customers used to go there especially to see Chris. They loved to hear the abuse and sarcasm he would hurl at people, and watch him spinning the spirit bottles, (Tom Cruise eat your heart out!) People were amazed to see that someone this rude and dressed so scruffily, could be so good at creating and making cocktails.

Mike was tragically killed in a fatal car accident in 1976. Subsequently the bar and restaurant were run by Chris and two other managers until the business was taken over by Mike's brother-in-law a couple of years later.

Unfortunately, the new boss's ideas and policies were completely different from those of Chris, and there was definitely a conflict in opinions and personalities. The arguments gradually got more frequent, especially with Chris' forthright approach and this made the atmosphere very strained.

The stress caused Chris to get alopecia, resulting in large bald patches on his head. It was time to seriously consider a career move.

The next step was what? He did not know. All he did know, was that it was definitely time to leave that particular job.

A comment from Chris:
'Oh Jude, I sound like I was a real shit when I was younger. But, ok then, on reflection, yes I was!'

****

The life history of my childhood and teenage years seem relatively subdued, compared to Chris'.

I was born on 29th June 1954 in Sussex. I, like Chris am an only child, and again not spoilt. Well, I don't think so.

We moved from Haywards Heath in Sussex to Norwich when I was seven years old. Actually, I haven't got a clue why we came to Norfolk, except that we took a holiday on the Norfolk Broads. My parents fell in love with the area, and as they were both mental nurses, they transferred positions to a Norwich hospital.

I went to a secondary modern school, my parents 'making' me stay on that extra year to take exams and obtain qualifications, when all I resolutely wanted to do was leave school, get a job and earn some money.

However, that year turned out to be the most enjoyable of all my school days, and the best thing I could ever have done. I sat 26 examinations, including typewriting, bookkeeping, shorthand and the usual academic English and Mathematics, which were compulsory. At the end of the year I gained good results. (Who said parents knew nothing.)

I never seemed to get in trouble much at school, mainly because I didn't get caught. In fact, the Headmaster made me Head Girl in my final year, so I was really the 'little blue eyed girl' as far as the teachers were concerned, and couldn't possibly do anything remotely wrong. Even if a teacher stormed in the room demanding to know, 'Who was making that noise?' I would say it was me, but he wouldn't believe I could possibly be the culprit.

Fortunately, I was never caught smoking behind the bike shed or found partaking in the odd fumble and snog with a spotty faced teenager!

I left school at 16 years old to begin employment in a well known bank as secretary to the bank manager and doing cashier duties. This job lasted for about a year, before I began to get bored and felt I needed a change. I handed my notice in and went to work at the Chamber of Commerce as a secretary. My duties included going to quite high powered meetings to take the minutes in shorthand, and organising functions.

This job lasted about another year and again I wanted a change, so got a job with a car dealer as his secretary.

My office was a garden shed, set amongst the fleet of cars for sale. My jobs here entailed all the book work, collecting cars and even petrol pump attendant (before the days of self service) in the garage on occasions.

I was always quite quiet in those days, so much so, people used to take advantage of my timid nature, especially my boss.

If someone was entering the office he did not want to see, he would hide. On one occasion, for example, he spotted two men walking towards the door he recognised as bailiffs.

He hid under his desk, adjacent to mine, so when the bailiffs entered the office asking to see the boss, I had to tell them I was very sorry, but the boss was out and not expected back that day. All the time I could see him out of the corner of my eye, crouched down on all fours, looking like a naughty schoolboy. God, how stupid was I?

Another time, he asked if I would like to go to London with him for the day, as he had a car he wanted to sell at the car auction.

He told me that whilst he was at the auction he would drop me off in Knightsbridge, so I could go shopping for the day. I had instructions to meet him back at Liverpool Street Station at 5pm.

If the car was sold, we would return to Norwich by train. If not, we would travel back in the unsold car. I arrived at the train station at 4.30pm, in plenty of time to meet him. 5pm came and went, and so did the train.

6pm came and went, and so did the train.

By this time, I was starting to get rather worried and concerned, mainly because I had spent all my money on clothes.

My boss never did turn up but, fortunately for me, a friend of mine who lived in Norwich did, and paid for my train ticket home.

The next morning my boss reprimanded me in front of the mechanics for not going into work the previous day. I just stood dumbfounded. Back in the office when we were on our own, he told me he had gone to Liverpool Street station and I wasn't there (liar) and, me being the fool, never said a word. Wow, how I changed over the years.

After several boyfriends, I had a relationship with a guy called David, a good friend of Mike's from Captain America's. One evening, while out for a meal with David, Mike and his girlfriend, they began discussing a staff shortage for the next day. As I did not work on Saturdays, I offered to waitress in the restaurant if it would help, pointing out that I had never worked in the leisure business before. Mike was obviously desperate, as he took me up on the offer. This was the beginning of my life in the catering industry.

I couldn't have been too bad as a waitress, as I carried on working there for a couple of evenings a week, but still continued with my full day time job.

After a few more months, my relationship with David finished and, as it turned out, his best friend was Chris Gudgin.

One Saturday afternoon Chris came into Captain America's for a meal, after he had spent all lunch time in a Norwich city centre pub and, consequently, was pissed.

Every time I walked down the restaurant to serve customers and had to walk passed him, he would grab my bum. I was not impressed, and thought 'Whoever is that creep?'

He certainly was not the best looking guy I had ever seen. I suppose the only remotely attractive part of his anatomy was his bum; it was one of those chutchy bums that needed to be tweeted.

The girl I was working with on that shift had known Chris for years, and assured me he was a really nice guy, although at that point it did seem hard to believe. However, when he eventually left the restaurant after a few more beers, he handed me his telephone number on a scrap of paper and asked me to give him a ring some time.

I shoved it in my handbag and forgot all about it for several days, until one evening I was out with a girlfriend. It was an uneventful boring night, I thought,

'Why not, let's give this guy a ring? I've got nothing better to do,' and here began our courtship.

That first date, I discovered Chris was not the hard nut he seemed to be, but was kind, thoughtful and actually quite a nice guy when you got to know him, and yes, I did fancy him, especially his bum.

The day I took him home to meet my parents was extremely worrying for me, as I knew Chris would not put on any airs and graces for anyone, let alone my parents. What you saw, was what you got. My father was a man of very few words and very strict, so I wondered what his reaction would be. I needn't have been concerned, he actually spoke to this scruffy, long haired man in depth and afterwards said to me,

'You will be OK with him; he will always look after you.' (Those words have stayed with me for ever.)

That statement from my father was a huge compliment for Chris, as all through my years of growing up, I realised, my father was never wrong about anything. He didn't say much, but the words that came from his mouth were always words of wisdom.

When we got married, I gave up my day time job, and worked evenings as a waitress at Captain America's so my shifts coincided with Chris', until the birth of our daughter Lucy on March 6th 1978.

When Lucy was a baby, we were quite short of money, and I needed to earn a little extra to help towards the household bills, so I began making cakes and fruit pies and selling them to the corner shop. From this small venture, orders started to escalate for birthday cakes and wedding cakes and even to doing outside functions.

When I was later offered a position to cook all the food for a take-away outlet in Norwich, I could not refuse. I was able to work my own hours, be my own boss, do something I enjoyed, and earn some reasonable money at the same time, and that was where I remained until the business was about to be sold and I was wondering what my next step was going to be. At the same time Chris was grumpy at work. Neither of us realised at this point that our lives would be changing forever in the not too distant future.

****

IN THE BEGINNING

Our long term friend, Harvey, had been in the restaurant business for some ten years. His catering enterprise began by winning £1,000 on a premium bond and he opened a burger van in Norwich, which rapidly became highly successful. He later opened restaurants in Norwich and another in Yarmouth – all with an American theme and which all proved to be extremely profitable businesses.

He came to our house one evening with an idea he put to us about opening an American theme bar specialising in cocktails - a concept which had never been seen in a pub in Norwich before.

All we needed were the right premises. After looking at a couple of pubs in the city centre and outskirts, nothing gave us that feeling of butterflies in the tummy when you just know you have the right place – much the same as buying a house.

We also viewed the Walnut Tree Shades, which had been closed down and boarded up for several years in the 1970's. The place was in a dreadful state of dirt and decay and obviously squatters had been living there. The pub needed a lot of money spent to completely renovate it before it could possibly be opened; however, we were still interested in pursuing this proposition further.

The talks with the brewery in obtaining the lease continued for several months, but eventually it wasn't a viable proposal to take on, so we decided against it and would just have to get back to the drawing board. Not long after this, someone did take the property over. They managed to get the brewery to spend money on the building and the pub reopened and was up and running again, but it only stayed open for about 13 months. It was at this time we returned for another viewing and another consideration of the possibilities of the property.

The Walnut Tree Shades is situated in the heart of Norwich centre, very close to the Market Place. Many years ago it used to be known as a market pub, meaning all the market traders drank there and fought there, along with all the other rogues in Norwich. It was a pub with a reputation - a bad one.

The pub is located down a small alleyway; there is no garden, and no driveway, just a small car park which belongs to the shops nearby and an amusement arcade, which was in the process of being built directly opposite the pub and owned by one of Norwich's lovable rogues.

One end of the alleyway is sited directly opposite the market place and the other end is Castle Street, housing several retail outlets and leading to the castle itself.

To enter the pub there are two separate doors leading straight onto the alleyway.

On the ground floor is the pub, the first floor is the restaurant and the second floor is the flat where we could live.

It would mean moving out of our terrace house, which we decided not to sell, but rent out, just in case things didn't work out, and then at least we would have a roof over our heads.

Harvey was going to finance the project - just as well, as we didn't have any money. He would help with the setting up of the bar, consulting with us about the food and menus, and the interior design, but would then be a sleeping partner, leaving Chris and I to run the whole operation, but with Harvey's input on any business matters (as long as we didn't ask him to work behind the bar).

The deal was set up, the rent was agreed, it seemed astronomical at the time, set at £10,000 per annum for five years, decreasing with the amount of beer we sold. Hopefully, with a lot of hard work, this should finally equate to about £6,000 per annum.

The lease was signed, we were set to go.

Chris handed in his notice at Captain America's, and whilst working out his notice, he told just about everyone who came in the bar where he was going, and what he was going to do, thinking (hopefully) that a lot of people would come into our pub to see him.

Two weeks before we moved into the pub we decided we must have a holiday before starting our new venture.

Unfortunately, we didn't have much money to our names, as we were going to have to furnish the flat at the pub. However, we scraped just about enough to have a cheap fortnight in Greece with our daughter Lucy. The downfall was, we were very short of spending money, so going out to eat on holiday was going to cause a bit of a problem.

We used to find the little back street restaurants, glance through the menu to see what was cheap, then order two small meals between the three of us.

If it was a meal that Lucy, who was then 6-years old, really liked, then we went hungry. You can't see a young child go hungry - well you could, but she would only whinge for the rest of the night!

The whole holiday turned out to be one of the best family trips we had ever been on. We walked everywhere, never drank (well, maybe just an odd one), certainly never ate much, but with all things considered it does goes to show you don't need much money to have a good time.

That family holiday in Greece restored our batteries and gave us time to get accustomed to the idea of what lay ahead. We returned to Norwich fully revived, fired up, and ready for the start of our new lives which would be starting in a couple of days time.

On Tuesday, June 12th, 1984, we moved into the pub. As you have to pay rent from the day the lease commences when you receive the keys, there was no time to waste in getting the renovations started and getting money in the till.

The first job of the day was a trip to the court for a premises license, as without that, we would be unable to trade and be unauthorised to supply alcohol.

Before I continue with the tale of opening our pub, here's a little useless information regarding license requirements.

The concept and acts of licenses changed over the years to a much improved regime.

Instead of a premise license, which only permitted the individual to sell alcohol in the specified building, in 2003 applicants had to obtain a personal license which was issued for ten years. It is separate from the license that authorises the premises to be used for the supply of alcohol. This one allowed individuals to work from one premise to another. Anyone who wished to become a designated premise supervisor of a licensed property selling alcohol had to apply for one.

Before obtaining a licence, each individual had to complete a basic criminal check and then sit an exam to ensure that he was aware of the licensing law and the social responsibilities attached to the sale of alcohol.

Everybody already operating a licensed premise, automatically received a personal license for the cost of £37, and didn't have to sit an exam as they were granted 'grandfather rights.'

Just as well, as Chris would have been extremely pissed off, having to return to school to sit an exam after working and running licensed premises for many years.

We planned to open the doors of the pub on a Friday night. The restaurant we decided to leave for a few months until the bar was up and running efficiently.

Electricians, carpenters and decorators were all there first thing in the morning. Obviously this had been organised previously, otherwise we would have been right up the creek without a paddle.

We had to strip off all the crappy pictures, posters, fluffy animals and bamboo canes that were strewn over the walls. (Plus the odd bra and knickers that were dangling from lamps from the party the previous tenants had held the night before their departure).

Next, all the lights and shades had to come down, so wires were hanging everywhere. The carpenters were sawing and erecting bar stools and making seating areas. Deliveries of glasses, an ice maker, cooling units, fridges were arriving; the whole place looked like a building site.

It was a hot day, so obviously the doors were open. People were walking into the pub, climbing over planks of wood, tools, boxes anything else that was laying around, trying to get to the bar and then saying,

'Are you open?'

Chris' reply to them, 'What does it fucking look like?'

By Thursday night the place was starting to take shape. The new Tiffany lights were all up and the majority of the American memorabilia signs had been put on the walls. The original Wurlitzer Juke Box had been delivered, and most of the equipment was installed. So far so good.

Our deadline was Friday, and we had to open the doors at 5.30pm. We had been surviving on MacDonald's and coffee to keep awake for the past couple of days. Our day's work had been starting at 7am, and finishing around midnight.

We began to feel we were in a no return situation,

God, are we doing the right thing?

What are our lives going to be like from now on?

Will we be able to work together?

Will we be a statistical divorce number?

How will Lucy cope with being brought up in a pub?

Will we turn into alcoholics!?

All these notions and thoughts suddenly started getting out of control.

It was time to pull ourselves together, stop panicking about everything, and say:

Hang on a minute; this is what we want to do; what we have dreamed of; we're going to see it through.

On Friday morning we started the big clean up. It was beginning to look less like a building site and more like the vision we were hoping to achieve.

Behind the bar was thick with dust. However when that was cleaned and the various sized glasses were put on the shelves; it began to look like a pub.

All the workmen had finished, packed up and left, all the alcohol was delivered and on optics, the pictures were being nailed and screwed down, otherwise someone would try and steal them if they weren't secure. Suddenly, I had an awful panic, we had been so busy getting the pub renovated and ready for opening, there was just one small detail we had both forgotten, we didn't have any bar staff.

Not only that, I had done plenty of waitressing, but I had never pulled a pint or worked behind a bar in my life.

The only member of staff we kept on from the previous tenant was the cleaner Chrissy who was going to work Monday to Fridays; everyone else we weren't very keen on; they just didn't seem our sort of people.

So a few phone calls later, we managed to get hold of an old friend who said she would come and help out, and as an added bonus, she had worked behind bars before.

At 5pm. we had half an hour before the big opening. 'Did everything look all right?'

'Have we got all the right drinks we need?' (Hey, what would I know?)

Still, no time to think about anything now, other than to quickly shower, change and slap some make-up on. Maybe a bit more than I usually did, - I didn't want to look as knackered as I felt!

Chris, well he needed a shit, shave and shampoo, and that was him all ready to go. With a bit of luck he may have put on a clean pair of jeans.

At 5.30pm we opened the doors. Our hearts were beating a bit stronger than normal; all the excitement and adrenaline were kicking in. I don't know why, because there weren't any customers beating the door down.

Say nobody came in all night? We hadn't advertised in any papers. However, we did tell a lot of people, and Chris was very well known. But did they really care what we are doing? Or would their curiosity get the better of them?

We looked round the bar,

Did it look American?

Are there enough pictures on the wall?

Are the lights too bright, or too dim?

Have we ordered enough beer?

Do we have all the spirits that people will ask for?

Have we enough glasses?

Not that we were feeling a little apprehensive! Oh no, everything would be fine. Yes, it would be fine!

We needn't have worried. Hilary and John had come along with Margaret and Melvin, Paul and Snowy (with his dog).

More people arrived and I suddenly got an odd feeling. We didn't know who those people were, and for an instant, it felt that those strangers had just walked into our home uninvited, and I wanted to tell them to leave, to get out of my house.

I had to get my faculties straight, this was a public house, and anyone may enter. All those thoughts rushed through my minuscule brain.

Yes, we had got it right. If it felt like home to me, then hopefully that was the impression people entering for the first time would also get.

People were piling in. Most of them we knew and were giving us encouragement. This was helpful for me, as the first pint I pulled, ended up over me instead of in the glass. Well, I didn't expect it to come out that quickly!

Chris was in his element. He was shaking cocktails, not throwing and spinning the bottles, or putting all the crap in the glass like the umbrellas that get stuck up your nose, sparklers, and those little fluffy toys you always get in your drinks in Spain, he would rather make it properly, pour it in the glass, and get the money in the till.

The night was going well, the atmosphere electric. We knew the vast majority of people who came in the pub that evening were either customers from Captain America's, or many of our friends. It felt as if we were holding a big party, except this time we were taking money.

The night drew to a close. It was nearly 11 o'clock. Chris and I just looked at each other, and because of the telepathy between us knew what we each were thinking.

Yes, we had cracked it, and yes we were absolutely fucked.

Everyone had gone, the glasses all washed, the ashtrays were cleaned, drip trays emptied.

We cleaned the bar counter, and swept the floor. Why? We had a cleaner who would be in the morning, that's what we were paying her to do. But then again, we couldn't leave it in that mess, not on our first night. We had spent all that effort renovating the bar to look something special and unique, we just couldn't leave all those fag butts everywhere.

The doors were locked, alarm set, then upstairs to the flat for a coffee with a Baileys in, and then to count the money.

Wow, did we really take this much? If we carry on like this, then brilliant, but I think maybe tonight was an exception, we were just very lucky to have so many friends who came and supported us.

Tomorrow we would have to do it all again.

****

A framed 'photocopy' of a Beatle's concert ticket.
Although the picture was screwed to the wall in the bar,
several people tried to remove it thinking it was valuable!!

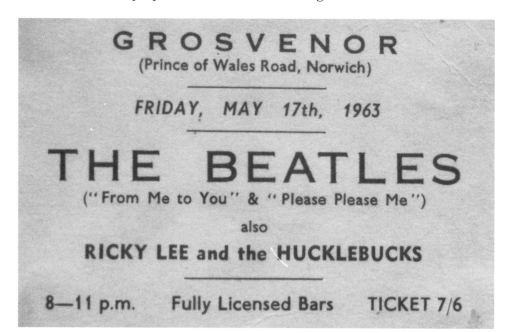

GETTING ACCUSTOMED

After the initial opening night, it was a case of realising our lives had changed forever. A routine would have to be established to enable the juggling of family life with a business. We were never naive in imagining pub life was going to be easy, but I don't think anybody can comprehend how much it takes over your whole life, and in the beginning, what a massive learning curve lies ahead.

Our 6-year old daughter, who was used to having undivided attention at home, also had to adapt to living in a pub. She was not able to go outside and play in the garden, or enjoy having local friends round to play – for her, those days were gone.

Her home now consisted of a top floor flat without any outside space and no neighbours nearby who had children to play with. However, at her tender young age, she was more excited about her new bedroom than having negative thoughts about her new life. I think we were more concerned, and knew it was still essential we gave her our time as much as possible.

The other family member who had to adapt to pub life after being used to roaming in our garden and beyond, and sit under a tree enjoying the sunshine, was our 8-year old cat, Pudin. Her life now consisted of sauntering up and down the corridor in our living accommodation or climbing out of the window onto the flat roof amongst the pigeons. She never ventured downstairs and had no wish to do so. In fact, she was totally lazy, spending most of her days sleeping, and so quite enjoyed her new life.

It transpired from a lady who apparently had perceptible psychic tendencies; and who knew the previous landlord; that an unhappy spirit had been in the flat.

We took her upstairs, to see if she felt any presence.

She did, but the spirit was happy, as someone was now living on the premises. Thank God for that! We certainly didn't want an unhappy ghost in our midst.

We never saw any visions personally, or heard any 'woooo's'. However, Pudin the cat, very occasionally around midnight, tore up and down the corridor, fur rigid, like something possessed. When these incidences first occurred we wondered what on earth she was doing. Eventually we put it down to the ghost making its presence felt. The large cupboard in the lounge was always excessively cold, - so it does makes you wonder.

One night in the restaurant, the chef's glass of drink flew off the shelf in the kitchen and landed several feet away. Another evening a glass went flying from the cabinet where the dessert glasses were kept.

No, the window wasn't open in the kitchen, no, the glasses didn't fall off, they flew. And there weren't any vibrations – ooh, spooky.

The restaurant remained closed for the first four months to enable us to concentrate on the bar aspect of the business. We were, however, offering bar food to customers during the lunch time sessions, and as we hadn't employed a chef yet, that was my job in the early days.

The hours of opening changed drastically over the years, but to begin with the law stipulated the bar had to close at 2.30pm until re-opening at 5.30pm. Thus began our daily work schedule of Chris working solo during lunchtime sessions behind the bar whilst I did the cooking and served the food.

Picking Lucy up from school and organising our meal was another drastic change to our life. Whereas we always used to have a cooked meal in the evening, this now proved to be impossible as Chris had to open the bar at 5.30 pm, so from now on our 'evening' meal was at 4pm.

Chris' subtle indication that he was required to open the bar at 5.30 pm came when he heard the yelling of some 'regulars' standing outside the pub waiting for a drink.

'Gudgin, come on, open the fucking bar.'

About four times a week the same regulars, after quickly downing a couple of beers, wanted to eat. We served food only at lunchtimes, but I did make an exception for these lads. Unfortunately, the time when they usually ordered food was when I had just got out of the shower and was still in my dressing gown.

That was no problem, I cooked their meals in the restaurant, still in my dressing gown and gave the signal so that they could come upstairs to collect their food.

I then joined Chris in the bar, completely clothed, along with the baby monitor (after putting Lucy to bed).

The first few weeks were quite exhausting; not only from getting accustomed to changes in our life, but also from all the jobs which still needed doing in the bar. There were more pictures to go on the wall; the bar also needed a few alterations to make it more workable. Music in the pub was a major factor, so acquiring more tapes (before the days of CD's) was essential.

Then, of course, there were all the mundane tasks of organising utility companies, insurance, banks, phones and other services - all vital factors in operating a business.

A crucial facet in running any business is the administration. The book work, wages (when staff are finally employed) and paying bills were all challenging jobs but proved to get easier as time went on.

Computers in the 80's were relatively unheard of for commercial use in small businesses or even as an essential commodity at home. Book work was written and applied by hand; advertising posters to be inserted in the windows were drawn free hand and written with a felt tip pen, so neat writing was requisite. Chris' diabolical handwriting meant he was never involved in the administration of the pub!

From employing no staff apart from a cleaner, it soon became apparent, as trade was rapidly increasing, that we needed some extra pairs of hands.

We began by employing Babs who had worked for Harvey in his restaurants for years. She could cook, waitress, do bar work, had managerial qualities, and she was a lovely person! She was an ideal candidate and proved to be a valued member of staff.

We employed a couple of bar staff to work weekend shifts; now it seemed our enterprise was really growing and we really were 'bosses'.

Throughout my working life, I had always been the employee or worked for myself; I had never been a 'boss' before. Having to tell people what was required of them, reprimanding them, complimenting them, attempting to be a decent boss so the work would get done, but not be a push-over needed to be learnt. This was another learning challenge which had to be conquered.

If you are unknown in the industry, and starting a business for the first time, it is often difficult to open accounts immediately with companies. They will still supply goods, but stipulate it has to be 'cash on delivery'. If there is money in the bank and a decent cash flow, then this system is fine. However, it is far more beneficial to buy, for example, the cases of beer, put the bill on account, and then sell the beer before you have to pay for it in 30 day's time.

As Harvey had been established in the restaurant industry for many years, with an excellent track record, and Chris with working at Captain America's for a long time, they both knew the majority of companies that would best suit our business for both the drinks and food, and could obtain the best prices.

As word got round that the Walnut Tree was open, the phone began to ring constantly, with representatives from various companies trying to promote their particular brand and keen for us to be a customer, or they just walked in the pub with their folders and samples hoping to win us over.

As the weeks went by, gradually a system and routine began to evolve and we didn't have to be in constant overdrive.

Once a week hygiene dictated a deep clean in the bar, shelves washed after being emptied of glasses and bottles, brass fittings polished, and equipment moved to clean behind.

Every day entailed renewing several light bulbs, on one of our 50 lights in the building.

Orders had to be phoned in for deliveries of cleaning products, food and beverages for the course of the week. This was a difficult problem to begin with, knowing how much to order; if it's not enough you run out, too much and it is negative equity; you need to know what drinks are popular, and what aren't.

Mondays seemed to be the favourite day for cold calling on the telephone. Numerous calls from utility firms trying to sell their gas or electricity, insurance companies wanting to give a quote in readiness for when the pub insurance is due for renewal and advertising agencies who are keen for you to spend hundreds of pounds placing an advert are just some of the phone calls we received weekly.

Often it was charities who want you to raffle a teddy bear in your pub.

'Why a bloody teddy bear?' – not really an enticing prospect to drinking customers in a pub - a case of beer for a prize would have been far more appropriate.

Then it might be a call from cleaning companies doing a really 'good deal,'- buy three cases of cleaning detergent and receive one free. With their extortionate prices, it's never a 'good deal!'

There was always a daily trip to Tesco to buy the burger rolls, bread, eggs, and other bits and pieces. Fortunately, it was only a couple of minutes walk away, as invariably something or other had been omitted and a second trip was necessary.

It took time to establish our weekly routine but gradually everything began to fall in place, customers were increasing and seemed happy with the unique atmosphere and ambience we had created at the Walnut. So we were feeling happier that our life in the pub was on the right track.

We would continue to basically work our butts off between Monday through to Saturday and then make sure we had a family day on Sunday when the three of us could spend quality time together before collapsing early to bed ready for the next week's onslaught.

After the mix between concerns, excitement and apprehension in the beginning, we were enjoying our new life as landlords in the licensed industry, but were under no illusion that many stories, trials and tribulations – good and bad were sure to transpire in the future.

In 1984 when we began our venture, we never envisaged we would remain in the Walnut Tree Shades for 25 years.

It wasn't actually 25 years; it was 24 years, 11 months and 2 weeks!

****

HISTORY

As my book is about our life in a pub, I thought it would be a good idea to throw in a few facts with regards to the history of the Walnut Tree Shades.

The Walnut Tree was built in the 17th Century and is a Grade II listed building. We are not sure how it got the name Walnut Tree Shades, one possibility which emerged was Gentleman's Walk, located at the end of the alleyway from the pub was once planted with Walnut Trees. Another, it was associated with cabinet makers.

Within the city walls there used to be extensive underground tunnels leading towards the cathedral and the Castle Museum and our pub was no exception. In the cellar of the pub was an underground tunnel, which had been blocked up many years ago, although we did briefly consider trying to dig our way through the tunnel to see how far we could get, but decided against that project!

Old Post Office Court where the pub is sited, once formed the entrance to a Tudor mansion, the home of Edward Rede, who was the mayor in 1521. It was this building that was later used as a post office in the 1840's which gave the name to the court.

There were three other pubs in close proximity to the Walnut Tree Shades, you didn't have to walk far to go to the next pub, it was a case of fall out of one and straight into the next.

Apparently, The Three Tuns and The Walnut Tree used to share the same outside toilet!

George Dady was the first recorded landlord at the Walnut Tree in 1830 which was classed as an unnamed licensed store selling wines and spirits. Because records show there are no ownership details, this leads us to believe it was a free house.

By 1839, the business was ran by his widow, Sarah Ann.

She was replaced by William Haylett Roe aged 35 by 1842, who adopted the pub name and was accordingly listed in Trades Directories.

William Roe died shortly afterwards, and by 1845 the licence was held by his wife, also called Sarah Ann. This was either a bizarre coincidence, or a very swift marriage.

By 1856 Sarah was aged 58 and 'Roe & Sons' were now holding the licence. This possible 'company' gives the impression of a family concern still handling the off-licence business. That impression is reinforced by the surprise return of Mrs Dady in 1859.

Sounds to me there were plenty of shenanigans going on in the pub during that time!

By 1864 the pub is listed as empty.

Mrs Dady's departure seemed to have ended the merchant era. It is plausible that the same lady was the driving force in the business, and outlived two husbands.

In 1867 the pub was taken over by Bullard's Brewery.

Edmund Cox was landlord from March 1867, followed by his widow, Mary Ann, from August 1878 to December 1883. From 1883 to 1938 there were another 17 landlords at the Walnut.

In 1938 The Landlord during World War II was Henry Johns. We received the following information from a distant relation of a customer who used to frequent the pub during those times.

The pub was very popular with US servicemen who were based in nearby Hethel, and Johns, along with his wife, were described as 'wonderful people'.

The customer, Bob, was apparently shot down during the war; when he recovered and returned to Hethel, and back to the pub for drinking sessions, the Landlord presented him with a poster, which illustrated a picture of a Walnut Tree on the corner with writing underneath, which had been displayed on the wall of the pub.

It read:-

A Woman, A Dog, and A Walnut Tree
The more you beat em
The better they be.
But down the Court in Castle Street,
There's a Walnut Tree you cannot beat
Because on Bullards Beer there's always a glut,
And the Landlord is a bit of a nut
Cosy Smoke Room – Bar and Snug
And the glorious sight of a well filled Mug
Whisky and Wines and Ales galore
And jovial folks with whom to jaw.
And at 10pm when it's time for kip
Here's a useful war time Tip.
'Go to bed hopeful, wake up thankful'

Someone had also pencilled in the bottom of the poster
'God save the King.'

The Walnut Tree in the 60's was classed as a Market Pub. Because it was located so close to the market place, it was able to open for extended hours on a Saturday until 4pm as opposed to the normal 2.30pm. This was to enable the market traders to have a drink or two after they had closed their stalls. The pub was one of half a dozen drinking establishments within a mile radius of the market place that had this privilege. However, this added benefit came with problems. The customers from the Walnut Tree and the Kings Head on the corner of Old Post Office Court were renowned for having fights and there was constantly trouble both inside the pubs and out on the street.

The market traders were obviously there, but alongside them were the mods and rockers who had been drinking all lunchtime and who then descended on the pubs with extended opening hours for a guaranteed fight.

I can remember when I was a child and used to go to Norwich on Saturdays with my mother, we would never walk anywhere near the Walnut Tree or the King's

Head because of the reputation both places had. I would never have thought then, that one day in the future I would actually be the landlady of the Walnut.

In the late 1960's the pub was home to a folk club, with visiting star performers, such as the Copper Family utilising the large upstairs room. (The room we used as the restaurant).

The names of the breweries who owned the Walnut Tree Shades changed a considerable amount of times from Bullard's Brewery, to Watney Mann, to Manns & Norwich Brewery, Norwich Brewery, Inntrepreneur, Criterion, Unique Pub Co., Grand Metropolitan, Spring Inns, Phoenix Inns and by 2001 onwards it was known as Enterprise Inns.

During our time at the pub we were owned by all of the above except Bullard's Brewery and Watney Mann, in fact the name of our landlord seemed to change so frequently, we used to forget who we were owned by sometimes.

In the Norwich Brewery days before we were there, the pub was used to trial new brews, and was probably the first pub to sell the disgusting Star Light Bitter (a low alcohol draught bitter).

The Walnut Tree was also the first pub to sell Budweiser on draught in Norfolk whilst we were the landlords, and was eventually the biggest selling outlet of the beer in the area.

Leonard Wales was landlord from July 1970, and finished sometime around 1975 when the pub was then closed for a time until there was a quick succession of three to four landlords from September 1977.

The pub had been closed for nine months before Nigel Hoare and Alan Armitage took over in 1978 and was then owned by Norwich Brewery.

Before the opening local craftsmen did a lot of restoration work, to bring the building and interior back to its original Victorian standard.

Some of the original furniture remained, as well as the impressive window screens, the oak backing of the bar, and advertising logos. All the furniture and features were still there when we took over in 1984 and remained when we left in 2008.

There was a spacious lunchtime restaurant, and rather than the conventional juke box, music was played on request, not like our customers who had no choice when or what music was played, if they didn't like what was booming out – tough.

The grand opening of the pub in 1978 was attended by Norwich City goalkeeper, Roger Hansbury.

In 1981 The pub was used by Anglia Television to film an episode of 'Tales of the Unexpected' entitled 'Blue Marigold' starring Toyah Wilcox.

After Nigel Hoare and Alan Armitage relinquished their license, the pub was closed for a further two years before it was taken over by David Turnbull.

The Brewery and David spent a lot of money on creating a restaurant on the first floor and refurbishing the bar. However he was only there for just over a year before he surrendered his licence.

As the saying goes, 'The rest is history'
We took over in June 1984.

In a list of licensees since the Walnut Tree Shades was built and open for business, we were the longest serving of them all – wow.

Not only did the Walnut Tree Shades operate with many different licensees all ensuing their own individual formulas for running a drinking establishment, but since the pub was first built and operating, the surrounding area and population was changing and increasing with time, making differences to trade and the way businesses were run.

At the time the pub was built, Norwich had a population of around 21,000 and was probably the largest provincial town in England. In 1870 it is alleged there were two pubs for every day of the year, with a few left over. By 1939 there was one pub for every day of the year. By 2008 the number of pubs in the city had drastically reduced.

During the 18th century, brewing became increasingly important and Norfolk malting barley was considered the best in the country.

By 1801 the city had six large breweries, supplying local needs, as well as sending beer to London for sale.

Inns and Taverns have always been an integral part of the history of Norwich's Market Place, known as Gentleman's Walk (located at the end of the pub alleyway). But in the 1920's and 30's many taverns were either destroyed or demolished to make way for the new city hall and market place which is now one of the largest open air markets in the UK, and has been responsible for much of the city's success.

Gentleman's Walk was closed for access of traffic in the 1980's and pedestrianised to be more in-line with Europe, and is now the busiest street in Norwich. However, in the evenings it is a different matter. It used to be packed with cars parked along the street and people walking – now it is often deserted and looks like a ghost town.

The opposite end of the pub alleyway is Castle Street. It used to be called 'The back of the Inns' getting its name from the several inns which were situated on Gentlemans Walk, the yards of which ran all the way through to that back lane.

During the late 80's Castle Street was also pedestrianised which stopped the access of motor vehicles. It did however, take them a lot longer than they originally anticipated, as they were only allowing access at certain times of the day. This would have made life extremely difficult for us residing at the pub, and not having the accessibility to come and go whenever we pleased, especially picking our daughter up from school.

We gave the council a choice. They either granted us a permit to enable us to drive in or out of the pedestrianised area at any time of day or night – or, they could supply us with a helicopter and landing pad as another means of transport. They decided against a flying machine, and gave us permits quite rapidly, as they were unable to display the new signs for prohibiting traffic until we were satisfied we would be granted access at all times.

During the 19th century the population of Norwich increased to over 80,000 in 1871. The city began to expand beyond its walls and the living conditions were somewhat unhealthy; with no supply of clean water there were epidemics of cholera and various other deadly diseases.

In the early 1990's the site of the old cattle market was excavated to build the Castle Mall shopping centre, an ultra modern scheme, erected on several levels, which at the time was the biggest site in Europe.

The 21st century has seen the landmark Forum building, housing the Millenium Library and a huge variety of shops.

During our period spent at the Walnut Tree Shades we were always aware of how many changes had taken place in close proximity to the pub and nearby surroundings, but that's nothing compared to the different kind of life and surroundings that previous licensees of our pub would have encountered.

One of our main problems in running a pub was the constant red tape and regulations involved, but we certainly never had to deal with wars, black-outs, bombings, disease, unhealthy living, debauchery, let alone the horse poo which was dropped on the streets!

If the walls of the pub could speak, I'm sure there would certainly be some incredible tales to be heard whether from travellers, prostitutes or the wealthy gentry!

****

A LESSON IN MAKING COCKTAILS

- *Always use good quality spirits.*
- *It is important to measure everything.*
- *Garnish the drink when appropriate.*

When to shake and when to stir cocktails:
- *Shake cocktails when they include fruit juices, cream liqueurs, syrup, egg or dairy.*
- *Place ice cubes in the shaker first. This will chill the shaker and cool the liquids as you add them.*
- *Use 5-6 ice cubes for one drink. When making two drinks at once use less ice to make room in the shaker.*
- *Don't overfill the shaker. Give the ingredients plenty of room to move around.*
- *Shake and shake and shake vigorously to a slow count of ten.*
- *Don't add fruit or fizzy drinks to the shaker but to the glass after straining.*

- *Stir cocktails that use distilled spirits or very light mixers. This is a more gentle technique than shaking, as many gin and whiskey cocktails are stirred because shaking is said to 'bruise' the spirit.*
- *Fill a glass just over half way with ice.*
- *Add liquors and other cocktail ingredients.*
- *Put a bar spoon (a long handled spoon will do) into the glass and stir it round and up and down for about 20 seconds.*

See – it's easy!

Please remember to always drink responsibly.

LAWS

From 1552 onwards, anyone who wanted to sell ale had to apply for a licence at the Quarter Sessions or the Petty Sessions. These were originally meetings of magistrates who met together four times a year (hence the name) to dispense justice and discuss the administrative needs of the county. In addition, alehouse keepers had to declare that they would not keep a 'disorderly house' and that they would prohibit games of bowls, dice, football and tennis.

In 1617, the requirement for licences was extended to inns. In addition, between 1570 and 1792 licences could be obtained directly from the Crown (from 1757 from the Stamp Office) rather than from local magistrates.

The licence act of 1753 required each licensee to produce certificates of good character, usually signed by parish notables, before they would be granted a license.

Licencing Laws prior to 2005 were first passed in response to the 'Gin Epidemic' in the 18th Century. Initially laws simply required that a responsible person be made the 'licensee of the pub' in order to overlook the establishment, and to ensure that drunkenness and debauchery did not exist.

The system was changed in 1828 with a new Alehouse Act, which controlled anyone who wanted to sell any kind of liquor by retail.

From the late eighteenth century breweries were increasingly buying pubs to increase their property portfolio, and putting in managers or licensees to run the outlets, but with strict stipulations. They had to buy all liquor and minerals through the brewery. These pubs were known as tied houses, those which remained free of any tie were free houses.

By the 1980's, about 90% of public houses were tied to one brewery or another; we were one of those pubs, although we did have the added advantage of only being tied to purchasing beer from the brewery and free to obtain all wine, spirits and minerals from our choice of distributor.

From the 19th to 20th century, licensing hours were gradually imposed, with blanket restrictions being applied throughout the UK and during world war one. These restrictions stipulated that a pub could only open between 12pm – 2.30pm and 6.30pm to 9.30pm. These laws served to try and stop soldiers and munition workers from getting too drunk and being unable to work to their best ability in serving the country during the war.

These laws were relaxed in later years, allowing pubs to open until 11pm Monday to Saturday and 10.30pm on Sundays.

Extensions were also granted on bank holidays. At the beginning of each year all licensees received a list which displayed all the extended hours of opening which was signed, stamped and approved by the council.

This formally stamped extension list caused a problem for us on one occasion. It was an August bank holiday Saturday, the sun had been shining all day – (for a change) and the Walnut had been busy all day and right through into the evening. People were standing inside and spilling outside the pub enjoying the warm night.

Chris was outside collecting glasses when a policeman marched up to him.

'You're breaking the law by serving after time, and you could be prosecuted.'

'What the fuck are you talking about; I'm licensed until midnight because it's a Bank Holiday and its only 11.15pm.'

'You don't have an extension, so you can stop serving now and I will be reporting you.'

Chris was fuming,

'You can just wait there while I go and get the information print out of all the extensions I have been granted from the council.'

By the time Chris had retrieved the list displaying all the extended hours of opening for bank holidays for the year, the policeman had begun to walk away from the premises.

Chris caught up with the policeman and passed him the list, demanding he took a good look at the official document. The policeman just glanced at the sheet, then glared at Chris,

'It's wrong, and you should have closed at 11pm.'

He continued to walk away and obviously, because we were right, we never heard any more from him.

On August 22nd 1988 new laws were introduced enabling drinking establishments to remain open at any time between 11am and 11pm, instead of previously having to close the doors between 2.30pm and 5.30pm.

Rural pubs often declined the opportunity to open throughout the day as it wasn't a viable proposition and wouldn't increase their trade. As far as we were concerned, the city centre pubs and many on the outskirts welcomed the extra hours and were going to take full advantage of the new law.

When we took the pub over in 1984 our licence enabled us to open the doors for business at 10.30am, unfortunately we soon discovered the only drinkers we attracted at that time were tramps – smelly ones at that, so we were constantly refusing them entrance.

After a few weeks we decided to open at 11am, hoping that would distract them, or maybe that they would find another drinking establishment to descend upon. Unfortunately that didn't work either, so after several more weeks of banning tramps and smelly people, we opened at 11.30am. This proved successful and the problem was resolved.

With the original closing hours at 2.30pm in the afternoon, we found that by the time customers had left the pub and we had cleared all the glasses away it was approximately 3.15pm, and the law stipulated we were unable to re-open again until 5.30pm.

We embraced the idea of been able to remain open during the afternoon with the extended new hours. We required only one member of staff to work during the new opening hours and would be able to take far more money than the cost of the bar person's wages during that time.

People no longer had to rush their drinks at lunchtime, especially on Saturdays or Sundays, when the vast majority of workers have time off. It enabled them to drink more sensibly, rather than feeling obliged to get as many drinks inside them as they could which contributed towards 'binge drinking.'

During the winter months with the old law, we needed the heating on all day; the building still had to be kept warm even during the closure period in the afternoon, so consequently with the new opening times it wasn't costing us any extra for fuel.

In 1994 Sunday trading was legalised for shops, although it didn't make a vast difference in town centres to begin with, as many had broken the law for years and been open for business on Sundays anyway. Over the next few years, more and more shops opened, until the city centre attracted as many people on a Sunday to do their shopping as on any other day of the week.

On 7th August 1995 Sunday licensing laws were relaxed to allow all day opening for pubs and other places selling alcoholic beverages.

Legislation meant pubs could open from noon to 10.30pm without having to lock their doors between 3pm to 7pm as before.

This never affected us as we never opened on a Sunday anyway. Even though Norwich was sufficiently busy enough for us to warrant opening our doors for food and drink, we always felt our sanity was far more important than increasing our turnover, and so we had the complete day off.

The only Sundays throughout the year we ever opened were in December when Norwich was busy with people embarking on their Christmas shopping. So we forced ourselves in to work and opened between the hours of 12pm and 4pm serving food and drinks.

We opened with a skeleton staff consisting of a chef and one waitress and they weren't too happy at coming into work either - we always had to beg someone to relinquish their day off. However, we always tried to put a smile on for the customers whilst we were open and because it was a Sunday we all felt a vodka and tonic or a lager during the afternoon would help the situation. Counting the money at the end of the day definitely put a smile on our faces and made the day worthwhile.

The Labour government fought hard to introduce new licensing laws amid opposition from the tabloid press, Liberal Democrats, the Conservative Party and even the police. After two years of debating, new laws were finally implemented, coming into effect on November 24th 2005. The laws allowed for local authorities to take more control of granting licences to drinking establishments rather than going through the courts.

It wanted to reflect the policy in the rest of Europe. It was hoped that, in doing so, binge drinking and the crime that often relates to it would lessen. Their idea that this would later lead to a continental style pavement café/bar culture was excellent in theory but in practice it was a different story, as many businesses who applied for a licence to have tables and chairs outside on the pavement were being declined.

Many people thought this new policy was a ridiculous idea. They believed that it would lead to more trouble and violence on the streets with excessive drinking, people running amok and town centres becoming no-go areas at night. It was portrayed in the press that the term 24-hour drinking, would mean hordes of people drinking constantly for 24 hours.

These laws were often referred to as 24-hour drinking laws. Pubs, clubs, supermarkets and restaurants all had to apply for extensions to their existing licensing agreements. A licence could then be granted for opening for any period of time during the 24-hour period, provided they closed for a minimum of one hour to clean their premises. In reality very few establishments opted to open long hours, the new law just allowed more flexibility.

To obtain extensions on our existing license came at a cost to us and every business selling alcohol. The pages and pages of forms which arrived from the council all had to be filled in and returned by a specific date. They were so complicated and trying to obtain information and get questions answered about certain points on the form was proving difficult.

Companies had sprung into circulation and were constantly telephoning to try and persuade landlords to allow them to fill in the forms because of their complexity; if paperwork wasn't done correctly, the council might not grant the new licence. Of course this came at a cost – an astronomical fee.

One Sunday, Chris and I attempted to fill in the twenty pages of information required. We moaned constantly, because at this period in time, we had the pub on the market to sell, and so had no interest in opening for 24 hours. In fact, it was increasingly difficult opening the amount of hours we did already, let alone extending them. However, it was important to try and decipher the best options for the next tenant.

Attempting to apply for the whole 24 hour opening was a decision we wavered on. It was unlikely that many establishments would be granted the whole 24 hours opening, so to avoid being refused our licence and then having to re-apply with the possibility of more problems arising, we opted for extended hours to 2am.

We had to think of every conceivable idea that a new licensee in our pub may want to promote. It could be sports, when they might want to open at obscure times for certain events; they may want to serve breakfast and so need to open early in the mornings, or to have performers and entertainers, or live music every day and evening; special occasions and bank holidays may all require longer opening hours: the list went on and on.

The questions and problems the forms created were far too difficult for us to attempt to fill in, to ensure that we were taking the right route. So eventually, we had to eat humble pie and make an appointment to see a solicitor and get him to fill in the incomprehensible forms. This privilege cost £2,500, an amount of money we certainly felt loath to part with, but we did obtain our license for extended hours, giving us the benefit of being able to open until 2am.

When the new licensing laws came into force and we were able to stay open longer in the evening, we noticed that customers still left around 10pm if they were going onto a nightclub, forgetting that the time factor was now no longer a problem. Pubs and clubs were open much later; it took customers quite a while before they got accustomed to the change.

During the old law of closing at 11pm our pub, along with probably every other pub in the country, used to have occasional 'lock-ins' when regular customers stayed behind for a late drink. This made them feel special at being allowed to stay and have a drink with the landlords after time.

As soon as the new law came into operation we continued to close at 11pm during the first half of the week, but would remain open if the bar was busy, especially at the week-ends. It soon became apparent with regular customers that, now they were allowed to drink legally, a lock-in was no longer necessary; the novelty value had gone and they often left the bar a lot earlier than they ever did during the old licensing laws.

The new licensing hours were extremely beneficial to us and did increase our turnover; although in the evenings, we did notice people were starting to come out later because there was no rush to leave the pubs by 11pm. The nightclubs were remaining open until 6am but also, at the end of the day, people only have a certain amount of resources to spend on a night out.

On 16th November 2004, a public health white paper proposed a smoking ban on almost all public places. This would be phased in gradually until there was eventually a total ban and penalties would be enforced.

There was a huge amount of tabloid press regarding the future smoking ban in pubs and clubs; on how businesses were expecting a downturn in trade. People would probably begin to stay at home more; jobs would inevitably be lost in the tobacco industry and also in the leisure industry.

Chris was asked his opinion by the tabloid press on smoking in dining areas and what system he operated for accommodating non-smokers in our restaurant.

Published in the local paper was his reply: 'If a customer comes into our restaurant and asks to eat in the non-smoking area, I don't tell them we haven't got one because our entire restaurant is a smoking area, I just sneakily remove the ashtray and seat them down at the table.'

After the weeks of tabloid complaining and opinions for and against smoking, it was inevitable that the law was going to be passed in the future by the government no matter what people's views were.

July 1st 2007 introduced the new law, making virtually all enclosed public places and workplaces in the UK smoke-free. The idea was to ensure a healthier environment so everyone could socialise, relax, travel, shop and work free from second-hand smoke saving thousands of lives a year.

The new smoke-free law was enforced by local councils who would fine anybody flouting the rule. It stated that the person with management responsibility is legally responsible for preventing smoking in his premises.

Smoking in premises came with a fixed penalty of £50.

Failure to display 'no smoking signs' was a £50 fixed penalty.

Failing to prevent smoking in a smoke-free premise came with a fine of anything up to £2,500.

With the smoking ban in all public places, the face of pubs was set to change beyond recognition over the coming years.

On the first day of 'no smoking' we wondered how many minutes it would be before a customer had to be reprimanded for lighting up a cigarette inside the pub. Amazingly nobody did. In fact, people were automatically going outside for a smoke.

However, the topic of conversation at the bar by customers moaning about not being able to smoke anymore in pubs got so monotonous that we put a sign up which stated if anyone was caught talking about the 'no smoking ban' they would be fined 50p. and all the money collected would be for charity. We collected nearly £100 in the first few weeks.

Chris and I both smoked and the majority of staff did as well, so this caused some initial problems as to when and where we could all smoke.

The restaurant staff wanted to be allowed to smoke on the fire escape, which I said was unacceptable, because the restaurant would be unattended and they wouldn't be able to see or hear the customers if they required attention.

One of the chefs I employed was particularly agitated with me, because I made him put on a different jacket other than his chef's whites if he wanted to go outside for a smoke, and seemed to blame me for the whole smoking ban because he was unable to light up as often as he used to.

After a short period of time, we all found a routine of being able to nip outside for a quick cigarette when we got a chance. And in a way the ban made us all cut back on our nicotine consumption, especially if it was raining or cold outside.

The days of 'lock in' drinks for customers were by now a distant memory. Now the regular customers who smoked stayed behind for a 'lock in cigarette.' However, we did have to be vigilant who was allowed this luxury, because neither the customer, Chris, nor myself, wanted to be fined for being in violation of the law.

Unfortunately, new smells were developing during opening hours in the bar, especially on warm summer days – farts and body odour. If Chris noticed, or should I say smelt it, as to who the culprit was, he got the air freshener and sprayed it deliberately close to the smelly person, just to make them feel a little embarrassed. Even having the doors open still did not deflect from the new smell which had arrived in the pub.

Our trade did slacken off to begin with; especially in the restaurant lunchtimes, since we were, even prior to the new law, one of the few eating houses that did allow diners to smoke. This therefore attracted a number of office workers and smokers on their lunch breaks, simply because it was possible to sit in comfort, and have lunch and a cigarette before they returned to work. After a time, people did get used to the idea and gradually began returning, because the law was universal and nowhere allowed smoking.

English pubs have always contained an aroma of a beer and stale smoke since the beginning of the traditional boozer. Times were changing; drinking establishments were spending money on refurbishments, special outside spaces with heaters were being erected and seating was put in to cater for smokers.

Decorating was taking place on interiors to cover the nicotine stains which had discoloured the paint work; new carpets were being laid inside pubs as the days of cigarette burns covering the entire area were gone forever and, finally, ashtrays had disappeared and the smell of stale tobacco was diminishing.

Needless to say, we didn't change anything at the Walnut other than take the ashtrays off the tables!

****

INTERVIEWING STAFF

Interviewing staff changed considerably over the years. Originally, in our early days at the pub, the employer was able to ask all kinds of personal questions to potential employees, such as their age and marital status, if they had any children, or if they were planning to start a family in the future. (Obviously this question didn't concern the male interviewee); what were their reasons for leaving their previous employment? The list went on and on.

If you didn't like the look of someone when going through the interview process, it was quite feasible to just point out you didn't feel they would be suitable for the position applied for, and didn't have to give a reason.

Interviewing changed drastically as the years passed by. The days were gone when you could virtually tell someone to piss off – in a polite way of course, and to stop wasting time. They obviously didn't want a job and most certainly were not suitable applicants. Now every word uttered had to be politically correct.

During the latter years we were unable to ask their age, which is a real problem when you have to be 18 or over to work on licensed premises. If they had any disability you had to make allowances in the work place for them, which was fine and I didn't have a problem with that. However, someone who was unable to read or write, or unable to carry or lift items, or communicate with the public to name but a few, would find it impossible to work in our small business and it wouldn't be fair for the employee involved.

There are a number of ways of advertising to obtain staff. Putting a poster in the pub window or toilets, in the local paper, where you were able to advertise for three consecutive nights for the price of two – it certainly didn't feel free.

The days before computers were used for job hunting and advertising, there was also the option of placing an advertisement in the Job Centre. Because of all the rules and regulations, you were not allowed to stipulate on the advert that you required a waitress, or a bar maid.

OK, so I required a waiting person or a bar person and, of course, I would employ a male; no, of course I'm not racist, and no, I didn't mind if they had a disability.

So with our advert in the Job Centre, we received several phone calls, saying they had suitable applicants enquiring about the job. Great, so send them along to see me.

Their offices, where prospective employees went seeking work, was about 10 minutes walk away. Oddly enough, the majority of time, applicants got lost walking from the Job Centre to the pub, or evidently decided they didn't want a job after all and didn't turn up.

One lady did arrive from the Job Centre along with her husband. She was applying for the waitress/er job. Every question I asked the women, the man kept butting in, and answering the questions for her. Eventually, I started to get a bit pissed off, so asked him,

'Who actually wants the job, is it you or your wife?'

To which he replied, 'My wife cannot speak very good English, so I need to translate for her.'

So I presumed the husband would have to be super glued to her while she was working so he could translate. I didn't even bother enquiring as to whether she could write in English – doubtful.

That was the end of her; the Job Centre received a very irate phone call, telling them that they were wasting my time and theirs by sending someone to be employed as a waitress who couldn't speak English.

The next hopeful who arrived was a youngish girl who was scruffy and wearing a woolly hat. Luckily I spotted the green hair sticking out from under the rim. Another quick interview swiftly completed. Thank you and goodbye.

That girl had tried to hide her hair: However, the next one was unable to disguise her black eyes, black eye shadow and bruises, or the various piercings through her nose, lip, and eyebrow, the tattoos and to finish it all off, some nice black nail varnish to compliment the skull and crossbow rings on every finger. (She probably had bells on her toes too). It was good-bye to her.

The girl with bright pink spiky hair, stud and earring in every conceivable place possible, very short dress and boobs nearly out (so what's wrong with that? - Nothing, except she weighed about 20 stone) and her dress was dirty and split.

She didn't get the job either.

An applicant arrived in the hope of gaining evening bar work. However, he had been tagged by the police for criminal offences, and was on curfew between the hours of 7pm to 7am. Consequently he was unable to work between those hours for the next three months. Another quick interview.

Frank will always stay embedded in my mind. He was of an ethnic origin. He came to be interviewed for the chef's position. During the interview he came across as a definite primadonna.

He had been there, done it, and I imagine got the teeshirt, and allegedly had worked in many top class restaurants – well, that's what he told me,

'Just leave me in charge and I will turn your restaurant around, I will make your takings increase dramatically. I will change the menu. You pay me a lot of money though.'

I didn't want the menu changed, and I liked the restaurant as it was, and he certainly would not be getting a lot of money, not the salary I paid.

So I told him he was obviously far too qualified for our small enterprise; his expertise would be far better used elsewhere. Basically, I told him a load of crap just so he would leave.

Unfortunately, I never managed to employ a chef from that particular advert, and therefore had to re-advertise.

Frank replied. 'I want to speak to the lady of the house'

'Why you not give me the job?'

'Because you aren't suitable.'

'I do you a good job, you pay me a lot'

'I don't think so, old pal'.

He continued to ring every day for a week, always asking for the lady of the house. The phone calls started to get very abusive and he demanded I gave him the chef's job.

'You give me job, or I take you to racial discrimination board'

'You do whatever you want; I just do not want to hear from you personally again.'

Fortunately that was the last I ever heard from Frank.

I always appreciated the fact that going for an interview can be quite nerve racking and stressful, so I always tried to put people at ease so they didn't feel intimidated or nervous. But it became so difficult sometimes when I sat opposite a potentially new employee and they sat with their head bent down, with their eyes focused on the table top, sitting half on, and half off the bench seat, as if they might suddenly get up and run away. They would swing a leg, twiddle their quite often dirty finger nails, without a smile, or acknowledgment, and when it came to asking them a question, the only response was, Yes or No, without elaboration.

'Do you have any hobbies?'

'Yes'

'Have you done bar or restaurant work before?

'Yes'

Sometimes a simple yes or no was even a struggle for them.

I often wanted to say, 'For Christ's sake, just look at me,'

I frequently felt I wanted to lay my head on the table, just so I am right up into their face, then they would have no other option than to look me in the eye.

There are many things that had to be taken into account during the interviewing process.

'Did they have a sense of humour?'

Was their appearance suitable?

Did they have experience in the leisure industry?

Were they a team player; would they go above and beyond the call of duty?

Did they have the right attitude to be a 'Walnut' person?

Being a Walnut member of staff meant having a quick response to remarks made from customers - whether flirtatious, cheeky or just plain rude, but not taking offence from the banter.

The regular customers who frequented the pub and restaurant were used to a particular way our staff had been trained; although they were polite, efficient, never rude, and mostly friendly, they were definitely not the 'yes sir, no sir' kind of staff.

Our 'Walnut' staff were cheeky to customers when the occasion demanded it, but wouldn't stand any shit from people if they were blatantly rude or obnoxious to them, and nor should they. However, they always knew they had our backing in unforeseen situations.

Staff had to put up with Chris' groping – well, only the female staff! The men just had to put up with him nipping their inside leg occasionally (no, not occasionally - often). He did like to undo females' bras - customers and staff, pull up their knickers from the back and give them a wedgy, and sometimes said, 'Show us your tits'.

On one interview I was conducting, I asked the girl in question for the reason she left her previous job.

'I didn't get on with the manager and I'm now in the process of suing him for sexual harassment.'

My good judgement meant I didn't employ her.

Whilst I was sitting with another candidate and writing down her details, I glanced into the restaurant and saw two customers I knew very well looking at me, trying to attract my attention. They were police officers in plain clothes from the local branch who often drank and ate in the restaurant. They were shaking their heads, miming 'no' to me and swiping their hand across their throats. I got the message – don't employ this girl.

So I told her I would be in touch soon if she was on my shortlist and – she left.

Apparently she was well known to the police for drug problems, so they were very interested to receive her most recent address and telephone number on a piece of paper surreptitiously dropped onto the table where they were sitting - she didn't get the job either.

I always interviewed prospective people in the restaurant on the first table, commonly known as Table One or the 'naughty table!' This was where all the hiring and firing and bollockings were done. So if I ever said to a member of staff, 'come to table one', they knew this meant they were in trouble.

Any staff working on the days I conducted interviews enjoyed having a quick look at the potential employees and taking bets on how long the interview would last, and whether or not I would employ them.

In the early days my interview process would range from about one minute upwards. One minute was just enough time to get their name and address and say I would contact them in a couple of days if they had been successful. These were always the disastrous ones, and their details went straight in the bin.

As the years went by, every aspect of interviewing changed and it all became politically correct. Under the new regime, when it came to the interview process and I knew instantly I would never be employing the particular person I was talking to, it was essential to make sure I went through the correct procedures. We had to get them to fill in the staff application form and had to ask precise questions. This took time, - wasted time. My one minute interviews had turned into at least ten minutes for a definite no-hoper.

I had to be so careful in the technique of questioning, as there was always the chance of being sued if I caused any offence by saying something which was politically incorrect.

Eventually, after having gone through the process of interviewing, and they had ticked all the boxes of expectations required, it was time to give them the good news and organise a starting date for their new employment.

So, with the interviewing procedure finished, with the member of staff employed, all they had to do was to commence their first day at work. That's if they bothered to turn up at all!

****

STAFF

Many, many staff came and left during our 25 years at the pub. Some started and finished so quickly they barely had time to take their coats off. The big majority were so insignificant that if, for one reason or another, I looked through past staff records at a later date, I would have absolutely no recollection of them whatsoever.

Some appeared to be a suitable applicant when they were interviewed, but not when they actually began to work. It sometimes only took about half an hour to see that a person was going to be of no use whatsoever in our establishment.

We employed a bar maid who couldn't add up a round of drinks in her head, and had absolutely no concept of how to give change from the till. By the time she had written down the price of several drinks and added them all up (using her fingers as an abacus) half a dozen or more customers could have been served.

A waitress started with us whose handwriting was so indecipherable that it was impossible for the chef to read the orders.

Many new members of staff turned up for work but didn't do anything constructive or even have any interest in learning the job, but just stood gazing vacantly into space.

Some people had to have our system explained to them over and over again and still they couldn't grasp it.

We were lucky in the fact that when we did employ good staff, many stayed for years and in a way became part of our family; although, as the saying goes, familiarity does breed contempt. At times, their attitude towards work did slacken, so they would just need a little boot up the bum occasionally to get them back on the right track!

One of the most important aspects of dealing with staff was gaining their respect. The results were more favourable and hopefully they were more loyal towards us and our business. They were less inclined to take a 'sickie' day off because they didn't feel like coming in, but would appear for work feeling under the weather and obviously genuinely unwell.

Being an employer meant being their confidant, their mother, father, their friend, someone they could turn to with their problems, whether personal or medical, giving them advice if they wanted it, even wiping their tears away and just making them feel better.

We heard many confidential stories from the staff over the years, the matrimonies, the boyfriend or girlfriend problems, the money worries, home concerns and pregnancies to name but a few.

Staff problems and conversations told to us in confidence were never disclosed to anybody else. I didn't agree with tittle tattle and I didn't like the staff doing it either. If I overheard anybody talking maliciously about another member of staff or trying to stir trouble, I would have no hesitation in pointing out, in no uncertain terms, that it was unacceptable behaviour. Of course, it happens in every workplace and cannot be avoided, because it's impossible to listen and be present for every conversation that takes place.

There were times when we were hypothetically kept in the dark by various employees when relationships were evolving amongst the male and female staff. Although they were trying to undergo a secret affair without anyone knowing, most of the time it didn't go unnoticed by us. As an employer, you become very vigilant watching staff and customers, just simple facial expressions and body language are easily apparent. It was obvious by noticing little sly glances between them, the secret smiles and whisperings, even an affectionate touch gave the game away.

We never mentioned to the couples or the other members of staff that we were aware of shenanigans; it was simply amusing for us to watch them, that was, until the relationship ended, then they would quite often ignore each other.

If a staff member did something wrong I would never give them a bollocking in front of customers or any other staff, I always believed this to be unprofessional and embarrassing for the person concerned. So, in these cases, I took them to one side, or to table one, and told them privately the error of their ways.

A motto of ours: Never ask anyone to do anything you wouldn't do yourself.

There wasn't a single job in the pub or restaurant that hadn't been done by either Chris or myself. Whether it was scrubbing the floor on our hands and knees, cleaning the equipment or washing up, we had done everything (except I did refuse to clean the public toilets and clear up any sick, as it made me gag.)

Chris did the toilet duties when necessary and had to wiggle his finger down the plug hole on more than one occasion to get rid of vomit – even writing about it gives me a sick lump in my throat!

If we wanted a particular job done by any of the staff we would always say,

'Please would you …….. as soon as you get time'

Rather than barking orders at them, this gained results far quicker and got the job done, rather than them thinking to themselves, 'Fuck you, I'm not doing that, it's not my job.'

'It's not my job' is another statement I would not tolerate. As an example, we did not always have a kitchen porter on duty for washing up, so the chef and waitress would have to do it. If someone needed some help then the restaurant staff would have to assist them. If the bar was busy but the restaurant was quiet, then the waitress would have to go down and do bar work or help them clear the empty glasses and then wash and put them away.

If a delivery of beer or food arrived then the staff would aide in putting everything away. Team work is a valuable asset and necessary in any business and that was what we attempted to achieve.

At the end of their shift, we would always say,

'Thank you' to them when they left, and 'Good job,' or, 'Well done' if it had been a busy night and all had gone well. If it hadn't been a good night, I may still say 'Thank you', but through gritted teeth.

Obviously all staff members liked to receive compliments and appreciation regarding their work, but we, as employers, received our 'thank you' from the staff on Fridays when I handed out the wages – I'm not sure why, not with the meagre amount we paid them.

****

Julia worked for me for about 10 years, during which time she got married, had two babies and still she kept coming back to work for me part-time.

I loved working with Julia, I didn't have to watch her every movement or check everything she was doing in the restaurant; in fact, we could work the whole evening without even having to communicate with each other. We knew how the other operated and could work completely as a team and the restaurant would 'nearly' always run smoothly.

She always had the same temperament - laid back, so laid back sometimes she was horizontal.

Her first job when she started on an evening shift was supposed to be checking to see whether we had enough prep for the amount of customers booked in for the evening then to replenish the wine rack, and do some of the cleaning duties on the list. Not Julia, her first priority was to put the kettle on, make a cup of tea and sit on the first table in the restaurant to read the paper.

That was Julia's bad attribute. However, I knew when the restaurant was extremely busy and she was working on her own, she could cope completely unfazed and do a professional job - except for the time when she made a banana split dessert and gave it to the customer, but had left out one vital ingredient – the banana. The customer kept eating, thinking he would obviously come across a banana soon, but to no avail, so he never even told Julia until all the ice-cream had been demolished that she had missed something out.

There was the time Julia put the water through the coffee machine to make a jug of coffee; it does generally help to put the coffee in first.

One evening, we appeared to have an abundance of foreigners dining in the restaurant. Taking a meal order from these customers always created a few problems. Often they cannot speak English and we were hopeless at any other language, except bad language.

They desperately tried to make themselves understood, whilst we talked slowly, but always in a cross between a Pakistani accent and a Chinese accent and making ridiculous sign language,

'Would you like beeg beer or leetle beer?' describing the size of glasses with our hands. 'You like cheeps or salard?' 'Yes, we doo beeef – moo.'

With so many foreign customers in the restaurant at the same time, this ludicrous scenario continued to progress throughout the evening. – not very well.

On one occasion, I went to clear a table and overheard Julia doing her poor interpretations to the people sitting at the next booth, when she glanced up and spotted me.

I made a few ridiculous facial expressions at her. She giggled, and tried to continue talking to the customers, but with tears coming down her face until she laughed out loud and could barely continue speaking,

'I am so sorry.'

'Eet is fine, eet is nice to see people happee in their work. Thank you', the German customer replied.

With that she had to make a quick exit out of sight to collapse in hysterics.

Well, we enjoyed the evening, even if the customers may have been somewhat bemused.

****

Jo, an attractive, intelligent girl was very popular with customers, and someone you couldn't help but like. She did have the odd 'blond' moment though. Like the time she made herself a cup of tea, but didn't think to ask if any other member of staff would like one. I said to her, 'Are you an only child?'

She looked at me blankly and confusedly, 'No, you know I have a sister!'

Jo was a happy waitress, she didn't panic when it got busy, she got traumatised.

One particular evening springs to mind. I arrived at 7.30pm, an hour after Jo's commencement. I walked in to find Jo panic stricken; she had one table in the restaurant and those customers were eating.

One hand was clutching her forehead, the other arm was just swaying, and she was looking extremely flustered.

'Thank goodness you are here, I've been so busy and its all gone wrong. I had to make a caesar salad, some starters, and even a milk shake, and then I had to take bar food downstairs, and it's been terrible'.

'So, come on, tell me, what else happened, you've only got one table in the restaurant so it's not exactly busy?' I asked.

'Well, it was dreadful, I had to make a prawn cocktail, and if that wasn't bad enough, I dropped it all over the floor in the middle of the restaurant. And well, I was just so embarrassed.'

On another occasion Jo made a liqueur coffee and took it to the table. Five minutes later the gentleman called her over to tell her it tasted very salty. Jo had picked up the salt container instead of the sugar one! The ironical thing was that some of the other customers on the same table also tried the coffee, and told him to drink it, as it tasted alright to them!

****

Charlie originally worked in the bar at Captain America's, but came to the Walnut a couple of months after we opened. He remained employed by us for the whole 25 years, apart from a short period off when he had a hip replacement at the tender age of 50.

Charlie worked by himself behind the bar on Tuesday evenings when we had the night off, and an occasional weekend if we were short staffed. He was extremely loyal and reliable and we could trust him implicitly to lock the pub up at the end of the session.

He had the same attitude as Chris, so he was the perfect candidate to be Chris' replacement in his absence. However, unlike Chris, Charlie would be much happier if he was supplied with plenty of coffee throughout the evening.

He worked at one speed, he didn't care if the bar was packed with customers waiting to be served; he carried on regardless at his slow steady speed. His remark if people started complaining about the wait was 'Fuck off then if you don't like it.'

At 10pm on the dot, despite the fact the bar might be three deep with thirsty customers waiting to be served, he would disappear for a 10-minute cigarette break.

We thought the world of Charlie; he was a valued and loyal member of staff, even if we did sometimes receive a detailed gory description and explanation of all his ailments!

****

Libby was an extremely intelligent girl, - but absolutely barking mad. At the time she commenced employment for us, she was also studying at university for a degree, so worked for us between lectures, and also a couple of evenings per week in the bar or restaurant.

Libby had a great attitude towards life which was evident in her daily routine. One priority of hers was to achieve something each day, and she would not be satisfied until she had accomplished her goal. This did not mean getting up in the morning and cleaning her teeth was an achievement, it had to be something productive. With Libby this could be starting to learn to play an instrument, studying poetry, or finishing an essay for university. Or she may want to attempt all those things - and this was all before going into work!

Libby could never decide what item of clothing to wear, for work or socialising, so she tended to wear everything – but all at the same time. Commencing at her feet, she wore wedged shoes, similar to callipers, with a sole that measured at least 10-inches. How, in God's name she ran up and down the stairs in them, let alone walk in them, I do not know.

She would wear trousers, a tee-shirt, a dress and possibly a jumper as well, then a shawl that could also be used as an apron, or sometimes as a kind of head scarf, or she might alternate the same piece of clothing throughout her working session. The end result was bizarre, but in a strange kind of way she did look acceptable for carrying out her duties.

However, one evening really took the biscuit, as she came to work behind the bar wearing a tiara. Our first thoughts - she cannot be serious.

Oh yes, she was.

The reasoning behind her strange attire was that she woke up that morning feeling like a princess, and wearing a tiara seemed to fit the bill. She continued to wear her headpiece for the whole shift, which was quite a mean feat in itself. The customers had great delight in taking the piss out of her; she didn't give a monkey's, she was a princess for the day.

Libby could never keep still. Whether the bar was quiet or busy she would dance behind the bar whilst serving drinks.

We were going on holiday one year, but abstained from telling the staff or customers our destination. So to keep them guessing, we began by sending a postcard of the Norfolk Broads which stated what a lovely time we were having on the river. This was sent to the pub on the day we left for our break.

On the flight to our destination, we stopped off at Bahrain to refuel, so another postcard was sent to the pub saying that the weather had taken a turn for the worst – now everyone would think we were on holiday in Bahrain.

Prior to our departure we had arranged for several of our friends to send postcards addressed to the pub. So with each passing day, the staff and customers received a card from Cornwall, Switzerland, Greece, Chicago, Spain and Germany all stating what a good time we were having and signed 'With Love from Chris and Jude.'

Not only were the customers and staff confused, but so was the postman who was also reading the postcards. Nobody had a clue as to our whereabouts.

Libby decided to go into a book shop, look at a map of the world, memorise it, then return to the pub and draw it on the very large mirror located at the end of the bar.

She wrote on the top, 'So where are they?'

She drew an arrow and then placed each postcard by the country or region from where they had received a card.

We actually went to the Maldives, but the postcard we sent from there did not arrive until a week after we had returned from holiday!

****

One young girl with a bad attitude washed up in the restaurant a couple of evenings per week. Although I did feel sorry for her, as she had been kicked out of her family home and had spent time in hostels and bed and breakfast establishments for the homeless, and had generally had a difficult time at the tender age of 15. By giving her a job and a chance in life, maybe she would get rid of the chip on her shoulder. She was always late and produced many excuses as to why.

She couldn't find any lipstick, so put red felt tip pen on, smudged it and consequently couldn't get it off, that's why she was late. Her clothes were in the washing machine and she had to wait for the cycle to finish before she could put on the still wet clothes to come into work.

A couple of times she arrived at work wearing knee length PVC boots, a very short PVC skirt, and bodice – definitely not suitable for washing up in a restaurant. The evenings she wore this attire I tried to keep her hidden out of sight from the customers!

I always seemed to spend the whole night nagging her to get on with work instead of smoking a cigarette or chatting on the phone.

However, even with all her annoying faults, I didn't want to fire her, as she was a sweet girl underneath her attitude, and I did admire how she was trying to better herself by attending a course at college; at last, she was beginning to grow up.

****

Heidi, a university student, was employed as a part-time waitress. She started working for us one October, so she had to rapidly achieve our high standards and be on the ball in time for the Christmas rush.

She did try to hide her fingernails from me one day, unsuccessfully, revealing her bright purple chipped nail varnish; I didn't say a word, I salvaged some nail varnish remover and a cotton pad, passed it over to her, 'Take it off now.'

She was hopeless at communication with customers, orders would be written down wrongly and meals would be taken to the wrong tables and items left off the bills. She may have been academically intelligent but, as far as I was concerned, waitressing was definitely not her forte. With Christmas upon us, and staff were not in abundance, I just used her as an extra pair of hands doing menial tasks that she basically couldn't mess up.

As soon as New Year and the festive events were over, we parted company with Heidi. Even she admitted how ineffectual she was at being a waitress and was quite surprised I hadn't fired her weeks before. Well – I would have done if it wasn't for the fact it was far too close to Christmas and I would have to go through the process of employing and training someone quickly, who could possibly end up as bad as Heidi.

****

Eileen was rather on the large size, probably because she kept eating everything available from my fridge, - the cheesecake, chocolate cake and anything that had many thousands of calories, although it never entered her head to pay for the food she consumed.

One evening she served a table of ten and decided she didn't like them, so when it came to giving them the bill at the end of their meal, she wrote on the bottom of the receipt, adjacent to the total price owed, 'Fucking bastards.'

That was the end of her.

****

A nice young seventeen-year old lad called Simon was employed as a washer-up in the restaurant. He had a pleasant disposition and was very helpful. However his big downfall was insisting on holding trays full of glasses or china in the air by his fingertips, which was all very well if you were professional but not if you were inept as he was. In the end I just had to fire him as I could not afford to keep replacing all the breakages.

****

Then there was Penny, another young schoolgirl who washed up. This girl was miserable, useless and couldn't even manage to clean anything properly; the crockery and cutlery seemed to end up dirtier than before she started washing them. She was fired, and that would be the end of her, or so I thought.

No, her mother came storming in to see me, retorting that I had upset her daughter so much that she had found her walking up the street in the middle of the night wearing just a nightshirt.

'I'm sorry but I really think there is an underlying problem which isn't anything to do with me; if she had done her job satisfactorily she would have remained with us.'

****

Bev, a very good friend of mine, was employed as a bar person. She was always late, (she was also always the last one to get ready if we all went out socially, as well!), but there was absolutely no excuse for lateness at work, as she only lived five minutes' walk away.

On one of her late mornings, her excuse was that she had missed the bus.

'Hang on a minute Bev; you don't have to catch a bus.'

Another morning, on walking to work, she had difficulty manoeuvring her way through the crowds as a brass band was playing on her walking route into the city, so she felt obliged to stay and listen to the music before the crowd dispersed. Then she was able to continue on her way – making her about an hour late.

She had a leak in her flat with a foot of water on the floor – 'Yes, so, - it will still be there when you go home.'

'But I can't, I need to wait for the fire brigade, and that could be ages'

She may have always been late for work, but when she did get there she was an excellent bar person, except the times she was busy chatting to regulars in the bar, -

but of course, that was all part of being a good barmaid, keeping the customers happy!!

****

Lisa was employed as a waitress, and did a pretty good job. I was able to trust her to work unsupervised and she was able to take some of the pressure from me.

One lunchtime the restaurant was fairly busy. At a table sitting by herself, was an elderly lady eating a meal consisting of a fillet of plaice with all the trimmings.

She suddenly rose from her chair, rushed into our prep area section, and whacked Lisa several times on the back exceptionally hard.

She swung round to see that the old lady was obviously choking; she couldn't speak, so her only means of communication in the apparent panic she was feeling was to hit the living daylights out of Lisa.

We realised by her actions that she wanted us to thump her on the back – so we obliged, but just hard enough for the fish bone that was stuck in her throat to come out; unfortunately she managed to throw up as well.

Christmas is the busiest time for the catering industry; staff need to be focused at all times, and ready to work their socks off. The restaurant is always packed, there are numerous office parties coming to dine, and there is a constant stream of taking orders and serving meals.

It is so busy, that even when it is time to go to bed, it is difficult to switch off from the daily events of work.

Lisa had this problem when she went sleepwalking during the night at home, opened the wardrobe door, held out her hands, and asked who had ordered a prawn cocktail.

****

Philip worked behind the bar; he was mad as a hatter always jumping about and acting stupidly, but was a lovable character. He had quite a skinny physique, with no manly muscles apparent to make him look masculine.

He worked from 11am to 6pm, Monday to Friday. When we went home in the afternoons he was working on his own behind the bar. This was never usually a problem as afternoons were relatively quiet and so it was completely unnecessary to have more than one member of staff on duty at a time. However one particular day, he was descended on by ten extremely large men, who were all ex-convicts from Wormwood Scrubs having a reunion.

Why they chose our pub I do not know. They were very loud, and most certainly not the kind of clientele any landlord would want to entertain but, on the other hand, would rather not have to tell them to leave in fear of any consequences that might prevail.

They ordered a bottle of champagne from Philip, who at this point was shaking with fear and had apparently gone a ghastly shade of green. He felt even worse when they didn't pay for their purchase.

He was too scared to ask them for the money, and continued to go about his work quietly, washing glasses, and serving the remaining customers left in the bar. Several had already departed after feeling intimidated in the presence of these burly men.

Philip was now too frightened to leave the security of standing behind a wooden bar counter to venture round to the customers' side to pick up more empty glasses. He didn't wish for any close contact with the ex-cons, let along any eye contact, and just kept praying for 6pm to hurry up when Chris would return to the pub.

By the time Chris arrived, the men had left. Philip was still very shaken and pale.

The next day, one of the burly, scar-faced men came in for a drink. Chris, without any hesitation, told him he owed £29.95 for the champagne he had ordered the previous day.

'Sorry mate, didn't realise we hadn't paid, ere you go,' and he took a wad of notes from his pocket and paid the outstanding debt.

Phew!

When he left he did mention to Chris he would be returning to see him soon regarding the protection that Chris was going to need in the future at the pub.

As I have mentioned before, Chris was renowned for undoing ladies' bras, either customers or staff – he wasn't fussy. He would walk past them, give a quick flick and it was undone.

The regular men customers were generally nipped on the inside thigh. It really hurts, but amazingly nobody ever took offence, they just tried to steer out of the way of his prying hands before he got to them. It was quite amusing, though, to watch customers jumping up, grimacing and usually saying 'bastard', as Chris walked past.

Philip obviously thought it would be a splendid idea to do something similar. However, he picked on the wrong person. It was Wendy, who also worked for us. One lunchtime, whilst they were working together behind the bar, he thought it would be a good idea to smack her on the bum. As soon as he had done it, he thought, umm, bad idea, and ran down the bar to get away from her. He got to the end, jumped up, banged his head on the door frame and completely knocked himself out.

Wendy didn't need to retaliate; Philip had managed to punish himself!

****

On the subject of Wendy, she was employed to waitress and work behind the bar. She was extremely efficient and hardworking in our presence, especially on a Saturday lunchtime session in the restaurant when it was always packed with customers for the whole day.

I always prided myself on the swiftness I could work, far quicker than most of the staff that were half my age, until I worked with Wendy, who whizzed up and down the restaurant like a car in a drag race - she was speedy.

Chris' favourite track on a particular CD was 'Love Shack', and boy, didn't we all know it. If he played it once a day, he played it several times, and sang along (which was painful). It was getting so monotonous that Wendy hid the CD. Chris hunted for ages without it being discovered, and was questioning everyone as to its whereabouts.

It was Wendy and Philip who 'borrowed' it. They bought a blank CD and recorded 'Love Shack' repeatedly over and over again. It was later planted back amongst the rest of the music, just waiting for Chris to find it.

On a bank holiday weekend, whilst the pub was closed, Chris and I went in to do a few mundane jobs - like scrubbing the floor on our hands and knees, jet spraying the outside area, and doing some ordering.

'I think we will put some music on while we work,' said Chris as he was rummaging through the CD's.

'Cor, look what I've just found; it's the Love Shack CD I lost;' It was immediately inserted into the machine.

Love Shack was playing, - full volume, Chris was singing – full volume.

Love Shack was playing again; Chris didn't notice.

Wendy and Philip had previously told me of their prank, so on the third time of playing, I was in hysterics and waiting for Chris' reaction. I didn't have to wait much longer.

'What the fuck's going on here; the CD's got stuck?'

When he ultimately realised what had happened and I told him who the culprits were he did, surprisingly enough, find it funny, but decided he would reverse the joke and play one on them.

He found the original CD – after I told him where it was hidden - and planted it back on the shelf.

Philip and Wendy were working the next morning. Chris was nonchalantly looking through the CD's and remarked that the 'Love Shack' one had appeared again. He put it on, and oh, what a surprise, the song in question was playing.

Giggling amongst themselves, Philip and Wendy waited in anticipation for the song to finish and then begin playing over, and over again – trying desperately not to laugh in front of Chris.

Of course it was the original CD with just one song of 'Love Shack'; they were confused and looked bewildered, until they were told that they were rumbled.

****

A lad in his early 20's was employed as a bar person. He worked the day shift and was left to work on his own in the afternoons while we went home for a couple of hours' break. The afternoon shift is generally quiet, especially at the beginning of the week, with usually about half a dozen drinkers in at a time.

He found this very beneficial as he had plenty of time during the afternoon to play the fruit machine. This was all very well if there was nothing else to do, except that the money he put in the machine was ours.

It came to light when Chris noticed on the till print out that the 'no sale' button had been pressed excessively. The only reason the till needs to be opened other than ringing in amounts of money is to give someone change, which would be either for the cigarette machine or the fruit machine, thus producing a 'no sale' on the print out. It would be normal for the till to be opened two or three times during the afternoon, but over twenty times, with only a few customers in the bar, caused alarm bells to ring.

On confronting him, he of course was adamant that everybody kept requesting change during the afternoon. We had no proof so; for the cost of a couple of pints, we got one of our regular day-time customers we knew well to sit at the bar and inconspicuously watch our bar lad whilst he went about his daily duties.

All was exposed when Chris returned to work. He found bits of paper in the bin with amounts of money written on and added up; this was subsequently confirmed by the customer unobtrusively watching him.

Instead of ringing up the rounds of drinks as people were buying them, he was adding them up on bits of paper, getting the money from the customer, ringing the 'no sale' button on the till, putting the money in the till and then taking it out again as soon as he got the chance later on.

He was fired.

The only consolation in this sad tale is, yes, a member of staff was stealing from us and, if we did hazard a guess, it was probably a couple of hundred pounds but, in a roundabout way, we retrieved the money as, whenever he wasn't serving, he was pumping 'our' money into the Fruit Machine.

****

Whilst we still lived at the pub we employed a cleaner who worked from Monday to Friday and then a different lady came and did the cleaning job on Saturdays. She was a pleasant lady, who did a reasonable job in the bar and afterwards she would give the flat a quick dust and vacuum, so I was happy with that.

At the end of each evening in the bar, Chris always stocked the shelves up with bottles of coke, tonic etc, so they all stood in a neat line. The chiller was also neatly stocked with bottles of beer so that everything was cold and ready for opening in the morning.

He noticed a couple of cokes were missing off the shelf, and a bottle of beer was gone from the chiller. Doubting himself, that maybe he hadn't filled the shelves completely, he didn't think anything more about it, and just replenished the stock.

This happened again the following week, and the week after that.

'Ha, it's the cleaner having it away.'

The next time she came into work, I waited until she had finished cleaning the bar and had gone upstairs to give the flat a clean.

As soon as she was out of sight, I went to the bar to check if there was anything missing. Yes, it was the same as all the previous weeks, two bottles of coke and a bottle of beer were gone.

I snuck quietly back up to the flat where I could hear her vacuuming in the lounge. Now was my opportunity to find the missing items; I located her bag and peered inside – this was something I would never normally dream of doing, as handbags are a personal and private possession. But then again, needs must, but I didn't feel guilty for many seconds, especially when I spotted the stolen goods.

I was mad, so mad. I stomped into the lounge where she was and glared at her,

'Are you OK?' she said.

'No, not really, I would like you to come with me - now; I am requesting that you reveal the contents of your handbag, as I believe it contains goods which have been stolen from the bar.'

She reluctantly opened her bag, and began apologising profusely,

'I've never done this before, please don't tell my family', her knees buckled under her and she fell, fainting to the floor.

'It's no good being down there, get up and then get out of my premises; you stole from me and just think yourself very lucky that I'm not calling the police.'

With that, plus a bit of nudging from my foot to get her back upright from the floor, she left. About an hour later she brought in a bunch of flowers for me as a thank you for not taking the matter any further.

It's a bloody good job I didn't see her come in with the flowers, otherwise I think there would have been a strong possibility I might have wrapped them round her head. Instead, I chucked them straight in the bin.

****

Jane worked for me part-time as a waitress for about six years. Her clothes, on occasions, could have done with a little ironing, but she always insisted that that was how they were supposed to look – it was the fashion. Chris often handed her a comb in anticipation that she might use it.

Monday morning was never Jane's favourite shift when the restaurant was given a thorough deep clean, which generally took a couple of hours to complete. She didn't mind the cleaning aspect of the job, it was the hangover and headache she invariably had which was the problem. The fact was that she had often been sick before she had left for work, and frequently rushed in to be sick again on arrival, before she even started doing anything.

Fortunately for her, she didn't complain – well not too much, because she didn't get any sympathy from me.

Jane's hangover miraculously vanished the Monday morning she moved a table to vacuum behind and found a £50 note on the floor. She ran down the restaurant screaming and waving the money, 'Look what I've found.'

However, I did make her wait a considerable length of time before I allowed her to claim her findings, just in case someone reported their loss.

They didn't and Jane enjoyed spending her £50.

Another Monday morning, I went into work with the worst hangover I have ever had to endure in my entire life. We had been to an LVA fancy dress ball on the Sunday. Unbeknown to me, I was drinking double vodkas all night, and had got absolutely trashed – we had a great time though.

Driving into work I felt completely vacant. Steve, our painter and decorator, was already at the pub painting the outside wall. After talking – or, should I say, attempting to speak to him, I discovered it was him buying the doubles (bastard). I felt a sudden urge to be sick after getting an intake of smelly paint fumes and so had to escape rapidly indoors to the loo and throw up. Did I feel better after that? – no!

That day I was covering the chef's day off, so had to tolerate the whole day working in the kitchen, doing the cooking and preparation. Every time I attempted to cook or chop anything I felt sick so, by the time Jane arrived for work, I was lying down on one of the restaurant benches looking green.

Jane thought it was hilarious after all the times she had come into work feeling rough and managed to carry on working, and here was her boss, laid out, looking pathetic.

She most definitely went beyond the call of duty that day; she helped get all the preparation work done in the kitchen and even cleared everything away and cleaned up at the end of the shift for me.

Jane got her own back the following week when she came in with another horrendous hangover. She took one look at a baking tray waiting to be washed up in the kitchen, got the aroma of the bbq sauce which the ribs had been cooking in and rushed to the sink and was sick.

So, for once, I helped her survive the shift and covered her work in the restaurant each time she disappeared to be sick again - and there were several!

After that I pointed out now we were quits, so no more sympathy from me.

****

I employed a waiter who was extremely good at his job and very meticulous. The women customers especially liked being served by him.

He also worked behind the bar quite frequently and, on one particular Friday night, I had just finished closing the restaurant and went downstairs to the bar. One look at the employee behind the bar, and it was patently obvious he was drunk. Chris had been working this busy evening with him so I remarked to him, 'What ever's going on with your barman? He's pissed.'

'But he can't be, as he hasn't had a drink all night.'

'Just look at him, he's all over the place.'

Towards the end of the evening session, Chris and the barman (well, mainly Chris) had to finish doing the last few jobs in the bar before the pub closed.

Chris then offered him a drink; he took one swig, and then it was all over for him – it was that one drink too many. He attempted to sit down, staggered, slurred and fell, landing on the bottom step of the restaurant stairs. When we woke him up shortly afterwards he was sent on his way home.

Chris was mystified and convinced our barman hadn't had a drop to drink all evening. The following week when he was tidying the cellar which housed all the beer, spirits and wine he heard a clinking sound behind the fridge. On pulling it out, Chris found twenty four empty alcopop bottles!

Now we knew how the barman had got pissed, and also the reason he always kept putting the bottle opener in the back pocket of his trousers instead of leaving it in the correct place on the shelf behind the bar, (much to the annoyance of Chris) and the reason why he kept disappearing downstairs into the cellar.

That was the end of him.

****

Sue has been a dear friend of mine since the early 1970's. We worked together at Captain America's, had our children at the same time, our mothers passed away within months of each other, and even our birthdays are in the same month. Over the years we have enjoyed laughs and tears together and had generally gone through whatever life throws at you with each other.

We worked together well, and I knew I could trust her implicitly. She was left in charge if we weren't there as she knew how to deal with problems the way I would like them resolved.

One day she stood on a seat in the restaurant to change a light bulb but didn't turn the switch off first. The light shorted and she got an electric shock which threw her off the seat into the gangway of the restaurant floor. Her body was shaking and her skin went a horrid colour of grey. She did manage to say that as she had had a coil fitted she would now be able to pick up Radio One!

Chris rushed her to the hospital, jumping all the traffic lights to get there, where she was given a CTU scan. Fortunately, she was fine and came to no harm.

Another time she took a sizzling dish of satay to a customer, which was boiling hot because of the oil in the peanut sauce and put it down in front of the customer. The plate slipped and the liquid went all over Sue's hand. She screamed and burst into tears with the excruciating pain. This was another trip to the hospital where the doctors bound it up and subsequently sent her home, ordering her to take a couple of weeks off work.

Myself, Sue, and Gerry called ourselves the trolley dollies. If we had a large party booked for the restaurant we used a spare table which sat up to four people. It was generally kept in the prep area and had to be wheeled down past all the customers before it reached its final destination at the end of the restaurant, enabling large bookings to sit together.

So whilst we pushed it past each table, we stopped and asked all the customers, much to their amusement, 'Any duty frees, perfumes, cigarettes or tobacco from our trolley?'

The trolley dolly 'duty free' table scenario continued for 25 years, and was used so often, even the regulars asked the staff in question pushing the table,

'Here come the trolley dollies. Have you got a carton of Marlboro?'

Dick, a friend of ours used to come in for a meal in the restaurant sometimes on a Friday night with his mates. They were always the last to leave but in the meantime Sue and Gerry used to earn a few extra pounds by giving them a flash of their boobs for 50p. a go.

I must stress that it was all harmless fun, especially as Dick's wife Debs also worked for me on a Friday night and would also do a flash for 50p.

****

Gerry was Sue's younger sister and also a very good friend of mine, and had also worked at Captain America's. She made everyone laugh with her antics and joke telling, and should really have taken up a career as a comedienne.

She worked both in the bar and restaurant. During the summer months when people were standing outside the pub having a drink, she would frequently lean out of the window and flash her boobs at the men. This backfired one evening, as one guy who was watching her from below, decided to climb up the drainpipe and into the restaurant through the window for a closer look.

We had been particularly busy one Saturday night; it was towards the end of the session when all the grotty jobs needed to be finished. The tables needed clearing; the restaurant and prep area needed cleaning down, and Sue, Gerry and myself were all pretty knackered, when Gerry started complaining of a stomach ache and wanted to sit down.

'You're alright, it's probably just wind, knowing you; let's get the work finished and stop being a lazy cow.'

She continued working but was still moaning; Sue said,

'Why don't you just fart, and then you'll be alright.'

However, she wasn't alright; she was doubled up in agony. So we took her upstairs to the flat where she went to the loo and had the biggest fart then smelliest poo ever. Sue and I gagged and rushed to the kitchen in the flat laughing, which does sound really mean, but the expressions on her face looked so funny, and the smell was disgusting.

Chris came upstairs to see what was going on and found poor Gerry sitting on the loo in the very smelly bathroom in absolute agony. He was wiping her brow and rubbing her back while Sue and I were of no use whatsoever. Chris was the hero in looking after Gerry that evening, as she really wasn't well and was off work for a couple of weeks recovering.

However, she did forgive Sue and I for being hopeless in looking after her and our lack of sympathy at the beginning.

Another time she walked into the restaurant with a fruit crumble, tripped, fell flat on her face and the crumble flew into the air and landed down her back.

One night Gerry started to walk up the stairs towards the restaurant with a tray of drinks when Chris stuck his finger right at the spot that women like the best (even though she was wearing jeans at the time)

She said, 'Ooh, you got right on my g.spot. Can you ring my husband and tell him where it is? Cause he hasn't got a clue.'

****

Ali worked in the restaurant occasionally if we were short of staff, but bar work was her forte, where the customers loved her. She was a pretty girl, with the special attributes of a wonderful caring attitude towards people and work.

One Christmas, it was the dreaded time to put up the Christmas decorations – the job Chris and I detested doing most. We stapled tinsel across the bar and stuck up a few hanging decorations and garlands and thought that would do.

However, Ali had other ideas. When we used to leave her in charge during the afternoon shift whilst we went home for a couple of hours, she decided that a few more Christmas decorations were needed. She put tinsel round every picture – there were at least 50 pictures in the pub.

More decorations were put round the top shelving of the bar. Fairy lights adorned the back bar, tinsel entwined round and up the banister rail of the stairs. Mistletoe and more tinsel was wound round the bottles; the jukebox had tinsel round it, along with the cigarette machine and the fruit machine. The wires which came from the ceiling for the hanging Tiffany lights had tinsel round them. There was barely a blank area without something on it or round it!

Chris walked in and his face said it all, 'What the fuck? It's like fucking Santa's grotto in here. You can't keep all this up.'

'Oh yes we can, it took me ages.'

It stayed up, but Chris gave her the job of taking it down after Christmas.

Ali used to work for us for a few months and then fly to Europe for the summer months; it might be Greece or France or wherever she fancied at the time and could get some employment.

She understood that I was unable to keep her job open whilst she was away but, fortunately, each time she returned, was always when I needed a new member of staff, so the job was hers. She left and returned eight times.

Each time she came back from her travels and walked into the Walnut, she always said she felt like she was home again, especially when she got a whiff of my perfume (OK, so I have worn the same perfume for over 20 years!) and she got the Jude smell – well, I hope she meant the perfume!

We loved her working for us and have remained friends ever since.

****

Wilko, a great barman, could charm the pants of any woman, and was known to everyone as the son of Gudge. Although he was in his early 20's when he started work with us, there was a strong familiarity in his facial features and certainly looked as if he should have been related to Chris. Wilko, however, was far more attractive than Chris, as his hair hadn't begun to recede - and a beer belly like Chris' hadn't yet developed.

Working in a bar as a single male, Wilko was in a prime position to pull the girls when they came in for a drink, and he wasted no time in chatting them up. It was also beneficial to our takings, as girls came in to see him. Unfortunately, they were not quite so thrilled if Chris served them; they much preferred Wilko drooling over the bar at them. There were not many occasions when he went home alone.

****

Cheryl worked behind the bar, was the same age as our daughter and there was a striking resemblance between them. This became evident when customers remarked to Chris, 'Your daughter is much better looking than you are, you ugly git.'

Being Chris' 'daughter' was very helpful to her sometimes; if male customers' were chatting her up or being cheeky to her and she wasn't interested in their innuendo's, she would call to Chris, 'Dad, can you come and have a word with these guys?'

One glance at Chris' face and their banter immediately stopped!

****

Neil worked for us for about six years and was one of the best kitchen porters we ever employed, but gave the impression of being so laid back he was horizontal. He used to saunter casually into work and if we had been busy before his arrival he could be confronted with a mountain of dirty pots, pans and crockery completely filling the washing up area.

I would leave him to get on with his job and go into the restaurant for about ten minutes, only to return to Neil's work area to find the majority of dirty dishes had already been washed and put away, cutlery would be glistening, and the whole area pristine with Neil sitting relaxing – and no, he hadn't thrown it all in the bin.

****

Linda was a sweet girl who worked in the restaurant as a waitress and also did bar work. She was very efficient, and a good employee. However, on occasions, she was so dippy and problematic, asking the most stupid questions that she drove me bonkers.

We kept a jug of hot water by the salad bar in our prep area which was used to fill the finger bowls when people ordered spare-ribs so that they could clean their hands after finishing eating. One shift she went to use the jug and noticed a dead fly floating in the water.

'Shall I tip this water out; there's a fly in it, or shall I leave it in there?'

She took some prawns out of the fridge, saw they were out of date and the smell was enough to knock you out, or gag, - or both, and asked me if she should throw them away.

'No, let's keep them. Why don't you have them for your lunch?' was my sarcastic reply.

'But they're off.'

Another time she went to clean and reset a table with cutlery after a table of customers had left, noticed the tablecloth was dirty and enquired as to whether she should change it for another one.

****

Shirley was employed to wash up in the restaurant, but was really helpful when the restaurant was busy. We would give her a tray with a list of drinks we required for customers and send her to the bar to get them.

On the way down the stairs she either attached the list to her suspender belt, or tucked it in her knickers, so when the bar tender asked what drinks she required, she pulled up her skirt and made him take the list from her underwear – in full view of all the bar customers.

On her hen night, she came to the pub in fancy dress with all her friends after consuming several drinks. She was getting louder as the night wore on. Some time later, her friends decided they would handcuff her to the post outside the pub and leave her there, whilst they were all inside getting some piece and quiet.

While she was sitting on the ground in the alleyway, with her legs tucked round the lamppost, a policeman walked past and asked if she was OK.

'No, my friends have handcuffed me to this post, and have left me all alone.'

He laughed and carried on walking up the street, leaving her handcuffed.

****

The zit kids were two 15-year old schoolboys, aptly named because their skin looked like bubble wrap – they suffered badly with teenage hormonal spots. They worked weekends either washing up in the restaurant or glass collecting in the bar.

This proved very beneficial from our point of view; although we always tried to be vigilant in spotting under age drinkers, occasionally some would slip through the net, especially the girls who had their faces plastered with make-up to make them look older, or groups of youngsters who would send the oldest looking to the bar for drinks whilst the others stayed out of view.

If we saw the zit kids talking to 'younger' customers, there was a good chance they were school friends, so obviously under-age, but they would also frequently give us the nod when they recognised younger people entering the bar who weren't yet 18.

****

When customers enjoyed drinking regularly in the Walnut, it's because they appreciated the music being played, the atmosphere and the ambience and were amused by Chris' mannerisms and personality; they basically felt comfortable and at home. Tim was one of those customers who loved the pub and drank there after he had finished work on a Friday.

Friday's being Friday's, the bar was always heaving with customers, so Tim would often go round and help Linzi the bar girl on duty until Chris arrived at 6pm. When an opportunity arose that we required a new member of staff, Chris approached Tim who was sitting at the bar with a Wild Turkey and coke in hand, and simply asked him if he wanted to work for us. That was Tim's interview. He commenced with us on a part-time basis to begin with and full time employment at a later date.

He was undeniably, 'Mr Clean.' Tim didn't give the bar a quick wipe over - everything and I mean, everything, was scrubbed and polished, equipment was moved and cleaned behind. In fact the bar was always spotless to the point of pristine when Tim was in control, with everything in its rightful place - and he got very cross if someone replaced an item in the wrong position.

He loved working behind the bar and often continued to stay when his shift was over. In fact, sometimes, he probably spent as many hours a week in the Walnut as we did.

He was an efficient worker and perfectly competent working a busy session on his own; however, we did receive a phone call one afternoon from him uttering just one word, 'Help.'

Mid afternoon a few Norwich fans had started trickling in, then more and more through both bar doors. A customer asked him if he was working on his own, when he said 'yeah,' the guy laughed and said he should go and take a look out of the door. There was a swarm of yellow and green, and many were heading towards the Walnut.

Tim got so busy that a customer had to dial our telephone number and hold the phone to his ear while he continued serving.

Chris got straight in the car and headed towards the pub. On arriving he saw hundreds – no, thousands, of people thronging the streets of Norwich.

'What the fuck's going on?'

The pub was packed to the rafters, Tim had completely run out of clean glasses but didn't have time to pick up the dirty ones and the poor guy was sweating profusely.

Not having much interest in football, Chris hadn't given a lot of thought to the fact that Norwich City had gone up to the top division and were arriving in the city that day for celebrations, hence thousands of people were coming to the city to see the spectacle; no wonder poor Tim needed help. By the end of the night, the only beer we had left on the premises was half a keg of Carlsberg!

One New Year's Eve, Tim and I had been working behind the bar for about an hour. We were singing and dancing as the band were playing whilst serving customers, when I remarked to him, 'Have you been bought a drink from anyone yet?'

'No, have you?'

'No, but I'll soon make sure we do; leave it to me.'

From then on, I made certain if the customers didn't offer to buy us a drink when I had finished serving them, I told them I would have a vodka and tonic and Tim would also like a drink. No one refused, so we managed to consume copious amounts of alcohol during the night and Tim thoroughly enjoyed his night working at the Walnut. He had got drunk and been paid as well!

****

Suzie worked full time as a bar person for many years and was a popular girl with the customers. One evening she was holding a house party which we were invited to. Chris arrived on his motorbike and Suzie immediately wanted to sit on the pillion. She did not listen to Chris telling her to be careful as the exhaust was hot. Unfortunately, she soon found out, as she leapt off the bike far quicker than she had mounted it. A bag of peas was promptly taken from the freezer to soothe the burning pain until she arrived at hospital for treatment.

After wearing tight fitting clothes from the day she commenced working for us, her attire was gradually changing. Her tops were getting baggier, and oversized jumpers were been worn, but it wasn't until she was over seven months pregnant that her secret was revealed, soon she was to have a lovely baby girl.

****

Emma was very meticulous in her work and dress sense and customers enjoyed chatting to her whilst she was working in the bar. They liked it even more when she walked out of the ladies toilet, continued picking up glasses from the tables as she worked her way all round the pub talking to the regulars as she passed through, until she eventually arrived back behind the bar – all the time with her skirt tucked in her knickers, exposing a bum cheek.

The customers certainly wouldn't have told her; they were enjoying the view. We thought they had seen enough, so not wanting to cause her any more embarrassment, told her she was hitched up.

****

A waitress and bar person who worked for us had a heart of gold and was extremely kind, but often drove me round the bend. She could talk the hind leg off a donkey, which I didn't have a problem with, until sometimes she forgot to serve customers because she was still in the middle of a conversation.

She was one of the culprits who brought in her own favourite music to be played in the bar whilst we were far away on holiday. She proceeded to dance and sing to the customers adorned with a straw tucked behind her ear for a microphone. Our usual blues and rock and roll music was replaced with WestLife and Abba. Chris was not amused when he found out on his return.

She had a habit of always calling us 'boss' – yes, I know we were her bosses, but it was unnecessary to say it each time she spoke.

'Morning, boss', 'yes, boss', no, boss', 'sorry, boss' – these phrases were used quite often.

At the end of every evening, Chris emptied the remains of the ice left in the bottom of the ice bucket in the gents' urinals; this also eliminated some of the smell lingering from men wee.

Towards the end of one particular evening, Chris asked her to go and chuck the ice in the gents' loo. Fortunately, Chris needed to pay a visit to the gents loo a bit later on and was greeted with a flood of water and ice strewn all over the floor.

'What the fuck did you do with the ice and water. It's all over the floor?'

'But you told me to chuck it in the gents' toilets, boss.'

51

****

Chris W, much the same as Tim, was another customer who had been drinking in the Walnut for a long time and loved everything about the pub.

Throughout the years we found that employing someone who enjoyed the pub on a social basis would be happy working there as well. So on many occasions we asked customers who we liked serving if they were looking for any work. Sometimes they did, sometimes, even if they didn't, Chris still managed to persuade them they did want an extra part time job.

Chris W. was a very conscientious worker and an excellent bar tender. He enjoyed working at the Walnut and socialised there too whenever possible. In fact he had so much affection for the pub he would have loved to have bought it when eventually we did go on the market.

He was a policeman in a former career, so was very capable of diffusing any difficult situation that might have arisen. On one of these occasions, Chris had no hesitation in breaking up a fight taking place outside the pub between four lads.

I've always found that men love to talk about fights they have been involved in, but with a slight exaggeration, and Chris was no exception. After a few drinks he tended to get verbal diarrhea (I mean that in the nicest possible way) but this fight he disbanded gradually increased from four men to six, to ten, to fifteen, then finally, undeniably twenty guys were fighting outside!

****

I arrived at the pub one evening to be told by Chris that I wasn't going to be very happy when I got upstairs to the restaurant, but would not elaborate any further.

Dubiously, I continued on my way to be greeted by the smiling waitress on duty that night.

'Evening, Jude.'

I just glared at her, shook my head slowly from side to side in disgust.

'You don't like what I'm wearing, do you? Have I got to go home and change?

'Yes – now'

Her attire was a short crop top exposing all her stomach, a pair of calf length leggings with purple stripe down the sides, and trainers, all in lycra. She had a smallish figure, but not drop-dead gorgeous, and if she was going to the gym, then her apparel may have been acceptable, but to serve food to customers in a restaurant - there was absolutely no way.

She went home very quickly to change, but felt rather hurt by my opinion, as she had bought her new clothing that day and thought she looked nice – whoops.

****

We had known Mark's parents since he was a baby. We used to frequent their very popular and successful pizza restaurant on a regular basis in the late 1970's. The years slipped by without us seeing Mark grow up, until one night he was drinking in the bar with his friend, extremely pissed. Andy, his mate, was trying to persuade the drunken Mark to make himself known to Chris. This was achieved eventually, and he went on to tell Chris, in his slurred manner, that he had done a lot of bar and restaurant work throughout the years.

'Good, you can work here tomorrow night as I'm really stuck for staff'.

Mark, in his drunken state agreed, until he woke up the next morning and wondered why he had agreed to this demand, especially when he arrived at the Walnut on Saturday night, still with a hangover, to be told it was the evening of The Lord Mayor's Procession, which just happens to be the busiest night of the year (apart from Christmas Eve).

'Chris, you bastard, you might have told me.'

He got through the night, then continued to work for us on and off, for several years.

If he went out for the evening with his mates, there was only one place he was happy in, The Walnut. As we had known him since he was in nappies he looked upon us as his surrogate Mum and Dad, especially after several drinks,

'Mum, look after me, I'm pissed, and he would lay his head on my lap at the end of the night and want to go to sleep.'

Before it got to that stage, we knew when Mark was getting drunk because of his accent. Even when sober he was well spoken, but this changed considerably the more drinks he consumed, until he sounded like a true perfect English gent, with definite OK yars being thrown into the conversation, and a vast vocabulary of words I've never heard of, but all spoken in the correct context (I imagine).

Then his facial expression progressed in what can only be described as 'stroke face,' when one side of his mouth drooped much lower than the other and he dribbled; then we knew he was on the point of no return. Since the mouth occurrence began, the term, 'stroke face', has always remained with him.

He would, inevitably, be sick somewhere in close proximity to the bar, in the loo maybe, although occasionally he didn't quite make it that far. Or he might try and go outside but throw up over the railings or in the alleyway; wherever the sick happened to land, poor Chris had to clear it up, but as Mark was his 'surrogate son' he didn't mind!

****

Sue was a sweet girl who washed up in the restaurant. One evening she came into work with fairly short hair; the following night, her hair was half way down her back – she had spent a small fortune having hair extensions. They were exceptionally realistic and she was thrilled with her new look.

A few weeks passed by and during the course of one evening, I kept noticing bits of hair on the floor. Somewhat bemused, I picked them up and threw them in the bin as this was not exactly hygienic in a restaurant. However, it soon came to light that Sue's hair extensions were beginning to fall out.

Needless to say, she was made to tie her hair out of the way so my restaurant floor didn't look like a hair salon.

****

We had known Mark (this is a different Mark from the previous one) for years before he came to work for us. He was a good bar person with a great personality and interacted well with the customers and staff.

His work was always impeccable until one particular week.

The week's events began when he was required to change a 1.5 litre of Bacardi on the optic - he didn't click the bottle in properly and let go; the full bottle dropped to the floor, smashing into hundreds of pieces, resulting in the bar floor being strewn with glass and flooded with Bacardi.

One quiet afternoon, with barely any customers in the bar, some thieves came in, unscrewed the fruit machine at the side, broke into the mechanics and stole the money - all completely unnoticed by Mark.

Towards the end of a Saturday evening Mark went into the cellar to change a keg of beer; unfortunately, he didn't put the valve back down correctly.

The pub was closed on Sunday so it wasn't until Monday morning when Chris descended the cellar steps to find the whole contents from the barrel containing 11 gallons of beer all over the floor.

Mark was a very expensive commodity that week.

Mark often came into the bar on a social basis but was irritated that there wasn't anywhere to hang his coat.

Chris never got round to buying any hooks, so Mark took it upon himself to buy them. He brought them in, and screwed them along the bar. Job done.

Early one Saturday evening, I was cooking in the kitchen after receiving a last minute call from the chef to say he wasn't coming into work. Therefore I was now the chef for the night, which ultimately meant the restaurant was now short staffed; so I was not in a particularly jovial mood, knowing full well we had a fully booked restaurant for the evening.

Julia answered a phone call and looking very concerned and a little scared, she relayed the message: 'Chris and Mark are in another pub, and aren't coming into work tonight. I did tell them they must, but they were insistent on staying out for the night and getting pissed.'

I was fuming, 'They're better be fucking joking.'

'I don't think they were joking; they sounded adamant' replied Julia.

At 7.30pm I stomped downstairs to the bar, to be confronted by a laughing, smiling, Chris and Mark both working behind the bar.

'You might think it was funny, but I fucking didn't.' I then stomped back upstairs to the restaurant.

Poor Julia was scared to talk to me; then Chris and Mark came upstairs to see me with their tails between their legs apologising profusely and said they would never have let me down – not like the chef did.

I did see the funny side – much later – however, at the time; their prank went down like a cup of sick.

****

A few of the staff looked upon Chris and myself as their father and mother and subsequently they were known as our surrogate children. They came to us with their problems, which we tried to resolve or to give advice and to point them in the right direction. They may have boyfriend/girlfriend trouble or money worries (no, they still didn't get a pay rise) or maybe just needed a shoulder to cry on, or maybe all those trials and tribulations at the same time. We were even called Dad and Mum.

One girl we employed was having difficulties for one reason or another and often came to me for advice after which I said she had better be one of my surrogate children. She was thrilled by this prospect and called me Mum quite frequently after that when she needed an ear to listen to her woes.

****

When the National Lottery began we decided to have a staff syndicate. Ten of our employees joined, each person paying £1 per week for a line of numbers of their choice, then any winnings would be evenly distributed between everyone. Very occasionally we won £10, but nothing significant, until one evening I stopped off at a corner shop into work to get the numbers scanned. The lady behind the till looked at me in surprise,

'Ooh, you've had a big win; I'll have to get the manager.'

My legs started to shake and, in a trembling voice, I asked, 'How much have we won?'

'108' came her reply.

'What thousand? £108,000?' I asked with heart thumping and speaking in a higher pitched voice.

'No, £108' she said, looking at me in disgust as if I was the most ungrateful person she had ever come across. Her reaction of distaste increased when I replied,

'Is that all?'

I laughed all the way into work then conveyed the story of our big win, equating to £10.80 each.

****

We were more fortunate than many establishments in the leisure industry because we didn't have a large turnover of staff; a vast number remained employed by us for years. Others started and finished relatively quickly, either because they were fired or because they didn't like working for us.

We were never under any illusion, realising that, without staff, we would not have been able to operate or produce the volume of turnover which was achieved so, to them, we are truly grateful.

No one was perfect – but who is? With staff, it was important to realise that each person had their own good qualities and attributes which were valuable to the working environment. Making our business successful far outweighed the little faults they may have had.

Not every member of staff employed by us has been mentioned; maybe they have been forgotten, maybe they did a good job but nothing eventful happened, or maybe something so bad happened I couldn't print it. But whatever the reason, each and every member of staff employed played an important role at the Walnut.

****

A SECTION FROM OUR COCKTAIL LIST – CIRCA 1984

Just look at the prices!

ALMOND AFFAIR Amaretto, Orange Curacao, O.J.
and cream   1.95
ALAMO Southern Comfort, grapefruit juice   1.10
APPLE KNOCKER Vodka, Galliano, apple juice 1.80
ALEXANDER BABY Rum, Creme de Cacao, cream
    1.80

The house special!

MARGARITA'S

FROZEN MARGARITA Large Tequila, triple sec, lime juice   2.40
STRAWBERRY MARGARITA Large Tequila, triple sec,
Strawberry liqueur, lime juice   3.20
KAHLUA MARGARITA Tequila, Kahlua, lime juice   1.70
MARGARITA BLUES Large Tequila, Blue Curacao, lime juice   2.40

B AND B Brandy and Benedictine   1.70
BLOOD 'N' SAND Scotch, Cherry Liqueur, Sweet Vermouth
and O.J.   2.10
BATTERY CHARGER Pernod or Ricard, grenadine topped with
soda   95
BETWEEN THE SHEETS Brandy, Cointreau, Bacardi and
lemon juice   2.50
BRANDY ALEXANDRA Brandy, Creme de Cacao, cream 1.80
BRONX COCKTAIL Gin, Sweet and Dry Vermouth, O.J. 1.60
BACARDI COCKTAIL Bacardi, lemon and lime, grenadine 1.10
BLACK RUSSIAN Large Vodka and Kahlua   2.20
BRAVE BULL Large Tequila and Kahlua   2.25
BLOODY MARY Large Vodka, lemon juice, Tabasco,
Worcestershire sauce, celery salt, and tomato juice   2.00
BANANA BANSHEE Banana liqueur, Creme de Cacao
cream   1.80
BLUE HAWAII Large Gin, Blue Curacao, pineapple juice,
coconut cream   3.00
BRANDY COLLINS Large Brandy, lemon juice,
sugar, soda   1.80
BLACK WATCH Large Scotch, Kahlua topped
with soda   2.25

Cream of the Coladas!

LOTSA COLADAS

**Puerto Rico's most famous drink,
blended long smooth and creamy**
PINA COLADA Large Bacardi Gold,
pineapple juice, coconut cream   2.30
BANANA COLADO Bacardi Gold, Large
Banana Liqueur, pineapple juice, coconut
cream   2.90
AMARETTO COLADA Bacardi Gold, Large Amaretto,
pineapple juice, coconut cream   2.90
CHERRY COLADA Bacardi Gold, Large Cherry Liqueur,
pineapple juice, coconut cream   2.90
MELON COLADA Bacardi Gold, Large Melon Liqueur,
pineapple juice, coconut cream   2.90
COMFORT COLADA Large Southern Comfort,
pineapple juice, coconut cream   2.50

Order doubles — mixers come free!

BAR CUSTOMERS

Over the course of our 25 years of pub life, there must have been thousands and thousands of different people who entered the pub.

The vast majority were completely inconsequential. They came in, ordered a drink, paid their money, stayed for just one or two beverages, or even remained the whole night, but there was no recollection of them afterwards, they were just faces upon faces disappearing into oblivion from our memory. Even if those people came in the following week and didn't say or do anything interesting, then they were again obliterated from our memories.

It took customers several months of constantly coming in the pub to have the privilege of being called a 'regular'. It sometimes took another few months before we could actually memorise their names, even then it was difficult. That aspect seemed immaterial, remembering their drinks and pouring them out as soon as they walked in the bar without them even having to ask for them was a far more important priority as far as we were concerned.

****

Andy (known to his friends as Larky) was a guy who frequented the pub often, and always drank the same brand of beer. He remarked one day that it had taken him four years to be acknowledged by Chris; he always felt he was serving an apprenticeship. His turning point came when he entered the pub and Chris immediately put his regular drink on the bar,

'There you go Larky.'

'Wow, I've cracked it; I've finally been accepted as a regular. It's only taken me four years.'

****

We were very fortunate that, although our pub was located in the heart of the city, we were known as a local pub to the customers because we had so many 'regulars' over the years that all knew each other or who got to know each other over a period of time.

A city centre pub doesn't generally have the same feel as a country local because of the passing trade you receive in a big city where people tend to go shopping for the day and just pop in anywhere handy for a quick drink or a bite to eat. Often you only saw them once, whereas country pubs rely on the local residents.

Many bars in the city are managed houses or chain pubs with some staff often lacking any charisma or personality, and certainly do not possess the individuality of a publican behind the bar, or the same regular staff working, who knew what people liked to drink without them having to ask. If they were spotted walking down the road towards the pub, the drink would be poured and on the bar ready for them as they walked in the door.

Obviously, we did have the one-time shoppers and tourists, which of course were good for our revenue, but the pub survived throughout the year with regulars and these were the people we felt it was essential to look after.

We listened to many stories from customers, and overheard numerous conversations that possibly we shouldn't have heard. To the regulars, we were their confidant, friend and often a councillor, giving advice when asked for it.

We heard their matrimonial problems and girlfriend and boyfriend arguments. We had to listen and be discreet, which was something Chris found quite difficult at times, especially if a customer came in for a drink with a person that wasn't their partner.

As a publican, it was important to gain the customers' respect, and with that endorsed, meant they treated the pub as their own personal drinking establishment and had a loyalty towards us and the bar. In fact it was like another home to many.

They loved to watch and listen to Chris being rude to customers, and liked abuse given to them as well, as they knew it was only an act on Chris' part. He was actually a nice guy underneath all the banter, but they still liked to see him grumpy. Even if he wasn't, he got blamed for looking miserable. People felt they had been accepted if they were given abuse from him. They wondered what was wrong with him if he didn't go round the bar and nip the men's inside thighs or try and undo a girl's bra, or make a few cutting remarks whilst passing, 'What the fuck are you wearing today? It makes you look gay.'

People often called Chris 'mate.' 'I'm not your mate, I don't even know you'.

He didn't like it if people called him 'Gudge'. 'Only my friends are allowed to call me Gudge, and you're not one of them.'

A lot of customers seemed to think we were their best friends, which was fine, except a lot of time we didn't have any recollection of who they were. Although I have to say, it was an accolade to think that customers had such a high opinion of us – even if we didn't know their names.

Some customers sat on their own, at the end of the bar next to the glass washer, and wanted to talk to Chris; not just talk - ramble on and on and on about nothing significant.

In Chris' words, 'That guy's boring the arse off me, why do they always sit that end of the fucking bar?'

Consequently, on these occasions, the empty glasses were stacked up by the machine without been washed, simply because Chris didn't want to be involved in a boring conversation with that person.

Women felt comfortable coming to the Walnut on their own for a drink, whether they were meeting someone later, or just on their lunch break from work. They said they never felt intimidated or threatened by anybody because of the reputation we had for not allowing any undesirables (if we could help it) in the pub. This was a huge compliment for us that we had created an atmosphere and ambience people were happy with.

Chris nearly had a heart attack one day in the pub when a guy came into the bar and asked him if he was Chris Gudgin.

'Yes. Why? Who wants to know?'

The guy went on to tell him he was his godson. Unfortunately Chris only heard the word 'son'. He went a whiter shade of pale; his jaw dropped to his knees; it wasn't until further into the conversation that he realised he was talking to his godson and not his son!

****

Customers who had once been part of our regular clientele, drinking over the course of many years, sometimes gradually came in less frequently or disappeared completely. People either moved away or settled down and had a family. So, as the years progressed and their children got older, the children themselves began coming into the pub, and we had great delight in portraying the antics their parents had got up to in the bar when they were younger.

Parents often told their children when they came to Norwich on their own that if they got into any kind of trouble, or just didn't have enough money to get home, always go to the Walnut and we would look after them – which happened on several occasions. The kids had either missed a bus or spent all their money, so we lent them some.

We had a group of lads who used to drink in the pub regularly, with one object in mind, to get as pissed as possible, have a laugh, and pull a bird at the end of the night. They were never any trouble, just loved to have a good time. We saw them mature, get married and have children. Some went on to run highly successful businesses and it was great to see them achieve their goals.

A few regulars from the Walnut have also gone on to running their own successful public houses and restaurants.

Jack, ran a thriving pub just outside Norwich, but long before he went into the licensed industry he was a regular customer in our bar. One day he sat in his usual seat and asked me, 'What are you drinking?'

'Water, why?'

He didn't believe me, and snatched the glass from my hand.

After tasting it, and showing a look of disbelief on his face, said, 'Oh, it is only water, I thought you were drinking vodka and that was the reason you always have a smile on your face.'

So Jack's assumption, was that I was an alcoholic drinking neat vodka, and therefore would smile constantly.

No, it was necessary to wear a constant smile in the pub to counteract Chris' grumpy face!

****

Chris never had trouble matchmaking in the bar. If a guy mentioned to Chris that he fancied a female sitting at the bar, Chris would immediately make sure the connection was made between them, although not always in the most tactful way.

'See that guy sitting the other end of the bar? Well, he wants to shag you – are you interested?'

Occasionally this worked, depending on the female of course.

He did manage to unite a couple using a more diplomatic approach. They dated and subsequently got married and had a daughter.

There were many customers over the years that came in the pub to celebrate an anniversary, saying that they had either met in the Walnut, or had their first date in the pub, or had their first meal together in the restaurant. Whichever it was, the Walnut has memories for people to treasure, and it is a mark of respect to us that, during our time as licensees, we may have contributed a small part in a small way, to customers' happiness.

Over the years it became apparent that clientele made identical remarks and repeatedly asked the same questions, to which there was always an instinctive or rejoinder comment.

Some customers may only have come in once and others a few times, but then there were the people who came in regularly every week for many years. But some of the events, the antics, the problems they caused us, the things they said, and incidences that occurred had a lasting memory for us.

If people were taking too long to decide on their drink order, Chris would offer them a piece of paper with the pub telephone number written on, and told them to phone him when they were ready with their complete order of drinks.

****

A lady may mention to Chris there wasn't any toilet paper in the ladies; he reciprocated by handing her a napkin informing her she could wipe away her drips with that.

****

If someone mentioned the price of drinks were more expensive in the Walnut than in another pub in the city, Chris would tell them to fuck off and drink there instead.

****

He had great delight in telling people we were probably the most expensive pub in the city – and also one of the best and that was why people came in.

****

A regular customer complained his beer was flat so Chris picked up his pint, blew inside the glass with a straw, making a frothy head, and said, 'There you go mate, it's fine now.'

The guy could not believe what he had just seen; there was sheer horror on his face. Chris reluctantly did replace it for a fresh pint!

A more hygienic way (no, on second thoughts, it's not that more hygienic) of putting a head on a flat glass of beer was to tear a piece of foil from a cigarette packet, roll it into a sausage shape, then spin it briskly round and round in the glass of flat beer – this created an excellent froth.

****

'My beer's flat!' Chris would take a sip from it, put it back in front of him and say, 'Nothing wrong with that' and walk away.

****

Live music from local blues bands was played in the pub on a Thursday night. Although the cost to us for putting on entertainment was, on average, around £180, we never charged admission on the door. Even so, people still complained about the price of alcohol we were charging.

Chris would have no hesitation in pointing out the fact they were watching a good band for free, and had the option to leave, but shouldn't even consider standing there watching the band without having a drink.

****

Women have an annoying habit of being unable to order a drink for themselves. They whisper to their partner first, who then has to relay the information to the bar tender – why is it that some women don't have the confidence to order for themselves?

Or people may be hanging over the bar waving a note, trying to attract the bar person's attention. When they are served, they don't even know what they want to drink. 'I'll come back when you are ready to tell me what you want; I'm off to serve someone else.'

People have a dreadful tendency to order just one drink at a time instead of presenting the complete order. I appreciate that many bartenders in various pubs can only manage to serve one drink at a time, but as far as we were concerned, this was too time consuming and frustrating, because the longer it takes to serve customers, the less money is going in the till.

If Chris was given the order only for the first drink and then silence from the person, he would be extremely prompt in saying (in his usual courteous manner), 'So, anything else? I can remember more than one drink at a time you know'.

The offending customer always seemed to respond with a blank, vacant look and couldn't quite believe what Chris had said.

****

Four people came to the bar and asked Chris for two vodka and tonics with ice and lemon.

'All the drinks we serve here come with ice and lemon; you don't have to ask for it.' This was spoken in Chris' usual sarcastic manner.

'Can we also have two pints of lager? Without ice and lemon, please.'

****

When customers ordered food to eat in the bar area, they paid the bar person, who then rang the meal requirement through on the internal phone to the restaurant.

A common phrase from the general public was, 'Will the food be very long?'

Chris' reply: 'It will be however long it takes to cook'.

or 'Do you want it cooked, or straight out of the fridge and slapped on a plate, and miss the cooking process completely?'

Or then there was the lady who ordered a portion of fries from Chris.

Chris picked the phone up to order them through to the kitchen. She asked, 'Who are you ringing?'

'McDonalds.'

Her mouth dropped open, a look of horror appeared on her face, 'You are joking?'

'No, but don't worry, they won't take too long to deliver,' replied Chris, trying to keep a straight face.

'But I don't like those skinny chips that come from McDonalds, I want the chips you normally serve here'.

She was getting extremely disgruntled, so Chris did put her out of her misery - eventually.

****

When a regular complained about his burger, Chris picked it up from the plate, took a bite and placed it back; 'Nothing wrong with that,' and walked away.

****

There was the guy with a twitch who drunk 3 pints of Holsten, then ordered another.

He started wandering around the bar trying to talk to people he didn't know. Getting no response, he tried talking to a post - no response there either! So he tried complaining to Chris, saying there was something wrong with the beer; it didn't taste right.

'Well, you've just drunk three pints of it, and as it came from the same barrel, there can't be anything wrong with it.'

'I want another pint,' stated the slurring twitch.

'Well you're not having one, in fact here's £1.20, the cost of the remaining beer left in your glass, now get out. '

'But why?'

'Because I said so,' replied Chris.

'But why? What have I done? For what reason?'

'I don't have to give a reason, it's my prerogative, just leave - before I show you how to use the door.'

'But why?' (He just wouldn't give up)

'You're fucking breathing: Is that a good enough reason for you?'

He left.

Chris' comment: 'Was I really that bad Jude?'

'Yes you were.'

****

Then there was the guy who ordered a pint of Newcastle Brown, complained about the cost and refused to pay and then subsequently asked if could exchange it for half pint of lager instead.

'No', rejoined Chris, because if you are already complaining about the cost of Newcastle Brown, you will complain about the cost of half a pint lager, so you can piss off.'

****

On more than one occasion, in fact many times, people have walked into the bar and appeared OK when they were served and then started to be rowdy, loud, or act like idiots; these were not people we wanted in the bar. So Chris just used to pick their beer up from in front of them, tip it down the sink, give them back the cash it had cost and tell them to 'Fuck off.'

****

If a member of our male staff or a regular male customer brought a lady in the pub on a first date, Chris would take great delight in going up to the table where they may be engrossed in conversation. Not waiting to be introduced, he would casually say to the lady, 'You know he's gay, don't you?'

Or he would be very blunt, and ask him in front of the poor unsuspecting lady, 'Have you shagged her yet?'

On the majority of these occasions, the guy had already warned the lady about Chris before they had even entered the pub, and told her certainly not to pay any attention to anything Chris may say. If the chap did forget to mention Chris' possible remarks, then that was his fault for bringing a girl into the Walnut in the first place; he should have known better.

****

There was the man who drank five pints of Holsten at the bar, took a bottle of 100 paracetemol from his pocket and proceeded to swallow the tablets. He announced to us what he had just done, but there was no problem as he had telephoned for an ambulance to come and get him!

****

An old lady, in her late 70's, came in practically every lunchtime for a light ale. She was always smart in her attire and tottered up to the bar and asked for her drink in a quiet, squeaky, high-pitched voice.

After rummaging in her handbag she would pass over 50p, - the correct money when she first began to frequent our pub. But, as the years progressed, obviously prices increased and the total amount for light ale ended at 95p. However, we only ever received 50p. and never had the heart to request any more from her.

We disallowed people eating their own food in the bar because we sold food in our restaurant which was available to eat in the bar as well. That is, unless it was 'Light Ale' (this was the name we gave to the old lady). She brought in her own homemade sandwich, sat and ate at a table in the corner of the bar and then went to sleep – often with her glass of ale in her hand, pointing precariously towards her lap. We used to give her a little nudge on the arm whilst she was asleep if she was starting to slide downwards, mainly to check that she was still alive.

One winter's day, she walked out of the pub door, tripped on the step and fell down. Fortunately she wasn't hurt, just a bit shaken, so we called a taxi to take her home and insisted we would pay her journey fee. We then found out that she lived nearly 20 miles away – 'Light Ale' was proving to be a very expensive customer.

****

Some customers were full of bullshit and told stories that were blatantly untrue, but still quite amusing at times – like Maurice, for instance, who had worked on Radio Caroline and owned a villa and a boat in the Bahamas, which we were welcome to use at any time. Then we called his bluff, and told him we were going to be taking some time off from work, and was the offer still open to have use of his villa? 'Um, Um, I'm very sorry, but I am in the process of selling it.'

'Umm, I see.' That was the last time he bragged about the villa.

****

We refused to sell a drink called snake bite in the bar, which was half lager and half cider mixed together in a pint glass. A pint of lager should be clear, but mixed with cider it turns cloudy and is therefore not very appetising to look at, especially to other customers that could see it and maybe think we were serving poor quality beer.

A snake bite made people drunk quicker and then throw up - another good enough reason not to sell it. It also congealed and separated in the glass if it was left for several minutes - so it left nothing to the imagination of what it was doing to your insides. No wonder it made people sick.

People would try to be clever when they ordered a snake bite. Instead of asking for it by name, they would request half a pint of lager, a half pint of cider, and an empty pint glass.

So obvious were their intentions that needless to say, they never received their request.

****

In the days before the smoking ban, I came down the restaurant stairs to the bar one evening when I was greeted with a strong aroma of a lighted joint.

I glanced at the customers to see if I could spot anybody smoking an illegal substance, but to no avail. I picked up the dirty ashtrays to empty, to see if there were any remains left; there was nothing. I told Chris, who was working behind the bar, that I could smell a joint but could not see where it is coming from and couldn't find any evidence.

He sniffed the air,

'I can't smell anything, but will have a look round the pub.'

He too was unsuccessful in finding the culprit, but by now the smell was very pungent. A few minutes went by until he noticed where the aroma was at its most prevalent. Tucked underneath a table, crouched far in the corner, was a guy with his legs folded under his chin smoking a joint.

Chris pulled him out by his leg, only because he couldn't reach his arm, and threw him out the door. 'You're banned.'

****

Chris opened the door of the pub when he arrived at work early one evening and immediately noticed a group of girls eating some chocolate brownies. He picked one up and shoved the whole thing in his mouth before the girls could stop him.

At the time he hadn't realised the brownie was laced with an illegal substance. About an hour later he was completely stoned and having great difficulty serving customers. Every time he took a drink's order from a customer and by the time he had walked to the other end of the bar he couldn't remember what the drink was.

That'll teach him for being greedy – Oh, no, it won't.

****

Richard, a fireman, drank regularly in the pub but was very embarrassed one day when a small fire occurred in the car park just outside the Walnut.

The fire service was called, Richard came hurtling down the length of the alleyway, hose in hand, until he got to the edge of the car park just outside the door of the pub, and discovered his hose wasn't long enough. His legs and arms went in the air and nearly fell backwards with the force of coming to an abrupt stop, only to see the customers and staff watching him. 'Of all places for that to happen, it had to be outside this fucking pub.'

We didn't let him forget this incidence and reminded him of it for a long time. Thereafter he was known as 'Fireman Sam.' 'Put any fires out lately Sam?'

'Got a longer hose yet?'

****

People can walk into the bar and appear, even to the trained eye, to be completely stone cold sober. They walk to the bar, order a drink coherently, pay their money and pick up their pint to drink and that's when it all goes wrong.

Taking a sip from their glass, they are suddenly as pissed as parrots, their legs go wobbly, they slouch on the bar with head in hands, dribbling, and cannot even

64

string a sentence together because they are slurring so much. 'Right, so who served him?'

'But he was fine when he walked in.'

This happened many times, and was quite funny to watch but, I must say, it was still quite a mystery how somebody can sober up just long enough to get a drink, but be unable to continue to act soberly.

The downside on these occasions was that the person subsequently had to be stood upright, steered towards the door and sent on his way hoping that he would be able to stagger up the road and out of sight.

****

A woman was sitting on her own at the bar one night, and had obviously had one too many drinks. She kept talking to all the men who were in close proximity to her but who were not in the least bit interested in what she had to say. However, her appearance was quite intriguing. It appeared, on first glance, that she had two sets of large boobs, one set placed just below her chin, the other pair where boobs are normally located.

She was so pissed she hadn't even noticed that her padded bra had moved upwards, directly under her chin, and her boobs were now braless; it was not an attractive sight.   ****

A rather large-built blind man, complete with his white stick, came into the bar one evening. He required assistance understanding all the different beers we sold because of his sight disability, which of course was no problem. Afterwards he proceeded to order a drink.

He sat on one of the stools at the end of the bar next to the public payphone, and began mumbling to himself and talking to the wall. It was becoming apparent he had already been drinking a lot.

He began by shouting out loudly the meals written on the menu board. He then asked for a telephone directory as he wanted the number for Anglia Television as he was going to sell them his story. Maybe the story was about a blind man who had suddenly regained his sight.

He put the telephone to his ear, pretending to make the call.

After collecting some glasses from around the bar area, Chris noticed the 'blind' man's beer was still there but he was gone. He asked a regular if he had seen him leave the pub. 'No, he fumbled his way to the stairs and continued up towards the restaurant.'

With the restaurant closed that evening and all the lights out, Chris went upstairs after him, only to find him at the top groping with the Venetian blind at a window (which he must have thought was a door) and was trying to open it.

'The restaurant is closed tonight. Come on, I'll help you downstairs.'

As Chris got to the bottom of the steps, still with his hand on the 'blind' man's arm, the man started getting verbally aggressive.

He tried to shake Chris' hand free and, at the same time with his other fist, took a swing at Chris' face; luckily, Chris moved quickly enough to avoid the full force of the punch and just got caught on the side of his head.

It was time for this guy to leave, but this was not an easy task when the man was built like a tank. When Chris finally pushed him towards the exit, he then had problems trying to hold the guy's arms down so he was not hit again. Then, at the same time, he had to try to manoeuvre around his body to open the door.

Eventually he was out, but Chris got the piss ripped out of him from customers. 'How could you? Chucking a blind man out of the pub!'

'Fancy getting hit by a blind man.'

****

Bob was a genuinely kind-hearted guy who Chris nicknamed 'Wobbly Bob,' fittingly called, because he often wobbled when he got drunk. If we had a live band playing he would stand in front of the musicians with his air guitar and play along with them, moving his make-believe guitar up and down, strumming the strings, shaking his head and jumping about. It was very amusing to watch, although not quite as good when he started singing as well!

****

Lulu was in her twenties, definitely not a lady; in fact, she was a 'rough bird.' She either came in on her own or with a couple of men who were equally as rough.

She didn't cause any trouble apart from being a bit loud on occasions after a few pints of beer. She wasn't the brightest spark intellectually but knew every swear word in existence, and used them in abundance. This became clear the day she came out of the toilets and shouted to Chris in such a loud voice that everyone in the bar could hear.

'Chris, there's two fucking girls, in the fucking toilets, having a fucking shag.'

Fortunately for us, she didn't continue drinking in our pub much after that. She was known to the police and didn't like the fact that quite a lot of the local police came in drinking socially, and was under the assumption they were watching her – which they probably were.

****

A very attractive Thai lady started coming in at lunchtimes for a drink, sitting at the bar and chatting to other male customers and accepting a drink if she was offered one. A man would come in to meet her, they would sit drinking for a while and then disappear. A couple of hours later she would return alone for another couple of drinks then leave.

There was nothing unusual about that until the next day when she came in again. She scrounged a couple of drinks from unsuspecting male customers, then a man came in to meet her and they enjoyed a couple of drinks together and then left. However, this time it was a different male.

This continued for a few more days with a different man on each occasion coming in the bar to meet her.

We were told from one of our regulars that he had taken the Thai lady out for a meal and then afterwards back home for sex, which surprise, surprise, he ended up paying for.

Now we knew exactly what she was up to. This was confirmed again when we found out another of our customers had, shall we say, enjoyed her company.

The Thai prostitute was banned for trying to run her business from our pub.

****

We had only been in the Walnut for a couple of months, when a customer who had been drinking in the pub since we opened, came in with some duvet covers to sell.

I was already considering buying some new bed linen, and the covers he was selling were exactly what I was after, and a good price, so I handed the money over and was very pleased with my purchase.

When I asked him if he had any pillowcases to match, he replied, 'No, but I can soon go and nick some for you.'

It was only then I realised how naïve I had been. No wonder the bed linen was cheap – he had nicked it all. That was definitely the last dealings I would be having with stolen goods from over the bar. What a great start that would have been as a licensee – being prosecuted for accepting stolen property!

****

Roddy was a very loyal customer of ours and came to the Walnut regularly for many years. He always stood in the same place at the bar with his newspaper, pint of lager and a constant supply of cigarettes. Well, that was until the smoking ban, then he had to go outside the door for a fag. He enjoyed perusing the betting pages and circling any bets he may be interested in. When it was Grand National day, or if one of the staff wanted to have a little tickle on the horses, it was Roddy who they went to for a possible red hot tip.

****

Every Friday night a group of regulars went out on a boys' night drinking session; they drank their way round several city pubs and usually ended up at the Walnut about 10.30pm – half an hour before we closed and then always haggled for a late drink after time.

One week Chris asked them if they would like to come in the following week and stay longer for a drink.

'Cor, yeh, thanks Chris.' Obviously thinking they could stay for a late night lock-in.

'Well, if you come in earlier, that means you will be staying longer drinking.'

'Bastard,' came the reply.

On another occasion the boys were in the pub for a drink. George went to the toilets followed shortly afterwards by Chris. He slapped George on the back. 'You alright mate?'

Unfortunately, it caught George unawares whilst he was standing at the urinal having a pee. George fell forwards, hitting his tooth, which broke on the tiles.

He returned to the bar to demonstrate to his mates what had just happened. 'Look, Chris has broken my fucking tooth.'

He showed everyone his front tooth, and with half of it missing, it certainly didn't look very attractive.

That friendly slap on the back cost Chris £200 for George to have his tooth repaired!

There were hundreds of regulars over the years, and many of them loved the pub as much as we did, and proved to be very loyal customers.

The lunchtime regulars either sat or stood in the same place every time they came in, and look very peeved if somebody unknown was in their usual spot.

Michael and Marty came in for a drink about three times a week and their seating area was the bench next to the juke-box. They enjoyed hearing all my gossip and news of the week but took great delight in telling me how much I smelt of burgers and chips, especially when it had been really busy in the restaurant, when the smell was even more potent.

****

Don and Marilyn were nearly always in on a Friday lunchtime. Don liked to initiate a conversation with the purpose of trying to wind people up; it was all in good fun and was quite amusing to listen to him in action. Don originated from Tobago so always took a long holiday to visit his family and, as he said, to top up his suntan because he was looking a bit pale – bearing in mind with his ethnic origin, he was dark-skinned.

****

Jason drank in the pub for years; he worshipped the Walnut and everything it stood for. After consuming several beers, he particularly liked hugging Chris and telling him how much he loved us both, which drove Chris mad, especially if he was really busy at the time and trying to go round the pub picking up empty glasses.

'Don't keep fucking hugging me. Yes, I know you love me, you've already fucking told me three times tonight.'

He did have a heart of gold and was very sincere in his loyalty to the Walnut, but that didn't stop him driving Chris to the brink sometimes.

***

Many photographs were taken in the bar by customers enjoying a night out. Sometimes they asked us to take innocent pictures of them – either pulling faces, raising their glasses for a toast, doing a moonie or flashing their boobs. Of course Chris felt obligated to assist them in posing for a shot.

Many copies of the pictures taken in the pub were brought in by the customers for us to keep in the Walnut photo drawer.

I received a phone call one morning from a gentleman claiming to be from the Sun Newspaper. He stated they knew we were in possession of a picture they would be interested in buying from us.

I thought it was a wind-up and didn't believe him for a second.

'What picture? We have lots of photos.'

He went on to say that the tabloid press were doing an editorial on a girl who had taken her ex-employers to court for sexual harassment, and the newspaper was delving into her background. He went on to say they understood we were in possession of a picture which revealed her standing by the juke box in an inappropriate manner and would offer us well in excess of £300 for the photo.

Still thinking it was a wind-up, I humoured him and denied any knowledge of having the photo.

A guy from the Sun appeared in the pub a couple of days later, asking again if they could buy the picture. Oh, so it wasn't a wind-up after all.

We bought the newspaper and there was a big spread about the girl in question, and the impending court case. They had attempted to be detrimental towards her, but without any input from us. We did find the innocent picture taken of her flashing a boob, rang her up so she could come and retrieve the picture from us and have it destroyed.

She came to collect the photo, bringing a bottle of wine for us as a thank you.

Yes, we could have received a few hundred pounds from the tabloids, but we had morals and felt an innocent photo would have been misconstrued.

****

We were away on holiday when 'Mr. Fuller' the main man from the brewery who produced the bitter we sold, Fuller's London Pride, came to the Walnut for a drink with the regional representative, Ron Finch.

He was visiting Norwich and calling at the various outlets selling his beer to see how sales were progressing and hear any comments received from customers.

Charlie, our bartender, served them with two pints of Fuller's London Pride. Ron took a few sips from his pint and continued chatting to Mr. Fuller. When Mr. Fuller picked up his glass, he looked at the beer, took a sip, and announced;

'This isn't London Pride.'

Charlie said that yes it was, he had pulled the beer from the correct pump.

Ron, who we know very well, was very embarrassed; firstly because he had started to drink his beer without even noticing anything untoward and, secondly, because he had been praising the Walnut to Mr. Fuller before their arrival, for the quality of beer we maintained, and for the excellent professional operation we were running.

Mr. Fuller was not happy, and insisted again that the beer being poured from the London Pride tap was a different bitter.

Charlie's investigation uncovered that someone had put the wrong keg on the connection!

On our return from holiday, Chris had to make some very apologetic phone calls to Mr. Fuller, begging absolution, saying it had never happened before and the incident would not be repeated.

Of all the times when something like that happens, it is always when somebody important makes an appearance.

****

Some individuals seemed to think the Walnut Tree was a gay bar, where that rumour derived from we have no idea. The only conclusion we arrived at is that Friday night was notoriously known as a boys' night out. So yes, the majority of customers were men.

When Chris (who wasn't sexy or hunky, and very definitely 'male') and another male bar person were working behind the bar, the comments from customers were often: 'You ought to get some fucking tits working behind the bar.' Or

'Employ someone worth looking at.' Or

'We're fed up seeing your ugly mush Chris.'

Not what you would expect to hear in a gay bar but, on saying that, when the Theatre Royal, which is only five minutes walk away, were showing the performance 'Rocky Horror Show' we were packed before and after the show with women and male customers dressed in scantily clad costumes, make-up, stockings and suspenders attempting to walk in stiletto heels – then, yes, you could be forgiven for thinking it was a gay bar.

****

Michael drank in our bar every Saturday. He had a very physical labouring job all week and abstained from drinking mid-week, but certainly made up for it at the week-ends.

With his strenuous job during the week he must have felt tired because he was always falling asleep. Not in a chair, but standing up.

He was sometimes leaning over the juke-box which made it really difficult if someone wanted to put money in to play some music. He sometimes slept leaning on the payphone situated at the end of the bar, which again, was a problem if a customer wanted to make a phone call. He often fell asleep at the other end of the bar which was fine, as it didn't obstruct anything used by the public, but if he went into a deep sleep with his head in his hands with one foot on the rail, he often just slid off the end of the bar with a thump and fell to the floor.

That woke him up – well for a few moments. He would get up, have a slug of beer from his bottle, then go back to the position of his head nestling in his hand and then he would start nodding off again.

His sleeping was much too frequent an occurrence and far too good an opportunity to miss so that a few pranks were often played on him.

The first thing he always did without fail when he woke up was to pick up his Michelob beer bottle and have a few slurps. So whilst he was asleep Chris used to exchange the beer for water. Michael would wake up, have a glug, just look at it, shake his head and – back to sleep.

Or Chris once put some Tabasco round the rim of the bottle which got more of a reaction as we got a grimace of disbelief on his face, a pout, a judder of the lips – then sleep.

If he stood snoozing at the end of the bar where the glass washer and sink were situated, it was quite amusing to splash little droplets of water at him; it used to make his head shake a bit, and one eye would open but this was still not enough to wake him completely.

Chris squirted some cream on his head once and put a cocktail cherry on top. Unfortunately, before he woke up, the cream had to be carefully wiped off as it began to melt and start dripping down his face. Although Michael was a great guy, if he had found out about that hoax he would not have been amused.

At around 9pm, one Saturday evening, Chris wrote with a black felt tip pen on Michael's sleeping head 'Walnut Tree'. Now, as the story goes, he left our pub about 10pm, went to a few more bars, drank a few more beers, walked through the busy nightlife scene at the further end of the city, then hailed a taxi to go home.

On getting in the back seat of the cab, the driver looked at him in his rear view mirror and said,

'Oh, see you have been to the Walnut Tree tonight, then mate'

'How do you know?'

'Cause you've got it written right across your forehead'.

Michael was not happy, in fact I had never seen him so angry, and that was a week later when he next came in our pub, so I wouldn't have liked to have seen him when he realised he had been all around Norwich for a few hours with 'Walnut Tree' written on his forehead.

He was so mad, I think he was pretty close to decking Chris and with the muscles he had, Chris would have been straight down on the floor.

So after lots of apologies and hugs, Chris was forgiven, and Michael still continued to frequent our pub – and go to sleep.

When he wasn't sleeping, or when he used to come in with a friend (even then he might doze off) we all used to chat and have laughs together, and he jokingly said that when he died he wanted his ashes in a Michelob bottle displayed behind the bar.

A few years later, Michael sadly passed away. Even while he was poorly and came in for a beer he never complained, although he never told anyone how seriously ill he was.

A couple of weeks after the funeral, we received a parcel in the post. On opening it, there was firstly a letter from the Funeral Directors' stating that it had been Michael's wishes for his ashes to be kept and put in the Michelob bottle herewith enclosed. Wrapped very carefully in tissue paper was a Michelob bottle, filled with ashes.

I immediately thought this must be a wind-up. Chris was a little more sceptical, and a part of him did believe it, remembering the conversation from way back of Michael's wishes in the event of his death; the letter was definitely official looking and printed on headed notepaper.

The letter and bottle with the ashes in had pride of place on the top shelf of the bar for all to see. A few weeks went by and all was revealed. It was a joke by a friend of ours (some friend), who received permission from Michael's widow to play this joke as she felt it would be something he would have enjoyed, especially as this was a way of getting his own back on Chris for all the pranks he had played on him.

Even after we knew the truth, and that they weren't his real ashes, but sand, we still left them on the shelf as a tribute to him.

****

This is the tale of a customer who used to come in the Walnut. When he first started coming in the bar we were in two minds whether to serve him or send him on his way; although he was clean and tidy, polite, didn't cause any disturbance or upset any customers, he just appeared eccentric.

It was difficult to understand what he was saying the majority of the time, as he spoke so quietly. So when I used to sit and chat to him and listen to all his stories, I always made sure I had turned the music volume down so I could hear him.

He would stride towards the pub, walk a few feet past, do a 360 degree turn – sometimes more than once, then walk back up the alleyway again. He often did this several times before eventually getting inside the pub.

When he managed to actually push the door open, he might change his mind, turn round a few more times, then walk away, or he would walk in one door and straight out of the other door. This could happen several times before he got to the bar to order a drink, only to turn round and go out of the door again.

As we got to know him, we had quite an affection and concern for his wellbeing. In fact we used to worry if he didn't come in for a few days, but when he did, we always made sure he left in time to catch his last bus home in the evening.

On his birthday he would have a steak in the restaurant, so we always bought him a drink to celebrate. However, he is the only person I know who has three birthdays a year (even the Queen has only two). He was being cheeky, thinking there was a possibility we would buy him a drink every time it was his birthday. We soon got wise to that little ploy.

One day he was walking down the alleyway at the same time as I was unloading the car with the new summer window boxes,

'Come on, you can give me a hand to carry these, you take one end and I will take the other.'

We walked a couple of feet, 'I can't do it anymore as my trousers are falling down.'

He was right, they were. 'Don't bother; I will carry them on my own.'

I definitely did not want to have the pleasure of seeing his underwear in the high street.

Every day, as I was leaving to go home, he would always ask me if I was cooking steak and kidney pudding for tea, and when I said no, he wanted to know what I was going to be eating instead.

He watched the staff and was a very good security guard! He loved telling us if any of the staff were doing something wrong in our absence.

Over the years he told us many stories which gave us lots of amusement:

- He lived in the Castle Museum eight hundred years ago.
- He said he was a virgin, and in the same breath told us he had triplets.
- Told me I was David Bowie's sister – oh no I'm not!
- He was buying a nightclub and getting planning permission for all the extensive work he wanted to do there. He was seeing his accountants and solicitors. He wrote down all our drink prices so he knew what to charge in his nightclub. And finally, would I do the bookwork for him?
- He was buying a travel agent's shop which had closed down, and was going to turn it into a funeral parlour.
- He was given a lobster from someone to cook; he ate the head and wondered why he was ill afterwards.

****

Occasionally, people would come in off the street and ask if they could use the toilets but then did not stay for a drink. Other people would walk in the bar, peer round as if they are looking for someone, then discreetly walk to the toilets and then back out of the door again.

If Chris spotted them before they exited the pub he would say in a loud voice, 'Toilet Inspectors are in. Are the loo's OK?'

'Yes, it was OK for you to use the toilets; thanks for not asking.'

'You didn't want to stop for a drink then?'

A few embarrassed people were seen walking out of the door.

****

At closing time in the majority of pubs, the landlord will either ring a bell, or call out, 'Last Orders at the Bar please,' or 'Time please.'

Not Chris, he would lower the music, and say, 'Enjoyed your company, loved taking your money, now fuck off.'

****

POPULAR WALNUT COCKTAILS

How to make the original
BLACK RUSSIAN

50 ml   Vodka
25 ml   Kahlua

Begin by filling an 8oz glass with ice
add Vodka and Kahlua
Stir

How to make a
HARVEY WALLBANGER

25 ml Vodka
25 ml Galliano
Orange Juice

Fill a 10oz glass with ice
Add Vodka
Add enough orange juice to
almost fill the glass
Stir
Float Galliano on top.
… …..
Substitute Tequila for Vodka
And you have a
FREDDY FUDPUCKER

SHAKEN BUT NOT STIRRED

Chris had worked behind bars for many years before we moved into the Walnut so completely understood the general running of a pub. He knew which drinks were popular, what prices to charge for the correct gross profit and, finally, how he wanted the drinks served.

Making cocktails was a skill he had learnt gradually at Captain America's. It was the first place in Norwich to specialise in making cocktails, and they wanted to build a reputation for creating these special drinks as soon as possible.

It was huge learning curve for Chris. If people asked for a drink he hadn't heard of before, maybe something they had drunk on holiday, or had read about in an article, he would discreetly look for the name and recipe in a large drinks' manual he kept hidden under the bar.

Dick, a good friend of ours, was in Captain America's bar one evening and asked Chris for an 'Anorak.'

This was a drink Chris had never heard of before, so he looked in his trusty book for the name, to no avail.

'That's a new one to me, what's in the drink?'

'It's not a drink you prat, I wanted an anorak or coat cause it's bloody freezing in here with the windows open!'

When we opened the Walnut, Chris, by now, had learned how to make the majority of cocktails in existence. This was reflected in our cocktail list at the pub which consisted of over 100 different creations, ranging from ice-cream drinks, to creamy drinks, to margaritas. There were drinks shaken, stirred and blended.

This was all very simple for Chris as he knew how to make them; I had never even worked behind a bar before, let alone made cocktails, so I had to learn fast, really fast, because in the early days of opening, it was just the two of us working behind the bar.

Before a restaurant menu or cocktail list was printed it was essential to check and double-check that there weren't any errors or spelling mistakes. Of course the professionals that we are, we always carefully read through proofs before the final publication.

We still managed to advertise a bloody mary on the list without the tomato juice (one of the key ingredients). A sirloin steak on the restaurant menu was spelt 'stake.'

Monday evenings, between the hours of 6pm – 8pm, we offered two cocktails for the price of one from the 'Top Ten' section on our cocktail list. It proved to be extremely popular, especially with the poor hard-up students. They came in droves and ordered their chosen cocktail, consequently also obtaining a free one.

However we soon discovered that they were sharing the drinks between two people – that wasn't the idea, one person was supposed to drink both cocktails. We changed the system so that when people ordered a cocktail we supplied a free drink only when the empty glass was returned to the bar. This proved to work to our advantage, except that we would spot maybe six people sitting at a table with only one person drinking. Chris soon sorted that out when it occurred. 'If you're not going to order a drink, you can fuck off.'

That worked, however most of them left as they didn't have any money on them – ah poor students.

Monday nights was always packed with customers enjoying cheap cocktails, and after so much practice, my expertise at shaking, blending and stirring drinks was as proficient as Chris' – on reflection, no it wasn't quite as good.

We started getting a bit pissed off when we realised, that yes, we were packed with customers until 8pm, but then everybody disappeared and the bar was deadly quiet for the rest of the evening. Or people would come in just after 8pm and ask if we were still doing cheap cocktails. On saying no, we had finished, they turned round and walked out again. This continued for a further few weeks until Chris said, 'Fuck it, we're not doing cheap cocktails any more, people take the piss and I've had enough.'

I have to say, though, I'm surprised he took that long to decide, especially given the fact Chris was always loathe to ever buy anyone a drink unless it was their birthday, let alone give free drinks away on a regular basis.

Chris' approach to training staff was completely different to mine. In the restaurant, I patiently explained our system in specific detail; how to prepare and execute various items on the menu, and my required method for working in the restaurant. If staff forgot how to do something, I didn't mind going through the routine again, unless they carried on making errors, then I did begin to get hacked off.

When a new bar person started work, Chris would briefly show them where everything was kept, then told them to get on with it and he would tell them when something wasn't done correctly.

If a bar person asked Chris how to make a certain drink, he always had the same answer, 'It's easy.'

Well, yes, it is easy, but not if you don't know how.

We kept a file containing the recipe, ingredients and the correct glass to use for every cocktail we served so all the staff were able to consult that for reference. Unfortunately some still managed to make a complete hash of assembling a drink correctly.

It didn't take long before Chris barked at them. 'Well put some fucking ice in the glass, not just two cubes,' 'Not that glass, this one.' 'You don't pour beer like that; look, it's flat.'

Our long term staff in the bar were used to Chris' ways and never took offence at his abrupt manner, realising he did actually know what he was talking about when it came to serving drinks and most of them eventually became proficient in keeping up with Chris' high standards.

A few members of staff pursued their own ambitions and later opened their own bars and restaurants, telling Chris that he had taught them everything they knew.

One guy who worked for us didn't quite have the same high opinion of Chris; he was about to serve a cocktail to a customer when Chris shouted, 'What the fuck's that you've just made?'

Immediately after that comment, the bar person grabbed his coat,

'If you're not happy with it, then make it your fucking self.' He walked out, never to be seen again.

On the restaurant menu was a section for adult milkshakes. As the name suggests, the drink consisted of a milkshake combined with different spirits - very yummy tasting and extremely popular with customers.

The drinks were printed in a list and told a story – although many people didn't realise, until I pointed it out to them:

Hawaiian Handshake - When you meet someone, greet them with a handshake.

Florida Fumble - You've become acquainted, so have a little fumble.

Georgia Grope - You have fumbled, now its time for a grope.

Seattle Spread - Enough groping; now you spread them.

Denver Dick - They are spread, time for action with Dick.

Pennsylvania Pussy - Dick's ready and waiting, let's get to Pussy.

New Jersey Jump - We'll finish off by having a Jump.

Some customers, women especially, were highly embarrassed ordering adult milkshakes, preferring to point with their finger to the desired drink on the menu, rather than say the name out loud.

On taking the completed drink to the table, I always knew which customer had ordered the milkshake, but still couldn't resist asking,

'Who ordered the Pussy?' or 'Who asked for a Fumble?'

Generally the reaction from customers receiving their drink was a giggle or a little snigger; occasionally a look of disgust passed over their faces.

I don't know, some people just don't have a sense of humour.

We often received visits from reps who tried to sell us the 'trendy' drink in fashion at that moment or ready made cocktails in a bottle.

Chris always had the same answer to these reps, 'Why the fuck would I want to buy that crap as they taste like shit and I can make them properly?'

They soon got the idea that the Walnut weren't in the least bit interested in their offers and left as quickly as they had arrived.

The rep from the company we used on a regular basis to buy our wines and spirits was called Flynnie (a good friend of ours, and I had known him since I was 15-years old). He called in the pub one day and his first comment was; 'Put the fucking kettle on and make me a coffee as I want to talk to you about the Smirnoff Vodka Christmas deal of the century.'

This company used to give points on purchases which equated to money – much the same way as Tesco's operates, so as he talked about the promotion and started punching numbers into his calculator we were starting to show some interest.

If we bought six 1.5 litre bottles, which is a case, we would get 18 points which equated to £18. We worked out that it was better to have points as opposed to the cash sitting in the bank earning next to nothing in interest and then use the 'points' money to buy more stock.

Flynnie worked out our yearly purchase of vodka and told us that if we bought 84 cases (504 bottles in 1.5litres, which was a whole pallet) we would gain £1,512 in points and could expect to have sold it all in just over six months; unfortunately I did not check his figures.

We decided to have the vodka delivered to our home to store in the garage as we knew there was no way it would fit in our pokey cellar at the pub. It wasn't until it all arrived and practically filled our garage we actually saw how much vodka there was, we thought; 'Fucking Flynnie, we'll never sell all that in six months'. We were right as he got his figures wrong – now there's a surprise because 18 month's later we still had vodka sitting in our garage.

The moral of the story is never trust a rep, especially one who has a fondness for Smirnoff!

****

RESTAURANT OPENING

The bar had been open for three months; the business was running smoothly and our clientele had increased with many customers frequenting the pub on a regular basis. Although food had been available in the bar since the pub was opened, it was now essential to concentrate on refurbishing the restaurant, especially as our first Christmas would soon be upon us when we would hopefully be busy and so be increasing our turnover considerably.

My days and evenings working alongside Chris behind the bar were coming to an end. His expertise had always been the drinks' part of the business, whereas my domain was the restaurant. He could continue to be grumpy downstairs, squeeze men's nipples, nip their inside legs and undo girls' bras but it was nearly time to take my happy persona upstairs to launch the restaurant side of the business.

My attention would be directed there full time. Well, apart from when I was doing the paper work, rotas, wages, hiring and firing of staff, housework, mother and a million other jobs. Now I know where the saying of women who multi task comes from – me.

But my most important job was to be happy at all times to make up for Chris' grouchy face!

It is quite remarkable that during the length of time we spent working together in close proximity, we never argued. That's mainly because I was always right!

But joking aside, we were very, very lucky to have such a good marriage and such an excellent working relationship and solved all problems and situations together.

The restaurant space was located on the first floor above the bar. The previous landlord had decorated the walls with blow up pencils, cuddly toys and a few bamboo fans in prominent positions. They would all have to go.

On the wall at the far end of the restaurant, the previous tenant had commissioned someone to hand paint a mural about 20-feet by 10-feet tall, of a huge Walnut Tree with miniature people standing at the bottom. That would also have to go.

The original furniture consisted of five wooden cubicles seating six people down one side of the restaurant, and four tables seating four persons down the other on the same level.

These were quite in keeping with the American theme we were hoping to create, so we decided they would stay. We would, however, raise the floor level on one side of the restaurant to break up the feeling of an open plan space, giving the appearance of a cosier, more intimate area.

The kitchen was located at one end of the restaurant; refurbishments were going to take several weeks to complete but we still wanted to continue serving food in the bar during this process.

We sealed the kitchen off from the dust and rubble which were obviously going to result when the workmen commenced the renovations. I was then able to continue preparing and serving food to the bar customers. I was continuously wiping the surfaces and equipment from the constant dust which was unavoidably in the air, and I'm sure the Environmental Health Officers would have been thrilled to see the working conditions during this time - not.

The first thing to be demolished was the mural.

With a hammer and chisel we bashed at it for hours, until we were finally down to bare brick.

It looked better already.

We never gave the mural a second thought until a couple of years later. Two women came into the bar, bought a drink, then struck up a conversation with us. It transpired that one of them was the lady who had painted the mural upstairs, and would it be OK if she took her mother to see it, as having moved away from Norwich, she had never viewed it?

Whoops, now we are in the shit.

We somehow managed to tell her it wasn't really in keeping with the style we had created for the restaurant, and although it was a shame to have it demolished, unfortunately it was necessary.

She was upset, and so was the mother, who had travelled far and wide to see her daughter's work. They left soon after.

The workman discovered the floor in the restaurant wasn't level; with some skillful carpentry the problem was rectified, and the raised seated area was complete

A new partition was built to create an area for food preparation and a working area for the waiting staff.

I bought pink, plastic shower curtain material (no-one would guess) for the base of the tables, then blue cotton material to make the top tablecloths, not really giving much thought to the time needed for the extra washing and ironing.

With the addition of window blinds to conceal the outside view of an ugly building, a lick of paint on the walls, new tiffany lamps and plenty of American memorabilia, the restaurant soon looked completely different and we were thrilled with the results.

With the restaurant nearing the finishing stages, we needed to finalize the menu and employ and train staff.

Our partner Harvey was incomparable in devising meals which would embellish our menus, and compliment the American theme we had produced in the bar and wanted to follow this through to the restaurant. He had created many popular dishes for all his restaurants over the years, so I had every confidence he would produce a successful and unique menu which would generate customers.

Chris' cousin Stephen designed the art work for our menus during all the years we were at the Walnut. In the early days before computers were common place, designs were constructed and drawn free-hand.

The menu design only changed a few times over our 25 years, when we created new meals or needed a price increase.

One of the Stephen's early designs was in the formula of a notice board. He typed our menu on various pieces of paper, i.e. the starters on one piece, chicken dishes on another, burgers on another, desserts on another and these were then cut into squares.

He also cut out iconic symbols of America, and placed them all on a notice board with tacks, so producing the effect of a busy bulletin board. After taking several photographs of the finished article it was printed and looked very effective.

The menus for the opening in our restaurant were ready; however, although the menu was ready, we hadn't actually had a trial run to see how we were going to cook the food, what actual ingredients we required, how it was all going to be executed and if the dishes were workable in our small kitchen.

As we had only a small area for cooking and preparation, the chef would be working alone without a flurry of other chefs assisting, so the meals had to be quick to prepare, not involve using too many pans for one particular dish nor need to be watched or stirred while cooking.

Items on the menu needed to be used over several dishes. It was no good, for example, having only one chicken dish, or one steak dish. If they didn't sell, food would be wasted and consequently thrown out, losing profit.

We hadn't employed a chef at this point, and even if we had, I didn't want to be in the situation of not knowing how to cook the food myself or having no idea how I wanted the finished article to look and taste.

Harvey and I went through the new menu together. The first item to cook was chilli. We combined components from a recipe he had always used in his restaurants, along with various ingredients I applied when making chilli. A large pot was made and tasted; we added a little bit of this, little bit of that – job done.

Gradually we worked our way through the menu, cooking everything. Deciding on the presentation for each meal was relatively easy and our thoughts were on par with each other.

The evening went well with Harvey and myself in the kitchen. Mind you, Harvey was continuously smoking, with the ashtray perched precariously on the window ledge along with a glass of Wild Turkey – good job we didn't have any kitchen or waiting staff, that would have been a great example to set them, smoking and drinking on duty.

The final meal to test was a 'lemon chicken'. We roasted six bloody chickens until we obtained the result we were aiming for. We stuffed them with whole lemons, sliced lemons, with rind on, rind off, lemons either up the bums, over the top, under the skin – in fact, in every conceivable area of a chicken, until we finally got the taste we were looking for.

By the time we had eventually finished cooking all the food on our menu, the kitchen looked like a walking disaster area; Harvey looked round at the devastation,

'I'm going downstairs for a well-deserved drink.'

OK, I thought inescapably, I would be clearing the mess away alone.

We were fortunate in employing Graham, a chef who had previously worked in one of Harvey's restaurants and so were confident in his ability to perform in the kitchen and produce high quality meals.

He continued to work at the Walnut for some time after our opening, and was an invaluable asset in achieving a good reputation for our food amongst all our new customers.

A good repute was an important aspect we were fully aware of when the restaurant first opened, and something which had to remain in the forefront of our minds throughout the years that followed.

Graham left our employment to open his own restaurant which was highly successful. I'm sure the chilli he served on his menu (my recipe!) – was the real reason for his success!

It's a known fact that customers who enjoy a meal in a restaurant will tell one person. A customer who has a bad experience in a restaurant will tell twenty people.

We were under no illusion that it is impossible to please all of the people, all of the time, but also realised that a bad word travels much faster than any compliments. Consequently, establishments rapidly close down through lack of customers and gaining a bad reputation. We certainly had no intention of being one of those statistics.

The next job entailed employing the waiting staff and training them to be efficient in the restaurant.

There has always been the preconception that bar work and waiting on tables in restaurants are demeaning jobs, only suitable for those people unable to get 'proper' jobs.

In my opinion, this couldn't be more further from the truth, and if done properly this type of work is a professional achievement. My philosophy in respect of serving customers is to be polite and courteous and to treat customers in a way you would expect to be served yourself.

Being employed myself as a waitress at Captain America's was an excellent insight into running a restaurant. Although I was used to been given orders from management, the roles were now reversed; I was now the 'boss' relaying instructions and stating the quality of work I expected from our new staff.

We never aimed to be a 'top class' fine dining food establishment, (not possible serving burger and fries) but service still had to be impeccable:

- Smile and give eye contact at all times.
- Customers should be greeted at the door within twenty seconds of arrival and escorted to their table.
- Customers should immediately be given a menu and asked if they would like a drink. This was the first priority, as customers are far more amenable with a drink placed in front of them, especially on excessively busy occasions when they may be kept waiting just a few minutes too long before their meal order is taken.
- Judge if customers wish to be served unobtrusively or if they would enjoy a cheeky repartee.
- Take their food order, beginning with the lady. Encourage them to spend more, offering side dishes and wine with the meal.
- Know the menu and how the items are cooked and presented, so that you are able to answer any questions. If a customer wishes to change something when ordering from the menu and it's possible, then do it – even if the chef's not happy.
- Offer more drinks throughout the meal.

- Always ask customers if everything is OK with their food; if it isn't try and resolve the problem.
- Never leave dirty glasses on the tables, clear finished plates as soon as the last person has completed their meal.
- Ensure you give the customers a pleasant eating experience, in a friendly professional manner.
- Finally, always acknowledge and say good-bye and thank you, as the customers depart.
- If they are happy with the service, hopefully you should be rewarded with a tip.

With our small kitchen and only one chef on duty at any given time, having to cook for a possible 45 people in our restaurant at any given moment, it was deemed necessary for the waiting staff to make the cold starters, salads and desserts and finish grilling the stuffed potato skins, garlic bread and toast.

So not only did they have to be trained in waiting at tables, they were also required to prepare the food, while not neglecting the customers.

Cor, I did make my staff work hard.

Obviously that was in theory, putting everything into practice was an entirely different proposition.

We decided against holding a grand opening event in the restaurant or even advertising the fact in the tabloids that the Walnut Tree Shades was open for dining upstairs.

We thought the best policy was to open the doors, discover the teething problems which were bound to occur, rectify them, and finally, adapt an efficient working system before we received a large influx of customers.

Obviously we did encounter a few problems; one continuously remained with us for 25 years - the difficulty of mastering the technique of multi tasking.

It was essential that the staff could jiggle their workload. They had to prepare any dishes required, get drinks from the bar and take orders from customers, but, most importantly, they must never neglect the diners. The technique didn't always work in practice.

If the waiting staff put bread or a portion of potato skins under the grill to toast, their attention might then be diverted to customers requiring drinks from the bar; on their arrival back in the restaurant they would then be greeted by the smell of burning toast. Some amicable customers may lightheartedly mention the smell, 'I hope the chef hasn't burnt our food?'

If customers were good-humoured, and were the same people waiting for their 'burnt' meal, I would teasingly take the burnt offerings to their table, 'Would you like these or shall I do some fresh toast?'

The hot starters may be ready to be served from the kitchen, but the staff may not have finished preparing the cold appetizers, as they had been getting drinks from the bar – multi tasking hadn't worked again.

It was a gradual process gaining a regular clientele in the restaurant; sometimes we were packed to the rafters, on other occasions we had no customers at all.

When we were content the service and quality of food was what we wanted to achieve, we began a small amount of advertising, just in time for customers to book for Christmas; whether it was shoppers, office parties or couples going out for a meal we were ready for them.

From then on, it was onwards and upwards and we never looked back.

****

THE CHEFS

The most important attribute for a chef is his ability to cook. Although his personality and character are vitally important these characteristics had to come secondary to his skill in the kitchen.

It was essential to employ a chef capable of running the kitchen on his own. He had to be able to cook for large parties without throwing a tantrum, and be particular with health and hygiene regulations. It was important that he wouldn't hand in his notice after a couple of months, so that I wouldn't have to start the interviewing process and subsequent training all over again. We also didn't want someone who wouldn't constantly phone in sick. If I liked his personality as well as his cooking ability this was a definite bonus.

Many chefs seem to think that they know how to run your business far better than you do, and try to demonstrate the fact by taking over the kitchen; they cook what they want to cook and not what you want without having any concept of profit margins.

I was not a trained and qualified chef, but by now was fully capable of running the kitchen single-handedly and producing good quality meals to the standard I expected from the chefs. The recipes, ingredients, and execution of each meal had been tried and tested by me – I knew how I wanted the food prepared and completed and didn't want someone coming in to change things to suit them.

We had a specials' board the chefs could use to create dishes of their own, as long as it was in conjunction with the American theme menu we were promoting.

Chefs often arrived for an interview with reams of papers displaying their qualifications and references. I wasn't particularly interested in how many certificates they had, I needed to know about their work experience, their references from previous employers, and their reasons for leaving. Their reply often made alarm bells ring when they told me they had had an argument with their employer, or didn't agree with their work ethics.

Many chefs are only used to working as part of a team in the kitchen, and never had to wash their own pots and pans, clean up after themselves, and most importantly, many only had to cook on one particular food station rather than compile and execute a complete dish.

Over the years I had plenty of experience interviewing chefs and listening to them bragging about how good they were, telling me that working in our kitchen would be easy compared to other places they had worked in and that they would be able to do it blindfolded.

A prime example of an employee exaggerating their experience in the kitchen was a young lad who worked for me as a washer-up. I allowed him to cook his own burger for his lunch and that was the only time he was ever permitted anyway near the chargrill or cooking equipment.

Apart from washing up the dishes, during the quiet periods I told him to grate blocks of cheese – which was boring and not the most stimulating job to do, but someone had to do it. However, that was no excuse for throwing half a block of cheese in the bin pretending he had completed the task. Thankfully I happened to notice, or several pounds worth of food would have been wasted. We parted company after that incident.

I received a phone call from another restaurant for a reference regarding the same young lad, who had applied for the head chef position and would I recommend him to run their kitchen.

'He wasn't a head chef; he was a kitchen porter, employed as a washer-up.'

I imagine he didn't get the job.

****

Some chefs did manage to convince me of their qualities and I subsequently employed them, only to discover they were completely inept, and didn't have a clue how to cook a burger, let alone a steak. Those chefs got their marching orders and left as quickly as they arrived.

****

Matthew was employed as a chef at the Walnut for just over a year before he opened his own restaurant in Norwich. During his time with us, he created a cake for our 1st anniversary at the pub and organised menus and food for special theme night's in the restaurant which were very successful.

He was a great guy with a wicked sense of humour; He loved children and used to amuse our, then 6-year old, daughter by showing her magic tricks during the quiet sessions.

****

One day Chris happened to look out of the pub window and saw a huge, bearded guy, wearing a kilt, walking towards the pub. 'I'd laugh if he's coming in for the chef's job'.

He walked into the pub and straight up the stairs to the restaurant, where I was waiting to interview a chef.

He strode in, fully kilted; his body frame filled the doorway, both the width and the height.

He said he had just arrived in Norwich looking for work, hence his attire. He appeared well-qualified and pleasant to talk to.

So what the hell, I employed him.

Jock (his nick-name) was friendly, diligent, and soon picked up our system of food preparation and our expectations for the completion of meals before service, and appeared to be a conscientious worker.

At the end of Jock's first week, Chris and I were going to London for the day to see the Rolling Stones in concert.

This is how the day in the Walnut went without us.

Jock had commenced work in the kitchen at 9am.

We left the pub at 11.30am.

Jock was in the bar at 11.35am and helped himself to 5 pints of bitter, drunk straight down, one after the other.

12.15pm he went to the wine fridge and helped himself to a bottle of wine, which was also drunk in record time.

1.30pm he started on the brandy which was kept in the kitchen for cooking.

Somehow he managed to work effectively during the lunch time session.

His shift finished at 2.30pm. until he commenced again at 5pm. For two and a half hours no one was sure of his movements or, rather, what his alcohol consumption was. During the evening several more pints of bitter, wine and brandy were drunk. At my expense may I add, as no money went in the till.

He was pissed, legless.

So pissed, that he kept dropping the steaks, burgers and ribs, in fact, every item of food he came in contact with.

My other chef Nick was working alongside him during the evening session, and started to feel very apprehensive as Jock began swaying a lot, especially as he was holding a large knife at the time.

Eventually he steered him outside onto the fire escape, just round the corner from the kitchen, where Jock laid down on the floor, spread-eagled with one leg hanging through a railing – he was out cold.

At least he was out of the way, so the staff could get through the rest of the evening without any more problems.

God, if only the customers knew what was going on behind the scenes!

When the rush was over, Nick went to look at him; he was still laid flat out on the fire escape floor, awake, well sort of.

Nick rang a cab, and with help from three other people, somehow got him standing up, and maneuvered him downstairs into the taxi. - Good-bye Jock.

Chris and I had had a lovely day in London, seen a good concert, enjoyed a nice meal and felt relaxed being away from the pub for a while.

At 11pm Chris said, 'I think I'll just give the pub a quick ring, just to make sure everything has been OK as it was a home football match today.'

Gerry answered the phone.

'Has everything been all right, no trouble from any customers?' asked Chris.

'Customers have been fine, just the fucking chef playing up.' replied Gerry.

Then we heard the whole story.

We thought that would be the last we ever saw of Jock.

Wrong.

The following day was a Bank Holiday, so weren't open until the evening. I was resigned to the fact I would be cooking that shift, as it should have been Jock's night to work.

We arrived to open the pub at 5pm; at the same time Jock walked down the alleyway. 'Did you have a good time at the concert?' enquired Jock.

'Yes'

'Were the band good?'

'Yes', came the curt reply.

Surely he was going to mention Saturday night's behaviour in a minute. We began walking inside the pub, while he continued to make idle conversation about the concert, without getting any response from us.

He began walking up the stairs towards the restaurant, 'Oy, I think we need to have a little chat first'.

'Oh about Saturday night, I've never done that before, and I can assure you it won't happen again.'

'No, you're damn right it won't happen again, because there is the door, so use it.'

'Oh, well, shall I come and pick my wages up tomorrow?'

'Now, lets' have a quick calculation shall we? You already had a £70 sub, plus all the unpaid drinks you consumed; I think we're about evens. So, goodbye.'

That was the last we ever saw of our drunken chef Jock.

****

The chef employed immediately after Jock lasted one lunchtime session.

Nick was showing him the working system, when he spotted a ramekin on the shelf, filled with brandy. - My brandy.

Nick quietly told me,

'I think we've got another drunken chef, he's been swigging the cooking brandy.'

It became very obvious over the lunchtime session that he was incapable of ladling a spoonful of chilli onto the top of a baked potato, without his hand shaking profusely.

He couldn't even carry a plate from the kitchen to the serving hatch without nearly dropping it.

That was the end of him.

****

The next chef employed only lasted for one evening. This time I was training him and although I have never claimed to be a qualified chef, and our restaurant is not fine dining, as long as the chef has a good basic knowledge of grill work and common sense, the work shouldn't prove too complicated.

This guy obviously could not cook, didn't want to cook nor, basically, do any work at all. When he asked if he could finish early to catch his bus home, I paid him and told him not to bother coming back.

I forgot all about him until a letter arrived a couple of months later from an insurance company, stating the evening he had been fired from my employment he had an accident getting on the bus to go home and was filing a claim against us.

So, what's that got to do with me? - He should have been more careful.

Fortunately, that was the first and last letter we received from the insurance company.

****

Another chef we employed could actually cook, but the stories he told us were laughable.

He reckoned he had been there, done it and got the tee shirt - twice.

He was paying a single man's tax allowance, but told me he was married. After trying to sort the problem out with the tax office, the true story was revealed, 'We were going to get married, but never got round to it.'

He said he had worked in many fine dining establishments all over the country – Oh, no, he hadn't!

He was trying to obtain a loan to enable him to finish renovations on his house, but decided a trip round the world was a better way to spend the money.

On his final shift before he started his alleged trip round the world, the staff thought he needed to be brought down to earth and leave the Walnut with some lasting memories.

He was about to change out of his chef's whites when the staff grabbed him by each limb, carried him outside and hung him spread-eagled over the fire escape, with his arms and legs tied to the railings in full view of the public. This was, of course, after stripping him first although nothing rose to attention as it was the middle of February!

The next addition was an empty plastic ice-cream tub which they perched strategically on top of his head. The staff filled tubs of cold water with a little added flour and ran outside in convoy to tip them on his by now shrivelled puny little body.

When he was completely drenched through, shivering on the railings, still tied up, the staff culprits went inside the bar to snigger.

He was left all alone for about 10 minutes, which probably felt like a life-time to him.

On being released, he squelched his way back into the bar for a well-deserved hot toddy, but he took the prank extremely well – so hats off to him. Apparently, he never did go round the world, but he did go to Southend - allegedly.

Apparently, he never did go round the world, but he did go to Southend - allegedly.

****

Then there was another chef employed by us who, for the purpose of this tale, I will refer to as Billy!

He lived in a village 20 minutes drive from the pub but, unfortunately, he didn't own a car so to get into work he either hitched a lift or commuted by train.

There was one occasion when everywhere was covered in thick snow, the trains weren't running and very few people were on the roads. That morning he arrived at work with plastic bin liners on his feet, and said he had walked all the way; it only took him two hours. Well, whether he was bullshitting or not, at least he was at work.

He seemed to spend more time scouring the racing pages and sneaking out to the bookies to place a bet than doing any kitchen duties and preparing meals.

Nick, the chef, was going on holiday for two weeks; Billy was going to work several extra shifts in the kitchen and I would cover the rest.

Billy arrived for work; however he never actually managed to do any shifts. Through the sobbing and tears, he managed to tell me his wife had left him and he didn't know where she had gone, 'Oh, what am I going to do?'

'Some work, - that would be a good start.'

No such luck. He sat down and sobbed.

What happened to the phrase, 'Leave your troubles at home when you go to work?'

'Why don't you just go home, sort yourself out, and I will see you at work tomorrow.'

See, I can be kind-hearted – sometimes.

That was the last we ever saw of Billy.

Nick was on holiday for the following two weeks; Billy had disappeared into oblivion, which meant I had to cook every single lunchtime and every single night, plus all my normal hours' work.

By the middle of the Saturday evening on my last shift in the kitchen, the restaurant was packed, I still had a list of orders to cook, but my brain and body suddenly went into melt down. I just looked blankly at all the orders which still required cooking and felt physically and mentally drained.

The end was in sight. I only had a couple more hours to work, but in the meantime I needed to focus again, bugger the customers – I needed a break, so I left the kitchen, walked outside in the air, smoked a cigarette and got my brain back into gear.

Two hours later, I was in the bar for a couple of well-deserved vodka & tonics.

****

Philip, a chef employed by us for nearly two years (unlike some incompetent chefs) was great.

If he was ever late for work, you could always rely on Philip to have a good excuse or an interesting story to tell.

On driving from his home in the country he saw some ducks crossing the road; unfortunately one of the baby ducks was lagging behind, so Philip thought he ought to help the baby duck find her mother. After eventually catching the baby, the duck family was by now in the distance waddling across the fields; unfortunately the nearer Philip got to them, the quicker they waddled. He did manage to unite the ducks, and felt very pleased with himself, even if mother duck hadn't noticed that one of her family was missing!

Another time when he was late his Alsatian dog had been into his neighbour's garden, into the rabbit hutch, killed the rabbit, and then proudly took it home in his teeth to show Philip.

He didn't want the neighbours to find out it was his dog who had killed the rabbit, so he crept into the garden, and put the rabbit back in the hutch, on his back, with his little paws in the air, so the family would think he had peacefully passed away in the night.

The next day the neighbour came to Philip's house, upset and absolutely horrified at what someone had done to their rabbit.

The rabbit had apparently died several days ago and the children had buried it in the garden, but some sick bastard had dug it up and put it back in the hutch.

'Oh, my God, that's awful!' He couldn't bring himself to tell the upset family it was his dog who had dug it up and he was the sick bastard who had put the rabbit back in its hutch.

Philip enjoyed playing a few tricks at work - like putting a little blob of tomato ketchup in Nick's work shoe.

The trouble was Nick didn't realise for a while, until his sock was feeling soggy and his toes were squelching as the ketchup was spreading around his feet.

He was not amused, especially when he took off his shoe, saw what looked like blood, and thought that he had inadvertently cut his foot.

Philip liked to leave notes everywhere, 'Beware when you open the fridge door' or, 'Be careful what may drop on you from above.'

This meant Nick always had to be very vigilant when entering the kitchen or opening any doors, especially after one occasion when a small tub of flour fell over him, along with a cup of water which had been strategically placed on the top shelf in the fridge, so when the door opened, down came the flour and water, all over Nick.

The best part of Philip's little tricks was watching him practice setting them up, seeing him covered with gunk, and constantly cleaning the floor after the mess he had made.

His favourite saying was 'Oh, my God',

He said, 'Oh, my God' when he received an order for meals, when there was a phone call, when you asked him a question, when customers walked in the door and, especially, if they were late punters.

'Oh, my God', when he received his wages and saw how much he had got. Or, should I say, how much he didn't get.

Philip was one of my favourite chefs; he was a lovely happy guy who we really missed when he left the Walnut.

****

There was an excellent methodical chef whom I employed, even after he told me about his temper in his previous employment which resulted in him pulling the sink off the wall and smashing it!

The temper tantrums were not prevalent during his time with us (which lasted nearly a year) but I did catch him with the cleaner's stiletto heels on one morning. Each to their own devices; however the cleaner wasn't too impressed when she found out he had been squashing his big feet into her tiny shoes.

****

I arrived at work early one morning expecting to find my head chef busy in the kitchen preparing for opening whilst training a new recruit – wrong. I could hear laughter and voices coming from upstairs. 'Yes, I won again, let's line them up for another race.'

They were both upstairs in our flat, playing on Chris' Scaletrix. 'Get your arses downstairs now.'

****

Then there was the chef who thought it a good idea to put the calculator in the microwave! The waitress on duty with him at the time told him he had better go and buy a replacement immediately as she knew I would be furious if I found out what he had done.

She was right, I was angry, and that was the end of him.

****

A chef on a morning shift left a note for the evening chef to make a batch of chilli when he started work.

He didn't feel like making it, so left a note for the other chef.

'Go fist yourself.'

****

On receiving our itemised telephone bill we noticed it was excessively high. We discovered one particular premium number had been rung several times, so thought we would ring it and find out who was on the other end. It was a sex chat line; next question, who was the culprit?

It didn't take long to solve the mystery, as the phone calls had all been made first thing in the morning when there were only two staff at the pub!

One staff member didn't have access to the phone, so it was obvious who was making the calls.

On confronting the other person regarding their early morning sex chats, they, of course, denied it but strangely enough the premium numbers ceased to appear on our bills after that. I don't even want to imagine what they did after that to get their early morning fix of sex!

****

A chef who should have been busy in the kitchen, stripping the chargrill down and giving it a deep clean had not been seen for about twenty minutes.

I found him sitting upstairs in the washroom reading his book.

I was not impressed, and his days were numbered.

****

We had a meticulously clean working chef, whose standards were exceptionally high, and as an added bonus he was a pleasure to work with. His first shift was a very busy lunchtime, but he had no problem in cooking and serving perfect meals every time.

He worked many manic shifts. When food orders were piling up he occasionally lay on the kitchen floor, flat on his back with his hands on his head, 'I've lost the will to live.' Then he got up again and continued cooking.

****

Pete was one of the first chefs to work for us. He was a lovely, quiet, unpretentious guy who worked methodically and never caused me any problems, except for one day when a customer complained her steak wasn't cooked enough. Instead of returning it to the chargrill for a few minutes, he put it in the microwave to speed the cooking process as he wanted to get home.

I was not impressed, and after the telling-off he received, it was the last time that incident occurred.

In conversation with Pete it emerged he was the lead singer in a band called the Boogaloos. They were the first band to play outside the pub on our 'car park gigs'.

Wow, what a transformation from our quiet unassuming chef! His voice and charisma on stage came from the depths of within; he was amazing to watch as he captivated the audience. The Boogaloos became a regular band at the Walnut, always pulling in a great crowd.

****

The correct procedure for disciplining staff changed over the years; if a member of staff did anything wrong in the early days they were just simply fired and that was the end of them. Later on it became increasingly difficult to sack anybody without first going through various different processes.

First a verbal warning was given; if the problem wasn't resolved by the offending staff member a written warning was processed, if this wasn't adhered to, sacking was the final result.

A letter had to be written to the employee inviting them to attend a disciplinary hearing. They were entitled to bring a witness along, then convey their side of the incident and the reasons why it occurred.

Another letter had to be written relating to the meeting and subsequent outcome. It was a long drawn-out process and fortunately something I didn't have to carry out very often.

Having to proceed with a disciplinary hearing wasn't a decision I came to lightly; but it was deemed necessary when a member of staff hadn't adhered to our employment policy.

When I handed him the envelope informing him he had to come for a hearing,

by the look on his face, I'm absolutely sure he thought I was handing him his Christmas bonus. 'It's not what you think it is, this is a letter inviting you to attend a disciplinary hearing.'

His face turned from a smile to a look of rage, 'Well, you can shove that right up your arse.'

I didn't shove it up my bum, but we did part company shortly afterwards.

****

This story about a chef employed by us for many years was told by the local paper. The headlines: 'PUB'S CHEF WHO STOLE, WARNED OF JAIL TERM.'

The article read:

'The former chef at a city centre pub has admitted stealing meat and drink from his employer over a four-year period.

He worked at the Walnut Tree Shades for more than a decade and has admitted he was taking food and drink home.

Yesterday, the Norwich stipendiary magistrate warned him he was likely to go to jail.

The case against ..... aged 39, was adjourned for a pre-sentence report to be prepared.

He was bailed in the meantime.

He admitted stealing frozen meat and alcoholic drink, worth nearly £1,230, from landlord Christopher Gudgin between September 1995 and September 1999.

A charge of burglary in private rooms at the pub, involving the alleged theft of £1,000 was withdrawn.

The prosecutor said police were initially called in to investigate an allegation of money going missing from the safe.

During the course of that investigation, items were found in the chef's vehicle and at his home.

He has never been in trouble before; he admitted to police that he had been stealing meat and drink from the pub for four years.

The exact value of what he had stolen was difficult to assess added the prosecutor.'

Three weeks later, a further article was printed in the evening paper. The headlines read: 'CHEF STOLE FOOD FROM PUB BY GOING DOWN FIRE ESCAPE.'

'A pub chef who stole from the landlord who had employed him for 14 years has been ordered to do 160 hours' community service.'

Norwich magistrates heard that the chef took frozen meat, wines and spirits home from the city centre Walnut Tree Shades over four years.

He could not explain the thefts. Frozen chicken and steak were found in his freezer and unopened drinks included champagne.

He had admitted stealing meat and drink worth nearly £1,230 retail value. He was ordered to pay compensation and costs of nearly £200.

The Chairman told the chef, who had never been in trouble before, that prison was normal for such offences, but in his case there was considerable personal mitigation.

The Prosecutor said drink and meat were found at the chefs' home by police investigating a theft of cash from the pub. He admitted taking them from the pub, saying he used to take them out by going down the fire escape. He could not explain why he had done it and was unable to eat the meat once he got it home. He did not have any conscious grievance against landlord Christopher Gudgin. There were glowing references before the court, including one from his new employer.'

Ummm, well, what can I say? – plenty – but I won't. What I will say is that it was a very sad and hurtful time for us, to think that a long serving chef who we classed as not only an employee, but a friend, had been stealing from us for a very long time.

Of course we had many chefs with star qualities who were a joy to work with but it was also important to recognize their negative vibes and pay heed to them.

I might arrive into work and notice the chef's body language - he is in a bad mood. Suspicions are confirmed when the waitress gives me a glance towards the kitchen and raises her eyebrows.

If chef's in a bad mood, sometimes the best policy is just to ignore it, because if you do ask what the problem is, it's either, 'nothing' or a grunt.

I always arrived at work and greeted the staff with a happy sounding 'Morning' or 'Evening'. One chef would ignore me completely if I didn't speak to him first.

I was always aware of the work load in the kitchen on a busy shift. If the restaurant suddenly filled up with customers who hadn't previously booked, they would all want to order at the same time; therefore the orders arrived in the kitchen to be cooked simultaneously.

Although I tried to avoid this happening by putting the meal orders in gradually, it still made one or two chefs very grumpy.

Although perfectly capable of cooking several meals at once, they used to pick the orders up, slam them down on the counter and mutter a few obscenities; then, instead of getting motivated, adrenaline pumping and working faster, they went into slow-mode.

When the meals were cooked they were practically thrown on the counter in front of the staff!

Last orders for food at lunchtimes were at 2.15pm and in the evenings at 10pm. Some chefs started clearing up way too early. They would put everything away, wipe down and mop the floor so that as soon as the clock showed 2.15pm or 10 pm, they could be out of the door with their coat on.

However, sometimes customers did come in and wish to order food a couple of minutes before closing time. Now this always made one chef very grumpy. He had to get everything out of the fridge again, (quite often put down on the work surface with a thump) moaning the whole time. Then after the cooked meals were nearly thrown at us, he would stomp out of the kitchen, ignoring everyone, without so much as a good-bye – straight out of the door.

Some chefs just didn't seem to realise that each meal cooked contributed towards paying their wages.

I employed a chef who was very good except that he would keep trying to change the recipes I had been using for years, and wasn't impressed that I wouldn't go along with his suggestions.

Our customers loved our chilli and diane sauce the way it was, so, as the saying goes, 'if it ain't broke, don't mend it.' However, I was quite happy for him to create dishes for our specials' blackboard if it was in keeping with our American theme of food.

He wasn't a popular member of staff, and I must admit, I didn't particularly like his personality either, however the quality of food he produced was good, and that had to be my main priority.

The staff were soon grassing him up. He spent all afternoon either reading the paper or making phone calls on my telephone, when I wasn't there. They saw him drinking beer whilst on duty - my beer, and not paid for.

It is impossible to confront any employee and accuse them of a wrong-doing if there is no proof. However, I soon had all the confirmation needed.

The chef, waitress and I had worked a busy Saturday lunchtime; it had been a good day without any problems.

I had bought some tiger prawns for the chef to create a dish during the quiet afternoon for the specials' board that evening.

Leaving my daytime girl to run the restaurant, I went home at 3.30pm for a very short break, before I commenced again at 5pm.

As soon as I returned, Jo the waitress, took me to one side,

'The chef's pissed. As soon as you left he went to the bar, had a pint of beer, didn't pay for it, then came upstairs with a bottle of brandy which he said was to make the diane sauce with. He has been obnoxious, and the kitchen's in a right state.'

'But, I've been gone for less than two hours.'

Before I accused him of anything, I thought it best to surreptitiously watch him for a while to see the situation for myself.

A quick glance round the kitchen confirmed that at least a third of the brandy had gone from the bottle; there was food all over the floor, up the walls, strewn over the work surfaces, and the chef was sitting in the dry store area with glazed eyes.

'What dish have you prepared with the prawns, so I can write it on the specials' board?'

'A thai broth' in a slurred voice.

'A thai broth, but our cuisine is based on America,' I said in a long drawn out voice and utter disbelief. 'A thai broth, but we don't have the ingredients to make a thai broth?'

No reply.

'Did you make some diane sauce this afternoon?'

'No, I didn't have time.' He shrugged his shoulders and staggered off.

Well, no wonder he was pissed. He had consumed a third of a bottle of brandy, plus the beer, and possibly anything else he managed to lay his hands on.

A few minutes later he picked up a small plastic squeezy bottle used for putting bbq sauce on top of the burgers. The bottle was frequently filled up from a five litre container using a funnel. This chef didn't bother with the funnel, he just poured the bbq sauce from the opening of the large container, straight into the small bottle. As a result, there was more liquid down the sides, on the work surface and on the floor, than where it was supposed to be.

I walked into the kitchen just at the moment he had picked a knife up to slice a burger bun, and told him to go home.

'You are drunk, and I know you have consumed the brandy because you certainly didn't use it for cooking; it's obvious you are incapable of working, the kitchen is filthy and your behaviour is unacceptable in the workplace. Working under the influence of alcohol is gross misconduct and a sackable offence, so you can leave immediately.'

He glared at me aggressively; the knife was being waved precariously and, for an instant, I thought he was either going to stab me, or take swing at me. Fortunately, he was too pissed to do either.

'So, you want me to go then? Well, you can just go fuck yourself,' was the verbal reaction I received, before he finally staggered from the premises.

The kitchen looked as if a bomb had exploded. I had to close the restaurant for forty-five minutes to give me time to clean the work-surfaces, walls and floors and then do enough prep for the busy evening shift ahead of me, as there was absolutely nothing cut or chopped. In fact, the fridge was bare, except for six cans of beer the chef had left behind – as if he hadn't had enough. I later found a bottle of Shiraz hidden which he had obviously helped himself to from the wine rack.

****

A good reliable chef worked at the Walnut for nearly a year when he decided to have a change of career. It wasn't until after he left I discovered he had been helping himself to steaks, various other items of food, and at Christmas had ordered all his vegetables for home from our wholesale supplier, and put on our bill.

****

Neil worked for 8 years as a chef in our kitchen; he was a loyal and reliable worker. He never had time off through sickness and always helped me out by working extra shifts without moaning and groaning. Well, maybe just an odd grumble now and again, but I let him off those ones.

We were very fond of him and he became our 'surrogate son' when we heard his trials and tribulations or just enjoyed a drink together at the end of the shift. He always called me 'Mum' and Chris was 'Daddy'.

He left the Walnut to work in another restaurant for a couple of years, but missed his 'Mum and Daddy', (we had missed him too) so returned to work for us again. But this time he worked full-time in the bar, and helped us in all other aspects of the business, either by waiting at tables or chef duties and by being in charge of the staff and running the pub and restaurant when we went on holiday.

****

Daren worked for us for several years and, although we may have had one or two little ding-dongs in that time, he never disappointed me with his meticulous cooking abilities and always received compliments from customers, especially for his fajitas which always created a 'wow'.

****

As you can see, some of the chefs employed by me left me with lasting recollections – some funny, some sad, some just plain stupid, and unfortunately, some were disgraceful; those I wish I could erase from my memory for ever.

Apart from a few bad chefs, I also had many who I employed for years and continuously produced excellent food, thereby retaining and enhancing our good reputation. I am fully aware that without a first-rate chef in our restaurant we wouldn't have had a business and for that I am very grateful and appreciative of them all.

****

WALNUT TREE SHADES
Restaurant

FIRST THINGS FIRST - STARTERS

	HAVE IT ALONE	SHARE WITH A FRIEND
LOVIN' SKINFUL - Deep fried potato skins filled with cheese, served with sour cream dip.	4.00	6.20
LOVIN' SKINFUL + BACON - As above plus chopped bacon	4.70	7.00
CHILLI SKINS - Deep fried potato skins filled with Texan chilli topped with grated cheese, served with sour cream.	4.95	7.00
HALF N' HALF - Half portion of Lovin' Skins and half portion of Chilli Skins.	4.75	7.00
BUFFALO WINGS - (Hot, hot, spicy chicken wings) to cool them down we serve them with celery sticks and a creamy dip.	3.75	5.50
WINGS N' SKINS - Hot spicy chicken wings and lovin' skins, served with celery, creamy dip and sour cream.	4.75	7.00
NACHOS - A plateful of Mexican tortilla chips, chilli n' cheese and jalapenos. Hot and spicy for all cool cats.	5.25	7.00
GRAND SLAM - A platter of Guacamole, tuna mayo, prawns in cocktail sauce, ham and a load of toast. (Only large size available)	- - - -	7.00
VERDE DIP - Guacamole served with toast and salad garnish.	4.65	- - - -
PRAWN COCKTAIL - The old faithful, but we have updated it a bit.	4.60	- - - -
BOWL OF CHILLI - Hot Texan chilli, topped with grated cheese, served with tortilla chips.	4.50	- - - -
THE FOURSOME - For four to share, four of our favourites, hot wings, skins, pot of chilli, half rack of ribs, tortillas and dips. (Only large size available)	- - - -	14.95

WALNUT TREE SHADES, OLD POST OFFICE COURT, NORWICH, NORFOLK.
T: 01603 620166

Our meals are not prepared in advance, so if you are waiting, please be patient - we want to be the best!

CHEQUES - All major credit and debit cards accepted. £10 minimum. Minimum charge for food per person - £7.15

RESTAURANT CUSTOMERS

Two types of customers came in the restaurant; the first sort drank downstairs in the bar first, great as far as we were concerned; not only were they spending money downstairs, they also came upstairs to the restaurant to eat, and generally continued to have another drink or two in the bar after their finished meal.

Then there were the 'restaurant customers' who entered through the door, walked through the bar without stopping, and went straight upstairs to the restaurant.

As soon as they had finished their meal they left the same way they had arrived – without stopping at the bar for a drink. Either they felt the music in the bar was too loud, (the restaurant volume was much softer, enabling customers to hold a conversation without shouting) or they didn't like the smoky atmosphere (in the days of 'permitted smoking in bars') or maybe they didn't like pubs full stop, but enjoyed going out for a meal, then straight home for a cup of Horlicks or cocoa.

We relied on word of mouth recommendations from customers who had enjoyed a meal with us to gain new clientele, rather than spending a vast amount of money on advertising.

Once the 'restaurant customers' had managed the trauma of having to walk through the bar and upstairs we generally managed to obtain repeat business, thus attaining loyal and regular customers for many years.

The menu board was located on the wall just outside the pub; new potential customers would quite often begin by studying the menu board, to see what kind of food we served, and if there was something they fancied to eat, or they might look at the menu and walk away, or appear interested, decide on venturing in, look inside at the bar, turn round, walk out and disappear up the road – gone.

If Chris happened to see people viewing the menu board he would often go outside and tell them the food was excellent; there was a really nice restaurant upstairs, and persuade them to such a degree that they daren't argue. They would follow him indoors, where he would near enough force them upstairs straight away, especially if he felt it a pointless exercise trying to get them to buy a drink first.

More often than not, customers were happy with their meal and pleased Chris had 'made' them go upstairs and consequently would return again and again.

We had many, many regular customers who proved to be loyal to our restaurant throughout our years at the Walnut. Some came in every single week, (apart from the times they were on holiday) others once a month, others might come in once a year and expect me to remember them.

Annual customers who came upstairs for a meal at Christmas on their work's party each year often said laughingly, 'Remember us from last year, you told us off?'

Smiling, as I replied, 'Of course I do, and you had better not be naughty this time, or you'll receive my evil glare or a wag of my finger', (thinking to myself, I have absolutely no idea who you are and no recollection of the previous year's events).

Trying to remember customers' names was an impossible feat for me, I just could not do it. I knew exactly what they liked to eat and drink; I knew which table they preferred to sit at in the restaurant, I knew the time they liked to come in and eat, but their names – impossible.

It was even more embarrassing if they came in and asked me to reserve a table for a later date; they knew me, - I recognised them – just not their name. My get-out clause here was, 'What name shall I put the reservation in?'

'Put it in my name.'

Umm, difficult, as it was essential to have booking details consisting of name, time, contact telephone number, and how many guests, all written in the reservation book.

My way of getting round this problem without causing myself any embarrassment was to write down either the meal they regularly ate or their usual drink, or if there was something memorable about them, or, if there was a nickname we had for them, then that was written down. It may have been, 'Famous Five', 'Miller boys', 'Moaner', 'In your Face'; however, I did make sure the offending customer couldn't see what was being written.

Customers like recognition when they enter a restaurant; it makes them feel important. They always received a warm welcome from me. Well, I had to make up for Chris' grumpiness downstairs; so, even though I may not know their name, they weren't aware of that and that's all that mattered; a smile would do.

I always knew their favourite table and sat them there, so they felt they were getting extra-special treatment.

I often wrote on the order pad what they were going to eat before they even told me. They would find this very amusing and said they were going to choose something different for a change – but, of course, they never did because these regulars were predictable.

We spent a long time sorting out meals we were going to produce and have on the menu - foods that complimented each other and which looked and tasted good, but there were customers who wanted something different to what was specified on the description.

Instead of peppers they want grilled onions.

One lady wanted lettuce on only one side of her burger bun.

Some wanted the garlic bread served on a separate plate, not with the meal.

Instead of hot sauce on the chicken wings, they wanted bbq sauce.

Instead of blue cheese, they wanted sour cream.

And these were just a few of the different variations requested which drove one or two of my chefs mad over the years and frequently put them in a bad mood. 'Why bother doing a fucking menu when people keep changing it?'

'Well, if it makes people happy and we are able to cater to their requirements, then that's what we will do; it's not a problem.'

That made them even grumpier, but as far as I was concerned, happy customers come back, it was their revenue which paid everyone's wages, so the chefs could either like it or lump it.

The regulars would treat me as their friend and expect me to stand or even sit with them at their table, chatting throughout their duration in the restaurant. This was fine if it wasn't very busy but sometimes there was so much work which needed doing, and other customers needing my attention, it was difficult to get away.

If the waitress I was working alongside could see I was tied up chatting to a customer and finding it tricky to make a departure, she would implement our plan of action. She would either interrupt our conversation by saying there was a phone call for me or say that someone was waiting to see me downstairs; these were great excuses for making a quick exit from chatting customers.

However, during quiet sessions in the restaurant, when I didn't have a million and one jobs to do, the waitress used to leave me to endure hearing customers talk and talk to me, until I might unobtrusively hold the menu in front of my face, trying to attract her attention by miming, 'Help me'.

She still wouldn't come to my rescue, just giggle from a distance and let me suffer.

However, there were many lovely customers who were enjoyable to chat to, to hear all their stories, tales of their holidays, or just about life in general.

It was essential to know at what stage each table had reached in the restaurant, and who or what required attention.

Maybe one table needed a drinks' order, another wanted their food order taken, another had just finished their starters and the plates needed clearing.

There might be meals ready on the serving hatch waiting to be taken to the table, or maybe all these tasks required a response at the same time.

The kitchen may have a back-log of orders to cook and a table may be waiting a few moments longer than they should be, so it was essential to be aware of this and inform the customers their meal would be along shortly, before they had a chance to query the fact first.

It was important to check customers were satisfied with their meal when they had been eating for a few minutes.

Another table may be waiting to order a dessert, another waiting for their bill, or a table waiting to pay.

There could be people leaving and it was always essential to say 'good-bye and thank you' as they departed.

To fulfil all those requirements, remember every detail, and be able to multi task are vital ingredients in being a professional waiting person. In fact, sometimes, it seemed there were so many jobs that needed doing at the same time, you felt that if you stuck a broom up your arse you could sweep the floor at the same time.

The evening could begin by running smoothly, everything going to plan, customers all having drinks and meals on time, when suddenly the whole system goes into melt down.

It always seems to happen in the middle of the shift, when suddenly it becomes evident every table in the restaurant requires attention in varying degrees, either drinks to obtain, orders to take, desserts to make, the list goes on and on.

These are occasions in a moment of panic when you seem to be running around like headless chickens and getting nowhere. In these cases we may run out to the back of the restaurant, out of view from the customers and scream. Then walk back through to the tables, saunter up and down the restaurant smiling as if everything was running smoothly and we were in complete control.

As long as the staff look calm and relaxed then this reflects on the customers.

If the restaurant was quiet, with several empty tables available, when the customers arrived they were able to choose where to sit. However, this tended to be far too difficult a decision for them to make sometimes. They stood gazing at each table blankly and wandered aimlessly in the restaurant conferring with each other as to which table they should sit at, until I had to intervene and make their decision.

They sat down obediently, and then requested to move to another table – so why didn't they sit there in the first place?

The restaurant area was too small to incorporate a bar space accommodating kegs of beer and the wide range of drinks we had on offer, so each and every drink ordered had to be fetched downstairs at the bar.

The first job for waitresses when customers were seated at a table was to get their drinks order whilst they decided what to eat from the menu. Some might want a drink; others on the table might say they don't wish for anything at the moment.

So the waitress might collect a tray and head off down the flight of stairs to the bar to prepare the drinks, which obviously takes several minutes. By the time she's headed back up the stairs to the restaurant and put the drinks on the table, one of the other people seated might have decided they now want a drink.

It's back down the flight of stairs to get their order. The same scenario was often repeated again, and again.

So I would banter with the customers, 'Look, I'm getting old and knackered and there are only so many times I can go up and down those stairs for an order of drinks.'

Trying to take the food order from customers was often very difficult, especially when they said they would like the same as the last time they came in. Well, if they couldn't remember what it was, I'm damn sure I couldn't. If they were frequent customers, then their usual requirements did register in my brain, (if not their name!)

Some women always seemed to have problems telling the waitress directly what she would like to order; whisper to her partner, who would have to relay to the staff the meal required. There may be questions about the order that need answering, 'Would you like fries or jacket potato?' or 'How would you like the steak cooked?'

We used to aim the questions at the women and try to get them to answer, but they still often told their partner the answer and not us, or sometimes they wouldn't even know if they wished for their steak to be cooked rare or well done and got the companion to choose for them.

Occasionally people would tell us that the last time they came in for a meal the steak was cooked a bit too much, but that they didn't like to complain on the night. This was so annoying because any faults can be rectified at the time; it's no good whinging on the next visit.

Many of the same comments heard from customers were repeated to us over and over again, although the customers thought they were being funny and original in their remarks. We just smiled sweetly and laughed with them or, if we wanted to be mean and embarrass them in front of their friends we would just say, 'Yawn, yawn, cor, never heard that one before – much.'

We always served finger bowls with warm water and a slice of lemon for the messy finger food. There were many comments from customers when this was put on the table. 'Is that lemon soup?'

'Could do with some salt and pepper.'

'The soup's not very hot, and tastes bland.'

'What's that? I didn't order any soup.'

Then there were the customers who didn't even know what the finger bowl was for. We would notice them trying to eat their spareribs with a knife and fork, carefully prising the meat from the small pork bones. We had to explain that the ribs would be much easier to eat if they picked them up with their fingers.

'How would you like your steak cooked?' the waitress would ask, (of course meaning, well done, medium or rare?)

'In the oven, please. Ha ha'

'Sorry, but we cook them on a grill, not in the oven.' Another phrase when asked how they would like their steaks cooked:

'In the kitchen please,' or

'Cooked on the grill please.'

'What dressing would you like on the salad?'

'Undressed please.' Or

'In a shirt and pair of trousers would be good.'

'What would you like for dessert?'

'I'll have you', would often be a reply from a group of men.

'Sorry, you couldn't afford me, I'm far too high maintenance,' would be the quick answer to that question.

When people were served their main course, and had been eating for a few minutes, the staff would always check they were enjoying their meal and that everything was OK for them.

'Lovely, thank you.'

When everyone had finished eating and the staff had cleared the plates the customer might decide to complain. Maybe the steak wasn't cooked correctly, maybe the chips were overcooked or undercooked. Whatever it was, why, oh why, mention it at the end of the meal and not when the staff enquired earlier if everything was OK.

They might say, 'Oh I didn't like to complain.'

You want to reply, 'So don't fucking do it now then'

But I always tried to smile sweetly, offering apologies, and pointing out I would have been happy to rectify any problems with their meal but unfortunately, as it has all been eaten, there is very little I could do at that stage.

There are, what we call in the trade 'professional complainers'. These are people who go to restaurants for a meal with no intention of paying. They have been known to put a creepy-crawly, or a hair on their meal just before they have finished eating and then expect a free meal.

Unfortunately, there is no proof if the meal was served with a hair in it, but I often questioned the complainer if the hair was the same colour as their own as our chef was bald and so it couldn't possibly have been his.

If the creepy-crawly was whole, I did tell them I wouldn't charge them for the extra side order, and at least it's a whole one and not a half one, otherwise they could possibly have eaten the missing half.

If it was a genuine error on our part we were more than happy to change their meal or deduct the cost from their bill and try to make amends with a complimentary drink. It was a top priority to keep customers happy so that they returned and this usually worked, but there were people for whom, whatever you did, it wasn't enough.

There are always going to be occasions in any restaurant, whether it is a small burger bar or a Michelin star restaurant, when someone is unhappy with their meal.

If someone was disgruntled, I would always say to them, 'What can I do to make you happy?'

That always seemed to confuse people and they never really knew how to reply. They mumbled a bit, but never mentioned having a free meal.

'The customer is always right,' is a statement made up by customers, because they aren't. They might complain that their steak is pink in the middle and they ordered it medium; if so, then that is the correct way to cook it. What they should have ordered is, 'well done', if they wanted a grey looking steak.

I never added service charge to our bills. If I went out for a meal, and received bad service, I wouldn't want to leave a percentage of my total bill for a tip if the service hadn't been satisfactory. So, in our restaurant, tips were left to the discretion of the customers. I believe that it made the waitress work harder, be more conscientious, and to deserve a reward at the end.

And there were big rewards at times, with customers leaving extremely generous tips. There were also times when people didn't leave anything, not because the service was bad – but because people were mean. There were the people who thought it funny to leave two pence on the table for a tip. If we spotted this in time before they left the building, I would have great delight in giving it back to them and saying, 'Excuse me, you left something behind. You need it more than we do.'

People who tried to pay with a credit card, only to have it refused on our electronic machine because of unavailable funds in their account, got so angry sometimes and said there must be a fault with our machine or, came out with, 'I can't understand it, there's plenty of money in my bank account.'

'Sorry, but it won't accept your card, so could you possibly pay with cash?' 'You don't have any money on you; well, maybe your friend could pay with their card.'

Many customers came in to celebrate special occasions. People might have their first date in the restaurant and then return for their anniversary.

We regularly had people celebrating their birthdays, and they often brought a cake in which they wanted served after their main meal. I didn't mind doing this, unless they brought in a really naff looking sponge which looked awful.

It was very embarrassing, when I had to walk past all the other customers in the restaurant with a cut-price tacky cake, candles glowing, and obviously attracting attention. When this happened, I tried to hide its appearance by cupping my hands round the cake before I arrived at the table and began singing 'Happy Birthday'.

I always kept banners to sellotape to the wall if I had prior warning of a special occasion. Mind you, the banners did get a bit tatty after a few years, especially when I had to keep changing the age on the banner by sticking another piece of paper on top.

I always cringed when a group of people started diving into the bags they'd brought in with them, producing confetti, balloons, and streamers. The mess they made was horrendous, especially when it was all over the floor as people got it stuck to the bottom of their shoes, and trailed it down the stairs into the bar.

I did ban 'silly string' from being used in the restaurant. It stained the wood on the furniture and was hideously sticky and messy. If I saw a squirty container, or heard the sound of a 'psst', I pounced on the culprit, 'Sorry, but no.'

We saw many groups of people celebrating different happy occasions; we also saw arguments between couples. They came in cheerful, were pleasant to serve and then you noticed the atmosphere changing between them. They may be glaring at each other in disgust or not talking to each other at all.

We did try to be discreet at those times, tending to leave them alone to sort out their problems, unless we had to venture to the table to either serve their food or clear away the finished meals, but then voices may rise. This was when it got quite interesting; we would go to the next table and pretend to clear some debris or just move the condiments around, whilst we tried to hear what the argument was about. Sometimes when the row got more intense, everyone could hear, until one of the couple, usually the woman, would grab her coat and stomp off in a rage, leaving the man looking pensive and embarrassed to pay the bill then leave the restaurant alone.

Kissograms were popular for a while with parties, and the person celebrating their birthday would often receive a kissogram previously organised by their friends.

If I was prewarned that there was going to be entertainment arriving, I always told the other customers in the restaurant what was about to happen.

Some people might be offended, in which case – tough, they would just have to look away. Others, especially the men, would be very pleased if they were going to see a half naked girl prancing around the restaurant; these ones invariably stayed longer than planned, just so they could watch, although sometimes the girlfriends weren't too impressed.

Kissograms arrived in many shapes and sizes to surprise the customers; there were roly-poly women, who were extremely off-putting if you happened to be eating your meal at the time.

For the person who had to endure the unglamorous lady sitting on their lap with huge thighs hanging over their legs, and an enormous pair of boobs in their face and then having to lick cream off her body it wasn't too thrilling either. This was even worse if she made him get on all fours and proceeded to spank him, either with her hand or one of her props – a whip.

There were a few attractive kissograms who came to the restaurant who the men enjoyed watching strip off. They would do an exotic dance whilst the victim was placed in a strategic position in the restaurant so she could sit on him, push her boobs against his body and make him squirt chocolate on her boobs which he had to then lick off - generally making him very embarrassed in front of his friends.

My chef was very happy when a kissogram arrived discreetly through the back fire escape door by the kitchen; she proceeded to get changed in front of him and asked him if he would rub some ice on her boobs to make her nipples stick out. Of course he obliged, all in the course of duty.

The end of November and throughout December was our busiest time for Christmas work parties and celebrations and, because our business was in central Norwich, we were inundated with people who came into Norwich to do their Christmas shopping, especially when it was late night shopping.

As soon as the shops closed on a Thursday evening, people piled into the restaurant expecting a table instantly; if there was a short wait they were grumpy. They had already been pushing, shoving and queuing in shops for the past few hours, so by the time they came to us their patience had dwindled. They were fed up, hungry and thirsty, and wanted to relax.

On busy shifts it was imperative to organise a table plan so I knew where all pre-booked reservations were going to be seated in the restaurant, and which tables were left available for walk-in customers off the street.

It could be quite a complex plan because I tried to 'pack them and stack them'. In other words – fit in as many diners as possible. If there were bookings for couples in at 6.30pm, I knew they would hopefully be gone by 8pm, so could therefore book another table in at that time. Four to six people generally took two hours to eat, so I worked other reservations to coincide with that time.

If people walked in without a booking, I consulted the plan and might suggest that there is a table available, but only for an hour, after which time another reservation was due in, so they would be unable to have a long relaxed meal.

It was the customers' choice if they wished to risk indigestion by gobbling their food. They might be offered the option of sharing a table with two other people who didn't mind someone joining them – that was when 'packing and stacking' really came into force.

Customers who arrived late occasionally rang us beforehand, informing us they were on their way and to please keep their table, or people would arrive and blame the taxi company for being late. Now and again we received an apology, but generally customers never said a word.

On these occasions, if no form of apology was forthcoming, I put my hand up and pointed a finger to my watch, 'You're late, good job you're not catching a train, as you would have missed it.'

I always delivered that remark with half a smile, but more of a grimace, and might just receive a blank look or chuckle from the guilty customers. They didn't understand my jokey sarcasm, or maybe chose not to, but from people like that I still never received an apology.

The customers who arrived late for a booking subsequently threw my whole table plan into turmoil; their late arrival meant they wouldn't be vacating the table in time for the next group of people booked, thus involving writing another plan and trying to jiggle all the bookings so everyone sat down on time.

I re-wrote those bloody table plans three or four times a night sometimes, just to ensure all the customer bookings had a table on their arrival.

Then, of course, there were times when reservations never turned up at all. This was the most annoying situation, because we had an empty table which could have been used for someone else so therefore had lost revenue.

I often used to telephone them the following morning and began by asking if we had made an error and written their reservation on the wrong date.

The most common reply was; 'I telephoned in the morning and cancelled the table.'

'Who did you speak to?'

You knew it was a blatant lie from the customer, because either Chris or I would have answered the telephone, but there's not much else you can say in that situation.

If they apologise and say they forgot to cancel the table, legally they should honour the cost of the revenue we had lost from their non-attendance, and I did sometimes point this out but never enforced it, because at the end of the day it just wasn't worth the hassle and only created bad feeling.

In late November, the Christmas decorations were displayed in the restaurant. Chris had to put up all the garlands and dangling ones because the ceiling is so high and a ladder is required.

I hated standing on ladders, and Chris detested putting up decorations; he consequently moaned the whole time, especially when we put on the Christmas CD's, playing all the Slade songs and 'Wish you a merry Christmas' - that made him whinge even more – bah humbug!

Customers expected a cracker when they were on their work's Christmas outing, so we obliged by supplying the cheapest crackers we could find. They usually contained a hat, a joke, and a plastic spider, if they were lucky.

I always warned customers before they pulled the crackers, that no expensive had been spared, so don't be too disappointed! In fact some customers brought in their own special ones if they had had previous experience of our rubbish ones.

Throughout December we were continuously picking up plastic spiders and the remains of crackers from the floor, hidden under plant pots or in nooks and crannies.

One year, instead of serving our usual American theme menu, we decided to do a traditional Christmas dinner consisting of turkey and all the trimmings and finishing with Christmas pudding.

We did it properly using good quality meat and fresh vegetables rather than the usual pre-packed, frozen food that many places served. We were pleased with the results and the customers enjoyed it. The following year we produced the same menu and the reservation book was full of Christmas bookings. It was all going well with many satisfied customers, until a party of twenty-four people arrived from one of the departments in a local building society and, for some reason, were not happy with our food.

I think they would have preferred frozen peas, instead of freshly made cauliflower cheese; granule gravy out of a tin, instead of proper gravy made with stock, and a frozen rolled turkey instead of a good quality fresh one.

They paid their bill, but it was obvious they weren't impressed, even though during the course of their meal I had asked if everything was alright.

We received a telephone call later on in the afternoon to cancel the tables which they had booked with us for another two occasions over the Christmas period, for different departments, totalling fifty people.

They had told the other people who were booked in at the Walnut, that the experience wasn't very Christmassy and there was no Christmas music playing.

I was furious, but there was nothing I could do about it. It just goes to show how true the saying is, 'if you have a good meal, one other person will hear about it. If you have a bad meal, ten people will hear about it.' However, in this case it was fifty people.

We never did a special Christmas menu after that event. Instead, we did a condensed menu for a set price from our usual main dinner menu, which gave new customers a taste of the food we cooked all year round, and so was a way of promoting our concept.

However there were customers who I only ever saw at Christmas. They used to say, 'We're back again.'

'Lovely to see you, but we are open all year you know, and not just in December.'

We had a party of 28 people from an insurance company booked in for their Christmas staff party. They had already consumed considerable amounts of alcohol in the bar before they came upstairs to the restaurant.

Trying to get them to stay seated at their tables was a mission in itself. They were constantly changing seats, talking to different members of their party, standing up, sitting down, and generally getting in our way, as we were trying to manoeuvre between them with more drinks that they kept ordering.

They had brought in their own Christmas novelty toys, streamers, silly string, whistles and balloons which were now all over the floor mixed with the beer they had spilt, making a complete mess.

We had a pre-order of the name and food each person had decided upon, making it far easier from our point of view to deliver the correct food to the right people when it was served. Because from previous experience nobody ever remembered what their order was. I found the best way of delivering meals to customers was to call out their name (as opposed to what the meal was). This was working well until I had one meal left and an empty seat at one of the tables. 'Where has he gone? His meal will be getting cold.'

'He had to go home, his tooth came out, and he was in agony.'

I didn't give this comment a second thought, just reflected to myself he would still be paying for that meal, even though he had left without eating it.

The remaining party appeared subdued after his exit and each time I was at their tables, either clearing plates or glasses, I kept hearing snippets of conversation regarding teeth.

They paid the bill without any question, although they didn't leave a halfpenny tip – bastards. Then the phone rang.

'I was in your restaurant with a group party this evening, I tripped on one of your tables and fell, breaking my tooth off; this is just to let you know I will be taking action and subsequently suing you.'

I pointed out that I would be taking pictures of the mess they had created, although I had relentlessly tried to keep the floor hazard-free, but had found it impossible with everybody constantly moving around. Also the copious amount of alcohol consumed would be relevant in any claim pursued against us.'

When the customers left the restaurant they were not happy and made a point of showing it by giving me no acknowledgement; they completely ignored me, even though I said good-bye to each person as they walked out of the door.

Generally, as customers departed, they usually made comments such as;

'Thank you for a lovely evening, we will be back soon'.

The department in the insurance company didn't come back, and I never heard any more from the tooth man.

A retail shop in Norwich booked their work's Christmas party for thirty of their staff. We knew the owners personally, so were happy to accommodate them and looked forward to seeing them.

On arrival they had a few drinks downstairs before coming upstairs to the restaurant where I greeted them and showed them to their tables. I gave them menus, but on turning my back towards the restaurant, was bombarded with sugar sachets and the contents which were being thrown across the restaurant; then slices of orange and lemons from their drinks were being hurled.

I wasn't feeling quite so jovial now and reprimanded them in the nicest possible way to behave like adults. They didn't pay the slightest bit of attention to me.

When they were served their meals they didn't show much interest in eating them, they found it far more amusing to see if they could hit one of their companions with a tomato, a rib, fries or burger buns, in fact anything that was on the plate, and who would end up the dirtiest.

The owner of the shop was the instigator, causing the most disturbance, so each time he threw something at the others they retaliated straight back, consequently he ended up covered in food, in his hair, down his back and all over his shirt.

Luckily for me, there were no other restaurant diners in, so at least I didn't have to keep apologising to anyone else. I just concentrated on retrieving finished plates as soon as possible before the whole place was covered in food.

They did leave a generous tip for the staff but that was no consolation for the clean up we had to do after their departure. The floor was strewn with food; it was up the walls, on the ceiling, and among the plants. I just thought,

'Never again.'

The following Christmas they telephoned to book another table for thirty people, and then the memories came flooding back to me.

'Yes, you can book but, and it's a big but, I do not want a repeat of last year's extravaganza. If you can promise me that not one item of food will be thrown, then you are more than welcome to come in.'

He said he could not promise, so thought it better that they didn't come to our restaurant.

The restaurant they went to that year had to spend about £200 having their upholstery cleaned after they had left and were subsequently banned from eating there again. In fact they ended up being barred from quite a few restaurants over the years to follow.

Another company enjoyed their Christmas party with us so much that they sent an extremely complimentary thank you letter to us, remarking on what a good night they had had and how impressed they had been with the service and food, and booked for the following year.

This time I was very happy to accept because, unlike the previous customers, these were well behaved and good fun to serve and look after.

I had learnt a valuable lesson in the art of avoiding temptation for big groups of diners; I now removed the sugar sachet containers from the tables before customer's even sat down, and only gave them enough sugar for an end of meal coffee.

On this occasion about an hour before the booking was due to be in, one of the party members came upstairs with some equipment and said they would be using it during the evening.

'What's that?'

'A karaoke machine, so we can all have a sing-song after the meal.'

Nobody had mentioned that they planned to put on their own entertainment; as I had other diners coming in for a meal that night, I was beginning to feel a bit apprehensive.

I managed to stop them using it whilst the other customers were in, but as soon as they had left, the party took over the complete restaurant. They had the music blaring, the singing was painful, and they were all pissed. They messed up every single table in the restaurant, spilling drink and sprawling everywhere – I was not happy, how things can change in a year. I was certainly pleased to eventually see the back of that particular party.

At least they enjoyed themselves, and I suppose that was the object of the exercise.

Trade in the restaurant changed dramatically throughout the year: the hectic Christmas was followed by January sales, then tourists in the summer, bank holiday customers, contrasted with the deadly quiet of February and March, when customers are few and far between.

During the quiet months, to give people an incentive to dine in the restaurant, we advertised in the local papers, 'Two meals for the price of one.' It was a good deal for the customer, everybody likes a bargain, and the increased trade was beneficial to us.

We hoped to gain new customers who had never eaten in the restaurant before or even knew we existed; they would enjoy a cheap meal then hopefully return. Even giving a free meal away, we made a profit –a smaller one, but it was better than having no customers at all.

The promotions always proved successful and we were a lot busier than usual, until we noticed people were ordering the most expensive meal on the menu – steaks. The profit margin was extremely low anyway, so we weren't gaining extra funds, we were virtually giving them away.

Time to change the concept of our advertising details, now all future announcements read,

'Two burgers for the price of one.'

This was a much improved idea, burger meals produced a good profit margin anyway, so giving a free burger away was still advantageous to our business.

Selling power was paramount, we needed to persuade customers to order a drink or two, encourage them to order an appetiser and a dessert, and to finish with coffee. This increased the spend per head and it was therefore well worth giving a free burger meal.

I hated doing these offers; I didn't like giving anything away, but in retrospect, if customers were going to spend money, be it on a smaller scale then, fair enough, as every little bit helps.

Some customers wouldn't order a drink from the bar, or if they did wish for one, it was a glass of tap water. They refused to have dessert or coffee, ordering two burgers, eating them, then leaving.

Sometimes pensioners tottered in, sat themselves at a table and rummaged in their handbags for the coupon which had to be produced when ordering. On handing it to me, they would say, 'We've come in for our free meal.'

There are professional coupon cutters – these are people that spend days going through all the papers, cutting out all the offers. It often took them a few minutes after being seated to locate the correct coupon and if they had left it at home, then these people left without ordering anything. 'We'll come back when I find the coupon.'

We tried to guess which customers were 'coupon cutters' on arrival in the restaurant, - invariably we were right. I'm not sure how we knew, we just did, they just looked like a 'coupon cutter.'

One evening six men were seated at the far end of the restaurant in one of the booth tables. They were drunk but not causing any problems – well, not at the beginning.

They rapidly devoured three pints of beer each, their voices got louder, their language was inappropriate for a restaurant environment, and other customers dining were not impressed by their manner.

I intervened in my still pleasant, but stern authoritive voice which, from past experience, normally had the effect required, along with my evil glare and a wag of my finger.

'Keep the noise and language down boys; there are other people in the restaurant to consider.'

Apologies were abundant, the men were quiet and everyone was happy.

That was until they started pouring their pints of beer over each other, which inadvertently spilled onto the unsuspecting customers seated at the next table –

they were not impressed, and I quickly told them I would resolve the situation briskly.

Within moments of the beer incident, while I was still trying to calm the other customer down and dissuade the irate man from interfering, the men started throwing the contents of the pepper pots towards the rotating fans in the restaurant, thereby making all the diners and staff, sneeze.

On reflection, it was actually quite funny; a restaurant containing thirty diners at different stages of their meal, all sneezing.

However, at the time, I was not happy and told them they could pay for their meal and leave immediately.

'But we haven't even had it yet.'

'You will get it, but wrapped in tin foil so you can take it away and eat it somewhere else.'

I obtained the money, which was not gently handed to me, but thrown in my direction, as they left the restaurant with their take away meal.

I received a letter of complaint from an 18-year old girl who had been celebrating her birthday in the restaurant the previous week with her friends.

I had been on holiday, but already been informed of the problems on the night in question by the staff before I received the letter.

Any criticism from customers should always be taken seriously and acted upon; there is always room for improvement however good you think you are. However, saying that, this was the only letter of complaint we ever received in 25 years of running the restaurant.

She was upset because we had run out of bananas so she was unable to have a banana split for her dessert and there were not enough spare-ribs available for all the orders on her table.

Although you always endeavour to have enough food for the dishes offered on the menu sometimes, unavoidably, you run out, on this occasion – we did.

I replied to her by letter, explaining how all our meals were cooked to order and how apologetic I was about the lack of ribs. Also the bananas we had available were not to the standard we require, so we didn't want to serve them to customers.

I finished her letter as follows:

'We try to be perfect all the time, but unfortunately, very occasionally, there is a hiccup, which we always attempt to rectify. However, on this occasion it is difficult, because we fucked up, you wanted a free meal and didn't get one, so you went away, pissed off, and thought you would write me a letter to spoil my holiday. Well wrong – because quite frankly, I don't give a shit.

As far as I am concerned, don't ever come back, and take your free-loading somewhere else, I don't want to see you in my restaurant again. So piss off.

I do hope this will not deter you from eating in our restaurant again.'

Yours faithfully,

From a Fucked off Landlady for spending my time writing this load of crap to you.

Yes, I did send her a letter apologising and begging forgiveness for her ruined evening, but the additional paragraph was omitted – obviously.

I showed the staff the derogatory unsent letter, asking if they felt it satisfactory before it was mailed, and had great fun watching their faces gradually changing from impressed at my grovelling and suitable wording, to absolute horror as they read further down the page. They looked at me, their jaws dropped open in total disbelief,

'You haven't really sent a copy of that letter to her – have you?'

'Yes of course I have, why, what's wrong with it?'

'You can't, Jude it's so rude.'

A table of six elderly people came in the restaurant one lunchtime. They ordered drinks and food and were sitting chatting whilst waiting for their meal to be served. One of the gentlemen suddenly clutched himself, turned a dreadful colour, then slumped onto the table. He was dead.

The ambulance was called and the paramedics took him out in a body bag. Unfortunately for the customers, they never got to eat their meal which was about to be served and, unfortunately for us, we never got paid.

About 6.30pm on a busy Saturday when the restaurant was packed to the rafters, a party of six people came in for a meal. They had previously reserved a table with us, wanting to ensure they had enough time to eat, as they were going to the Theatre Royal to see a show afterwards.

They ordered their meal and enjoyed having a drink, when they started looking at their watches in anticipation.

There was rather a backlog of meals waiting to be cooked in the kitchen, so I explained their meal wouldn't be too much longer and apologised for the wait and, in the meantime, I would give them all a complimentary drink.

They seemed satisfied with that until another five minutes elapsed and they still hadn't received their food. Now they were very disgruntled, so after telling the chef to get a move on and get their meal served, I went up again and apologised profusely, promising they would still have plenty of time to get to the theatre. I would even drive them there if necessary – the place was only about five minutes' walk away.

They were still not happy, in fact they were extremely angry, and all ate their food in silence.

Before they finished their meal, they asked for the bill. I was in the preparation area when they got up to leave. I heard them speak to the waitress, after which they practically threw the bill and money at her before their departure.

On questioning the waitress, the happy people had paid the bill but deducted all the drinks consumed because they were so angry at having to wait for their meal, so were just paying for the food items.

I was furious. Yes, they did have to wait a little longer than usual, but I had already bought them a round of drinks and offered to drive them to the theatre; they had no right to knock another £20 off the bill.

I would get my own back.

The following morning on a Sunday when people enjoy a lay-in in bed, I phoned them up. They were thrilled to hear my voice at 7am telling them they had no right to be so rude to my waitress. They should have spoken to me regarding the matter of deducting the cost of drinks from the bill.

'I didn't want to speak to you because all you did was smile at us each time you came to the table.'

'Would you have preferred it if I had a miserable disposition then?'

No answer from the happy customer. 'Did you enjoy your meal when you received it?'

'Yes, there was nothing wrong with the food.'

'In which case you had no legal right to deduct £20 from your bill. I'm sorry your evening was spoiled but I did go out of my way to make amends, therefore I will be sending you a bill for the outstanding amount.'

There was moaning and groaning on the other end of the phone,

'Do what you like, I'm not paying.'

In my most pleasant, chirpy voice I said good-bye, and they would be hearing from me shortly.

I had no intention of sending them a bill for the money due; it would have been more trouble than it was worth, but it did give me huge satisfaction to have a little dig at them early on a Sunday morning.

On the subject of smiling, I did have a habit of walking down the centre of the restaurant, nodding at each table of customers giving them a big smile on the way – representing the impression of a nodding dog you see in the back of car windows. The staff enjoyed taking the piss at me, so no wonder those disgruntled customers hated my pleasant disposition.

Snowy and Corky ate in the restaurant every Saturday lunchtime on table one (the hiring and firing table). During their meal of bacon and eggs, Corky loved to sit and moan about life in general, or just grumble about anything that agitated him at the time, although he was somewhat loud.

'Corky, everyone can hear you in the restaurant.'

He just laughed, lowered his voice for about a minute and then up went the decibel level again. Snowy would just retrieve his magazine which he kept hidden under the seat cover from the previous week and barely listen to Corky rambling.

One Wednesday evening, two regular customers came in the restaurant, instead of sitting at their usual table, they asked if they could have a word with me first. One of them took one of our 'lovin skins' (a jacket potato with the potato scooped out and filled with cheese,) out of his coat pocket; wrapped in a paper napkin.

'We came in two weeks ago for a meal whilst you were on holiday, and this was one of the 'skins' served to me. It only contained a small amount of cheese, instead of the usual large helping, so I kept it in my fridge so I could show you on your return.'

'I am very sorry, you should have mentioned it to the staff at the time; they would have rectified it for you, I will make amends and give you some complimentary ones this evening.'

'I didn't like to cause a fuss.'

My thoughts, so why the bloody hell are you doing it now then? Did I really need to look at a two-week old potato? Just telling me would have been sufficient.

But I did manage to keep my mouth shut and proceed to tell him I would give the chef a bollocking for serving it in the first place.

He was happy with that and they continued to come in the restaurant every week for their 'skins.'

Table eight was a small side-by-side seat facing towards the restaurant, also known as the gropers' table, aptly named because over the years we spotted quite a lot of shenanigans going on underneath the tablecloth that draped over customers' laps.

The customers didn't think we noticed anything untoward going on, as the men would deftly have a little fumble under their partner's skirt; the women would reiterate by slipping their hand between the man's inner leg, but we were far too clever and knew instantly what was going on, mainly because of the look on their faces as they were enjoying themselves.

We liked the customers to leave our restaurant satisfied after a pleasant dining experience, so never mentioned that we knew what they were up to.

A guy came in occasionally and sat on table eight, I don't think he groped himself – but you never know. He was never any trouble to serve, but was just one of those people you didn't particularly like.

He ordered a steak diane which is served on a hot sizzling plate. When we told the chef who the meal was for, he immediately put the sizzler on a high gas ring to make it extra hot. So when the time came to serve his meal in the restaurant, it was so hot that when it was placed in front of him, he disappeared behind a cloud of steam for over five minutes. When he eventually came into sight, the sweat was dripping down his face from the heat off the plate. He just glared at us,

'Are you taking the piss?'

'Of course not, you did ask for your steak to be cooked well done.'

A husband and wife ate in our restaurant fairly often always booking a table first and stating that they did not want to sit at the small two-seater table; they had obviously been married a long time!

They were customers who appreciated special attention and did enjoy a long drawn-out conversation with me, totally unaware there was a restaurant full of customers requiring attention – but it made them happy.

They always ordered the same thing off the menu, but whinged about something on each occasion they came in, which did tend to get annoying after a while.

The husband moaned that the previous time the ribs were bigger. Although we always tried to get consistency in the size of the pork ribs, they did come in various sizes sometimes, so customers had to be grateful when they did receive a large portion, while still getting them for the same price.

'I wish you sold custard because I don't like cream or ice-cream on my dessert.'

So I bought custard especially for him; then he decided he didn't want custard anymore on his dessert.

'The fries are small and crispy and not as good as they usually are.'

When new potatoes are in season that was our only option for fries, so, yes, they were a bit smaller, and, yes, you do get some crispy bits.

It wasn't his intent to have money deducted from the bill, he just liked moaning, and that was just his way. Basically, I never paid any attention to him.

Over the years he mellowed, the moaning stopped and we began to receive compliments – result.

Haz and Jan loved the Walnut, both the bar and the restaurant. They enjoyed the music and always came in on a Thursday night for a meal before going downstairs to listen to the live band playing.

Haz loved trying to wind me up, each time I asked if their meal was OK, he always gave me the same reply;

'No, its crap.'

'Good, I'm glad it's the usual standard, we wouldn't like you to enjoy it for once.'

Several drinks later, Jan occasionally got a little wobbly on her feet, but never failed to delight us with her big smile.

They are a lovely couple and on their wedding day enjoyed a few drinks and meal in the restaurant after the ceremony. I really pushed the boat out and bought special wedding banners, confetti and fresh flowers for the table.

Two guys who came in regularly for a meal used to love trying to wind me up and have a banter during their stay, constantly telling me the food was rubbish when I asked if everything was OK.

They ordered a bottle of wine which they were drinking by the time I served their meal. 'Jude, this wine's off, I think it's corked.'

No, it's just crap wine, the quality we usually serve to our customers; it's just one grade better than vinegar.'

'I'm been serious, the wine really is off.'

I still didn't believe him, and why should I, as every time they came in they always teased me, remarking the food was rubbish and tonight wasn't any different, except they were moaning about the wine.

It took him a few more attempts, saying there really was something wrong with the wine. 'Jude, just try it – please.'

'Yuk, Oh, you really weren't joking this time, the wine is corked: that'll teach you for been cheeky to me every week!'

We were fortunate in the fact that we only had a handful of 'runners' during our whole duration at the Walnut. It's an annoyance I'm sure every restaurant in the land has had to endure at some time or another.

One minute the customer is seated at the restaurant, your back is turned or your attention is drawn somewhere else, the next moment he has gone without paying his bill. We would run up the street in anticipation we may catch him, no such luck.

However, on one of these occasions two of our regular customers had been dining in the restaurant at lunchtime. The lady left first, returning to work. Shortly afterwards I suddenly noticed the man had gone without paying for their meal.

I wasn't too concerned, as I knew they would be back again soon for a meal. Luckily they were, so I mentioned their misdemeanour,

'Have you come in for another free meal?'

After looking somewhat bewildered, it emerged that the man thought the lady had paid and vice versa; consequently no money had been forthcoming. After many apologies, his bill was paid.

A family regularly ate in the restaurant and were always very pleasant to serve, until they left without paying their bill.

Again, I wasn't too bothered; I would mention their forgetfulness the next time they came in.

Not quite so fortunate on this occasion – I never saw them again, - bastards.

I was in the prep area section of the restaurant, obstructed from a view of customers when Pete, the chef on duty that evening, saw a man walk in the restaurant and sit at one of the large tables, set up for six people. He remarked he looked a bit dodgy, although the staff's idea of dodgy customers and mine sometimes didn't agree.

He looked OK from a distance, in a seated position at the table and didn't appear to be an impending problem. He wasn't shouting, wasn't drunk, but just sitting quietly. I gave him a menu and tried to pick out any oddities for myself. From the waist upwards everything appeared normal. His attire consisted of an acrylic turtle neck jumper, slightly faded and a bit scruffy but on the surface he was reasonably presentable.

I asked if he would like a drink, 'A beer please'.

That was a result, the guy had manners, so should not be any problem; just a man on his own, wanting a meal and a drink. It started to go downhill when he ordered his meal.

'I want a steak, with chips, peas and carrots.'

I wondered what had happened to the manners; they were short-lived.

'I'm sorry, but we don't serve peas and carrots, how about a mixed salad?'

'I want peas and carrots.'

His voice had increased in decibel level; his aggressive tone alerted the other customers in the restaurant sitting in close proximity to him. Why I didn't tell him to leave the premises at that point, I do not know.

However, I persevered, and eventually got his order, sirloin steak, (I'm glad he said sirloin, as that was the only cut of meat we served at that particular time) and home fries, which again I had to describe in great detail. They were fresh potatoes, sliced, which don't have the same appearance as a chip as they are round, not like McDonalds long thin kind; however, you will really enjoy them. Then mushrooms would be a good idea as we do not sell peas or carrots.

Our steaks were cooked on a chargrill, and as he wanted his steak cooked well done, it was going to take about 10 minutes at least.

A few minutes went by, I glanced in the restaurant, he was out of his seat and talking to two customers, who I have to say were looking rather uncomfortable.

Oh, God, what is he saying to them? I watched from a distance, then saw the lady on the table pass him a piece of meat from her plate; he then returned to his table.

He had a slug of his beer, got up again and started talking to another table of customers.

'What is he up to now?' It was definitely time to intervene.

I went to the first people he had been having a conversation with, to ask what had been said.

The female replied, 'He came up and asked if he could try a piece of my steak, as his hasn't arrived and he was hungry.'

I glanced towards him again, he was talking to yet more customers; he picked up their can of beer and began swigging it.

I went straight up to him and got hold of his arm, at which point the aroma of BO, stale urine, stale beer, and a musky stench, (a haven't had a wash in a long time smell) became overpowering.

I presumed that, having been out in the cold, and then entering a warm environment had made his body temperature rise, producing the overwhelming pong.

I steered him back to his table and asked what on earth he thought he was doing; it was unacceptable behaviour to disturb other diners, let alone asking to try their food and drink their beer.

'I'm hungry, where's my dinner?'

Ok, so Pete the chef was right, he was a dodgy customer and why the hell hadn't I listened to him in the first place? 'Pete, hurry with that steak; he's being a pain in the arse,'

'Oh God, he's up out of his table again.'

I rushed up to him in the restaurant and got there just in time before he descended on some more unsuspecting customers. 'Will you sit down now at your table, or you won't be getting anything to eat.'

I placed the meal in front of him and turned back to the husband and wife who were sitting immediately opposite him, and offered my apologies on his behalf. The woman lent over to me, smiling, and spoke very quietly. 'Just glance round slowly and look at him now.'

He was undoubtedly enjoying his meal, as he had his head down and was eating the steak grasped in one hand with home fries in the other dirty hand. He was shovelling the food into his mouth without stopping for breath – and dribbling.

I just looked in desperation; I apologised yet again to the customers, pointing out that this was not a normal occurrence. Luckily they all seemed to find the whole affair very amusing.

I was convinced he had no intention of paying for his meal, so without offering a dessert or coffee, I totalled his bill and put it directly in front of him.

He rose from the table and went towards the exit. This was the first time I noticed the flies on his trousers were undone and poking out from the zip was no, not his willy, but a toilet roll!

A fleeting look at his table revealed the bill still there, but no money - what a surprise.

I had had enough of the whole saga by now and felt I couldn't put the customers through any more scenes of disruption, so I let him go down the stairs towards the bar, with me in hot pursuit, and then I would confront him for the money.

With a gentle hand on his shoulder – I really didn't want to touch his smelly body at all; I told him it would be a good idea to pay for his meal before he left.

'I want to go to the toilet.'

'OK, so do what you have to do in the loo, then you can pay your bill.'

He came out of the toilet and went straight to the exit door where Chris and I were waiting. 'I don't have any money.'

'Well that's just great, you came in the restaurant, upset all the customers, tried to eat their food, drink their beer and ate your meal with your fingers and then tell me you don't have any money to pay for it. You can just sit down there and wait for the police to come.'

For once he was obedient.

The police arrived and on telling them the situation, they looked at the guy, 'Um, I recognise you, we arrested you a couple of evening's ago for smashing windows at the railway station and then you spent the night in jail: looks like you are going back there again.'

When all was revealed, it turned out the guy broke the windows at the train station, waited for the police to come and arrest him, then he confessed to the crime, and said he was homeless and wanted a bed for the night and, of course, breakfast the following morning.

So I presumed he was getting rather peckish so descended on our restaurant for a free meal, and was quite happy to be arrested.

Quite sad on reflection, that some homeless people need to go to such lengths to get a hot meal and a bed for the night.

No chance we would ever receive any compensation for lost profits then?

'No'.

A husband, wife and two children parked their car outside the pub and came upstairs to eat. The husband and wife were very pleasant; the two children, aged five and seven, were the kids from hell.

They never sat still at the table, used to crawl under every piece of furniture in the restaurant, pulling the tablecloths as they proceeded on their crawling journey. When they were bored with that game, they went to each unoccupied table and moved the condiments, or emptied the sugar sachets all over the tables.

They managed to sit at their table just long enough to eat their meal or, rather, drop most of it on the floor treading it in, and more often than not spilt one or more drinks over the tablecloth.

When the children had finished eating and destroying the restaurant they were allowed to play outside the pub by their parked car. Their favourite game was standing on the parents' car, hitting it with a squash racket kept in the boot, or pulling the retractable roof up and down.

When this got boring they chased each other round the car park and thumped each other until one started crying.

For obvious reasons I called them 'the kids from hell' which the mother overheard me say one evening.

I noticed the car had been parked outside and called through to the other waitress on duty,

'The kids from hell are about to descend on us.'

Unfortunately, just as the words came out of my mouth, the mother walked through the restaurant door and heard my remarks. Good job she had a sense of humour because she laughed, agreed with me they were hellish kids and, from then onwards, each time they came in the restaurant for a meal she would say, 'Here come the kids from hell.'

A smartly dressed lady in her seventies regularly came in the restaurant; staff enjoyed serving her because she always left a large tip. She always walked in with several shopping bags and, being rather infirm, asked the bar person if he would carry her bags upstairs; she would insist on tipping them £5. Although it was never a problem to help her, and a tip wasn't necessary, she was adamant.

She tipped the waitress anything from £5 - £10, which was gratefully received, but the total cost of her meal generally only came to about £9 or £10, so she was often spending more money on tipping than eating and drinking.

She enjoyed chatting to the staff, so we presumed having company was probably far more important to her than money. It was the same scenario when she was assisted downstairs at the end of the meal there was another £5 tip.

After a few months her visits were less frequent; the last time we saw her in the restaurant she entered without any bags, which was unusual as she was generally laden.

She wasn't the smart articulate lady we were used to seeing. When it came to paying her bill, she rummaged through her purse to find enough money to pay the bill and told the waitress she didn't have enough cash left to leave a tip. Although the waitress said it was absolutely no problem, she had been more than generous over the previous months, the lady insisted on giving her some jewellery instead of a tip. Although she refused, the woman was resolute and put the jewellery firmly in her hand saying she would be offended if it wasn't accepted.

We never saw that lovely lady again, so whether she ran out of money or passed away we will never know.

I received a letter in the mail from a woman claiming to have eaten in the restaurant a couple of nights previously along with three other people. She went on to complain that the waitress was rude; everything had seemed an inconvenience to her. She had been served warm, flat beer, the plain chicken wasn't plain as requested, the restaurant was dirty, the toilets were unclean and there wasn't any loo roll.

The whole evening was very off-putting and she was hoping for a reply from me soon.

I read the letter out loud to the other staff and watched their faces drop, especially the section regarding rudeness. The first area to investigate was to see which waitress was working on the night in question.

It was me!

The staff thought it hilarious that the boss had received a letter of complaint about her; they heaved big sigh of relief that they had no involvement in the matter.

I was a little mystified to say the least, how could anyone say I was rude?

I began my investigation into the matter. I retrieved the copy bills to look through the orders. Firstly, we didn't even have a table of four in on that particular night, they were all couples and one table of six. And secondly, there wasn't an order for plain chicken.

Aah aah, a prime example of a scam, but they picked on the wrong person. It was obviously someone trying to receive complimentary free meal vouchers as means of compensation for a disappointing meal.

I telephoned a few other restaurant owners we knew quite well to see if they had received a similar letter. It transpired that an American restaurant in Norwich had received a complaint about their sweet and sour chicken dish – they didn't even sell sweet and sour. A Mexican restaurant also had a complaint regarding their burgers – something else not on their menu.

This person certainly hadn't done her research very well, by way of studying the various menus and food each restaurant was serving, but her game was up.

The police were called and they took the letter containing the woman's address away as evidence; it didn't take much investigation before the police paid her a visit.

She received a warning, but no court appearance or fine, because she wasn't actually asking for any money in her letters and was therefore not doing anything illegal other than being a bloody nuisance to proprietors.

For a couple of years most Friday nights, a party of between four to ten people descended on us in the restaurant. Their main priority for their visit was the cocktails; food was secondary and just a way of lining the stomachs.

They were great fun and very entertaining to watch after several drinks. Their favourite cocktail, a Long Island Iced Tea, consisted of five full measures of different white spirits, served in a pint glass topped with coke.

Consuming one of these cocktails isn't a problem, but anymore than two can generally tip you over the edge, and then you're sick.

How they drank four or five without being ill, I do not know, but we did see the consequences of their actions.

They enjoyed dancing up and down the restaurant gangway – luckily by the time they usually got to this stage they were the only customers left, so weren't upsetting anybody else's evening.

They played wheelbarrow races down the aisle.

They threw themselves down on the floor, legs and arms flapping, moving up and down like a caterpillar then combining all the actions into a half circle shape; this was their interpretation of sizzling bacon in a pan.

We often assisted helping them downstairs at the end of the evening for fear they may fall, by which time their legs had turned to jelly and they could barely stand, let alone walk. There was the time one of them lay on the bench seat fast asleep and had to be carried out over someone's shoulder.

We had just finished working a very busy lunchtime session and were in the process of closing, when the door opened and in walked twenty people. 'We would like to eat.'

Our restaurant had instantaneously been taken over with people sitting down at tables and spreading themselves across the whole restaurant, cameras and lighting gear strewn everywhere. 'I'm really sorry but the restaurant is closed until 6.30pm.'

'Don't you know who I am?' came a rather snooty voice.

'Yes, I do know who you are; however, we are still closed.'

After grunting and moaning and realising they wouldn't be eating at the Walnut, they picked up their equipment, stomped down the stairs, through the bar and out the door.

I had just turned Esther Ranzten and her entourage away from our restaurant.

A table of seven men I knew quite well were waiting for their meal. I came upstairs with a tray of drinks and was about to put them on the table, when one of the guys moved his arm and knocked all the drinks off the tray, all over his trousers – he was soaked.

Although it was his fault, I felt dreadful and extremely apologetic. I suggested if he took his trousers off I would put them in the tumble dryer so he didn't have to sit with soaking wet trousers on.

The restaurant was full with customers, so he discreetly slid his trousers off under the table and passed them to me for drying. It only took a few minutes to go upstairs and put them in the machine.

When I came down, the guys were beckoning to me for attention. The other six men had also taken their trousers off and were all sitting at the table in their pants and that was how they stayed throughout their meal.

After several drinks; on their departure they weren't quite as discreet, as they stood in the restaurant aisle putting their trousers back on in front of the remaining restaurant customers!

For the thousands of meals and customers we must have served over the 25 years, its quite remarkable that there was only the very odd occasion when either food or drink got spilt or dropped on a customer. Of course accidents did happen, it's inevitable, and you just had to hope the customer understood it wasn't done on purpose.

On one occasion there were some people having a business lunch. I placed a portion of wings along with the dip of blue cheese in front of one of them. Unfortunately, the dip slipped off the table onto the man's lap. I apologised profusely and told him to follow me into the washing up area so he could clean up by the sink.

He was not happy; the blue cheese dip was a nice white creamy colour spread all over his trouser groin area, resembling something else! And it didn't smell too good either. I did offer to wipe it off for him, he grumpily declined the offer.

I have often seen people spill food down their trousers, shirts or skirts, if this was white clothing, it made the stain even more obvious. If I saw them looking at the damage, I always offered to get some soapy water and a cloth to wipe the worst off. However, sometimes I didn't get back quickly enough to shout 'No, don't do that,' they had already put one of our red paper serviettes into a glass of water on the table to wet it and begun rubbing the stain on their clothes; the dye from the napkin came off onto the material, making the soiled mark worse. It was generally the men who did this and couldn't understand why their white shirt was now a lovely shade of pink and ruined.

I went for a flying visit through the air one evening in the restaurant carrying a couple of ice-cream desserts to a table, tripping on the strap of a lady's handbag sticking out in the centre of the aisle. I flew through the air and landed about three tables further down the restaurant, flat on my face, but still with the desserts completely intact.

Feeling extremely embarrassed, and still lying on the floor, I looked up at the customers sitting at the table where I had landed and said, 'Just passing, hope you are enjoying your meal.'

They just glanced at me, paying no heed to the fact I was laying flat out on the floor. 'Yes thanks', then they continued eating, as if the incidence was a normal occurrence!

Nigel and Fanny were frequent customers, and really nice people; they enjoyed the restaurant food and loved to drink in the bar. They came in one evening and announced that it was their anniversary and jokingly said they wanted a romantic table with a candle. 'Cor, you'll be bloody lucky.'

They didn't come across as a couple who would be impressed with a flamboyant setting for a romantic meal; just as well, as the best I could offer them was a tomato, cut in half and put on a plate with a doyley with a little birthday candle in the middle. They thought it was hilarious, and it stayed lit, on the table, the whole meal.

A table of six middle aged people were eating in the restaurant. One of the women was enjoying several vodka and tonics – and it showed in her manner. After four or five vodkas she complained I had forgotten to put any vodka in the last drink. I assured her there was definitely vodka in her glass; however, she was not convinced and told me to put another shot in.

Anything to oblige, I did as I was told. She again said there still wasn't any spirit in her glass and wanted to complain to the manager.

'She won't tell you any different you're already talking to her.'

That didn't go down very well, at which point her husband stepped in and said he would like to come down to the bar with me to watch me personally pour her vodka and tonic.

No problem, so again I obliged. She drank that one but still didn't look particularly happy, although she was by now extremely drunk, which I think proved my point that there was definitely vodka in her drink. They left soon afterwards – thank God.

A few days later we received a visit from weights and measures, which wasn't unusual, as occasionally they would come and check licensees were selling the product being advertised and not displaying an expensive bottle of spirit containing a cheap substitute. Something we never, ever did, so we didn't have any cause for concern when we did receive a visit.

Generally they took samples of three different spirits, which were paid for and took them back to their laboratory to check the product, and then send us the results.

However, on this occasion, their only interest was the vodka; they had received a complaint from someone, which they have to act upon.

Memories came flooding back of the drunken woman who was adamant she wasn't getting vodka in her drink. It transpired the customers in the restaurant were coal merchants, obviously used to dealing with people from weights and measures so thought they would try and get us into trouble.

It didn't work because there was absolutely nothing wrong with the vodka we were selling.

Tim and Wendy dined at Captain America's every Saturday night when we worked there. As soon as the Walnut opened we had their valued custom in the bar and restaurant every week for 25 years (apart from the very odd occasion when they fancied an Indian curry or were on holiday).

They had a specific routine which never changed. They came in the bar on a Saturday night laden with shopping bags, would have a drink in the bar, buy another one which was brought upstairs to the restaurant and always sat at the same table, in the same seat.

Tim always ate the same meal every single week, Digby always had a chilli hot dog, but didn't like kidney beans (Tim ate those). Wendy however, used to alternate between three different dishes. The times she ordered a chicken caesar salad inevitably seemed to be when I was really busy; it was the most time consuming meal I had to prepare.

We watched their son Digby grow up from a baby to an adult, and never, ever, saw him misbehave, in fact he was the best behaved child I have ever come across. Mind you, every Saturday when he was very young he did have a new toy, game or book to play with, that may have helped.

They were a lovely family and I really enjoyed chatting to them. They loved to hear my week's events of trials and tribulations in the pub, especially the funny stories, making Wendy laugh till she cried.

They were such loyal customers of ours and on our leaving party, Wendy took nearly one hundred pictures of the day's events and people who attended. She also presented us with a poem she had written, which summed Chris and I up perfectly and is an accolade we will always treasure. The poem can be read towards the end of the book.

Customers sitting at the far end of the restaurant directly under the air conditioner did sometimes get dripped on when the unit had a build up of condensation. I was always ready to rectify the situation – when there's a problem, there's always a solution.

Firstly I gave the customers an umbrella to stop them getting wet; this was always appreciated as their food didn't get spoiled.

Secondly, I got a broom, wrapped the bristle end with a cloth and wiped all the drips off the air conditioner.

Job done!

Nigel owned 'Nigel Alexander's hairdresser's, just round the corner from the Walnut. He often took short breaks to Italy so Chris asked him if he wouldn't mind bringing back a whole parmesan cheese, an expensive ingredient we used a lot in the restaurant. 'No problem.'

On arriving home, his first words to Chris were, 'You bastard, asking me to bring back a whole parmesan cheese, you're taking the piss.'

'Why, what happened?'

Nigel had gone to the speciality cheese shop in Italy and ordered the parmesan. The guy collected a barrow, disappeared into a back room, reappeared, and struggled to manoeuvre a gigantic whole parmesan, costing well in excess of £600.

A very embarrassed Nigel briskly changed his mind and ordered a small piece cut from the 'whole' parmesan.

We thought a whole parmesan was the same size as Edam – oops, wrong.

We were forgiven by Nigel, and remain good friends to this day.

We bought a bottle of sauce back from America which we thought the regular customers may appreciate – or not. It was called 'Fucking Hot Sauce.'

Tabasco sauce is hot, but not compared to this one.

Chris had great delight in telling regular customers to taste the sauce, tipping a little on their finger without revealing what they were trying, then watching their faces show pain, go bright red, sweat and then take a large gulp of beer before they could speak. 'Gudgin, you bastard, what the fuck was that?'

Of all the customers who Chris insisted should undergo the tasting experience, not one person could handle the heat of the sauce.

A family of six were dining in the restaurant one Saturday lunchtime; the mother asked if we had any Tabasco as her young son liked hot spicy food, bearing in mind he was eating a bowl of chilli, which is already fairly hot.

I gave her the Tabasco, and showed her the bottle of 'Fucking Hot Sauce' in case her son would like to try it, but I advised her to use it very sparingly, and to keep her hand over the name so he couldn't see it.

He used a quarter of a bottle on his bowl of chilli and didn't even break into a sweat. He was seven-years old.

Comments and complaints were, most of the time, taken seriously and acted upon. A night of charming customers could be marred by one disgruntled person spoiling the whole evening for us, giving us concern as to why that person hadn't enjoyed their meal, what were we doing wrong and how could it be improved. These doubts might continue for several days worrying about that one person when so many other diners had gone away happy and content.

We valued our regular restaurant customers, enjoyed their banter, and equally took pleasure in reciprocating. We have so many recollections to look back on, some good, some I would rather forget, but each and every one, did, in their own way, contribute to making our time at the Walnut memorable.

****

Another section from our
EVENING MENU

BURGERS GALORE

All our burgers are cooked medium <u>unless</u> you state otherwise. They all come garnished with lettuce, tomato, onion, dill and mayo, or tell us to "hold the garden".

Choose from a 6 oz. (175g) or 8 oz. (225g) (uncooked) made from finest ground beef. All served with a choice of jacket potato or home fries.

	6oz	8oz
PLAIN OL' BURGER	7.15	8.15
CHEESEBURGER - With melted cheese.	7.65	8.65
PRAWN BROKER - Atlantic prawns in cocktail sauce.	8.45	9.45
BEANFEAST - With melted cheese and baked beans.	8.45	9.45
BURRBURGER - (The wh-what?) Coated in Cajun spices and topped with fried peppers, onions and cheese.	8.45	9.45
VERDE BURGER - Topped with guacamole	8.45	9.45
HOG'S BREATH - Topped with melted cheese and garlic mushrooms.	8.45	9.45
SMOKEY JOE - Topped with tangy bar-b-que sauce.	7.95	8.95
BELLOWS FALLS - (Don't mispronounce this) Topped with cheese, salsa and jalapenos.	8.45	9.45
MEX TEX - Smothered in chilli con carne.	8.45	9.45
BURGER DIANE - Covered in a sauce of mushrooms, brandy and Worcestershire sauce.	8.45	9.45
NEW YORKER - Covered in melted cheese, with a side pot of chilli.	8.45	9.45
HICKORY - Covered in melted cheese, BBQ sauce and grilled onions.	8.45	9.45

To add bacon to any of the above .60

FOR THE CARNIVORE

RACK OF RIBS - A slow baked sheet of baby back ribs finished in a bar-b-que sauce with a side pot of coleslaw	13.00
STEAK DIANE - Tender sirloin, covered in a sauce of mushrooms, brandy and Worcestershire sauce, served on a sizzle plate.	13.95
DELMONICO STEAK - 8oz (225g) ribeye steak with hot Cajun spices, served with mushrooms.	12.95
CHICAGO STYLE HOT DOG - (All beef frankfurter.) Covered in melted cheese and fried onions OR chilli.	8.00
DRACULA'S LAST WORDS ("Can you steak me?") - 8oz ribeye steak topped with mushrooms, grilled onions and cheese, served on toasted garlic bread.	13.50
SIRLOIN STEAK - (Looks like steak, smells like steak, must be steak!) - In fact, finest British beef, 10oz (275g) served with grilled tomato.	13.50

ALL THE ABOVE MEALS ARE SERVED WITH A CHOICE OF HOME FRIES OR JACKET POTATO.

BEEF FAJITAS - We provide the warm flour tortillas for you to fill with a combination of beef, sour cream, guacamole, salsa and chopped salad.	13.25
BURRITOS - 3 floured tortillas filled with chilli, topped with melted cheese and salsa, served with coleslaw and salad garnish.	8.25
CHILLI CON CARNE - Just the way you like it - if you like it hot! Topped with a sprinkling of cheese and served with tortilla chips.	8.25
OR Served with rice	8.25

Your servers' wages are pathetic, and THERE IS NO SERVICE CHARGE included. Tips are gratefully received and go directly to your server.

LEASE/RENT REVIEWS

The lease for our pub was, I imagine, not too different from any other commercial lease inflicted on a tenant. If you want to take on a leasehold business then you have no option but to sign on the dotted line and agree to abide by the rules.

The lease from the brewery was available in terms of 5, 10, 15 or 20 years. It is a protected business agreement with the security of tenure.

There are varying kinds of ties inserted into the agreement, some tied for just beer, some tied for beer and wine, and others could be tied for beer, wine, spirits and minerals.

The retailer was also responsible for all non-structural repairs.

There was a five-yearly open market rent review subject to annual indexation by the Retail Price Index which can move the rent up or downwards. During our term at the pub the landlords only considered one option when the rent review was due, and that was to put the rent up.

Annual rates for commercial and domestic property changed throughout the years. In 1984 when we took over the pub they were called 'rates'; the amount paid was based on a uniform rate set by central government and collected by the local council. Properties were assessed on the rateable value, a valuation of annual rent value which required us to fill in endless forms detailing each specific area of sales relating to our income.

At the time when we were assessed by the council, we hadn't opened the restaurant, so our turnover was substantially lower than what we hoped our future income would be. Our rates were set at £1,800 per annum, which doesn't seem a lot now, but was relative to prices being charged for a pint of beer.

In 1984, when our lease commenced, our landlords were Norwich Brewery. The lease we signed was one of the last of that type of specific agreement, called a Turnover Lease. We weren't on the usual fixed rent for a period of five years. Our rent began at £10,000 per annum and decreased with the quantity of beer we sold. The more beer we bought and sold, the lower our rent became.

We had taken on a pub where previously sales of beer had been low, so our increase of trade equated to the rent reducing to approximately £6,000 per annum.

Towards the late 1980's when trade was at its peak, not just for us, but for all licensees and retailers who were enjoying a boom time and making money, we were ordering so much beer that the landlords thought we were ordering and then reselling it on to other licensees. They couldn't believe for the size of our pub how much beer we were getting through, - no, we weren't running a wholesale business, just being successful.

Mind you, the boom didn't last and we were hit with the recession in 1990.

Our lease stated that the brewery were responsible for all structural repairs and were responsible for painting the outside of the pub every five years.

They commenced the redecoration outside the pub in 1985 and began by taking all the signs down advertising the Walnut Tree, including the plaque with Chris' name on, in preparation for the work.

Chris went to New York with Harvey, our partner, for a week's holiday, subsequently leaving me to run the business which was no problem as I had good staff to help me.

However, customers were very bemused and rumours were rife in Norwich, because when people came in the pub for a drink and asked me where Chris was, I replied, 'I have no idea; I've not seen him for a few days.'

'But all the signs have been taken down outside; he hasn't left you has he?'

How I managed to keep a straight face I do not know, but I carried on with the charade the whole week, still saying I hadn't seen him.

I wasn't telling a lie, just not quite the whole truth.

When Chris did return, customers remarked, 'Thought we'd seen the last of you, you miserable git, might have known you would never leave Jude.'

Needless to say, Chris had to find something to complain about regarding the outside painting of the pub; he wasn't happy with the colour of the paint on the doors. So he made the decorators strip the doors and redo them until he was satisfied.

In 1989 we received our next rent increase. It was supposed to be in accordance with what is assumed to be a fair maintainable trade for the size of the premises. After much arguing, they set a figure of £24,000 per annum, bearing in mind we had been paying approximately £6,000 a year, this was an outrageous figure and we felt we were being penalised for running a successful business.

Apart from the rent increase, Norwich Brewery leases ceased to exist and were changed over to Inntrepeneur 20-year leases. This was the first time a pub company had offered 20-year leases, so it was thought that it would be beneficial to all licensees. Unfortunately, there were plenty of new clauses which had not been evident on the Norwich Brewery agreements.

Under the new terms we would now be responsible for all structural repairs, pay for decorating the internal and exterior walls and replace or restore the roof, if necessary. (Thank God we had the bar floor replaced with maple wood when the lease was originally signed with Norwich Brewery – they paid).

Under the terms of the new lease they would allow us to sell a 'guest ale' – which enabled us to buy an ale from a distributor of our choice; this would be at a cheaper cost than if it was bought from the brewery.

We were also entitled to receive the full amount of income from our one fruit machine instead of previously giving the brewery half the profit we received. – big deal.

With the vast increase in rent, and the new lease making us responsible to pay for – well, everything, our partnership with Harvey was no longer a viable proposition; at the end of the financial year there would not be a sufficient profit to split between the three of us. Harvey agreed that the best option for us was to buy his share of the business and for us to run the operation on our own.

Harvey had originally put all the money up required to start the pub and over the first five years we had gradually been paying him back our half share of the ingoing costs. Now we basically had to start again from scratch, but this time doing it on our own.

The bank agreed to give us a loan enabling us to pay the amount agreed upon with Harvey. It was quite scary to have a huge financial burden but we were optimistic that with the level of trade we had already achieved and it was the boom period for trade with people spending freely, the loan could decrease rapidly after a couple of years.

With the financial outlay to Harvey we approached Inntrepeneur, who very kindly (with sarcasm) agreed to only charge us £18,000 rent for the first year, increasing to £24,000 for the following four years! What a great help that was going to be after paying £6,000 per annum.

Chris and I signed the lease, begrudgingly, but we knew the business inside out; if we kept sustaining the present level of trade, we would still be able to have a reasonable income after the loan was paid.

The regional representative from Inntrepeneur came to introduce himself within the first week of our 'new lease.' He was in his mid 20's, freshly graduated from university, and spoke to us as if it was our first day of operating a pub. He went on to tell us how much we should charge for a pint of beer and suggested options which bore no relevance to our business.

Chris was not impressed and had no hesitation in telling him, 'Hang on a minute, we've already been here five years, if I charged the figure you are suggesting to sell a pint of beer, the business will have gone bust in a year's time, so don't bother visiting me anymore, because I am quite capable of doing it without your brainless suggestions.'

He soon left, looking as despondent as a little puppy dog and never bothered to return, which was fine by us.

The first year without Harvey as our partner was profitable, and we were able to repay a good proportion of the loan to the bank.

However, this good fortune did not continue. We received not one, but several of the dreaded brown envelopes in the mail from the Inland Revenue stating how much tax we were required to pay. We knew we had tax to pay but not to the sum of £72,000, with the first half due by the end of January – two months away.

We were horrified, so immediately got in touch with the accountants who told us they would look into it. A week slipped by without any communication from them, after several phone calls, we still had had only evasive conversations.

I telephoned the tax office to see if they could offer any information regarding the extortionate amount. I knew if this problem wasn't sorted out quickly we would not only have to pay the figure stated on the bill, but might be liable for extra penalties and interest on the amount unpaid.

We were so worried about the situation, by the time I got to speak to a tax official, I was in tears, stating the demand of money was wrong and we didn't have that kind of funding available to pay the bill.

'The amount must be paid by 31st January, or you will incur penalties and interest will be charged.'

We were left with no option. Firstly we had to beg the bank for a huge loan to pay the first half's tax bill. Fortunately they obliged, as they knew a considerable amount would be refunded from the tax office shortly. Secondly, we decided we required new accountants.

The tax bill was paid; we were in debt up to our necks, and with the possibility if trade decreased for any reason, the business could go under and we would also lose our house which had been used as collateral against the loan. So feeling pretty miserable, we decided that - OK, we owe all this money to the bank; we may as well owe a bit more, so we booked a two week holiday in the Maldives - and off we went.

It took nearly a year, but eventually the tax situation was resolved. We were refunded a big fat cheque, which went straight to the bank, and couldn't have come at a better time because trade was beginning to slow down. Not just for our business, but there was a general decline in every trade. It was evident a recession was imminent.

We had suffered the past four years with a rent of £24,000 and under the terms of our agreement the brewery were supposed to begin negotiations for a rent review six months before the due date.

Since the last rent review five years before, many things had changed in the business environment. There was a recession in the early 90's which apparently was not as bad as the previous one at the start of the 80's. (supposedly by far the worst in recent memory) that really consoled us.

Even so, the two year recession obviously had a drastic effect not only on our trade but on everyone in the country, so this would be reflected in talks regarding any increase in the rent imposed on us.

In 1990 the community charge, commonly known as the poll tax, came into force and increased our rates to over £3,000 per annum.

In 1993 poll tax was scrapped and replaced with council tax which was based on the estimated market value of property and assessed in bands of value.

For our premises this meant the top floor of our building comprising of the flat was classed as the residential area so would now incur a separate band of value to the commercial section of the pub and restaurant.

After appealing to the Council, we managed to get the residential rate lowered from where they had fixed it. We pointed out the only access to the flat was walking through the bar so we should therefore not be penalised for having a city centre dwelling and should not pay higher rates. Naturally, with any change of legislation, prices rise and our pub was no exception with an annual rate's bill again increasing to over £4,000 per year.

The early 90's saw the opening of The Castle Mall, located about 500 metres from the pub. It was a large indoor shopping and entertainment centre with shops, cinema and eating establishments which consequently had an effect on our trade, especially when it first opened, attracting tourists and locals.

Wetherspoons bar opened in Norwich in 1993, an establishment already well known in London, selling drinks cheaper than we could purchase them for. This had the effect of attracting customers into Wetherspoons, and making people query the prices we were charging. Chris was quick and to the point with his response, 'Fuck off there and drink then.'

We couldn't compete with their prices so had to suffer the consequences of losing some customers.

We received a letter from the landlords regarding our next rent increase stating the required figure was set at £35,500 per annum– an increase of £11,000. We were expecting the amount to go up, but not by that much. After we had picked our jaws up from the floor and read the letter again in disbelief, Chris phoned them to come in and see us.

Two guys arrived from London to negotiate an agreed figure. From their briefcases they took out spreadsheets, folders and calculators and pointed out the data from their head office records which showed we were selling a vast quantity of beer; the increased rent to be paid was relevant to our beer sales and size of the property for a fair maintainable trade.

However, the landlords had no idea how much the restaurant turnover was, or how much we sold in wines, spirits and minerals, so were basing their predictions solely on beer sales.

When rent reviews are in progress there is always an option for the licensee to take the matter to arbitration, meaning all our figures would have to be disclosed to the landlords and the arbitrators. We weren't keen to take this option because of the financial cost in having solicitors and the fact that we would also be liable for the landlords costs if we lost the case.

So we tried to call their bluff by asking them,

'How much total turnover do you think we actually take a year?'

They got more spreadsheets out of their briefcases, bashed some numbers into their calculator and came up with a figure which was nearly bang on target to the amount we actually turned over per year.

Damn, so it was definitely no use giving arbitration even a second thought. We tried to look shocked at the figure they showed us and told them they were way off track. We told them we would not be happy paying the increased rent so would now be considering surrendering the lease, handing back the keys and walking away from the pub.

'OK then, but under the terms of your agreement, you do have to give three months' notice.' Ooh that told us!

We contacted a professional dealing with rent reviews who would negotiate with the brewery; he told us to leave it to him and he would do all the communications.

He was true to his word; after a couple of months of hard negotiation on his part, he managed to get the rent fixed at £28,000 for the next five years, which was still an increase of £4,000 but certainly a vast improvement on the original figure.

The following five years saw many changes with the entertainment industry in Norwich. More and more chain bars, pubs and clubs were opening in Prince of Wales Road, a street leading towards the train station which had previously been relatively quiet during the evening, as most of the premises were offices and only a couple of bars had existed. Gradually, as a property became vacant it was snapped up by companies and investors pouring huge amounts of money into creating modern drinking and dancing establishments.

Just past the train station another development was in the process of being constructed at the small cost of £75 million. Known as Riverside Leisure Centre, it consisted of cinemas, a bowling alley, nightclubs, a health-club, shops and bars.

Along with Prince of Wales Road and the Riverside complex this area changed the face of the evening economy in Norwich.

People could travel from other cities to Norwich at night by train, arriving in close proximity to the action and so had no cause to venture into the city centre. With parking available close by even during the day the shops attracted more people away from the centre of Norwich.

It was becoming evident that more individually owned pubs were changing hands more frequently in Norwich, run by managers as opposed to licensees standing behind the bar – the days of the local pub seemed to be numbered.

We did wonder sometimes how other licensees could afford to have managers running their pubs, and still make a living. 'What were we doing wrong?'

As an exercise, we asked our accountant to draw up a few figures to see if it was a viable proposition for us to employ a manager, enabling us to take a step back from the business, have some quality time instead of working 12 to 14 hours a day, and be like many other licensees, just overseeing the business.

The accountant's prognosis showed that, without us working at the pub, trade would probably drop off by at least 10% because we had built up a huge clientele of people who came in to see us (or customers came in to be abused by Chris). There would be more wastage of food because we were vigilant of costs; that would probably be another 10% off the profit. The main cost was obviously the extra wages, firstly for a manager who wouldn't work as many hours as us and for more staff to cover the extra hours.

When all the figures were added up, the diagnosis showed there would barely be any profit at the end of the year. Ok, so that idea was straight out of the window. We won't get a manager, we would just continue working as before, which was no problem at that point because we enjoyed the life and challenges, and quite honestly wouldn't have been happy with someone else looking after the pub anyway, when it had been 'our baby' for all this time.

However, we still could not quite work out how other licensees managed it and we couldn't. Oh, well, ho hum.

With Prince of Wales Road open and in full swing boy, did we feel the crunch, especially at the week-ends. Of course it was a novelty for people to venture into new places. It was the happening, the social scene, and it was obvious that trade would drop off, not just for us, but also for other pubs in Norwich.

This downturn continued for many months, until gradually customers started to drift back into the centre of Norwich for the evening, especially the older customers – people in their early 30's who decided that Prince of Wales Road night-life wasn't for them. It was too crowded, there were too many idiots wanting to fight, and too many large groups of lads or girls out for the night with the sole purpose of getting as drunk as possible and then throwing up.

To begin with we were concerned about the decrease in turnover but soon came to realise that the new area of night-life was actually doing us a favour. People on stag nights and hen nights were no longer coming in, fine by us; football supporters and opposing teams didn't come in, as the football ground was also close to the latest drinking area; also fine by us.

Obviously, we still had to be vigilant as to who we served in the pub, but it wasn't such a big issue as in previous years. The number of large groups no longer came in – good, because it saved Chris the job of refusing them entry.

Although there was a noticeable decline in trade and decreased turnover, we no longer had as many idiots coming into the pub, which made our life much less stressful, especially at the week-ends.

Our next rent review was in 1999 when memories came flooding back from the previous arguments regarding the increase.

The letter arrived, (bearing in mind we were now paying £28,000 per annum) - they wanted to raise the rent to between £42,000 - £45,000 per year.

Chris' comments: Well, they could take a running jump and stick that figure where the sun doesn't shine!

We made a phone call to the landlords telling them they had better come to Norwich to see us as soon as possible, and in the meantime, to come up with a more sensible offer, as they must obviously have typed in the wrong numbers.

Chris happened to see a guy suited and booted, carrying a briefcase, walk down the alleyway at the time our appointment was due. 'Are you from Enterprise Inns?'

'Yes'

'Have you been to Norwich before?' asked a grumpy Chris.

'No, this is my first time.'

'In which case, before you come in the pub, you can get in my car – now. I am going to take you for a drive round Norwich and show you which areas have developed since our last rent increase, as you obviously have no idea.'

I don't think he dared to argue and quietly got in the car.

Chris drove him past Wetherspoons, then along Prince of Wales Road, pointing out the extra drinking establishments opened since the last rent review. He finished his tour by showing him the vast Riverside complex which was nearing completion and would have a detrimental effect on trade.

By the time the guy got out of the car after contending with Chris' erratic driving and forthright talking, he was shell shocked. He managed to recuperate enough to say he would take into consideration the comments Chris had made, but that the business was still trading at a fair maintainable level for the size of the premises and, even though the turnover was slightly down, he thought there wouldn't be much room for negotiation.

Seeing the look on our faces, he left soon after.

We contacted the same negotiator we used for our last rent review, who agreed the amount was astronomical, especially taking into account all the aspects of the new developments, so we left the job in his capable hands.

It took several months of letter-writing backwards and forwards, the amount changing each time, until a final figure of £32,000 per annum was agreed.

Were we happy with the result? Of course not, but our hands were tied and there were only two other options. One was to take it to arbitration. Not a good idea. Although trade had dropped, it wasn't actually as bad as we had made out to the brewery.

The other option was, hand the keys back and leave – and we weren't ready to do that either.

The following five years were relatively insignificant as far as trade was concerned. Our next and final rent increase was due before we left the Walnut.

The boom time of the late 1980's would never ever return and we were under no false illusion it would. We were grateful for maintaining a good level of trade, when many publicans were struggling to survive with ever increasing overheads.

We kept staff to a minimum; we worked constantly and tried to keep the outgoings as low as possible which all contributed to making a profit at the end of the year.

When the rent review was drawing near, it was time to reflect on the past five years in readiness to argue and negotiate the figure we were approached with from the landlord.

The letter arrived, the rent was increased to £35,500 per annum, a rise of £3,500, set for five years before the next review was due. From past experiences with the landlords, this was not the figure we were expecting to receive; they generally commenced proceedings with an astronomical amount before the hard negotiations began.

We telephoned the negotiator who had acted on our behalf on the previous rent reviews, for his opinion on the figure requested from Enterprise Inns. His immediate response was, 'Accept it now.'

We did accept it, without any arguments, which actually felt quite strange. We were so used to getting stressed and irate and having to go through the hassle of communications and negotiations, eventually arriving at a sensible figure – this time it was easy. Enterprise were at long last beginning to be more realistic on the rent they were charging tenants.

****

MUSIC

A major factor of the Walnut's popularity was the music. We didn't play the usual pop, garage style, hip-hop or whatever other style of music was trendy in pubs and clubs at the time. Chris loved the blues and had collected hundreds of tapes before CDs made them obsolete.

He obtained blues albums from every artist imaginable and bought any new releases as soon as they were released and played them in the pub, one or two regular customers supplemented Chris' collection by updating him on the latest blues albums being released.

People came in for the music, they knew what to expect, and were always asking questions about a particular song and artist being played at the time.

We had a music system behind the bar which controlled the sound for downstairs; the same music was piped to the restaurant, although it was played at a much lower volume upstairs. Chris had the music so loud sometimes that you could not hear yourself think, let alone talk.

If he spotted a customer trying to make or receive a phone call, he would turn the volume up even more, just to aggravate them. Unfortunately for everyone else, he would often forget to turn the volume down again.

Chris had problems with his hearing, due to years of working in a loud environment so, subsequently, the music that sounded quiet to him, was excessively loud to everyone else. On those occasions when I came downstairs for whatever reason, and had noticed the sound had gone up to an extreme level, (and the staff and customers were looking at me in desperation), I would wait until Chris' back was turned then discreetly give the volume knob a few downturns, hoping he wouldn't notice.

Unfortunately, if he suddenly realised, he would turn it up even louder. I often spent the whole evening trying to turn the music down to an acceptable level just so the floor wasn't shaking.

As well as CDs being played constantly, we also rented an original Wurlitzer jukebox that played one record for 10p. or nine records for 50p. – that was 10p. and 50p. 'old money,' in old coins.

So to play the juke box, first you had to exchange a modern day coin with the bartender for one of the obsolete 50p's. from behind the bar where we kept a small collection of coins.

Unfortunately, we lost several because one of my dippy bar staff was handing them to customers as change from the till.

The juke box played lots of old classic 60's songs which customers would choose when the mood took them.

The Wurlitzer Jukebox was made in the early 1970's and only 2,000 were produced in total; it was also one of the last Wurlitzers to be made in America as the company went bust whilst they were still in the process of manufacturing them.

It sat in the corner of the bar with the lights glowing, and watching the records drop onto the turntable was a topic of conversation for many customers, especially those who saw it for the first time.

After renting it for several years we approached the company we hired it from with a view to buying it. After several phone calls, we managed to persuade them to allow us to purchase it for £2,500.

Every business at some point or another has a dreaded visit from the VAT office, and we were no exception. On one of these visits as she was inspecting the books and punching figures into her calculator, the VAT inspector noticed that the juke box didn't appear to be making any profit. It took quite a lot of explaining that modern jukeboxes charged £1 per song and ours cost 50p. for nine records; then we had to show her the workings of the jukebox to explain why it was non-profit making.

We went on to tell her that music was played from the CD player, which, of course, was free to listen to and if by any remote chance the juke box was played as the only source of music for the whole period we were open, the total amount that was possible to take from the Wurlitzer would still only be about £10.

There were often days when the jukebox wasn't played at all, so eventually she was satisfied we weren't trying to fiddle the books or avoid paying VAT.

The jukebox broke down after many years and had to leave the pub and retreat to a jukebox hospital to be repaired. The space it usually took up looked so bare; we needed something to put in its place. We managed to find a little plastic blow up jukebox that was an exact replica of our original. Somehow it just didn't have the same presence as the original, but it did cause some amusement to customers when we made up a story that we had come into work in the morning and the proper one had been stolen and a plastic one left in its place.

The proper jukebox broke down again two years before we left the pub, and although the lights were all on, it just wouldn't work. We knew several experienced people who attempted to fix it, but to no avail.

Now the jukebox was just an ornament, until we found a man specialising in repairing old music players, so the jukebox was again removed from its pride of place in the pub.

It never returned to the Walnut; instead, it came to our home. Just at the point it had finally been repaired, was the time we sold the pub, and we certainly had no intention of leaving it behind as part of the fixtures and fittings.

Not only had we grown fond of it, but also it had cost us a lot of money because to bring it back to complete working order was £1,200. It was a good job Chris was sitting down when he found out how much the bill was, as he had an idea it would probably cost in the region of £500!

The pub had been operational for six years and trade had gradually been increasing throughout that period. The music we played was popular amongst the customers, so we knew blues and rock music was right for us, but we felt it was time to move forwards with the music and start to consider various options. We decided to put on live music, especially as several people started coming into the pub enquiring if we ever put on live bands; there were only a couple of large venues in Norwich that had live entertainment at that time.

Bands were also coming in with a copy of their demo CD for us to play to see if we would consider letting them play in the pub. The majority of these were dreadful, but the occasional one sounded professional, and the type of music we liked, so these were kept to one side for future reference.

Chris spent some time wandering, looking pensive and studying the downstairs' area, wondering where would be the best place to incorporate an area to have bands playing. A few weeks went by and he suddenly had a brain wave – unusual for him.

If we stripped the benches from the end of the bar where the seating area was, then raised the whole area up a further 20cm and put a wooden railing round the edge, it could be the stage. If we also purchased some tables and chairs to replace the benches, these could be removed when a band was performing – brilliant.

Before any changes could be made and building operations commenced we needed to obtain permission and a special music licence from the council to enable us to play live music on a regular basis.

Dealing with the council was never simple or prompt. There were three sets of forms to fill in, which entailed writing in detail the number of nights we were requesting live music to be played, the number of musicians we expected at any one time and the hours they would be performing as well as supplying drawings of the bar area and the proposed site for the music.

When this was completed, one copy had to be sent to the council, one to the police, and one to the fire officer, to await for any objections. It had to be published in the paper and notices put on the public highway to see if any resident or member of the public would object. With that all done it was now a waiting game to find out the results.

In the meantime we received a visit from the Fire Officer who told us we were only allowed a maximum of 140 people (including staff) in the building at any one time because of the size of the area in the bar.

We were pleased with this result, especially as there was no way 140 people would fit into the pub anyway, unless they were standing on each other shoulders. 100 people in the pub and it was packed to the rafters, so I think he was extremely generous – however, we were certainly not going to argue with him.

He also stipulated that signs were required on the wall showing a map of the bar area; some of the lighting had to be changed for emergency exits and more fire extinguishers needed to be put in.

The council were very strict on noise levels in residential areas; however, in this respect we were very lucky, because nobody lived in close proximity, so loud music wasn't going to upset anybody.

The police were happy with the situation and didn't place any objections because we had always had a good reputation and our pub was never a cause for concern with them; a lot of them used to drink in the pub anyway.

Eventually we received confirmation that permission was granted and we were now able to have live music - at a price.

Every year we had to pay a fee for playing taped music to the 'Performing Rights Society'; this increased drastically when we had live music.

While we are on the subject of the Performing Rights Society, I will just bore you with a few facts regarding this licence.

The Performing Rights Society was founded in 1914 and is a collecting society for UK songwriters and composers. It authorises the public performance of all songs in the society's catalogue.

It is a non-profit making organisation which distributes the income received to all its affiliated members - the writers and publishers of music. This is regardless of whether the music is performed live or by recorded means, whether it's from television, a jukebox or through the internet. It is a legal requirement to obtain a licence and this privilege cost us in the region of £900 per annum.

PPL – Phonographic Performance Ltd. is a music service company working on behalf of performers and record company members. It is also a legal requirement to obtain a licence from the PPL at approximately £90 per annum; this allows the broadcast of sound recordings and music videos through public performance and the media.

So with that smidgen of knowledge out of the way, let's move on.

The fire officers had stipulated that we had to make changes to the wiring and the emergency lighting.

The building alterations commenced for the stage area after which we laid a new carpet and bought tables and chairs. This area could now be used as a stage in the evening then as a separate section for people dining during the day.

It was essential to get good musicians and bands in the pub who people would enjoy so that they would want to return in the weeks and months to follow. We also aimed to attract new customers who had never been in the pub before.

The first band to play live at the Walnut was the Charlton Brothers; the band members were already popular in Norwich so we knew we would have a successful evening – we weren't wrong.

It was advisable and proved beneficial to use bands recommended to us either from individuals or other bands who had previously seen them play elsewhere. Fortunately we only had about three or four bands that didn't go down well with the customers, or us, in 15 years of live music in the pub – those particular musicians never got invited back for a second gig.

The bands loved playing at the pub; they enjoyed the ambience. Their music was appreciated by the customers and we usually attracted a good crowd to listen to them.

We got to know the bands really well over the years and enjoyed having a drink and chat with them after they finished playing, although sometimes we ended up getting home about 2am because one drink turned into two, three or more.

We were fortunate in having some very professional musicians playing over the years and, occasionally, there would be a guest appearance from another musician who was in the area or who just wanted to come and play a couple of numbers with the band who were playing that night.

Paul Tinkler, a professional performer and accomplished blues guitarist and singer, has performed with many bands, one being the John Slaughters Blues Band and has spent some time touring Germany.

He enjoyed playing at the Walnut with either his own band, 'The Part Time Blues Band,' or with a few other musicians who would be advertised as 'Paul Tinkler and friends.'

Some of Our Favourite Bands that Played at the Walnut

'Eygpt'
(Photographs
by Purple
Promotions)

1994 celebrating a decade at the Walnut. With 'World's Apart' (Photograph by Archant)

'4D Jones'
(Photograph by Dave Gutteridge)

Albert Cooper was chauffeured to play a gig at the Walnut in a 1965 black cadillac
(Photograph by Archant)

'Tea'
one of Spains
top rock bands

Keno Kings
(Photograph by
Terry Wisbey)

Bar interior

2004 Chris loves his jukebox
(Photograph by Andrew Blundred)

Tim getting ready to open the bar

A busy night at the Walnut

Ho Ho Ho - it's Christmas

Some of the memorabillia that
adorned the pub walls

Last Orders at The Walnut Tree Shades

May 22nd 2008 our last day at the Walnut

Customers enjoying the farewell gig on May 4th 2008

Jude and Chris
It's all over - retirement begins now

Restaurant interior

Jude busy in the prep area
(Photograph by Wendy
Fullam)

See... Chris does smile
occasionally
(Photograph by Archant)

Chris and Jude passing on the stairs
(Photograph by Archant)

Chicken Caesar Salad
(Photograph by Wendy
Fullam) 'her meal'

Paul arrived at the pub to play one Thursday evening; it wasn't until he had unpacked his guitar that Chris noticed him,

'What are you doing here tonight?'

'We're playing'

'You prat, its next week you're booked here.'

'Oh shit,' said Paul, 'I've just rung Stuart to tell him to get his arse here. He was at home eating his tea; he thought it was next week we were playing, I'd better ring him and tell him he was right after all.'

On another occasion Paul told us he had an old friend coming down to Norwich, a brilliant bass player and suggested getting a trio together, including himself and Larry Tolfree, a drummer who has played and toured with Peter Green's Splinter Group, Joe Jackson, and David Essex, to name but a few.

We were good friends with Larry, who is such a lovely guy and is fascinating to talk to about the places he has visited to play gigs and also the bands he has drummed with over the years.

Paul's bass player friend turned out to be Jim Rodford, who originally performed with the Kinks, the Zombies and the Animals in the 1960's and went on to play and tour with Argent, Lonnie Donegan and many others.

Their first gig as a trio at the pub was held on a Friday night when people are generally out socialising and tend to move from pub to pub having a drink. Not this night, because people were flocking in, listening to the band and then staying the whole evening.

It was a fantastic night and the place was packed with everyone enjoying the music, in fact there were so many people that they were practically lined up at the bar, watching in awe.

We loved it as much as the customers did. We all talked about the gig for weeks afterwards and couldn't wait for the next time they would be able to play at the Walnut.

However, another gig was only possible on half a dozen more occasions over the next four years, as Jim Rodford was touring; so it was only in between tours that they were able to play at the pub when they became known as 'Off The Cuff'.

We got to know Jim really well over the years. One evening, just before they started playing in our little pub, he told us that the previous night he had performed at The Royal Albert Hall with an audience of 4,000 + people, probably earned a huge amount of money, but was quite adamant that he enjoyed playing at the Walnut more because of its intimacy and atmosphere. It certainly wouldn't have been for the money he received from us - £180 to be shared amongst the entire band.

The Dalling Brothers, included John Langham with his bushy beard, who played lead guitar; he was a great blues singer and had been playing locally for years.

He always brought his dog to the pub, who lay sprawled on the floor in front of the stage the whole evening, and would never attempt to budge, even if the place was packed. That part of the floor was his area and he had no intention of moving for anybody.

Scottish Stuart played bass guitar and was such a lovely guy with his really thick bushy beard, so when they did the ZZ Top number, 'Cheap Sunglasses.' The band all wore their black sunglasses to look the part!

Another up and coming musician was a lad of 16 years old called Martin Trimble, a lead singer who played with Larry on drums and Steve Jinks on bass. As soon as he started to play the guitar and began singing it made the hairs stand up on the back of my neck – he was absolutely amazing.

By the time he was 20-years old he formed his own band called 22-20; they wrote all their own music and lyrics and got better and better all the time (if that was possible). He eventually went on to much bigger events - touring the world and playing to massive audiences. He had a couple of hit albums and appeared on television talking about his music and what he had achieved. There was also a Vauxhall advert on television that played the sound track to one of his songs.

Another young lad, Olly Brown, played his first gig at the Walnut Tree, at only 16-years old; he had the makings of an excellent blues singer and each time he performed at the pub his confidence grew; his singing and guitar playing was incredible to listen to.

His father acted as manager and did an excellent job at promoting him - he went on to play large venues including Glastonbury and played to packed audiences.

Whilst touring he played with the Paul Jones Blues Band and Walter Trout and Aynsley Lister, among others. He was quoted in the 'Classic Rock Magazine' as being one of the best and brightest guitar heroes performing in the world today.

The Keno Kings were a popular local band who played the blues. Mick, the lead singer, was an excellent harmonica player and performed several numbers whilst having the odd drink or cigarette and still managing to sing or play the harmonica at the same time.

He had a perfect routine with one particular song; he took his tobacco pouch from his jacket, rolled a cigarette with one hand whilst he was singing, licked the paper just at the exact moment he was going into the next lyric, then lit the rolly, taking in a huge suction of nicotine and showing pure satisfaction on his face.

When the bands played in the pub I used to record a few songs on my video camera and then pan it round the pub to incorporate the customers watching and listening to the music. However they often just used to stick their tongues out when they spotted the camera in their direction.

One particular evening, when the Keno Kings were playing, I had the video on record whilst looking through the view finder, but I couldn't make out what Mick was doing. He was singing, but at the same time patting his jacket with his hand, rummaging through his pockets, and kept looking all around him on the floor.

I kept following him with the camera, which was still recording, whilst he continued to walk round the stage, still singing, but obviously looking for something.

He was again patting his body and his trouser pockets and lifting up a towel that was hanging over a rail while moving the bass player out of the way so he could see that area of the floor.

Unfortunately for him, on that particular song he had to play quite a long harmonica section and he was grimacing extensively all through it, mouthing, 'ow' 'ow' every few seconds.

He eventually finished singing to a loud applause from the audience, at which point I switched the camera off. 'Whatever were you looking for during that song?'

'My fucking tooth fell out; I was trying to find it and the pain was excruciating when I started playing the harmonica.'

When I played the video back you could actually see his tooth drop out onto the ground, it was hilarious.

No wonder he was in agony playing a harmonica with a missing tooth!

Albert Cooper is well known in Norwich for his musical performances. He is a wonderful man with so much character and stories to tell and people adore him. He has been playing for over 50 years and has a great love of the blues and jazz.

Whenever he played – which wasn't that often - people travelled from miles to come and see him perform. The only problem we had when Albert played at the pub was that although we were packed to absolute capacity, we never took a vast amount of money. Chris called it, 'geriatrics night' as many of the audience consisted of the older generation and consequently didn't drink much. Chris always used to say on these evenings, 'The only thing missing tonight is the smell of piss and Dettol, and the reason they don't drink much; as their colostomy bags would get full.'

However, the crowd used to love hearing Albert talk and talk, and talk, – about nothing in particular before embarking on the next song, but when he did sing, he received the biggest applause any band ever received in the pub.

Even after performing for over 50 years, Albert still used to get nervous before he played, so to help him relax he had a drink or two before and during the gig. He had a jam jar that travelled everywhere with him and that's what he used to drink his wine or brandy from. People also bought him several drinks during the course of the evening (which were much appreciated).

One evening, he drank so much, he was pissed as a parrot, and only managed to sing four or five songs in the first set of the performance. The band, which consisted of his son on keyboards and three excellent musicians, had an easy night, they just waited in anticipation wondering if Albert would stop talking, and get on with playing a number - he eventually did.

Albert came to the Walnut the following day, full of apologies. 'Oh dear, it must have been the customers' fault for buying me too many drinks!'

It goes without saying that Chris forgave him; especially as he always jokingly say's he is Albert's 'love child'.

Worlds Apart was another favourite band of ours who played on a regular basis at the pub. The lead singer, Eric, was like Jekyll and Hyde.

By day he was a very quiet, reserved guy, and was actually a boyfriend of mine for a short time when I was 16 years old, (we only ever kissed and cuddled though, or maybe just had a little fumble!)

However, when he got on the stage to perform, a different character emerged - a rock singer with a tremendous voice and the moves to go with it.

They were a popular band to play at the Walnut on New Year's Eve and we used to be packed with customers who wanted to rock their way into the New Year.

The lead guitarist, Terry, often used to leave the stage with his guitar and walk amongst the audience whilst still playing. One time he went into the ladies' toilets – guitar strumming and singing - until he returned to his position on the stage.

When the song had finished he announced over the microphone that there wasn't any loo roll in the toilets so could I put some in there please!

A band called Egypt had been recommended to us, so we decided to book them for a gig one Thursday night. They arrived and started to unpack their equipment. We took one look at one of the band member's waist-length hair in a ponytail and another wearing a Stetson hat (very old time rock and roll) and thought, Oh my God, what has turned up?'

However, speaking to them before they performed, the guys seemed really nice (which just goes to show, never judge people on appearances). They travelled abroad frequently and played in huge venues.

Alan, the bass player, had also performed with many famous artists including Tony McPhee and Billy Boy Arnold.

They started to perform and 'wow' – this was now my favourite band. It was loud, very loud, in fact the decibel level reached 116 – the accepted level should be 80! Whoops.

Eric's guitar solo was verification of how professional he and the band were. (He was the one with the ponytail).

They played on a regular basis at the pub and we became good friends with all of them. We had plenty of time to get to know them because they never wanted to leave at the end of the night, 'Come on Chris, get the drinks in' – and a bit later on, 'Get another one in Chris, go on, one more for the road.'

We were lucky if we got home by 2am when Egypt played.

Alan spent a lot of time promoting various bands and obtaining gigs for them. He was really helpful to us because if he came across a band who he knew would go down well in our pub, he would put them in contact with us.

One of those bands (called Tea) lived in Spain. So several times a year they would fly over, and spend several days performing at various venues in Norfolk. They were fantastic professional musicians, and always attracted a large audience. Watching George strum his guitar with his drumsticks on one particular song was quite fascinating to see; he insisted it was easy, and just his little party trick. Yeah right - I can't play a guitar with my fingers, let alone a pair of drumsticks!

We got to know them really well. Even though only one band member spoke fluent English they were great company and, again, never wanted to leave at the end of the night.

Alan recommended a young up and coming band who he had watched perform and thought would go down well at the pub. We trusted his judgement and agreed to allow them to play one evening.

The customers seemed to be enjoying the music, although Chris wasn't overly impressed and most definitely went off them completely when they began singing Slade's 'Merry Christmas!'

At the end of the evening we sat outside having a drink when we overheard some customers discussing the band; they turned to us and asked Chris for his opinion, Not beating round the bush, Chris replied, 'I thought they were crap.'

Unfortunately the people who had asked Chris for his opinion of the band turned out to be the parents' of one of the kids in the group, and they were not overly impressed with what they heard. Chris' thoughts on that were, 'Well, they shouldn't have asked if they didn't want to hear the truth.'

They did improve as they matured, were more experienced, and changed their music direction to rock and blues. So, if the opportunity had arisen, Chris would have booked them to play at the Walnut again.

We received a phone call from a guy called Ben Ruth who was an agent for many bands both in the UK and abroad; he said he was in a predicament and wondered if we could help.

He had a set of three bands over from the United States in our area and, unfortunately, one of the venues prearranged for them to perform at had double booked for the Saturday night so he wondered if we would be interested in letting them play at the Walnut.

We weren't particularly bothered about booking live music for Saturday evenings because we were always busy that night anyway, so it wasn't necessary to spend resources on a band. 'How much is that going to cost me, I only pay £180, and I'm not paying for three bands?'

We told them if they couldn't find another venue we would allow them to perform at our pub – for the cost of £180 in total for all the musicians.

Saturday arrived and so did the bands, consisting of eleven musicians, - they wouldn't be ending up with much money between them! However, being as they were getting such a small pittance in cash terms, we agreed to give them all a meal of cheeseburger and fries and drinks. See, we're all heart. They would not receive much money, in fact a minuscule amount, but at least their bellies would be full.

Brother Big Bad were from Minneapolis. Their music is described as, 'being defined by searing guitar licks, witty lyrics and memorable pop hooks. Their huge funk sound grooves superbly – and immensely fun.'

In between Brother Big Bad and Fluttr Effects sets, Meg Hutchinson sang solo with her lyric-based, contemporary acoustic style. She was an award winning singer, songwriter and has played at several prestigious music festivals in America.

'Fluttr Effect' were formed originally in 2002. They advertised themselves as a unique sound resulting in an adventurous, experimental take on art rock, gothic rock and progressive rock with sounds from eclectic sources.

They had so much equipment and instruments that they were unable to fit them all on the stage area, so they ended up spilling onto the far end of the bar.

We were used to seeing our regular bands produce their drum kits and guitars from their protective cases when they arrived at the pub to play, but this night we just stood in trepidation looking at their instruments as they were being unpacked and wondered what the hell we had let ourselves in for.

There were drums, guitars, percussion instruments, acoustic cellos, and a machine that we had never seen in action before called a midi marimba. It looked like a giant keyboard, but instead of keys there were twelve large different coloured pads, operated with two sets of mallets in each hand and tapped in the same way as a xylophone.

They were one of the most fantastic visual bands we had ever seen. When they commenced singing and playing, it appeared as if they were all totally lost in their music (which seemed to take them over).

The sound from the cellos and the visual effect of the performers was amazing; the girl playing the midi marimba was unbelievable to watch. She had four mallets in each hand and as each pad lit up with the music she had to hit them.

Sounds easy, except the pads and lights were flashing on and off at such a speed that to watch her movements using all four mallets at the same time was absolutely awe inspiring.

What a night we had. The customers loved it, and so did we.

All the members of the bands were really nice people and we enjoyed chatting to them at the end of the evening, however I somehow thought that would be the first and last time they played at the Walnut, especially as they only received £180!

As the Walnut Tree was adorned with American memorabilia, we decided American Independence Day seemed a fitting occasion, and a good excuse, to stage an event at the pub.

We had built up a good reputation since we began putting on live music which was proving popular with customers and had increased our clientele, so we thought it a good idea to have a band outside in the car-park to celebrate July 4th.

The car-park was owned by the shops adjacent to the pub. We obviously had no legal right to use it, but as the shops would be closed in the evening, we didn't think they'd mind.

We had a good relationship with the shop managers so when Chris approached them, none had any objections and said they would probably come along for the evening and enjoy the entertainment.

Hypothetically we also needed planning consent from the council for live entertainment in an outdoor area. We knew they would most definitely turn our application down because of the expected noise level, we would be using someone else's property and also running electricity cables to the equipment would give them cause for concern with health and safety regulations.

So we decided not to inform them and risk the consequences.

July 4th arrived, and fortunately the weather was good, a vital point, as it would be far too risky to allow the band to play outside even if there was a drop of rain; they could end up as fried musicians.

Chris ran a couple of cables from the kitchen window, across to the flat roof on one of the shops where lights would be attached, and continued the cable to the end where the band would be playing and the amplifiers plugged in.

A popular local band the Boogaloos played on our first gig in the car park. The outside was packed with people and a great night was had by all. We received no complaints from the environmental health noise department, so all in all the event was a resounding success.

The following summer customers began to enquire whether we would be hosting another 'car park gig.' We gave the idea a couple of minutes thought then decided that as we had got away with it once, why not do it again.

The only problem with putting on live entertainment outside - well apart from not having permission from the Council, - was the weather. If the forecast was precarious over the next couple of weeks, it wasn't even worth considering, so a date was set when the weather seemed more settled.

We promptly had posters printed and began informing everybody of the forthcoming event. The day the posters arrived Chris, I and Suzie (one of our bar girls) started to pin them on the walls in the pub, when one of our regulars came in for a drink.

Unfortunately he happened to be someone from the noise pollution department at the council. Although we knew him really well, as he often drank in the pub and enjoyed the music we played, we weren't sure he would approve of our outside gig.

Whilst Chris kept him talking, I whispered to Suzie to quickly take down the posters without the guy seeing – phew, that was close.

The evening arrived and again we were so lucky with the weather. Chris ran the cables from a 13-amp plug in the kitchen, across the roofs and everything was set up ready for evening.

The evening was another roaring success with hundreds of people turning up to enjoy the night's entertainment. In fact it was so successful and the long term forecast was favourable that we decided to hold yet another 'car park gig' two weeks later.

Again we were packed with people. The sound travelled several hundreds of metres which attracted more customers; as they were walking along the streets they could hear music playing and followed the sound to the pub.

A pub had recently opened on the next street to the Walnut and we had been having a few problems with the owners regarding the sound levels of their music at night.

They had erected speakers outside their building and were playing music so loud that it could be heard in Lucy's bedroom, keeping her awake at night. Ironically, although our music was loud, it couldn't be heard upstairs (well, maybe just a bit) and therefore didn't affect her. Lucy was only 10-years old and wasn't complaining about the noise as she enjoyed listening to the other pub playing Kylie Minogue, 'I should be so lucky.'

I, however, wasn't happy and asked the new pub owners if they would keep the music down; they paid no attention and didn't see what the problem was.

After repeatedly going to see them I eventually made the manager come back to the Walnut with me and enter Lucy's bedroom so she could hear for herself how loud their music was compared to ours.

Two weeks after our second 'car park gig' our friend from the environmental department turned up at the pub looking slightly apologetic.

'I'm sorry, but we've had a complaint about your outside gig so I've got to give you a bollocking. You mustn't hold any more events unless you apply for permission first. Look, I'm really sorry, but we do have to act upon any complaints received so I will unfortunately be sending you a formal letter.'

I suppose we had been rather greedy doing two outside gigs very close together, but had been lucky and got away with it up until now.

It later came to light that the people in the pub over the road were the ones who complained – bastards, a bit of retribution on their part after our complaints to them.

We promised we wouldn't hold any more outside events, but under our breaths thinking, well, not until next year anyway.

The council sent a letter to us stating:

'It is alleged that, on several occasions in the past, you have held outside public entertainments consisting of more than two performers. A complaint has been received by this department over the last occasion, and I would warn you that it is an offence to have public entertainments without the benefit of the appropriate licence. Any further instances of this nature which come to my knowledge and are substantiated will be reported to the Director of Administration with a recommendation for prosecution.

Although I understand it is your intention to apply for a public entertainments licence for the inside of your premises the department would not be in favour of a licence to cover outside events.'

Quite a severe bollocking, but his hands were tied; he was only doing his job and still continued to come in the pub in a social capacity.

We did pay heed to our telling-off and didn't hold a car-park gig the following year, mainly because the weather was so unsettled throughout the summer, it didn't seem worth it.

The pub over the road soon closed down so they wouldn't be creating any further problems.

The following year was the beginning of hosting an outside gig every summer until we left the pub; there was only one occasion when the weather turned against us and the band had to be moved indoors to play.

The high walls surrounding the car-park created a great acoustic sound from the bands and although the area where the musicians played was pretty drab with rubbish bins in one corner, and wasn't an ideal setting for watching a band, the atmosphere was always electric when our rocking musicians started to play.

We had several bands playing outside - The Boogaloos, the Barry Homan Band, the Keno Kings, Beyond Duplication, Worlds Apart and Egypt; each one created a fantastic atmosphere and never failed to disappoint the crowd.

One summer we held a Rock n' Roll Extravaganza featuring the 'Rollercoasters'; many more musicians turned up and played during the evening, making an exceptionally fantastic night and an occasion which was talked about for many weeks.

We never received any more complaints from the public regarding our car-park gigs and luckily didn't get any more bollockings from the environmental department.

Before we implemented an application to have live music in the pub, New Year's Eve was much the same as any busy night throughout the year except there were Christmas decorations and the odd Christmas CD being played. Chris hated this with a vengeance, that was, until he bought a CD which brought a whole new meaning to Christmas.

It was extremely rude with artists singing about Rudolph being fucked by Santa Claus and Hanky the Christmas Poo. This CD was played far too frequently for my liking, as Chris enjoyed watching people's reaction when they suddenly took note of the lyrics been sung.

Mind you, I certainly wasn't too impressed with him one Saturday lunchtime when he put the CD on to play, whilst old age pensioners and children were upstairs in the restaurant eating. I flew downstairs and barked at Chris. 'Turn this fucking CD off – now, there are children upstairs.'

'Whoops, sorry.'

I'll give him bloody sorry.

When we first took the pub over, New Year's Eve was always a good night and we were always busy with customers who had a great time. We found after a few years people started to drift off to nightclubs around 11pm to celebrate the New Year in. In fact the final year before we began to put on live entertainment, when midnight arrived there were only six people left in the bar, so there was plenty of room to sing Auld Lang Syne, although the atmosphere wasn't quite what we were hoping for!

The Charlton Brothers were the first live band to play on New Year's Eve and created a fantastic atmosphere.

We decided to sell tickets for the evening's events at £1.50 each; that way we were able to control the number of people and also regulate who we allowed in. If someone enquired about buying tickets and we didn't like the look of them, we said we were sold out.

This system worked extremely well and we continued using the same practice every New Year's Eve, although the price did rise gradually to £3.50 per ticket.

Some years the tickets were sold quickly, other times we really struggled to get people to make a commitment. In fact one year, by lunchtime on New Year's Eve, we had only sold twenty tickets and thought we were heading for a disastrous evening, but fortunately by 9.30pm the bar was packed with people who just turned up and paid for a ticket on the door.

At midnight I always supplied dozens of party poppers for customers to pop and make a horrendous mess everywhere, and Chris would shake a bottle of champagne, spraying it over everybody. The poor cleaner certainly had her work cut out when she next arrived on duty.

Employing staff to work on New Year's Eve was always a nightmare, I had a rule that if they worked on Christmas Eve they could have New Year's Eve off. Unfortunately, some had families and couldn't come in; others were away for Christmas or they basically didn't want to work.

The restaurant was always closed on New Year's Eve so that was the one night of the year when I could work behind the bar and not have to worry about the restaurant. I had spent the whole of December being nice to customers, serving hundreds of meals, so New Year's Eve was a night I could enjoy, be cheeky to customers, and have a drink.

We didn't allow the staff to drink in excess whilst they were working, but we did make an exception for New Year's Eve, well, we all wanted to be part of the celebrations as well.

Chris generally drew the short straw and had to stand by the front door all evening collecting tickets from people as they came in.

The bands that played on New Year's Eve, - Boogaloos, Egypt, World's Apart, and the Barry Homan Band, always made the evening a special occasion and the Walnut was renowned by customers for always rocking into the New Year.

I cannot leave the music chapter without giving a mention to John who used to come in the pub every Thursday evening to listen to the bands. He was called 'our promotions manager.' His topic of conversation was music, or music, or even music. He was on the verge of fanatical when it came to talking about bands. The people he had seen play, where they had played and how good, bad or indifferent they were, plus the names of each member of the band, what instrument they played and where they would be playing next were meat and drink to him. When he saw a band that hadn't played at the Walnut before and thought they would go down well with our clientele he was more than happy to pass on the relevant information to us. Thus, we called him our 'Promotions Manager.'

****

AMUSEMENT ARCADE

When we took over the pub in 1984, the amusement arcade opposite the pub was still in the process of completion. We didn't have any reason for concern nor realise there were going to be problems. However we were soon to found out what lay ahead.

Part of their licence agreement necessitated closing on Sundays and the whole place had to be sound-proofed.

At the time Silver City opened in 1986 we were still living upstairs in the pub so on Sunday mornings Norwich had the appearance of a ghost city with tumbleweed fluttering along the street! We had previously enjoyed long leisurely lay-ins after working hard all week and a quiet day without any interruptions.

The opening of the amusement arcade meant the end of our peace and quiet especially on Sundays when the owners were in breach of their agreement by opening; we would be lying in bed hearing numerous loud sounds from the arcade machines; kids shouting and yelling outside and riding up and down the alleyway on motor bikes and pushbikes, and the sounds of footballs being played with tin cans.

When the weather turned warmer the arcade opened all the windows and doors. We were not impressed, but politely asked the owner if he would close the doors and windows and try to control the kids outside who were causing the disturbance, to which his reply was, 'They're nothing to do with me; they're outside my building.'

We had never encountered problems in the alleyway until the arcade opened, but unfortunately for us, events continued to get considerably worse as the weeks and months went by.

We observed the youths sorting out bags of clothes, selling goods which had been shoplifted; we saw them selling and smoking drugs, and although we tried on numerous occasions to talk to the owner it was to no avail.

If the owners had kept a tighter control of what was occurring inside and outside his premises, had kept the noise at a lower level and kept the windows and doors closed, we would have been quite happy for him to open and shut when he wanted. We didn't want to have any grievances against him, we just wanted to get on with running our business and have a decent relationship with him.

This proved to be impossible and the arcade was beginning to have a detrimental effect on customers who began complaining about the state of the alleyway and about youngsters being abusive as they walked past.

Regretfully, we decided to take matters further and contacted the environmental noise pollution department regarding the noise level from the fruit machines which could be heard upstairs in our flat.

Using their sound monitor it was evident the noise was an unacceptable level, so the council said they would take measures with regard to ensuring the arcade kept its doors and windows closed and was fully soundproofed.

We contacted the city council and the local MP about the arcade being open on Sundays and the consequent trouble it was causing in the area.

In July 1987 Chris and I had to attend a formal meeting at the council along with the owner from the arcade, his solicitor and members from the planning committee who stipulated that the conditions on his planning application must be adhered to or enforcement proceedings would commence.

We took a petition to the meeting with 96 names and two letters from nearby residents objecting to the Sunday opening of the arcade centre.

It certainly appeared the city council were on our side and against the establishment.

The meeting went well from our perspective in gaining some assurance regarding the future, but the relationship with the owner from the arcade failed to improve.

Between July 1987 and January 1988 the arcade remained closed on Sundays, but in the meantime the owner had been busy trying to receive permission from the planners to have the ban lifted; however we had also been busy collating another petition and letters from people opposing Sunday opening.

In January 1988 there was an article in the local press with the headline: 'ARCADE SET TO STAY SHUT ON SUNDAYS.'

'Planners look set to refuse permission for Sunday opening at a Norwich amusement arcade – for the second time in six months.

The council had received a 48 signature petition and two letters from opponents who believe it would create a disturbance.

Now officers are saying that permission be refused and that enforcement action should be authorised to make sure the arcade stays shut on Sundays.

The owner said if the application was refused, he would appeal to Whitehall.'

He did remain closed for sometime on Sundays and we made the most of the tranquillity.

In 1986 around 8am on Christmas Day we were woken by the sound of loud voices and a rumbling noise outside the pub. 'What the fuck is going on outside?' said an infuriated Chris.

We got out of bed and looked out of the window to see the owner and his son walking up the alleyway with a wheelbarrow and two large containers full of coins from the amusement machines – unbelievable - even on a Christmas morning we were being disturbed.

Things went from bad to worse; there started to be a congregation of youths hanging about every day in the alleyway, getting very abusive towards us and our customers who were walking past.

One of the kids had an argument with his mate one day, and then took his aggression out by breaking one of our pub windows.

The alleyway began to look more like a dumping ground with litter, cans and sweet and crisp bags and with graffiti on the walls.

The youths were often shouting and yelling at each other which invariably ended with a fight occurring between them, with some resulting in quite serious injuries.

It got to the stage when it wasn't safe for Chris and I to walk down the alleyway. We were receiving open threats from the youths, who were quite frightening, especially when our 8-year old daughter was with us, witnessing them swinging bike chains at us, swearing and being abusive.

This was also having a detrimental effect with our customers and they, like us, stopped walking down the alleyway instead walking the long way round in the opposite direction.

One evening we witnessed one of the rogues who hung around the arcade throw a bike through the jeweller's shop window located at the end of the alleyway. A quick phone call to the police with a description of the culprit soon saw him arrested.

Not long after that particular incident, it was late one evening, and I was upstairs in the flat. I could hear banging outside at the end of the alleyway. When I peered out of the window, I witnessed another youth from the arcade continuously smashing his foot into the fire box until it broke.

Another phone call to the police ensued and the guy was subsequently arrested and taken to the police station, unashamedly denying having anything to do with it. However, they took prints from his trainer and found fragments of glass in the grooves.

I was asked to attend the station to make a statement regarding the episode, which wasn't a problem until they asked which foot had been used to break the fire box.

'Umm, the left one.'

'Or was it the right foot?' said the police officer.

'Giving it a lot of thought; ah yes, I remember now, it was the right foot.'

The police were happy with the finished statement, especially as the guy was already well known as a trouble maker to the police; a criminal conviction was definitely on the cards for him.

One lunchtime several customers, along with a few of our long time friends, were in the pub drinking when a couple of kids opened the door, stepped inside and shouted, 'Gudgin you're a wanker.' Then ran off.

This episode happened twice more, by which time Chris was beginning to feel exasperated and went outside to have a word with them.

They had obviously anticipated Chris would eventually go outside, because there were fifteen youths lying in wait to attack him with pool cues. He didn't stand a chance with the amount of kids present, and received serious injuries to his eye and head.

Some friends of ours were in the pub at the time, unaware Chris was outside getting beaten up, until they noticed him through the window. They rushed outside to help, unfortunately one friend ended up with a pool cue being pushed straight into his eye, causing a very nasty injury.

Chris and his friends managed to get away and back inside the pub to call the police, who arrived quickly and immediately entered the arcade to discover the kids were swapping clothes to avoid recognition.

However, the youths were arrested and taken to the station for questioning.

Chris went upstairs to the flat to clean the blood which was splattered over his clothes and inspect his eye which was already beginning to close up.

He was dreadfully shaken so remained upstairs. The police came and took a statement from Chris saying that the youths would be prosecuted in due course.

The next day Chris' eye was completely closed and one half of his face was swollen and going a ghastly shade of black.

He didn't want to go downstairs to the bar and opted to remain in the flat, which is where he stayed for nearly a week. Apart from his eye giving him physical pain, the incident had shaken him psychologically to the point of feeling scared about being in public or walking outside.

After a week, Chris' eye was looking much better, the swelling had gone down and the various shades of black, purple, yellow and green were fading from his eye and face area, so it was time for Chris to return to work and normality in life and put the incident behind him.

Harvey, our partner, came and collected him one evening and told him they were going out for a few drinks. Chris wasn't very keen but realised he had to go out at some point to overcome his anxiety. After several beers had been consumed he felt much better and was ready to get back to normal.

After the drinking session, Chris was soon back behind the bar and serving with his usual friendly manner! The troublemakers also stopped hanging about outside the arcade (probably because some were serving time in jail) so the alleyway, at long last, began to feel safer to walk down.

The arcade was eventually sold to a new owner who was very strict on the clientele he allowed to use the centre. He didn't allow children to enter his premises during the school term and ran an exemplary business, so at last our problems with amusement arcades were over.

****

OUR FAMILY

Sadly, my father passed away when I was only 26-years old so never lived to see his only daughter and son-in-law achieve their successful business. However, I know he has always looked down on us and would be so proud.

My mother was a godsend to me in the early days at the pub, she helped me with the ironing and little household chores which needed doing. To Lucy she was her Big Nanna who kept her occupied during the school holidays and Saturdays, took her out and spent quality time with her.

She was a wonderful mum who I adored but, sadly, she developed senile dementia over a period of time and had to spend her final five years in a nursing home which was a dreadful period in my life. I visited my mum three times a week for all those years to chat about the day's events and to try to obtain some recognition from my lovely mum who didn't have a clue who I was.

Chris' parents enjoyed visiting the pub every Saturday night when they played the fruit machine all evening; the other customers never got a look in when they were there.

Chris' mum was full of life and enjoyed nothing better than having a laugh and joke with staff and customers. She could talk the hind leg off a donkey, whereas Chris' dad was the quiet one and was content to sit with his beer and listen to everybody else chatter.

They often went on holidays in their caravette and sometimes took Lucy away for the day during the school holidays which was lovely for her, spending time with her Little Nana and Grandad and visiting new places.

All our parents had passed away several years before we finally left the pub but I know they were all so proud of us and their granddaughter Lucy.

Moving into the pub and starting a new life was relatively easy for our six-year old daughter Lucy, especially as she didn't even have to change schools.

To her it was quite an adventure, living over a pub, in the middle of the city and her newly decorated bedroom with her favourite 'My Little Pony' wallpaper was all she needed to make her very happy.

I tried to donate as much time as possible to her when she came home from school until bedtime but, obviously, as she got older her bedtime got later, so it was necessary to leave her upstairs watching television on her own whilst I went downstairs to work.

I always felt so guilty at leaving her but tried to go and see her for a couple of minutes at every available opportunity. She managed to amuse herself in my absence by rearranging the lounge furniture, covering everywhere with blankets and making an indoor den and putting all her toys inside.

Another time she found some paint and thought it a good idea to decorate the inside of the cupboard in her bedroom, which also contained the water tank, then climb inside with her toys. When I popped upstairs to see her she was nowhere to be found!

Call it mother's intuition but I had a feeling she was up to mischief one evening, so I crept quietly along the corridor in the flat and opened the lounge door to find

Lucy sitting on a chair, just about to light the remains of a cigarette which had previously been stubbed out in the ashtray.

I should have made her smoke a packet of 20 cigarettes one after the other, but I didn't like clearing up sick so I gave her a lecture instead.

She had a friend who lived within walking distance of the pub and they spent quite a bit of time together. One day she asked if she could go and see her friend to watch the Indiana Jones' video we had just bought her.

It was several weeks later I happened to open the Indiana Jones' video case to discover a porn video there instead.

Guess what was inside the porn video case!

When Lucy used the extension telephone in the flat, a light would flash on the main phone in the restaurant, so I was aware of how long she chatted to her friends.

One of her favourite occupations to amuse herself was telephoning the local radio station to answer questions on various quizzes. In fact, she rang so often the DJ broadcasting on air called her 'Lucy with the buzzing phone.'

Our telephone often picked up interference, thus making the phone buzz, hence the name.

I didn't mind her ringing the radio station as long as somewhere in the conversation she mentioned the Walnut Tree to gain some free advertising.

One evening Lucy was talking to the DJ live on air at the same time as a member of our staff picked up the other extension phone in the bar. She was under the impression she was speaking to the chef in the restaurant, 'Can I have a cheeseburger and fries please?'

The DJ could barely speak through laughter, when he managed to compose himself, 'To all our listeners who are wondering what on earth is going on, I had better explain; Lucy with the buzzing phone lives at the Walnut Tree Shades in Norwich which sells great food and someone obviously wants to order a cheeseburger and fries.'

She used to go in our private kitchen and make 'things'. She would collect some ice-cream wafers from the restaurant, put a blob of squirty cream on top, add a cherry, then go into the bar and sell them to customers for 10p each.

If she got adventurous she would try and make chocolate crispies and sell those. By the time she had finished cooking, the kitchen would look as if it had been burgled.

During the summer she would play tennis against the wall outside and get customers to play with her – but charge them 50p for the privilege.

She would climb out of the window in our living accommodation onto the flat roof outside and play on top of the adjoining shop's roof tops. An extremely dangerous activity, as there was a huge drop over the edge which could have resulted in a major catastrophe.

Even though I continuously told her not to go outside, did she pay any attention? – No. It wasn't until staff from neighbouring shops informed us, 'Your daughter's on the roof again.'

I had to run upstairs and grab her indoors yet again.

She liked to swing on the banister on the stairs and make the staff jump when they walked out of the door, nearly giving them a heart attack.

We returned to the pub after enjoying a Sunday lunch in a neighbouring restaurant to discover a pigeon hunched in the corner of the entrance door. He obviously wasn't well and made no attempt to fly away. 'It looks sick, please let me take it inside and give it something to eat,' said Lucy.

'It's only a pigeon, they're like rats with wings, I don't want it indoors.'

'But please, please Mummy; we can put it in the laundry room.'

We put the pigeon, which Lucy had named Polly, in a box, gave him some bread and water, and retired for the night.

The following morning, Polly was lying on his back, stiff as a board, with legs in the air – dead. I just thought, 'Oh God, Lucy is going to be so upset, there's going to be tears.'

The first thing she said on being woken up, 'How's Polly?'

'Not too good, I'm so sorry Lucy, try not to be too upset but he died during the night.'

I expected floods of tears and having to console a devastated daughter. 'Oh no, well you could turn Polly into pigeon pie then we can eat him for tea!'

Lucy went to school not giving a second thought to Polly and I assured her tea would not be consisting of pigeon.

School holidays was a difficult time, as I hated leaving her so much on her own, so tried to make work appealing to her in the restaurant. She could feel involved and be with me at the same time. I would get her to polish the cutlery and wrap them up in napkins. I let her press the start button of the dishwasher and got her to polish the tables before we were open.

However, it didn't have the desired effect and after about ten minutes of hard labour she just kept asking, 'How much have I earned so far?'

To give her incentive for helping in the restaurant, picking bits of tissue and rubbish from under the tables, I used to hide a few coins for her to find; that project always got her motivated.

We didn't have time to take her to a fireworks' display on Guy Fawkes' Night. On our first year at the pub, not having the luxury of a garden, we obviously couldn't have a bonfire. So with a pile of sand in the car park we performed our own little display of fireworks outside the Walnut.

A friend from school was spending the evening with Lucy whilst her parents had gone to the theatre and would pick her up later to go home. It was company for Lucy and at least one evening I didn't feel guilty about leaving her upstairs alone, so thought I would leave them to their own devices.

However, I didn't anticipate they would help themselves to the Baileys, attempt to make rice pudding with Baileys instead of milk, concoct some imaginative cocktails then get drunk - they were only about 12-years old!

When the parents arrived to pick up their daughter, I had to point out the girls had enjoyed a lovely evening but were somewhat tipsy.

Not going to bed until late every night, I found it extremely difficult getting up in the morning to take Lucy to school, so consequently was late on several occasions. I was called into the headmistress' office one day and reprimanded like a naughty schoolgirl. 'Would you please make sure Lucy arrives to school on time in the future?'

'I'm very sorry, and will try to do better, but I find it so hard to get up in the morning.' She wasn't impressed.

It was much easier when Lucy was in her final years at school. She managed to get up on her own, get ready, say good-bye to me whilst I was still in bed, go into the bar and help herself to the odd shot of Jack Daniels, or vodka, or gin to take to school in a bottle, catch the bus and arrive on time every day.

Of course, I was totally unaware of her nicking the odd spirit until she revealed her misdemeanour in later years.

When Lucy was a little older and stopped creating havoc in the flat she found the love for books and sat for hours reading; until it came to doing homework, then she wasn't quite so keen on the schoolwork reading material.

When children are teenagers it is a massive event being allowed into the city without the supervision of parents, so we always had an endless stream of Lucy's friends arriving at the pub to see her.

Most of them lived in the country, so coming into Norwich for the day was a really big deal. The city for Lucy was second nature as I had allowed her to walk to nearby shops on her own since she was about ten-years old, but always with the strictest instructions she had to be back in ten to fifteen minutes' time, and only to visit that one particular shop without venturing further.

By the time she was a teenager, she was confident and self-assured walking around the entire city centre.

Throughout her upbringing I had a feeling of guilt, much the same as any parent in business or full time employment, trying to make a better future for all the family. There were never enough hours in the day and if Lucy wanted me to do something for her the reply was often the same. 'I'm busy,' or 'In a minute.'

Lucy never did anything really bad when she was young other than causing havoc in the flat and generally misbehaving sometimes, no, on reflection - many times.

Yes, of course, she caused me a few problems and heartaches over the years – much the same as most young adults, but ultimately grew into the most wonderful daughter and best friend I could ever wish for, producing two beautiful grandchildren Joel and Mia and marrying Scot, who we are proud to have as our son-in-law.

****

PLANNING APPLICATIONS

The Walnut Tree is a grade II listed building so making any structural alterations or extensions was impossible as planning permission would never be granted. Having said that, we never had any reason or the necessity to knock down walls or change the original design of the pub – we liked it as it was.

It was beneficial in some ways to have an old building because, as new laws and regulations were enforced regarding access for the disabled, we were unable to change the size of the front door or put in a disabled toilet because of the structure of the building. This saved us a vast amount of money. Of course, it goes without saying, we always assisted people with wheelchairs into the pub and there was just enough room for them to squeeze into the toilet area.

Fortunately for us there were only two occasions when we had to put in planning applications. Dealings with the council and their administration always seem such long drawn-out affairs and are never straightforward.

In 1988 we decided the exterior of the pub needed some refurbishment and enhancement to cheer up the dingy looking alleyway. We came up with the idea of erecting some canopies to place over the restaurant windows.

We knew planning permission would be required before the blinds were erected, so asked a member from the planning department to inspect the premises and give us his thoughts before we put in an application.

We showed him the plans and drawings for the shape and size of the canopies, which he seemed quite happy with, although he indicated planning permission would only be granted if we changed the shape of the awnings to arched instead of square to keep in character with the windows on the ground floor.

We didn't have a problem with that suggestion, so took the drawings and instructions to a canopy manufacturer, with the view that by the time planning permission was granted, the canopies would be made and ready to adorn the exterior of the pub.

We were thrilled with the finished result of the canopies, and even more so when they were erected. It made a massive difference to the appearance of the pub and although we still hadn't obtained our planning application approval, we weren't too concerned that permission wouldn't be granted.

We should have had a better understanding of how the council worked, but I suppose were still a little naïve in the many areas of red tape involved concerning a business environment.

We had interpreted from the council officer on his visit that permission would be granted if we altered the shape of the canopies, which we did – we were wrong.

The tabloid press even published the story, with the headlines:

'NO LIGHTS FOR THE SHADES.'

'City Centre pub, The Walnut Tree Shades wants to build illuminated awnings over its front door, and first floor windows, but the idea was thrown out by Norwich planners. The planning sub-committee laughed as the council officer joked, 'It's all in the best possible taste.

They would look like a typical Watneys. I thought they were going out of fashion.'

How dare they?

We had spent a lot of money having the canopies made so certainly had no intention of taking them down, even if we hadn't obtained planning permission.

They remained in their prominent position above the windows in full view of everyone to see.

We never heard another peep from the Council regarding the planning permission for 12 years.

During the 1990's, to be in line with Europe, alfresco dining was becoming popular. Drinking and eating establishments in Norwich started having tables and chairs outside for customers, and an increasing number of streets were being pedestrianised. It made business sense for cafes and bars to expand their clientele and enlarge their seating area outside.

The ownership of our pub didn't extend to outdoor space. With no garden and certainly no pleasant view the outside area, at first glance, didn't seem particularly appealing.

However, there was still room to place three tables and twelve chairs outside the front door of the pub on the paved area in the alleyway without obstructing people walking past. We decided to apply for planning permission.

It entailed putting in an application and filling in several forms, stating the size of the area we intended to use, plus the hours of day and evening the furniture would be kept outside.

A notice had to be displayed outside the pub to see if any member of the public would oppose the application. A notice was published in the paper stating our intentions and when the committee would be meeting to discuss any grievances and decide on whether the application should be allowed.

After several weeks it was confirmed we had received no objections and planning permission was passed – but with restrictions.

The tables and chairs must be taken indoors at the end of every evening; they must not extend over a certain area to avoid obstruction of the alleyway. To ensure this didn't happen the furniture must be roped off with some form of structure.

One obstruction in the middle of the alleyway adjacent to our tables was a metal post erected by the council. One morning when the brewery were delivering the beer, Chris was guiding the driver of the lorry so he could reverse down the alleyway to offload the kegs. 'Back some more.' 'Keep coming back.' 'Bit more, Oh, whoops! You've just knocked the metal post over.'

Now there was much more accessibility for people to walk through the alleyway. The council didn't think so and put another post up!

For the privilege of putting tables and chairs outside the cost for the first year was the meager sum of £5 – a bargain. It did, however, gradually creep up each year until 2007 the cost reached £90.

In 2001 someone complained to the council about the noise and water dripping from the several air conditioners located at the end of the alleyway owned by the bank and shops.

A member from the council came to investigate the complaint and examine the air conditioners.

Unfortunately, while he was inspecting the alleyway, he decided to continue walking a few more feet and scrutinize the exterior of our building, consequently he noticed the canopies and our cooler unit and extraction vent, essential equipment needed for the kitchen.

The cooler unit and extraction vent were erected before we even took over the pub. Although we did replace the vent at a later date for a new one, apparently we still needed planning permission. We received a severe letter from the Council:

'Planning permission is required for the cooler units which you have installed, and I have no record of listed building consent or planning permission being granted for these works. Additionally I have noted that canopies have been fixed to the windows when planning permission was considered but then refused. So these must therefore be removed.

You may apply retrospectively for consent of the canopies and units but the size and design of the units is unsightly and inappropriate and detracts from the special interest of this building and character and appearance of this part of the conservation area. Similar concerns relate to the canopies. It is unlikely; therefore that planning permission would be forthcoming.'

We were absolutely furious with the contents of the letter. Yes, OK, so planning permission had been refused for the canopies but we put them up anyway and they had been erected for the past 12 years. As far as we were concerned, they were bloody well going to stay there.

We got an engineer to give us his opinion on changing or moving the cooler unit and extractor. To install smaller ones would cost many thousands of pounds.

Both items of equipment were essential in the running of our business; there was no realistic way they could possibly be taken down permanently, and we had no intention of doing so.

Chris telephoned the council, saying that we would only consider taking the units down if all the other properties in the alleyway removed their's.

The outcome of this story, - nothing changed.

The canopies remained where they were, so did the extractor fan and cooler unit and we never heard another word from the council.

****

HOW TO MAKE A
STREET MACHINE

First of all you need to buy a cocktail shaker

25ml Bacardi
25ml Apry (Apricot liqueur
50ml grapefruit juice
50ml orange juice
splash of grenadine

Half fill the shaker with ice
then add all the above.
Shake well.
Strain the contents into a 10oz glass ¾ full of ice
Garnish with a slice of orange and straw

HOW TO MAKE A
WHISKEY SOUR

50ml Bourbon
50ml Lemon juice
25ml sugar syrup (or to taste)

Half fill the shaker with ice
Add all the above and shake.
Pour it all into an 8oz glass.
Serve with a slice of lemon and a cherry.

You can substitute Amaretto, Galliano or Scotch
for the Bourbon

PHONE CALLS

Before the days of having the advantage of ringing 1471 to discover the number of the previous caller on the telephone, we had a spate of dirty phone calls, quite a common occurrence in businesses which employed a majority of female employees.

It wasn't concerning in any way, in fact it was quite amusing to hear a grunting voice on the other end attempting to be sexy and giving an account of his fantasies.

In one phone call I received the guy began talking about my tits, asking how big they were – well, anybody who knows me, realises my breasts are just a tad bigger than the size of fried eggs! So I told him they were 36DD and was that big enough for him, thinking the person on the other end of the phone was a friend of our's trying to wind me up.

He continued to talk about my boobs and how voluptuous they must be; I was baffled, and desperately trying to associate the voice with someone I knew.

'Who is it? Stop messing about; you know I've only got little boobs which are definitely not a size 36DD.'

As his conversation got more passionate and he began fantasizing in depth about the sexual acts he would enjoy carrying out with my boobs, I realised this wasn't someone I knew, it was a dirty old (or young) man on the other end, probably talking to me whilst pleasuring himself at the same time. I slammed the phone down.

Another memorable phone call I received was a guy enquiring if my name was Jude. 'Yes, how can I help?'

'I would like to congratulate you on your centre-fold picture in the Forum magazine.'

'What picture? I don't know what you're talking about.'

'Well, you do own a pub in the centre of the city don't you?'

When I said yes, he went onto say there was a naked picture of me balanced on top of the bar in a provocative way.

'I think you've got the wrong person, I can assure you it's definitely not me.'

He went on to ask me if I would like to pose naked whilst he took pictures of me.

'No thanks,' and I slammed the phone down.

I immediately rushed out to buy a copy of Forum magazine (strangely enough from the top shelf) to discover a centre-fold picture of a naked girl called 'Julie' who showed no resemblance to me – thank God. At least the guy on the phone didn't know me personally from coming in the pub.

'Julie,' was standing on the bar counter, which did have a similarity to our pub layout, her legs and bum spread-eagled over the top of the beer pumps in a sexual manner.

I had obviously misconstrued his conversation when he enquired if I was Jude.

I told Chris he could call me 'Julie', if he wished!

****

A SECTION FROM
THE WALNUT COCKTAIL LIST

SOURS NEWYORKER'S FAVOURITE EARLY EVENING LIVENER.

Sours are shaken with lemon juice and sugar, you choose the spirit and the size. Bourbon, Rye, Scotch, Apry, Amaretto, Blackberry, Cherry, Galliano and Melon. Regular 1.95 American 3.30

RUSTY NAIL Scotch and Drambuie	2.50
RUM RUNNER Rum, Banana and Blackberry liqueur, lime juice and grenadine	4.00
STREET MACHINE Bacardi, Apry, grapefruit juice, O.J. and grenadine	3.00
SCORPION Brandy, Bacardi Gold, lemon juice, orgeat and O.J.	3.20
SINNER Large Gin, lemon juice, cream, sugar and O.J.	2.95
SLOE COMFORTABLE SCREW Southern Comfort, Vodka, Sloe Gin and O.J.	4.00
SINGAPORE GIN SLING Gin, Cherry liqueur, lime juice and soda	2.90

WINE COOLERS

White Wine, over ice, and a splash of your favourite liqueur, Melon, Cassis, Apricot or Cherry.

2.75

TEQUILA SUNRISE Tequila, grenadine and O.J.	2.00
TOM COLLINS Large Gin, lemon juice, sugar, soda	2.80
VOODOO (for 2) Bacardi Gold, Bacardi, Dark Rum, Apry, O.J. Curacao, pineapple juice, lemon juice, grenadine, orgeat	7.00
WILD JAFFA Vodka, Cointreau, Galliano, lemon juice grenadine, sugar	3.20
YELLOW BIRD Bacardi Gold, Creme de Banana, Galliano, pineapple juice and O.J.	4.30

LIQUEUR COFFEES

Available at the bar at all times topped with lashings of whipped cream. Irish, Royale, Amaretto, Galliano, Jamaican, Russian, Scotch, Mexican, Sambuca.

From 2.50

or be wild and different Galliano and Kahlua, Tequila and Kahlua

3.85

WILLIE '61' BLACKWELL

SYNDICATE

In 1996 the rent and rates had increased significantly since we took over the pub. We had survived the recession and since then trade had improved each year so we felt confident that we were running a successful business. The time felt right to try and buy the freehold of the pub.

We had heard Enterprise Inns were considering the future strategy for the whole of their estate as new regulations were being brought in. In future breweries would only be allowed to have a certain amount of pubs, so would either have to sell some to another brewer or sell them individually.

We approached the brewery enquiring if they would consider selling the freehold to us.

We received a swift reply, and were told, in no uncertain terms,

'We are not in a position at present to consider the disposal of any properties on an individual basis, but our interest was duly noted.'

That meant no, and obviously they were not interested in any kind of negotiation, so subsequently we had to continue paying the extortionate rent and be tied to purchasing their beer.

In 1999 we were approached by another publican with regard to setting up a syndicate consisting of successful operators in the licensed industry with the view to collectively trying to buy the freehold of our properties.

We knew that three years ago the brewery had no intention of even considering selling our pub to us but as a cooperative body we may have more chance of arousing their interest.

Eight successful pubs located in and around Norwich joined the syndicate with a view to purchasing our individual properties.

A lot of work was involved in consolidating the business plans and finance. Each pub had to be valued according to the current market and on this basis each owner had to arrange their own finance to make sure payments could be made to purchase the property.

Each member of the syndicate had to source their own finance to the value of 60% of the proposed acquisition price. The brewery would advance finance to the value of 29% of the acquisition price and, finally, each member had to provide their own (unborrowed) funds to the value of 11% of the total price.

The Walnut was valued at £275,000 but we knew the brewery would want in excess of the lowest valuation figure. We needed to secure a loan for a much higher sum for the freehold and consequently would require a huge loan from the bank.

We had meetings with the bank manager, showing him a business plan we had produced and how we expected our trade to increase over the next three years, along with expenses which might be incurred.

He appeared impressed and this was confirmed when he told us the bank would be prepared to lend us £195,000. We ascertained from another brewery we were able to secure a loan of £95,000, and with our own funds of £35,000 this made a top valuation of £325,000.

It would leave us with absolutely nothing in the bank, but the repayments on the loan would actually work out cheaper than our rent was at present. In addition, we would have the added advantage of being able to buy beer from any wholesaler at a much cheaper price.

It was common fact that licensees of a freehold property were able to buy beer at over £50 a barrel less than we were paying, which when calculated, meant the money we would save in the course of the year would actually cover the cost of the loan.

With all the exacting calculations and obvious concerns about borrowing vast amounts of money, we were confident that if our business continued to grow, we would own the freehold in just over ten year's time and this would prove to be a nice pension plan when we retired.

The remaining seven pubs arranged their finances and loans in much the same way, so everybody had a base valuation and a top valuation (the highest figure we would be prepared to go to).

A letter from our consortium was produced and forwarded, stating the proposed financing package of the eight pubs and the offer to purchase the properties (which came to just under three million pounds). This was based on the lowest valuation figure.

The letter was received with distaste from the landlords; their reply was straight to the point: they wouldn't give any serious consideration to our proposals unless the offer was in excess of five million pounds. They went on to say the gap was far too large to warrant any further effort on our part and it would be in our best interest not to pursue this route any further.

They basically just laughed at us for even going to all the effort of adopting a proposal in the first place. Even with our top valuation of £3,725,000 from the eight pubs in our syndicate, we still had a massive short-fall of over a million pounds.

On reflection, why would they consider selling eight of their most successful pubs in and around Norwich when they were guaranteed a regular income from rent and beer and would still own the property?

After all the months of meetings and planning involved in our consortium, that was the end of our syndicate and we would therefore be remaining a tenant.

****

LICENSED VICTUALLERS ASSOCIATION

The Licensed Victuallers Association was a members' organisation which looked after the business interests of self-employed licensees in the licensed trade.

A landlord of a pub is known as a licensed victualler, the name deriving from a victualler of goods in the retail trade. The association helped with every aspect of the business from applying for extended licenses to assisting with any legal problems.

There were associations based in every region; they were made up of committee members, a Junior Vice Chairman, Vice chairman, Senior Vice chairman who were licensees and a President was from the breweries, spirit companies and allied trades.

They met every month to discuss a range of concerns in the licensed industry and campaigned against relevant issues from the smoking ban to energy costs and aimed to influence the decisions that affected licenses by working for reform of the law.

The LVA was founded in 1864 and still holds a black tie Steak and Kidney Pudding dinner every year. The pudding was 2lb in weight, and after eating it; along with several glasses of port, Chris' belly looked like a beached whale when he arrived home!

In 1981 the British Institute of Innkeeping now known as the BII was formed, which offered legal and business advice, and access to extensive support and savings within the licensed industry. It was extremely beneficial to us in matters like staff problems, pursuing the correct procedures and any legal implications which could evolve.

In our early days at the pub, being newcomers in the industry, we were still outsiders within the circle of publicans. We were always so busy running our pub, we didn't have time to socialise with other licensees so, in a way, in the celebrity stakes, we were in the Z list!

After a few years we received more recognition and were no longer in the Z List; in fact, we were nearly A list! We had gained respect from working so continuously hard at our business, and became good friends with several other publicans enjoying their company at special events and social gatherings.

We attended several LVA functions which ranged from luncheons and week-ends away for the men, to balls with posh frocks and D.J's.

Chris may have been scruffy in his attire for work, but he could scrub up nicely when the occasion arose.

Unfortunately, he had a change of heart on the first ball we attended after taking over the Walnut; instead of a crisp white dinner shirt and bow tie, Chris wore a white tee-shirt with a printed motif on the front displaying a bow tie and waistcoat!

I can't remember how he managed to get more involved with the LVA, but he was voted to stand on the committee, joining the monthly meetings to discuss any current issues affecting the licensed trade.

They organised functions and events which all committee members were actively involved in. One of Chris' jobs was to arrange the flower buttonholes for each of the committee members to wear on one of the LVA luncheons. Not a difficult job: order the flowers, pick them up and take them to the event.

He brought them home to discover there weren't enough. 'Oh shit, now what am I going to do?' 'No problem, I will pick some flowers and greenery from the garden and make some.'

It didn't take long, and he was quite pleased at how professional they looked.

The committee members were all adorned with their buttonholes and none the wiser that some weren't from a florist. It wasn't until much later on in the afternoon when the place was warming up and everyone had consumed a copious amount of alcohol, enjoying each other's company and the ambience of the day, when a smell began to linger amongst the men.

His beautifully arranged buttonholes had a strong aroma of cats pee; the greenery he had used from the garden was attractive to cats – apparently.
'Where the fuck did you get these buttonholes from Gudgin, they stink?'

He had to come clean and tell them the truth that he hadn't ordered enough.

They never asked him to organise the buttonholes again!

After spending time as a committee member, the next promotion was Junior Vice Chairman, then the following year Vice Chairman. It didn't entail any more work on Chris' part; he just had to wear chains round his neck looking like a Lord Mayor on any LVA functions.

Chris didn't have time to be as actively involved as he felt he should be on the committee. With so many new regulations coming into force and other publicans concerns about reforms and economic climate survival, he decided to step down and concentrate on being more obnoxious at the Walnut.

****

BAR ROOM BANTERS

Every couple of months, a local paper distributed in Norwich and Norfolk, published an article asking for views from the general public on various topics which had made the national news headlines recently.

Chris was invariably contacted for his opinions on various issues:

Q. The Government has announced four new trial sites for GM crops in Norfolk. Would you be worried about eating genetically modified food?

A. It does not bother me at all if food is GM or not. If it's food, that is good enough for me.

Q. What do you think about The Sun newspaper coughing up £40,000 to bring fugitive Ronnie Biggs back to Britain?

A. Leave him where he is, we don't need him back. At the end of the day, he's a bank robber.

Q. Do you think the Government should pay for a new national football stadium?

A. You could probably write on the end of a pin what I know about football. The FA should put their own bed in order. It's like me making a screw-up and asking someone else to solve the problem for me.

Q. Are you surprised to hear one in three nurses is ready to resign because they are 'emotionally exhausted'?

A. Most bartenders will tell you they are emotionally exhausted as well. I'm not surprised to hear though, with the long hours they work. I think the Government should pay to send them on a big holiday - that would help relax them.

Q. What do you think about Deputy Prime Minister John Prescott staying in a £1,264 a night room in Bali – paid for by taxpayers?

A. If I could afford it, I wouldn't mind staying there, but not with the taxpayers' money; he is not worth it.

Q. A survey has shown fast cars really do give men extra pulling power after women said men were more sexy if they owned a sports car. Do you think it would boost your sex appeal?

A. I do actually have a fast car. I drive a Golf VR6 and no, I don't think it makes me more attractive – not at my age.

****

ANOTHER SECTION FROM
THE RESTAURANT EVENING MENU

CHICKEN FEED

LOUISIANA CHICKEN - Chicken bosom coated with Cajun spices and chargrilled, served on granary with Dijon mayo, lettuce and a pot of coleslaw. — 9.75

TERIYAKI CHICKEN - Chicken chest mildly marinated, gently grilled, served open faced on granary with a salad garnish and a pot of coleslaw. — 9.75

CARIBOO CHICKEN - Chicken breast chargrilled, topped with bar-b-que sauce, bacon and melted cheese. — 9.95

THE POULTRYGEIST - Chicken bosom, grilled and topped with cheese, peppers, jalapenos and grilled onions, served on toasted garlic bread. — 9.95

ALL THE ABOVE MEALS ARE SERVED WITH HOME FRIES OR JACKET POTATO.

CHICKEN CAESAR SALAD - Made the way it should be, with Romaine lettuce, Caesar dressing, croutons, anchovies and fresh parmesan. — 9.75

CHICKEN FAJITAS - we provide the warm flour tortillas for you to fill with a combination of chicken, sour cream, salsa, guacamole and chopped salad. — 13.25

SOMETHING FISHY

TUNA AND PRAWN SALAD - Well that's it really. Tuna mayo, with some prawns and a plateful of salad with a taco shell. — 9.25

SCAMPI - Crisp battered pieces with home fries or jacket potato and goodbye sauce. — 9.25

FISH OF THE WEEK - Look on the blackboard to see what's been caught.

SAMPLER RIB PLATTERS

PRAIRIE PLATTER - (Ribs n' Wings.) Half rack of baby back ribs and 10 hot spicy chicken wings. — 12.50

DETROIT DUO - (Ribs and Teriyaki chicken.) Half rack of ribs and a marinated chicken bosom gently grilled. — 13.95

RIB N' RIBEYE - Half rack of ribs plus an 8 oz. ribeye steak and battered onion rings. — 13.95

FROM HERE TO MATERNITY - (Or making the most out of sweet nothings.) Half rack of ribs, an 8 oz. ribeye steak and prawns, but don't expect too many. — 13.95

IF YOU ARE ON A DIET,
OR JUST DON'T WANT POTATOES, WE WILL CONCOCT YOU A HOUSE SALAD INSTEAD - BUT REMEMBER TO TELL US, WE WON'T ASK.

VEGETARIAN

VEGETARIAN NACHOS - A plateful of Mexican tortilla chips, topped with cheese, jalapenos and side pots of salsa, sour cream, guacamole and salad. — 8.25

VEGETARIAN BURGER - Choose any topping from the Burgers Galore section to accompany your finest no-meat burger. Prices as 6oz. column.

VEGETARIAN BURRITOS - filled with something vegetarian. Served with coleslaw and salad garnish. — 8.25

SALADS & SIDE DISHES ▶
OVERLEAF

GOING ON HOLIDAY

Anybody with an individually owned business enterprise will fully appreciate the stress involved organising a holiday; there are so many factors and considerations to overcome before actually envisaging going anywhere.

Are the staff trustworthy and capable of working efficiently without the bosses there to crack the whip?

Who is going to be left in charge?

What problems are you going to return to?

Will anyone call in sick?

What equipment, if any, might break down?

Will any staff argue and fall out?

When it comes to taking a break, this is the time you wish you were an employee. Employees can book the time off from work when it suits them and start to wind down several days beforehand. They can think about what to pack and what new clothes to buy and finally, at the end of the last day's work, they can just walk away from the job with no concerns or cares until they get back. Oh, what bliss that would be.

So, being the employer and all the above to worry about, you go ahead and book a holiday anyway. We were quite fortunate that, for the majority of the time, we had a good team of employees who we knew would work consistently well in our absence and would be capable of overcoming any unforeseen eventualities which may occur.

I was always particular and methodical in trying to organise everything possible before we went on holiday. I knew we could relax more if every contingency had been anticipated before our departure, so all the staff had to worry about was going about their normal daily routine of work.

The rotas had to be arranged to make sure there were enough staff working on each shift. Obviously, with the amount of hours Chris and I worked, we had to do a bit of grovelling to get the staff to work extra shifts. Fortunately most of them were very obliging and only too pleased to get rid of us for a while. Once the rotas were finalised, the wages had to be prepared and handed out to the staff, although they never complained about receiving their wages a week early – funny that!

Everything was ordered in advance - beer, spirits and minerals. Chris did his most hated job - going to Cash and Carry to buy the tinned items for the restaurant and the cleaning materials.

Ice-cream and frozen goods were pre-ordered.

The only goods which the chefs needed to order on a daily basis were the meat and vegetables, which on a few occasions they forgot to do, then wondered why they weren't delivered the next day.

I drove the staff mad by leaving lists pinned everywhere – just to make sure they didn't forget certain jobs which required attention in our absence.

There were lists for the cleaning jobs I wanted done if it was quiet – that was often a waste of time, as it was far more enjoyable chatting than cleaning out fridges etc.

There were lists for suppliers' phone numbers, another one for tradesmen if anything broke down, then all the lists on the fridges and freezers which required filling in each day for monitoring the temperature of each appliance. Then I might think of a few more last minute requests and write another list.

It was essential that one particular person was left in charge of staff and the running of the business in our absence. We were fortunate in employing some very loyal staff who were extremely willing and capable, and actually enjoyed taking on the extra responsibility.

This worked well if we were away for a short break, but for a two week holiday it was more practical to employ the services of an extra person with experience of running a business. We couldn't expect the staff to work the same hours we did, so this necessitated an extra person to work a large number of hours.

The person in charge had to be shown my system of cashing the tills, the banking routine and the bookwork which, of course, entailed several more lists of instructions in case they forgot how to do it.

That's why we never had the need for decorating the premises; I just put another list on the wall!

With everything (hopefully) organised, we were able to prepare for our holiday.

Packing was usually a last minute job, and on one occasion, I was so busy trying to sort out last minute problems, I only managed to pack thirty minutes before we were leaving for the airport. I literally, went to the wardrobe, grabbed some clothes still on their hangers, chucked them in the case with some underwear – job done.

Quite a revelation when we arrived at our destination and I hadn't a clue what items were packed but, surprisingly, there was everything I needed.

We were due to depart on holiday to America in the early hours of a Sunday morning. The bags were packed, and everything connected to the business side of things was organised.

Just after 11pm on the Saturday evening I was upstairs in the flat cashing the till, hoping the customers would leave soon to enable us to have a few hours sleep before our departure, when Chris received a phone call from the Chief Inspector at the police station.

He went on to say he had just received an anonymous phone call from a member of the public, saying there was a bomb planted in the pub. He insisted we evacuated everybody immediately, and re-enforcements and bomb disposal unit were on their way.

Chris thought the phone call was a wind-up from a customer and replied, 'Yeh right', and put the phone down.

On telling the customers still in the bar about the phone call and having been told to evacuate the bar, they didn't believe the conversation either and were under the assumption that Chris wanted everyone to clear off as he was going on holiday the next day and wanted an early night – of course, they just carried on talking and drinking their beer.

Chris came upstairs and told me about the phone call – I didn't believe it either and carried on counting the cash from the till.

It wasn't until he saw several police officers walking briskly down the alleyway that he realised, oops, this wasn't a prank phone call after all.

The police asked Chris if he had looked in the toilets for anything resembling a bomb. 'No, how am I supposed to know what I am looking for, is it big, round, and black with bomb written on it?'

'No, it could be as small as a cassette tape.'

'Well, it's your job, best you go and have a look.'

On reflection, Chris decided he really must phone the Chief Inspector and apologise for not believing him, genuinely thinking it had been a customer playing a stupid prank.

As you can imagine, the Inspector wasn't too impressed.

After thoroughly inspecting the building, they found nothing and left. So much for an early night before our holiday!

Arriving at the airport the following morning, security as usual was very rigid. When it came to the questions asked at the check-in desk. 'Did you pack your own luggage?' 'Has it been left unattended?'

It did cross our minds whether we should mention the fact we had had a bomb alert in our premises the previous night – we decided against it.

It always took a few days to switch off from business mode on holiday and to catch up from sleep deprivation before it was possible to relax, wind down and lose the tension which had built up.

We always had a great time on our holidays and enjoyed everywhere we visited. It was so nice to have quality time together and not spend every waking hour working.

We never spoke about work whilst we were away and tried not to even think about it. That was until a couple of days before it was time to go home. Then my tummy would start churning and my thoughts began to return to work mode. I would start to think about the mountain of mail I would soon be contending with, all the bookwork and banking which would have to be sorted out, and then worry about what problems we may return to.

I always hated walking in the pub for the first time after our holiday - trying to judge the staff reactions, to see if they were happy, moody, and were they all speaking to each other?

The first question we always asked, 'So, any problems while we were away?'

The usual answer was, 'No, everything was fine.'

Except for one occasion when we had driven directly from the airport and straight into work, only to be told by the bar person that I had better go in the restaurant quickly as the chef wasn't happy and was about to walk out. 'Ooh, welcome home Jude.'

Did I receive a, 'hello', or 'did you have a nice time Jude?' No, of course not. His first remark to me; 'The fucking chef who worked lunchtime didn't clean the microwave and didn't leave any fucking prep done for me.'

'Have you run out of anything yet?'

'Well no, but that's not the point, I'm pissed off and on the verge of walking out.'

There's a part of me that really wants to say, well, fuck off then, but on a quick perusal of the reservation book and it's a guaranteed busy night, I don't want to be without a chef in the kitchen. So I zip my mouth and say I will get the problem resolved but, in the meantime, 'What needs doing, and I will help do it.'

However, it would generally take a couple of hours before one or two stories would evolve, sometimes even a few weeks later and various tales would be related and these were usually from the customers.

We always played blues music in the pub; it's what the customers liked, what the pub was known for. However, a couple of staff had different ideas, and brought their own music in to play – very loudly. Unfortunately it was often Madonna, Take That, or Abba, with a few more pop tapes in between. Chris was not impressed when this story came out a few weeks after our return from holiday. 'You wouldn't have brought that music in to play when I was here, so you don't fucking bring it in when I'm away.' - Ooh, that told them.

Sue, my best friend of nearly 40 years, stayed with her partner in the pub on one of our trips away. She also worked for me and was left in charge of all the duties and staff. She wrote me a diary of every occurrence that happened in our absence, and there were many, so after reading it I felt as if I had relived the whole experience with her.

Like the morning the fuse box on the wall downstairs in the pub caught fire. They immediately used the powder fire extinguishers to put out the flames and anyone who has used one will appreciate the amount of mess they make. Yes, they do the job and put the fire out, but, God the aftermath.

Every glass, bottle, picture, (and there are plenty), and piece of furniture was covered in powder, from downstairs in the bar and up the stairs to the restaurant, where every table and surface was covered in a layer of dust.

Whilst they waited for the electrician to arrive, everywhere was in darkness. The washing-up area, where there aren't any windows, was pitch black; every plate, cutlery, glass and container had to be washed by candlelight.

The bar had to be stripped down and, again, every solitary item in the place had to be washed and wiped.

I have to say, hat's off to all the staff though, because they managed to open the bar and restaurant by the evening.

There are times when you can be really proud of the staff for all mucking in and getting the job done.

The day this occurred was the same day we rang the pub to see if everything was OK.

'Yes fine, no problems at all.'

They didn't like to inform us of the day's events and spoil our holiday.

On our return we heard a couple of rumours as to why the pub had been closed for the day; firstly, the staff had a party the previous night and couldn't be bothered to open the following day and, secondly, there was a huge fight in the bar and the place had been wrecked. Ooh, people do like to gossip!

We bought a little village house in France, so tried to grab a few short breaks over there when we could. A trip departing on a Sunday from Stansted airport and returning Wednesday just in time to commence work at 6pm was ideal.

It was quite strange having breakfast in France and a few hours later being back at the Walnut working for the evening.

Our little trips didn't entail too much organising or lists to be pinned on the walls. We just had to make sure there was a staff member to oversee the business, cash the till and lock up.

Carcassonne airport, which is our nearest airport to land, is very small, with one plane in and one plane out at a time.

On one of our short breaks while sitting at Carcassonne airport ready to go home we saw our luggage go past and thought, Ha, our plane must be arriving soon. A little later the luggage returned back to where it had started. We were somewhat bemused, until we heard the announcement over the tanoy, the flight was cancelled – until Saturday!

Now we were in the shit, as everything at the pub was only organised until our return on the Wednesday. So there were no wages done, no ordering, and no staff to cover all our shifts.

We managed to book another flight from a different airport for the Friday. Our next priority was to ring the pub and tell them we wouldn't be home for another two days. 'Yeh right, bad joke, don't believe you, and will see you at 6pm.'

I have to say, it did take quite a bit of convincing to persuade them that we were actually stuck in France.

After a long phone call organising the wages, which of course the staff needed, saying what to order the next day, and calling on extra staff at short notice to come in and cover our shifts, everything was organised and nothing more could be done from our end.

So we opened a bottle of wine and made the most of our extra couple of days' break.

The staff were all brilliant in pulling together in the time of crisis, and worked as a team to make sure everything was run efficiently in our unforeseen absence.

Another time we were on holiday a customer in the pub was pissed and had fallen asleep on one of the bench seats; Neil, our chef came down from the restaurant and said, 'What's up with him over there?'

He walked over to wake the guy up, gave him a little shake of the arm, that was all that was needed, the guy fell on the floor. He wasn't asleep - he was dead.

The ambulance was called but, in the meantime, the bar girl on duty suggested that someone should maybe try and resuscitate him.

'Fuck that, I'm not putting my mouth near him, you don't know what he's got, where he's been, and what he has died from.'

The bar girl did however give him the kiss of life, but to no avail. I'm damn sure I wouldn't have tried to bring him back to life either.

When the ambulance arrived he was carried out of the pub on a stretcher. Apparently, he died of a drug overdose.

Neil, with his very dry sense of humour kept saying all evening, 'It's dead in here tonight, it feels like a morgue.' 'Anyone fancy a stiff one?'

After discreetly dimming the lights up and down, 'I think there are ghosts in the bar.'

Tim, our barman, had been in charge whilst we were on holiday and proved he was a super hero in our absence, so obviously couldn't wait to relay this story to us on our return.

All our pictures in the bar and restaurant were screwed securely to the wall to stop people attempting to steal them. Generally it had the desired effect, except for one picture which attracted attention from several customers who had previously tried to take it.

The picture in question was a concert ticket, signed by each member of the Beatles. However, not only is it a large magnified ticket, but a photocopy, worth absolutely nothing in value terms. If it had been an original then, yes, it would probably cost several hundred pounds to buy.

A couple of men in the bar obviously thought it was valuable so they inconspicuously managed to unscrew the picture then legged it up the road.

Tim, along with a customer, suddenly noticed what they had done, so immediately went in hot pursuit. The guys had ran as far as the market place, where Tim managed to catch one of the men and hand him over to the Police. Unfortunately, it was the guy who got away who still had the picture, but after a little gentle persuasion, the arrested man 'shopped' his mate and the stolen print was retrieved.

'How dare they try and nick something when I had been left in charge, no way was I coming back to the pub without the picture.'

Well done Tim.

****

YOU HAVE GOT TO BE KIDDING

Chris received a letter from The Hazel Grove Ladies Guild, in 1999.

'During a recent visit to Norwich I regrettably had cause to frequent your establishment to partake of lunch. I cannot state strongly enough how appalled I was by your dreadful behaviour towards the female staff. I witnessed constant touching and groping behaviour towards the female staff employed, who were quite clearly perturbed by your seedy actions.

I have been actively involved in women's groups for the past forty five years but have yet to witness the blatant and public humiliation you subject your staff to in your endeavours to satisfy your perverse habits.

Yours is a low class establishment patronised by low class clientele, I witnessed a drunk falling off his stool and your staff should not be exposed to such individuals or your degrading behaviour.

I will be returning to your establishment with a witness and then taking official action.'

We read the letter and laughed, it looked official, the comments were quite apt, but we knew it had to be a wind up from someone we knew – or was it?

Two months later a letter arrived from solicitors, with the reference heading: The Hazel Grove Ladies Guild.

'This practice has been commissioned to act on behalf of the above organisation in respect of allegations of sexual harassment against yourself toward members of female staff in your employ.

Section 26 of the Sex Discrimination Act 1991 require an employer to 'conduct his or her management of employees with reverence, fairness and decency as he or she would reasonably be expected to afford commissioners of goods or services tendered as part of the principal function of the business or organisation in which they are employed.'

Your individual behaviour has on occasions been in breach of the above legislation to an extent that we have been commissioned to commence court proceedings against you.

As required by law and as your right as a defendant you will be provided with the detailed evidence we intend to present prior to receiving a formal summons to appear.'

Again, a very official letter, and an excellent follow-on from the previous correspondence. The female staff employed at the time thought it was hilarious telling Chris he had better stop trying to undo their bras and to stop giving them a wedgy with their knickers whilst working, as you never knew if the Lady from the Womens Guild was in the bar just waiting for any opportunity to see his perverse behaviour.

Strangely enough, we never heard any more from the Hazel Womens Guild.

We received an official letter from Norwich City Council, Environmental Health Department, dated 9th Feb. 2000. It read:-

'Following a visit to your premises on Monday 7th February by one of my Inspectors, I would like to draw your attention to the following points:-

1 Your staff all looked rather grubby, a weekly wash would suffice.
2 There was a large male turd behind the door of the ladies WC.
3 The cellar door was so narrow that it would be very hard to get through if you had a hard-on at the time.
4 Toilet paper is not suitable to dry hands on in the Gents.
5 You continually scratched yourself during the visit.
6 A used tampon was located in your ice maker.
7 There were teeth marks in a block of cheddar cheese in the fridge.
8 The steaks in your freezer were dated August 1973.
9 A used condom was removed from the Hellmans Mayonnaise.

Kindly deal with the above as a matter of urgency.'

There was not a shadow of doubt this wasn't a wind up, mentioning our steaks were only 15 years out of date!!! Also this was confirmed when I noticed it was signed by the 'Invironmental Health Officer.' The culprit should have been more careful with the spelling.

When Lucy, our daughter, was 15-years old she went out socialising in Norwich on Friday and Saturday nights with her friends.

She came home one weekend to tell me she had met a guy and would be going on a date with him the following Friday. I was a reasonably liberal mother, but insisted on a few ground rules. I wanted to know who she was with, where she was going and always specified a time for her to be home. She informed me he lived in London during the week, and was over 40-years old. As you can imagine, I went ballistic. I knew if I banned her from seeing him she, like all teenagers, would see him anyway behind my back.

I kept quiet and never mentioned any more to her for the rest of the week about the forthcoming date; in fact I didn't even tell Chris what her plans were and who she was seeing, I knew what his reaction would be – far worse than mine.

Friday night came and Lucy started to get ready for the date. She tried on various outfits and asked my opinion as to which one she should wear. 'I don't care; you know I'm not happy about this, and I want you home by 11pm at the latest.'

'I'll bring him to the pub for a drink so you and Dad can meet him.'

'Don't bother; I don't think your Dad would be too impressed.'

She left soon afterwards, I felt sick in my stomach all evening just praying she wouldn't bring him to the pub, for the simple reason I still hadn't mentioned a word to Chris.

It was a busy evening with regular customers and several friends drinking in the pub.

About 11pm Chris and I were having a drink, chatting to his friends, when Chris spotted Lucy walking down the alleyway towards the pub with someone. They both walked into the pub hand in hand, gazing lovingly at each other.

Chris immediately went behind the bar – he was not happy; his facial expression revealed his anger.

Lucy began to introduce Winston to all our friends. Chris just glared as they were all shaking his hand and talking to him.

As soon as Chris and I were in close proximity, Lucy introduced Winston to us. He shook our hands saying how happy he was to meet us, and he had journeyed from London for the night to be with his little lady. He proceeded to put his arm adoringly round Lucy's shoulders and tried to prompt Chris into conversation by telling him he worked with computers and began talking about computerised tills. Chris was not interested, and couldn't even bring himself to speak to him.

Winston and Lucy sat down at a table, far too close to each other, passionately gazing into each other eyes. I could tell Chris was absolutely livid as he walked round the bar, aggressively putting the tables and chairs away.

This job was done at the end of every evening, but tonight the tables were being moved far more forcibly and belligerently than usual. Chris continued into the Gents toilet closely followed by one of our bar staff. 'What's up Gudge?'

'What's fucking up? Don't say a fucking word to me.'

Chris walked back behind the bar and noisily continued to put glasses away and chuck rubbish into the bins; in fact he took his aggression out on anything other than the boyfriend.

I just kept glancing at Lucy and the boyfriend in disbelief.

What did she see in him? He wasn't good looking; he was old, shorter than her and stocky in build.

Lucy announced she wanted to go with Winston to a club and would be home by 1am. 'You're not going, we are locking up soon so you will just have to say goodbye to him now.'

With that they both walked out of the door, and Lucy said she would be back in a few minutes. That left just our friends and bar staff in the pub.

Snowy, a good friend of ours was in the pub and reacted to Chris' obvious annoyance. 'You alright, Gudge. I see Lucy has a new boyfriend.'

'No, I'm not fucking alright, a new fucking boyfriend, I would rather have you for a fucking son-in-law.'

'Ah, Chris, that's the nicest thing you have ever said to me.'

Snowy walked away laughing.

Ten minutes later, the door swung open and in walked a laughing Winston and Lucy, 'April Fools.'

The whole escapade had been planned by Snowy. Winston, a friend of his, agreed to play a prank on Chris and had actually driven from London especially for the night's events.

It had previously been organised that Lucy would meet our friends in another pub, who would be with her the whole time. The escapade nearly backfired when Snowy began to get a little concerned that Lucy and Winston were getting on far too well – that wasn't part of the plan.

A great April Fool's prank; we fell for that one, hook line and sinker, and Winston was such a good sport for even considering taking part.

We shook hands, and were quite happy to pose for photographs and chat to him. Then I wanted to go and throttle our daughter for making me a nervous wreck the whole week.

****

THERE'S TROUBLE AHEAD

One Thursday night the live band were in the middle of their set, when a women on her own who had drunk a bit too much – no, far too much, was standing in front of the stage area being abusive to the band. Everyone is entitled to their opinion, but not loudly so that everyone can hear or enough to upset anybody else who is enjoying the music.

Chris quickly decided it was time for this woman to leave, so approached her with the notion of steering her towards the exit door. She was having none of it, and refused to leave. More gentle persuasion was needed, well, until she began fighting with the intention of trying to hit Chris.

She was swinging punches at him but, of course, he wouldn't retaliate as she was a woman. He managed to grasp her arm firmly and lead her outside the pub whilst she was still screaming and trying to fight.

He came back indoors and was immediately followed by the woman in hot pursuit, still yelling, and shouting. Again Chris managed to get her outside hoping this time she would leave the surrounding area.

No such luck, she continued to be a nuisance and kept coming in the pub door. Chris got her out twice more until he decided the best option would be to remain outside until she had completely gone.

He had to pin his body against the door so she couldn't try and get in again; then she proceeded to the other door and attempted to get in that one but, to no avail, as a customer was standing on guard duty to help Chris out.

She continued to swing her arms and fists with the intention of hitting Chris. He couldn't retaliate by hitting her, but when she tried to kick him in the groin, he stopped her by grabbing hold of her foot; unfortunately she fell to the ground, straight on her bum. 'Now will you fuck off?'

Eventually, after some more swearing and commotion, she decided she was getting nowhere with Chris, so staggered up the alleyway and disappeared round the corner.

Although the following incident wasn't related to the pub, we received a visit from the police asking for any information we had in connection with a tragedy which had occurred in Norwich.

The incident was published in the local paper, with the headline:

'MANS LAST HOUR IS STILL A MYSTERY.'

It went on to say,

'Big Issue Seller – murder victim's final hour is still a mystery to police – despite two weeks of extensive inquiries.

At least 12 officers working on the case have managed to figure out some of his movements the night he was brutally kicked to death, although are still unsure where he went after he left the Walnut Tree Shades at about 10pm.'

Unfortunately we were unable to assist with any information regarding this dreadful incident other than the guy had been in the pub on his own and nobody had noticed anything untoward.

In the 1960's the Walnut was renowned for its bad reputation of constant trouble. If someone wanted a fight or wished to cause one, he went there. This was a regular occurrence, especially at week-ends with fighting inside and outside the pub. The bad name and memories associated with the Walnut throughout the previous years of trading remained with many people, and some undesirable individuals occasionally still tried to come in when we took over the premises.

Chris had a reputation in his younger days for being a hard nut. Although he had never fought in the Walnut in the 60's, there were several occasions when he had been thrown out of pubs and clubs in Norwich for fighting, so his status, although superseded, was as the person not to cross. This proved very beneficial during the early days of taking over the pub.

Strangely enough, we were popular with the Norwich CID, and they spent many hours in our pub, on and off duty. If they were working (undercover!), they sometimes nipped in for a drink, but would stand facing the large mirror located at the end of the bar so they could watch who came in, and if it was someone known to them could inadvertently then observe him.

With the police using our establishment regularly this automatically stopped many unwanted people coming in, so they did us a huge favour and made life a lot easier in keeping the riff raff away.

Sporadically a few customers would comment on the fact, 'This pub would be alright if the fucking police weren't here all the time.'

Chris was very prompt in his reply, 'I'm quite happy with them being here, and you know what to do if you don't like it, fuck off'.

With our pub situated in the city centre, always packed with people drinking especially on Thursday, Friday and Saturday nights, it was inevitable there were going to be occasions when a fight occurred.

During the early days, there were several individually owned pubs in close proximity to us. Often people going out for the evening would begin by having a drink at one particular pub and then continue to another, on what was commonly known as the drinking circuit.

There were half a dozen popular establishments where people consumed a drink in each until closing time at 11pm, when people would finish off their evening by going onto a nightclub.

The Walnut could only hold a small number of people compared to many other pubs who encouraged large groups of people. We never liked to promote big parties, as a large noisy band of individuals would appear to take over the pub and upset our usual clientele.

Thursday evenings was renowned for hen and stag nights when girls would enter the pub adorned with balloons stuck to their clothes, feather boas strewn round their necks and antlers on their heads and then throw confetti everywhere.

The boys would come in with blown up condoms over their heads so they could hardly get in the door - sometimes dressed as women or school girls - order their drinks, try and consume the whole pint, then leave to go onto the next pub.

This would be fine, except the majority of time they didn't finish their drink, but tried to take it with them, which necessitated Chris having to run up the alleyway in hot pursuit in an attempt to retrieve the glass.

That's when trouble could start; people didn't seem to understand that glasses cost money. It was against the law to walk the streets drinking, let alone with our glasses which could reflect on our business if windows were broken.

'Come on boys, leave the glasses behind.'

Most of the time they swigged back their pints and handed the glass over. On other occasions they would be more obnoxious and continue walking or just throw the glass on the floor smashing it.

'Now what are going to fucking do about it?'

'You can give me a £1 to replace it,' replies Chris.

Sometimes this worked and they chucked some money at him. Other times, if there were too many of them, Chris thought it wasn't worth getting his head punched in for the sake of a couple of glasses, so would give up, tell them not to bother to come in anymore, and be grateful for retrieving the majority of the glasses.

If a crowd were leaving our pub who had been causing a nuisance and appeared as if they were looking for trouble, we would look to see which direction they were heading and telephone the pub in that proximity to warn them a group were heading their way, so they were forewarned.

They also did the same for us so Chris could immediately stand outside the door waiting for their arrival to inform them there were far too many of them, so they couldn't come in. It was far easier to stop them before they actually got their foot in the door.

In our 25 years at the pub we were very fortunate in only having half a dozen nasty fights compared to so many drinking establishments in Norwich who regularly had to restrain a fight every weekend.

There were often occasions when a customer may have had one too many drinks and started getting obnoxious, talking to other people in the bar, or just being a bloody nuisance, then it was time for them to be shown the exit door.

There were times people weren't in the slightest bit drunk but still a pain in the arse through just coming in to cause trouble.

It was important to constantly keep a watchful eye on all customers. To be alert to their behaviour and body language, and also aware that somebody just walking and accidentally bumping into somebody else can cause a potential problem if that person isn't very hospitable.

When we took over the pub, our first 'regulars' were four Scottish men who came in every lunchtime, sat on the stools at the bar and stayed for two or three hours drinking. They didn't cause any trouble, they didn't smell, they weren't scruffy – they just weren't very nice people and we didn't like them, especially after a few drinks when they got a bit louder and their strong accent made them even more difficult to understand.

So instead of banning them and causing any possible consequences, we decided to ignore them. If they were waiting to be served drinks we ignored them and would serve everybody else first. If they tried to uphold a conversation with us, we walked away.

After a few weeks of making them feel uneasy and definitely unwelcome at the Walnut, they got fed up having to wait such a long time for a drink, so eventually found another pub to drink in and that was the last we saw of them.

In the early days before we had the luxury of staff, Chris and I worked behind the bar. If people were being obnoxious it was always me who approached them, either to ask them to keep the noise down or ask them to leave. This proved a favourable judgment as the majority of men wouldn't attempt to hit a woman or retaliate as much as they would a man.

However, when a group of men came in one summer's evening they were not quite so obliging. I spotted them outside the pub standing in a circle with their drinks. As they finished, instead of putting the glasses down on a table they thought it a much better idea to smash them on the floor.

I took out a dustpan and brush and handed it to them, 'You dropped them, you can pick them up.'

The men surrounded me, 'You fucking pick them up yourself.'

I glanced round at the big, burly, loathsome men, and thought, 'Um, on reflection, maybe I will' so I bent down and picked up all the broken glass.

Walking back inside the bar, Chris said, 'Whatever were you thinking of, don't you know who they were.'

'No,' but he was about to tell me. They were a gang of lads who were renowned for causing trouble in the city, I'm glad I didn't argue with them because they wouldn't have had any hesitation in giving me a good hiding.

It is against the law to serve anybody intoxicated; the licensee also has the prerogative of refusing to serve any customer and doesn't have to give an explanation why.

Chris refused to serve many customers over the years, for either been drunk, loud, smelly, or he just didn't like the look of them. People who may have caused problems in the past were all banned. However, the problem we came across, they may have been banned from the pub, but a week or so later it was difficult to remember what that person even looked like, let alone their name, especially if they weren't particularly significant. So if they had come in the pub for a drink, we probably wouldn't even remember they were barred and serve them.

When people were banned they often asked how long they were banned for; Chris always had the same reply. 'As long as you are breathing.'

We had a couple of instances when people got upset if they were either banned or thrown out of the pub. In their anger whilst walking away from the pub, they would find something hard and big and chuck it through one of our windows, then run away. We were just so lucky the people sitting by the window didn't get hurt, just sprayed with fragments of glass.

This was an expensive inconvenience, as the window had to be boarded up for security reasons until it could be replaced by professional glass contractors the following day. To claim on our insurance policy was not feasible as by the time the excess was deducted we may as well have paid the total amount due.

A guy we nicknamed, 'Shaky' because there was a slight resemblance between him and Shaking Stevens, came in regularly for a drink. After a while he got to be a bloody nuisance; for no particular reason except he was in the pub and we didn't want him there, Chris banned him.

He must have lived locally as we often bumped into him in the street and each time, for several years, he would ask if he could come back to the pub.

'No.'

I was standing at a busy checkout desk in Tesco one day, when I heard a loud voice from Shaky who was standing in a queue about twenty feet away from me, 'Oye Jude, am I still banned from the pub?'

Everybody turned round and stared as I called back, 'Yes.' An embarrassing moment.

The guys from the local police station became good friends of ours and one day suggested to Chris it might be a good idea for him to learn Taekwondo as a means of self defence in cases of emergencies. There were often courses held at the station so on the next available date the police said Chris could go with them.

They picked him up one afternoon and left me to run the bar. There were several customers drinking and I was enjoying the afternoon, having a chat in between serving.

Mark, a guy we knew came in and was going to do some upholstery work on the bar seat covers for us. I was standing chatting to him while he was measuring the seats until another couple of men came in. I served their beer and a few moments later noticed them talking to Mark, but not in a particularly amicable way. Voices started to get somewhat raised but I couldn't make out what the problem was as they had only been in the pub about ten minutes.

Suddenly a large glass ashtray was grabbed from the bar by one of the men and swung onto the side of Mark's head; he immediately retaliated by trying to take a swing at the guy with his fist. However, the other one took out a bottle of ammonia and sprayed it in Mark's eyes, consequently temporarily blinding him.

I quickly dialled 999, requesting immediate assistance from the police; in the meantime all hell was breaking loose, there were glasses being smashed, another ashtray was chucked and punches thrown; I ran round the bar, screaming at them to stop and get out.

It's amazing in times of crisis how the adrenaline kicks in; there is no fear, just anger, and although my body is small in stature, the booming voice that exited from my mouth in attempting to diffuse the situation, was enough to scare a heavy weight champion.

The police quickly arrived and the two guys were arrested. Mark paid a visit to Accident and Emergency to get his head stitched and his eyes looked at.

I had nearly finished cleaning the glass debris and blood from the floor and bar counter when Chris and the CID arrived back from their self defence lesson.

'What the fuck's been going on here?'

Bloody typical, while my beloved husband was out with the police all afternoon I had to contend with the worst fight we had had to endure since taking over the pub.

We had a live band performing in the car park outside the pub; the place was packed, inside and out with people drinking, dancing and enjoying the hot summer evening.

Chris had gone outside to collect empty glasses which had been placed in every conceivable spot and was piling them on top of each other which resulted in having several stacks of glasses clutched to his body in both arms.

He headed towards the door, when he came face to face with Jack – another publican who was a very good friend of ours and could at times, be as grumpy as Chris, if that's possible.

Jack had been moaning about the band, and thought it a good idea to try and wind Chris up about the music.

'Don't fucking wind me up, you can see I'm busy.'

Jack raised his arm holding his bottle of Becks in readiness of pretending to pour it over Chris.

'Don't even fucking think about it.'

Chris was still clutching several stacks of glasses in both arms while Jack still had his arm raised to soak him. With that, Chris lifted his leg up and caught Jack right where his 'meat and two veg' were located.

Jack dropped to the floor clutching his groin in pain.

'I told you not to mess with me, fucking serve you right.'

After that, Chris went inside the pub still armed with the stacks of glasses.

The following morning, Interflora arrived with a delivery of flowers for Chris. A single red rose bearing the inscription, 'Love you lots, Jack.'

We were never renowned as a pub which attracted football supporters because we were situated at the opposite end of the city football stadium. In that respect we were fortunate in not having too many concerns on the days of football matches.

During the early years of trading, our usual regular customers came in for a drink before and after a match, but as our pub was located a little bit tucked away we missed the opposing team supporters.

We were always on our guard if Norwich were playing Ipswich at home, as they were two rival teams who didn't like each other, and would always be looking for an excuse to fight.

The only time we suffered a football related situation, was when Crystal Palace came to play Norwich. Unfortunately a crowd of their supporters found our pub. This resulted in the worst fight we ever encountered at the Walnut in all the years of being publicans.

One person wound somebody else up, and before we knew it, there were glasses thrown, ashtrays being hurled across the bar and fighting broke out.

Whereas we had always previously tried to diffuse a situation before it got out of hand, this instance was a case of ringing 999 for emergency assistance, clearing as many glasses and ashtrays as possible from the bar to avoid them being thrown or smashed, then just standing back to let them get on with it, as there were far too many people involved.

The police arrived just as the fight had disbanded – bloody typical.

We had to close for a short time to clear the floor of glass debris and thank our lucky stars nobody was seriously hurt.

We always had a good relationship with the HA (Hells Angels), and a few had been very good friends of ours for many years. The HA had subsidiary organisations in probably every city, and although we never had deep conversations regarding the HA, we knew we could count on their help if needed. Even when our daughter was young and began socialising in the city, we knew she could always call on them if necessary.

One or two would regularly drink in the pub, but on a few occasions, if they were having a get-together, we would hear the rumble of the bikes arrive outside the pub, and were consequently inundated with fifteen to twenty HA. Ok, so it was quite a large crowd of men, but we certainly weren't going to refuse them entry!

Their appearance and black leather attire did scare a few customers, and several often left swiftly. Saying that, they were generally far more polite and congenial than some men wearing suits, and most definitely would never, ever give us cause for concern.

There was however, just one time when a biker did behave unacceptably; he was standing at the bar with a pint of beer, then decided he would wee in his glass!

One Monday night, Chris was working by himself behind the bar, the restaurant was closed and no other staff members were on the premises.

It was a quiet evening with only half a dozen customers drinking at the bar when two guys from a rival 'gang', dressed in leathers came in and started to be obnoxious to Chris, telling him it was their patch and HA weren't allowed to come in.

Chris replied, 'I can allow in who I like, and it's not your pub, it's mine, so you can fuck off.'

Chris' comment: 'What I wanted to say, but decided against it was, 'What's HA; does it stand for Housing Association?'

They continued their abuse, shouting obscenities to Chris and then one of them pulled a cosh from his jacket and slammed it down onto the bar top.

Behind the cellar door, Chris kept a baseball bat (just in case), and this was nearing the time he may have possibly needed it for self defence. However, to get as far away as possible from being hit with a cosh, he stepped back against the closed cellar door – duh. So no hope of telling them to hang on a minute while he got the bat out from behind the door.

Fortunately for Chris, these were only scare tactics and they turned round and walked out of the door.

We had cause for apprehension one weekend evening. The bar was packed, and half a dozen bikers entered– we knew they weren't HA as the motif displayed on their jackets revealed it was another gang.

The atmosphere in the pub was suddenly subdued; there appeared to be an air of distaste because of their presence as they walked round the bar, seemingly looking for someone.

Chris decided it would be more favourable serving the bikers than refusing them a drink. It wasn't until he served all the drinks he realised there were four more bottles of drink ordered than the number of bikers present. A few minutes later he discovered why.

There were two bikers at each end of the alleyway on guard or watch duty.

Now we were worried and apprehensive as to what trouble would be encountered. We realised that they were on the hunt for their rivals who they thought were drinking in our pub – all I could say was, thank God they weren't and, luckily for us, they finished their drinks and left and so did their guards.

On a busy Saturday evening, four guys came in the bar and were on their second drink when one of the men thought it a good idea to try and stop the ceiling fan with his hand. Chris immediately told him to stop, but he paid no attention, and continued to lift his arm up to try and stop the fan working.

Chris walked round the other side of the bar and asked him to leave. He began to get very mouthy, at which point, Nick, a friend of ours who was drinking in the bar, had no hesitation in going to Chris' aid. As he went to apprehend him, the guy picked up a pint glass from the bar.

Chris went to grab the glass, but his hand slipped and his thumb went inside the glass and it broke, cutting the heel of Chris's hand.

Nick and Chris managed to get the guy outside, fortunately the others followed and that was the last we saw of them.

Chris' hand was bleeding quite badly, so he went behind the bar to get a tea towel and wrapped it round the wound tightly. He continued upstairs to the restaurant to get a plaster and asked one of the waitresses if she would put the band-aid on.

He took the tea towel off; the waitress nearly passed out when she saw Chris' thumb was literally hanging off his hand.

'I think you need a lot more than a plaster.'

We left the pub extremely quickly for a speedy ride to Accident and Emergency who said he would be seen quite promptly. Unfortunately, I had to leave him there whilst I went back to the pub to finish the evening's work and lock up.

As soon as all the customers and staff had left, I went straight back to the hospital to find Chris with the thickest, biggest bandage I had ever seen. They didn't apply any treatment to his hand other than wrapping it up and said he needed to be taken to another local hospital for an operation.

On arriving at the hospital, doctors told him they were unable to operate on his hand until the following day, but it was advisable to remain in hospital; Chris flatly refused and said he wanted to go home. They gave him strict instructions not to have anything more to eat or drink.

On arriving home, my darling husband paid no attention to the instructions he was given at the hospital, immediately lit up a cigarette and drank a cup of coffee.

A little later, he went upstairs with full intentions of going to bed; unfortunately he began to feel faint. Luckily he was beside the bed as he went a paler shade of white, then completely passed out, half on, half off the bed. I managed to get his heavy lump back onto the bed and immediately phoned 999 for an ambulance.

They turned up fairly quickly, by which time Chris had come round and was properly tucked up in bed. I wanted them to take him to hospital for the rest of the night, even though he didn't possess any pyjamas, but my pig-headed husband was stubborn and said he was going to stay at home in his own bed.

The paramedics were really helpful and said I could ring if I was concerned during the night, or if Chris took a turn for the worse.

I was so worried about him all night, I didn't get a wink of sleep, and Chris didn't get much either because everytime he started making a snorting noise I kept asking him if he was OK.

'Well I was, until you woke me up'.

It was a long intricate operation. They gave Chris the option of watching the procedure – he declined – not wanting to see his hand being put back together again and took the decision to just lie back, with a shot of morphine, listening to Jim Morrison and The Doors on the radio in the theatre.

After twenty internal stitches and about thirty external stitches, his thumb was put back where it belonged. A few days in hospital and a big bandage later he left, along with instructions he would be unable to work or use his hand for three months.

Our staff were all really helpful, and between us managed to cover Chris' bar shifts in his absence, although after spending a week at home on his own, Chris began to get stir crazy and fed up with his own company.

He decided that although he was unable to do any physical work in the bar, he was capable of chatting to customers. However after a few weeks of doing that, he started to drive the bar staff mad, moaning if they made a cocktail wrong, saying the beer wasn't been poured correctly, that the shelves needed stocking up, and just generally whinging about anything or anyone.

Eventually, the staff decided they couldn't take any more of grumpy, interfering Chris, so they wrote on a piece of paper, - 'Chris £10,' placed it in the till, took the money out, handed it to him and told him,

'Fuck off to another bar and have a drink.'

That worked, and got rid of him for a couple of hours.

It was a difficult few months for both of us, what with the extra work load I had to contend with, and for Chris, it was extremely frustrating being unable to drive, work and tolerate physiotherapy on a regular basis to enable movement in his thumb and strengthen the muscles.

Eventually Chris, the grumpy old git, was back working behind the bar and life was back to normal, although he did think twice about putting his thumb in a glass again.

The upside of that story, Chris received a cheque for £2,000 from the Criminal Injuries Board – although he would rather not have received the injury in the first place - all for some prat messing about with the fans.

Another particular incident involved a drunken woman being a nuisance to other customers, trying to obtain a free drink and dancing round the bar. Chris decided enough was enough and asked her to leave. She paid no attention and continued flinging her arms around in an attempt to dance.

Chris gently took hold of her arm and steered her towards the front door, she forcibly tried to resist by grabbing the door and keeping her feet firmly on the floor.

Chris managed to get her outside and closed the door behind her. She was having none of it and proceeded to enter by the other door, so again Chris got her outside and told her to clear off.

We thought she had gone for good until she suddenly appeared in the restaurant; she had walked out of the pub door, up the fire exit stairs, through the door, past the staff, and strode downstairs into the bar.

'You won't fucking give up will you?' said an annoyed Chris as he got hold of her arm, and this time chucked her out of the door, closing it sharply behind him. However, he wasn't quite quick enough to get to the other door as she got in yet again.

Not to be outdone, Chris locked one of the doors and stood by the other one until after much abuse, she left.

Under the terms of our licence for playing live music we were supposed to employ door staff. We never paid heed to this requirement; it was an expensive commodity we could ill afford, especially as we were already paying for a band to play.

The only time we employed someone to keep an eye on customers was the few days before Christmas. Then we used Nick, a friend of ours, who was first-rate in dealing with any potential problems which might arise.

He came to work dressed in his usual attire of jeans and jacket, didn't stand out as a bouncer and just wandered inside and outside the pub keeping an eye on everyone, taking the pressure from Chris so he could focus on serving customers during the demanding Christmas rush.

One Christmas Eve, Nick had been working at the pub all day and although it was the usual hectic session with customers drinking as much as possible and being very festive, there hadn't been a hint of trouble all day, so Nick left the pub around 4pm.

He had only been gone about twenty minutes when half a dozen guys came in with the deliberate intent of causing trouble.

They were drunk, loud, obnoxious and altogether, not very nice people, who were known in Norwich as troublemakers. When Chris asked them to leave, they started giving him verbal obscenities and took a swing at him after which a scuffle broke out.

A few months later, we took our very excited 14-year old daughter to the UEA to see the band Aswad. We had all been looking forward to the evening, but it all went horribly wrong as soon as we walked in the hall.

The place was packed, but the first people we caught sight of were the guys who had previously caused trouble in the pub. For the first part of the evening we stood inconspicuously in front of a speaker lodged in between two security guards, all the time watching to see where the troublemakers were.

We could see them, but fortunately, as yet they hadn't noticed us. We felt so uneasy as to any forthcoming consequences that were bound to occur, especially having our daughter present; we went home before the band had finished – much to Lucy's disapproval.

Chris was sitting on the bottom of the stairs which leads up to the restaurant having a few minutes break, when a big hefty guy came in the bar. He glanced round the pub until he spotted Chris then immediately approached him.

'Are you the gov'nor?, as you need someone on the door for football.'

'No I don't,' said Chris, still sitting down and making no attempt to get up.

'Yes you do.'

'No I don't, and if I do need any door staff, I employ people I know.'

'Fair enough' and fortunately, he left the pub.

A few days later, it came to light, a gang were running bouncers as a protection racket at various pubs in the city.

A week later they began drinking in the pub and became quite friendly towards us, and it soon became evident, if we did have any problems with customers; at least they would be on our side.

We knew Concord (named because of the size of his nose) and his family really well, and they all occasionally drank in the pub. Concord was often the cause of an altercation with customers especially after consuming too much alcohol. He head butted a few people, threw several punches, and consequently was chucked out by Chris on more than one occasion.

However, Concord always came in the next day, apologised, saying he wouldn't do it again.

Umm, well not until the next time.

Obviously over the course of 25 years there were a few little scuffles that paled into insignificance. With Chris always alert and aware of any raised voices between customers, he would promptly stop any impending problems before they led to further confrontations and tell them to continue their disagreement outside the pub; however I do think that we were extremely fortunate in only having a few really nasty fights in the pub.

****

HOW TO MAKE A

RUM RUNNER

*You will need to use your
kitchen blender for this cocktail*

*25ml Bacardi or dark Rum
25ml Crème de Banana
25ml Blackberry Liqueur
25ml Roses lime juice
splash grenadine*

*Put all the above in the blender with
enough ice to make a slush.*

*Serve in a goblet glass
Garnish with a wedge of lime and straw*

HOW TO MAKE A
MUDSLIDE

*25ml Vodka
25ml Kahlua
25ml Bailey's*

*Fill an 8oz glass with ice.
Pour in all the above.
Stir and enjoy.*

TOILET TALK

I don't like talking toilets but unfortunately toilet incidents are all part of running a pub. Some sections you may find revolting (they're not for the squeamish) so don't read - but I bet you will.

Vandalism of our property was also a problem we had to contend with. There were times when we arrived at work in the morning to find graffiti on the outside walls which had to be removed swiftly, otherwise one piece of artistic work soon multiplied to several. The same prognosis went for the toilets - when somebody wrote a piece of senseless rubbish on the walls, it had to be removed.

For some obscure reason, men seemed to enjoy the art of ripping the urinals or sink off the walls in the gents' toilets.

There was a separate toilet for men to have a poo, so why they shit on the floor instead of sitting on the toilet or rip the seat off was beyond me. However, Chris solved this problem by cutting the door in half so everybody could see under and over it.

This wasn't very popular with the majority of men who wanted privacy, but did prevent the idiots from causing unnecessary misdemeanours.

The ladies' toilets weren't much better; the women enjoyed ripping the wallpaper off the walls, littering the floor with the contents of the toilet roll holder, leaving used tampax in the corner of toilets, and if that wasn't bad enough, somebody pooed on top of the toilet seat for three weeks on the trot, and left finger marks where it had been rubbed in.

It must have been the same person doing this disgusting act, and watching women coming in the bar on the nights it was happening, it was impossible to think who, in their right mind, would do something so revolting.

Another time, someone either put a foot, or fist, in the side of the wall in one of the toilets and made a small hole. To rectify the damage would mean completely decorating the toilets, and as the hole was quite small Chris decided to abstain from repairing it.

Several weeks went by, the hole got bigger in width and length and deeper inside the wall, then a smell began to linger even after the toilets had been cleaned. The smell got increasingly worse until it was quite unbearable, and by now it was apparent which location the aroma was coming from.

A contemptible person had obviously had a poo, picked it up and put it in the hole, but done it very neatly as there was no evidence of poo from outside the hole.

Chris was thrilled at having to retrieve the smelly culprit; this time the wall was swiftly repaired.

While I am talking about poo, another revolting job Chris sometimes acquired was trying to clear the floaters in the toilet. The turds would be so big they refused to flush away so Chris had to chop them up to get rid of them.

I made two golden rules before we moved into the pub, I didn't mind doing any jobs required in running the business. I would scrub floors, clean, wash up – but, I would not, under any circumstances, clean the toilets.

I wouldn't even use a public toilet myself unless I was really desperate so I definitely wasn't going to clean them. My other golden rule was vomit. Even hearing somebody talking about sick makes me gag, so no way was I ever, ever, going to clean up after somebody was ill.

Poor Chris had to contend with all the grotty jobs of poo and wiggling his finger round the plug hole to get rid of remains of sick after somebody had thrown up, or they didn't make it to the loo and it was all over the floor.

Even typing this is making me want to gag!

I had to break my golden rule when Chris was away for the day. A customer came in one lunchtime who wasn't very well. She tried to reach the toilets but failed, and subsequently started being sick at one end of the bar continuing to the other end, leaving a trail of vomit on the floor as she rushed through, then completed her final exodus of sick all over the fruit machine.

Where was Chris when I needed him?

I asked all the staff if anyone would clear it up.

No such luck, they were all squeamish, so I had no option but to do it myself. Armed with a bucket, cloth, rubber gloves, mask, not even looking at the sick, trying not to breathe in the smell, - I did it, but gagged the whole time.

Another time someone was ill in the Gents' toilet, and Chris wasn't present to clean it up. Looking pitiful and with the offer of buying a customer a couple of pints of beer to help me out, worked wonders. Job done.

Toilets seem to be a favourite place for people to carry out sexual activities, Yuk, I don't even like having a wee in a public toilet, let alone sex.

Chris went in the gents' one day and saw a guy and girl having sex in the gents' toilet. (bearing in mind, with the door cut in half, they weren't enjoying much privacy)

'You alright in their mate?'

Just a short time later, they were sitting outside the pub with a drink and smoking a cigarette. Chris walked outside picking up glasses and saw the couple,

'It's always good to have a fag after sex isn't it?'

The poor girl blushed to the shade of a tomato.

A customer came out and told Chris there were two girls in the same toilet; clearly doing whatever it is that two lesbians do together, so he turned the lights out so they were in pitch darkness. After they had groped (excuse the pun) their way out of the darkened toilets into the bar they were greeted with a cheer, 'We know what you've been up to.'

Apart from having sex in the toilets, another major concern in any licensed premises is drugs. Whether it is drug dealing or drug taking, they are both serious offences and not something you wish your pub to be renowned for.

Obviously people don't 'skin up' or snort cocaine at the bar in full view of everybody, they are going to disappear into the toilets instead to partake of this activity.

A few people were caught red-handed and instantly shown the exit door but I wouldn't like to hazard a guess how many went undetected.

COURT CASES

The local press published an article regarding details of this court case, headed:
'Landlord says Man hit him.'
A man punched a pub landlord in the face after being accused of smoking cannabis in the bar, it was alleged yesterday. He appeared to be smoking a cannabis 'joint' as he stood at the bar of the Walnut Tree Shades pub in central Norwich, city's Crown Court was told.

The landlady of the pub, Jude Gudgin, said she asked the man to leave when she smelt the joint but he refused, saying it was a normal cigarette, and returned to his seat.

Her husband Christopher then went over to him and grabbed his wrist to get a closer look at the cigarette.

Mr. Gudgin said he was satisfied the cigarette contained an illegal substance and again asked the man to leave, saying he would call the police.

The man then hit him in the face with his right fist, cutting his forehead and causing his cheek to swell.

The man denies causing Mr. Gudgin actual bodily harm.

He told the court he was smoking a king size filter cigarette and showed the landlord. He asked for time to finish his drink before leaving.

Mr. Gudgin then grabbed him by the scruff of the neck, pulled him off his stool and pushed him towards the door, said the man.

He could not remember intentionally hitting Mr. Gudgin, but said it was possible he might have flung up his left arm.

Police witnesses said they noticed blood on the man's left sleeve and around his wristwatch. No cannabis was found on him when he was searched.

A verdict is expected today.

In court, Chris and I were both called to the dock to give evidence.

It was a terrifying experience, and after forty-five minutes of being questioned and cross examined we were the ones who felt like the criminals.

After hearing all the evidence, we would have to return to court for the verdict.

Published in the tabloid press under the heading:

'Man on harm charge cleared.'

'A man who was alleged to have punched a pub landlord in the face after being accused of smoking cannabis in the bar, was acquitted at Norwich Crown Court today.

He denied causing actual bodily harm.

As you can imagine, we were really pissed off with the verdict – so much for trying to be vigilant; and that's all I'm going to say on the matter.

Outside the pub were three plastic tables and 12 chairs to enable customers to enjoy alfresco dining or a drink. It wasn't the best view in the city, being tucked down an alleyway; there was a clear outlook of the car park and brick walls on the adjoining buildings. I tried to make it a bit more pleasing to the eye with flowered window boxes, but these were often used as ashtrays. However, the view didn't seem to perturb the customers, especially when the smoking ban came into force, as it gave them somewhere to sit and smoke.

This was the article published in the local paper with the heading: After fine for assaulting boy, landlord says: I'D DO IT AGAIN.

A Norwich landlord who was found guilty of assaulting an 11-year old boy he suspected of vandalising his pub said today he would do the same again.

Chris Gudgin, of the Walnut Tree Shades, was fined £1,000 by Norwich Magistrates and ordered to pay £100 compensation to the boy and £100 costs.

The boy's mum said her son had been traumatised and left too scared to go into Norwich after the attack.

She said he was left with a black eye and bruised cheek after Mr. Gudgin slapped him.

But Mr Gudgin who denied a charge of common assault at Norwich Magistrates Court on Monday, said he did not hit the boy.

He said he had suffered a week of vandalism and was sent over the edge when one of the tables outside the pub was knocked over.

Mr. Gudgin said: 'I got hold of the back of his clothes and warned him that if he did it again I would contact the police. But I never hit him.'

'I feel I have been fined for trying to protect my property; I admit I was angry at the time but I would probably do the same thing again.'

The boy was riding his bike down Castle Street when one of his friends accidentally knocked over a table.

Mr. Gudgin claimed the boys had knocked the table over deliberately and ran after them but the boy in question was the only one he caught hold of.

The boy's mother said her son was really upset by what happened, especially because it was the first time he had been in the city on his own. He thought everyone was kind, but he won't go into the city now.

She said her son had trouble sleeping and breathing after a spate of nosebleeds caused by the slap. She added: 'He has changed since it happened and I didn't want him growing up thinking there was no justice in the world. I was so angry when it happened and wanted this man to know that no one gets away with hitting my children.'

On the day of the alleged assault after Chris had gone home for a couple of hours later on in the afternoon, a policeman came to the pub requesting to see Chris regarding the incident with the child. The bar staff told him he would be returning at 6pm, so the officer said he would call back later.

The policeman didn't return, Chris forgot all about it, as it was such a minor episode and part of a day's inconsequential trials and tribulations in running a business.

The following Saturday, during the lunchtime session, Chris received a phone call from the police saying they would like him to attend the station to make a statement regarding the incident the previous week.

It took Chris a few moments to even recall what they were talking about. He replied by telling them he was busy at the moment, but if they came to the pub he would recollect the incident to them.

'No, we require you to come to the station as soon as possible as the statement needs to be recorded.'

He arrived there at 3pm, and was immediately arrested by the officer on duty; they read him his rights and took him down to a holding cell.

The policeman in charge of the cells knew Chris, 'What are you doing here Gudge?'

'What does it fucking look like? Evidently I've been arrested for alleged grievous bodily harm'.

At least the officer didn't lock Chris up inside the cell like a real criminal; he allowed him stay outside on a bench.

'I think you need a solicitor, would you like me to contact the acting solicitor on duty here, before you make a statement?'

So Chris waited, and waited, and waited for the solicitor to appear, time was slipping by, and he needed to be back at the pub by 6pm.

'So where's the solicitor? I've got a business to run and haven't got time to sit here all day.' Chris was not happy.

The solicitor never turned up as she got rushed to hospital with labour pains and was about to give birth.

The police let Chris out on bail and told him to come back on Tuesday morning to make a statement.

Over an anxious weekend and a few phone calls later, he kept thinking, 'I'm in the shit'

Chris made a statement at the police station with the facts of the alleged incident, which completely contradicted the story the 11-year old boy had related.

Chris was let out on bail again and told to report back to the station in two week's time.

Now we were concerned, this didn't look good; in the worst scenario, a publican can have his license seized if he has a criminal record

The first essential decision was to employ a solicitor who specialised in criminal law. We managed to obtain the best solicitor in Norwich, who was a friend of ours and would act on Chris' behalf. He said the outcome didn't look very promising. Chris was on bail for six months before a date was set for the court case.

Three weeks before the date of the court appearance, we were on holiday. The past few months had proved to be an extremely anxious and worrying time for both of us, so a short holiday was a good opportunity to try and relax and enjoy a stress-free break.

Whilst sitting on the beach, I read an inappropriate book under the circumstances, called 'The Jump', about a prison where inmates were killing each other and chopping their heads off! Chris asked if he could read it when I was finished. 'No, I don't think it's a very good idea.'

On our return we immediately rang the solicitor for the latest update before the court case.

'It doesn't look good Chris, you could be looking at a three-month jail sentence.'

Words cannot describe our feelings and emotions - anger, rage, upset, anxiety. Having to go through the past six months of apprehension about what the outcome might be, and the allegations which had been made out of a minor incident.

When the day of the court case arrived, I felt a nervous wreck, and Chris was really worried, obviously wondering whether he would be spending the next few months behind bars.

Chris stood in the dock at the Norwich Magistrates Court, and answered the questions fired at him by the prosecuting solicitor in a very professional manner.

He explained his version of the story, also mentioning he had previously suffered several weeks of vandalism, and yes he had been angry when it occurred yet again, but although he had grabbed hold of the boy's clothes, he most certainly never touched his face. Chris was eventually allowed to stand down from the dock.

The whole episode with solicitor's fees and costs cost us in the region of £3,000 for trying to protect our own property.

We were obviously hoping the press weren't aware of the court case so the whole episode could remain a low profile – wishful thinking.

The following day, published on all the fly sheets displayed outside newsagents,

'NORWICH LANDLORD FINED FOR COMMON ASSAULT.'

A journalist had interviewed Chris and asked him, 'If there was repeat of a similar incidence in the future, would you take the same course of action?'

To which Chris replied: 'Probably.' And not, 'I'd do it again.' which was the headline of the article printed in the newspaper.

We were obviously not happy at seeing the article spread across the front page of the paper, creating a vast amount of interest in Norwich but surprisingly, and very movingly, we received a huge amount of support amongst other business owners, our customers, and the general public.

We arrived at work the following evening to discover one of our regular customers had printed dozens of stickers which he displayed all round the bar, toilets, windows, in fact anywhere he could find a space, written with the words,

'Chris Gudgin is innocent.'

Chris also received telephone calls from the general public, even old-age pensioners, offering their condolences and remarking how disgusted they were with the outcome of the fine.

A letter was published in the local paper from a member of the public saying they sympathised with Mr. Gudgin who appeared to be the victim of the nineties' laws, relating to youths under the age of 16.

The letter went on to read:

'Here are a few points I find disturbing:

1. What are ten year old boys doing riding around Norwich unaccompanied by adults?

2. How is anybody allowed to ride a bike in Castle Street, where 'cycling prohibited signs' are clearly displayed?

I am from the same age group as Mr. Gudgin and when we were the same age as the boy we were certainly not let out of our parents' sight. If we were caught riding bikes in the city centre, knocking tables over, we would have been given the same treatment by a policeman as Mr. Gudgin gave this boy. We would have learnt our lesson and Mr. Gudgin would not have to resort to violence to protect his property.'

Another letter arrived to us in the mail from a lady who worked in a 24-hour service station, who felt compelled to write to us offering her complete approval and the utter disgrace of the fine, when we were only trying to protect our property.

She went onto mention the times she had been abused, had property vandalised, and been threatened by youngsters at work.

She ended her letter with the words;

'Thank you for your actions.'

Another local magazine also printed an article outlining the details of the court case and how Chris had received a fine of £1,000 for just grabbing hold of a boy.

The article went on to say:

'According to the press (via the boy's mother) the boy is 'mentally scarred,' and 'has lost his faith in adults' ……… what a load of proverbials. ….Had it been me and I told my mum, I would certainly have got little sympathy, and probably got a rollicking off me dad!'

The fact remains, however, that Chris Gudgin is out of pocket, has a criminal record, and received awful press coverage, just for trying to protect his property.

There, but for the grace of God, go many of us.

Even the brewery was sympathetic and donated a free keg of beer for us to sell as reparation for the outrageous court costs we had incurred.

The Licensed Victuallers members were always quite generous with their cash when they were out on a social evening, and purposely held a 'small gathering' at the pub to try and compensate for some of our loss.

For a few weeks we were excessively busy with additional customers coming in to offer support; even people we hadn't seen for some time were making the effort to come into the pub to be empathetic and buy a drink.

It was really touching to have support, especially after all the past months of worry and stress, and it was certainly an experience that Chris, especially, never wanted to replicate.

He just had to remember that next time kids were vandalising our property, he had to stand back and let them carry on.

****

A SECTION FROM OUR COCKTAIL LIST IN THE 1990's

TEST TUBE SHOOTERS

2.95

all served in a 50ml Test Tube (approx).

ANABOLIC STEROID Midori, Triple Sec, dash Blue Curacao
ANGRY FIJIAN Banana liqueur, Baileys, Malibu
B.52 Kahlua, Baileys, Grand Marnier
BITCHIN' Midori, Archers, Triple Sec
D.O.A. Frangelico, Archers, Cacao, Baileys
FOKKER FRIENDSHIP Cassis, Creme de Grand Marnier, Archers
KRAZY KAT Banana liqueur, Kahlua, Malibu
MELON BULLET Midori, Rum, Triple Sec
ORGASM Cointreau, Baileys
NUTTY RUSSIAN Frangelico, Vodka
TEST TUBE BABY Amaretto, Tequila, dash of Baileys.

BEER BY THE PITCHER

Pitch in with a 4 pint jug but only pay for 3½ pints of any draught Lagers or Bitters

Plus a selection of U.S. Premium and Continental Beers always available

PARTY PITCHERS

A one litre pitcher of these and you're anyones!
HARVEY WALLBANGER, FREDDY FUDPUCKER, PLANTERS PUNCH, APPLE KNOCKER, PINA COLADA, CHEE-CHEE
8.00

SANGRIA

Made to a traditional Norfolk recipe and served in a 1/2 litre jug
3.95

FLOWERS

When the bar opened in 1984, a flower arrangement was delivered every Monday morning and placed at the end of the bar counter.

If looked after and watered regularly, it generally kept for a week, that is, unless a customer began to interfere with the arrangement by pulling petals off the flowers. A petal or two was sometimes not enough for some culprits; they ate the whole flowers until all that was left were stems and a couple of leaves.

Eventually, I decided enough was enough and that was the end of putting nice seasonal flowers on the bar.

Outside the pub were half a dozen hanging baskets; sited on the first floor, well out of reach of potential vandals. They were only plastic but actually looked effective, and brightened up the dingy alley way.

We received through the post, a letter and application form to enter in the yearly flower event of Norwich and Bloom, a competition for all businesses in the city with a chance to win a trophy and subsequent publicity for presenting the best flower arrangements outside their premises.

Chris thought it a good idea at the time to enter the Walnut Tree into the competition, it didn't mention on the application form the flowers had to be fresh. So after filling it in and sending it off, we forgot all about it.

A few weeks later, it was a warm sunny evening, Chris decided to give the hanging baskets a drenching of water, as they were looking a bit dusty, and thought they needed a little livening up.

He had just finished and put the hose pipe away, when four very mature people stopped outside the pub, and looked up at the windows. With clipboards in hands, they started talking amongst themselves, periodically glancing upwards and looking very bemused.

Chris walked outside, and asked if he could help. One of the ladies said, 'Mm, you have caused us rather a problem; we are from 'Norwich In Bloom' and are judging all the plant and flower boxes in the area. We are looking at yours, and although you have obviously just watered them as they are still dripping quite considerably, they do appear to be plastic; no one has entered plastic plants before.'

Chris replied; 'Yes, but they do look good though, so what's the problem?'

The judges scribbled something on their clipboards then shuffled away. Needless to say, we didn't win anything.

We arrived at work one morning to discover two of our plastic hanging baskets had been stolen. It never ceases to amaze me that people can go out for an evening, walk along the road, look up, see some crappy looking hanging baskets containing plastic plants and then climb up the drainpipe to nick them.

If they were good quality flowering containers, I could possibly understand them being stolen for their own home - but these baskets – no, ridiculous.

I never got round to replacing them during the following week, which is just as well, because the following Monday, we discovered the rest of the hanging baskets were hitched on the railings outside the pub. Somebody, or more than one person, had climbed up the drainpipe, unhooked them all, but instead of stealing them, they left them behind but at a lower level.

They probably looked at them and decided they didn't want them after all!

Another time, we came into work on Monday morning to find one hanging basket on the pavement outside the pub, completely trashed. Looking up, the rest had disappeared.

To reach the baskets in the first place was a difficult task, needing a ladder to climb up the drainpipe or having mountain climbing skills.

Amazingly, all the baskets were retrieved; some were lying at one end of the alleyway, the others were in the opposite direction strewn on the ground.

The following spring I decided to make some window boxes with fresh flowers to place outside the pub windows behind the grates, and hoped they wouldn't get stolen or vandalised.

The best place to buy plants was at the auction in Aylsham. They were cheaper than the garden centres and good quality. As I needed enough plants to fill six window boxes, price was an issue. Unfortunately after spending the morning buying and filling the car with numerous plants, I managed to get a speeding fine on the way home. My cheap plants proved to be extremely expensive.

While I'm on the subject of speeding fines, I actually accumulated two in that same week – on the same camera. But then Chris got caught, and so did Lucy, all on the same damn camera during the course of the same damn month.

The colourful window boxes were very successful and I was quite pleased with my horticultural expertise, so I continued creating both summer and winter displays.

Amazingly, in all the years they were positioned outside the pub, they never came to much harm. Occasionally we found a glass amongst the plants, several cigarette butts, or an odd plant may have been pulled out, which was quickly shoved back in again. Watered with left over beer, they seemed to thrive.

At 8am on a Sunday morning, (an unearthly hour when we didn't go to bed until about 2am), the phone rang, Chris reluctantly got out of bed to answer it, 'Sorry to disturb you, it's the police here, but there is nothing to worry about.'

'So why are you ringing me then?' replied Chris.

You have some broken windows at the pub. We already have an officer at the scene, so if you could come and attend to getting the windows boarded up, we will meet you down there.

'Fucking great,' said Chris as he grumpily dressed and started banging about,

'That's all I fucking need at this time of day, and on a Sunday.'

I kept quiet and snuggled back down in bed, as he left slamming the door behind him.

Twenty minutes later my phone rang,

'You're not going to be happy Jude, there are two windows broken, they attempted to break three, but the plant box wouldn't go through the third window. The first window is smashed with a window box laying half in and half out of the pub. At the last window, they managed to throw the plants and pot completely inside the pub, so we now have an indoor garden. There are plants and earth all over the bar floor, and all the plants have been completely trashed.'

He was dead right – I wasn't happy.

The only consolation, from our point of view, was the vandal who did the damage managed to cut himself badly. There was blood on the broken glass, a pool of blood on the floor and a trail of blood all the way up the road, round the corner, up another road, round a bend and up a hill.

The police took DNA from the blood, but in the meantime someone rang to tell us he had the name of the culprit as he had overheard him in a pub bragging about the incident.

We forwarded the name to the police, who were still waiting for the DNA results to come back from the lab. With those obtained, he was subsequently arrested.

We were quicker than the police in solving a crime!

His excuse for doing this damage was that Chris had allegedly tried to run him over on the Saturday night in his car. With Chris' driving, I wouldn't have been surprised, but, at the time this alleged incident was supposed to have occurred, we were both at home drinking a cup of coffee.

The guy was off work for nine weeks with his injury – Aah! Shame!

His court appearance resulted in him receiving 80 hours community service and £200 compensation to us for the excess on our insurance claim.

It took three years before we began to receive the £200 compensation at £10 per week.

The speed at which we found the criminal and solved the crime, obviously impressed the police, as we received a phone call from the detective, saying they were having problems tracing some gnomes which had been stolen from a garden, and could we help!

****

TRY AND MAKE THESE COCKTAILS

SEX ON THE BEACH
now don't be rude - it's a drink!

> 25ml Vodka
> 25ml Peach Schnapps
> 25ml Pineapple juice
> 25ml Cranberry juice
>
> Use your 'new' cocktail shaker
> Put all the above ingredients in the
> shaker with enough ice that will fill
> an 8oz glass.
> Now you must shake and shake and shake.
> Pour it all into the glass

HOW TO MAKE A

MARGARITA

> 25ml Tequila
> 25ml Triple Sec or Cointreau
> 25ml lime juice
>
> Put ice in the shaker along with all the above ingredients.
> Shake and shake and shake.
> Get a margarita glass or something similar.
> Rub a lime slice around the outside rim of the glass
> and dip in salt.
> Now strain into glass.
> Garnish with a wedge of lime.
> Or
> If you prefer you can have it on the rocks

GUN SIEGE

Chris had left home to arrive at the pub for 6pm. He drove into Castle Street sited next to the Walnut to be confronted by police cordoning off each end of the road with masked tape, and numerous strategically parked police cars.

'What's going on? I need to drive past to get into work'.

'Sorry sir, you can't come through here. We have a situation at the pub and the road has been closed.' replied the policeman.

'But it's my pub; I'm the landlord, you'd better let me through.'

By the time he had parked the car, the SWAT team were already in the alleyway. Two men had their arms and legs spread-eagled on the ground, with guns being held to their heads and body and surrounded by half a dozen SWAT team members, all armed with extremely menacing rifles.

Chris walked into the pub quickly, to see customers and staff all looking out of the window at the events happening outside.

Lucy, our barmaid (not our daughter Lucy) was working that relatively quiet afternoon shift.

She had noticed two men in their early 20's sitting in the corner of the bar, deep in conversation and fiddling with a couple of objects on the table, which at this point, didn't give her any cause for concern and she thought no more about it.

She had been talking to another member of my staff, Chris W. who had come in for a drink on his day off, when she glanced over to the table where the lads were sitting and saw what she thought was a gun.

Lucy was a bit of a worrier and panicked at the best of times, so seeing a gun horrified her. Terrified, she whispered to Chris W. what she thought she had seen. He used to be a police officer and so was experienced in dealing with a possible difficult situation. He moved his seat round, still remaining inconspicuous; to catch a better view of what, if anything was going on at the table.

Yes, - they now had two guns on the table, were intently looking at them, turning them round, inspecting them in great detail, and putting their fingers in the trigger point.

Not wanting to cause any alarm to them, or panic anybody else, he moved away and out of earshot to call the police, and relay the situation.

They instructed Chris and Lucy to stay calm, not to alert any customers and, most importantly, not to disturb the two men with the guns; they would be sending undercover police down immediately.

Within minutes a couple of plain clothes police officers walked into the pub. The two guys had already put their weapons in a bag and were just leaving the premises from the other door.

The SWAT team were already waiting in the alleyway. The guys were immediately pounced on, and were laying handcuffed on the ground, when Chris arrived.

Front page headlines in the local paper the following day along with pictures displayed: CITY STREET IN GUN ALERT.

'Uniformed officers, CID and armed police were called to the Walnut Tree Shades.

The area was sealed off; two men were challenged by officers and were subsequently arrested after leaving the pub just before 6pm.

Two imitation firearms were seized.

No-one was injured in the incident. The two men will be interviewed by police today.'

The two lads were from the Art College and had bought two paint guns for projects they were involved in. They were trying to work out the instructions for loading the paint into the guns and how they subsequently worked, never realising the consequences of their innocent actions.

This caused a big debate in the media afterwards, demanding that imitation guns should be banned from shops because of the consequences that could arise, and the possibility of innocent people being shot.

Had those guys pulled out the guns from the bag when they walked out of the pub, there is a very strong likelihood they could have been shot. - SWAT men do not miss.

****

ENVIRONMENTAL HEALTH

Environmental Health Officers are employed by the Council to inspect all food and catering establishments which sell food to the public. They have the power to close an establishment down immediately if the standards are not up to health and hygiene regulations set by government law.

When they enter a business it is usually unannounced without having first made an appointment. They walk in, introduce themselves as the Environmental Health Officers and show their card by way of proof of identity, announcing they are here to inspect your premises.

In our early days they generally appeared every six to twelve months; although we were always vigilant in our cleaning regime, they never seemed to be fully satisfied. We never saw the same officer twice, and each one seemed to have different ideas as to what was acceptable.

On one visit they told us eggs should be kept in the fridge, six months later the next officer told us not to refrigerate them.

Another time they said food should be chilled at less than 8° then at a later date it was 4° or 5° at best practise (a technical term).

Nail brushes must be by the sink. Later they were classed as being unhygienic.

Regulations and systems were always changing, and we had to abide, whether we agreed or not with their rules.

The best way to deal with the EHO was with the utmost courtesy; disagreeing with their suggestions and recommendations was definitely inadvisable. It was much easier to agree with everything they said and promise to immediately rectify any problems they found - which of course we did.

If they found major faults in the premises, the usual action would be a warning to make improvements. A letter would be sent, stating each item in detail they weren't happy with. It made a 'suggestion', which when translated, meant you were not legally bound to rectify the fault, but they would prefer it if you did.

The letter may have 'recommendations', meaning it was advisable the grievance pointed out was improved before the next visit from an officer.

The worst letter from them was an 'Enforcement Notice' stating if work was not carried out by a specific date, action would be taken in the manner of a fine and possible court appearance and finally closure of business if the problems were not resolved - I hasten to add that this never happened to us.

If that scenario happened, it nearly always made headlines in the local paper - and bad publicity is something no business wants to receive.

We always had a plan of action ready when the EHO descended on us. They were greeted with a big smile and a look that tried to display how pleased we were to see them – although inside it was a feeling of dread, churning tummy and fear and thinking, 'Oh shit, what are they going to tell us we are doing wrong this time?'

Whilst they were removing their outer coat or jacket, undoing their big black holdall bag, putting on a protective hat, a white coat and latex gloves in preparation for inspection, the bar person rushed upstairs to the restaurant to warn the staff,

'Environmental are downstairs.'

'Shit, shit, quick everyone, you know what to do.'

The large bins used in various positions for food waste never had a lid on, for the simple reason it was so much easier and quicker to chuck the food straight in the bin, rather than messing about manoeuvring a lid, which was, in my opinion, unhygienic. However, we did keep the lids in a cupboard all ready for emergencies – this was one.

That was until the last visit we received. She noticed the bins with their lid perched precariously on top, and then proceeded to tell me it was no longer necessary to put lids on during service as it was unhygienic.

I smiled, 'Ooh, the chefs will be pleased, as they find it really annoying with the lids on all the time.'

I certainly wasn't going to tell them the truth that the dusty lids had only been on there for about three minutes.

If there was time before the EHO descended in the restaurant, we had a quick double check in the fridge to make sure all food items were stored on the correct shelves, dairy produce at the top, cooked meats, then raw meat at the bottom.

Every tub of food had to display a sticker showing the date it was either made or bought in and the use-by date.

Checks were made to ensure that every tub and container was covered in the fridge with either a lid or tin foil.

There had to be soap by the sinks.

Spray sanitizers had to be by the work surfaces.

Checks were made that all the temperature and log sheets were filled in.

Chef had to have a hat and apron on.

The ashtray and staff cigarettes had to be hidden.

With the EHO downstairs, and about to ascend on me in the restaurant, I always got a bit panicky and paranoid, although ninety nine per cent of the time, food items were dated and covered, the temperature sheets were all filled in; there was soap, but you could bet there would be something not done correctly.

Obviously during our 25-years we had many visits from the EHO. When we first opened the restaurant they came every six months, as they did with most new operators in the industry.

But, as the years progressed, the inspections were less frequent until there was only an annual visit, then it was about every eighteen months, then two years lapsed without seeing anybody.

We were obviously maintaining a good level of health and hygiene for the visits from them to be rare.

The Environmental Health department is an essential commodity and I am in total agreement with the work they carry out in establishments. There are far too many premises that do not achieve hygienic working environment, and these should be clamped down on.

EHO has a job to do which entails helping the employer maintain the correct procedure in their business, thus benefiting the public and avoiding any problems which may occur.

They made many suggestions and observations to us over the years, some were useful, however, some were a little daft.

They noticed a patch of what they thought was grease outside on the fire escape, just beside the empty frying oil containers.

'Is that grease on the floor? It's a hazard and needs to be cleaned immediately before an accident occurs.'

Trying desperately to keep a straight face and without smiling, 'No, it's water, look it's raining.'

In the dry store area, the officer found an 8inch diameter round empty hole, which originally had a small extractor fan in before it broke, and was then removed. Positioned just below the ceiling, the hole went through the wall into the washing-up room.

'You should block that hole up because vermin could run up the wall and through the hole into the next room.'

'Yes of course we will get that done.'

But under our breaths thinking, 'Why would rats run up the wall to get to the other side, when all they had to do was travel along the floor and round the corner for a couple of feet?'

The electric fly trap located in the kitchen had a container at the bottom to catch the dead flies.

The EHO remarked on one of their visits; 'There are two dead flies in here.'

'Yes, but that's what the container is for – that's where the dead flies drop into.'

'Well just make sure you clean it out regularly.'

'Of course we will.'

If there had been fifty dead flies in the trap, then I could understand her point – but just two.

They suggested the fly trap be moved from the kitchen where it had been positioned for the past 23 years to the wall on the walkthrough from the preparation area towards the washing up room.

Two slight problems with that suggestion,

1. There wasn't a power point to plug it into, but yes, one could be put in.

2. The fly trap would be protruding from the wall, a hazard for anybody walking past from the restaurant which consequently could possibly cause an accident.

'The inside of the microwave has some dirty food stains; the floor has a few crumbs and a couple of bits of food debris which should be removed immediately.'

'But it is 1.30pm, in the middle of a busy lunchtime session, and at the end of service everything will be cleaned down and the kitchen left spotless.'

The only time a commercial kitchen can be pristine clean is when it is shut.

They suggested we stripped the whole kitchen, removed the tiles then sheet all the walls with stainless steel, making it far easier to maintain the cleaning regime.

Yes, I totally agree if we had a bottomless pit filled with money, unfortunately, that was not the case so the tiles would have to remain.

They would check the shelves in the bar were clean, running their white glove along it to see if they retrieved any dust, suggest stainless steel shelves would be easier to clean as opposed to our wooden ones.

Chris would try and politely (difficult for him) point out that the whole of the back bar was the original from the early 1900's and it would be sacrilege to replace it with stainless steel.

Chris would stand over the hole in the floor behind the bar where the wood was beginning to rot, so the EHO didn't detect it.

This was a job we were going to rectify and new flooring laid – but not yet. When it was a hazard that someone could possibly fall through – then the job would be done.

'The toilets could benefit from redecoration.'

'Actually this job is already in the pipeline and the decorator will be commencing work here shortly.'

As the years went by and the visits from EHO were very rare, the regulations and system began to change from the early days when their main priority was inspecting the cleanliness of the premises. Now the administration for maintaining records regarding health and hygiene was equally as important.

We ended up with so many lists on the walls; the whole place was adorned with them, and there was barely any necessity to redecorate because there was hardly any paintwork showing.

There was a list by every fridge and freezer which had to be filled in and signed twice a day with the temperature of the equipment.

Cleaning rota lists were in the kitchen, prep area and washing up room which were filled in when each job had been completed.

There was a list to mark down the temperature of the cooked food before it was served.

A delivery list had to be signed when frozen goods were received, after having checked the quality and the temperature of each item.

Then there were all the notices strewn on the wall displaying Health and Safety in the workplace, fire regulations, colour coding for food storage, chemical lists, and any other sheet of information necessary to display.

Every business had to carry out 'Risk Assessments' involving looking at the entire company and establishing where the hazards were, how to control them, and what procedure you would put in place.

This had to be written in great detail and ranged from the dry goods, chilled and frozen foods in the restaurant, from delivery, checking the temperatures, storing correctly, defrosting instructions, preparation, cooking, reheating to serving. Looking at hazards from cross contamination and pest control to waste disposal.

The bar also had to be assessed by looking at all the risks to staff and customers, from picking up glasses, how to stand when pouring beer, to tripping over a step or slipping on the floor.

When the 'Risk Assessment' came into force, many companies were jumping on the band wagon, offering to carry out the assessment for you, at a cost of around £500 for the bar and restaurant. The phone was constantly ringing with companies trying to persuade you it was necessary to have it done professionally.

For that cost, I thought – no way, I'm not stupid, I will do it myself.

Which I did, although it took me about three solid weeks' work to complete.

If a customer requested a rare burger, (by law, all burgers had to be cooked to a temperature of no less than 70° for two minutes or 75° instant heat), they had to sign a disclaimer letter relinquishing us of any responsibility if they went down with food poisoning. It was very embarrassing handing out this letter to customers and seeing the expression on their faces of disbelief, however rules were rules and we had to abide.

Chris had been eating rare burgers for the past thirty years or so and never been ill once so I don't think there would ever be a problem with our quality burgers.

The council started a scheme in 2006 for businesses in the catering industry called 'Safer Food, Better Business.' Premises were inspected, then awarded stars, ranging from nil to five stars. The findings and comments from the EHO would be published on the internet, so any member of the public could look and see if they would be happy to eat in a particular eating establishment. An excellent idea and ensuring establishments kept high standards.

The council sent out large manuals with instructions for owners and managers detailing all the new requirements. They were running courses every month at the City Hall on how to fill in the information. The Council telephoned me to attend the course;

'I'm very sorry, but I'm on holiday, I will attend the next one.'

However, the next one was in December when I was far too busy in the restaurant with Christmas bookings. So I apologised profusely and said I would definitely be there for the next course.

Or maybe not, because I put the next one off as well and made a feeble excuse as to why I was unable to attend.

My life was busy enough running a business and anyway it wasn't rocket science to understand. I had already filled in the book, trained the staff, taken on board the extra administration – job done.

Strangely, I didn't get any more phone calls asking me to attend a course, so I thought they had either forgotten or given up on me.

The manual contained various sections on hygiene, cleaning, preparation, fire safety procedures and staff details and each one had to be filled in, in great detail.

This felt unnecessary extra work as far as I was concerned, as every staff member who commences employment with me is trained to my exacting demands in all the above areas anyway.

So after spending time with each member of staff and reciprocating the same basic training, they all had to sign a letter that they fully understood the working routine and what was expected of them.

We already had, a 'Fire Risk Assessment Book' which I composed years previously, displaying in great detail: the risk of fire, where all the fire extinguishers were kept, how to use them, and graphic fire safety notices on the wall and instructions for emergencies – but again this all had to be entered in the manual.

There was a managers' section showing all the different elements of training I had done with the staff. There was a page for each employee which had to be filled in, stating when they commenced work, what their job entailed, the date they had been trained and when they would need a refresher course.

I already had all this information filed for each staff member, so this was another job which had to be duplicated.

Extra administration entailed filling in a Daily Diary of the day's events; any problems that may have occurred during the day written down and how the situation was resolved. So for example: If the fridge broke down, what procedure would we take?

We phoned the engineer, he came and fixed it. Job done

Then there was a monthly summary to incorporate the previous four weeks' happenings, along with a comments' area for anything that hadn't been resolved satisfactorily during the past seven days.

What happened to the days when EHO visited premises with the sole intention of checking the cleanliness of eating establishments and if they were contravening the health and hygiene regulations and standards? Now it appeared that their work-load had increased as much as ours by having to spend time going through the manuals to check that procedures and systems were in place and kept up to date, as well as having to inspect the cleanliness in the restaurant and bar; this was certainly proved to me in the last visit we ever received in 2007 before we sold the pub.

The EHO entered the pub at about 11.30am, and for once her visit was at a convenient time. The restaurant wasn't open for another fifteen minutes, everywhere was pristine so I had absolutely no worries or concerns she would find anything untoward.

She introduced herself, so while the bar staff kept her talking downstairs we did our usual quick double check in the restaurant. However, she wasn't interested in staying downstairs in the bar; she asked to see me.

Greeting her with a big smile and offering her a cup of coffee she sat down at a table in the restaurant.

Looking extremely sullen, she explained in no uncertain terms the reason for her visit.

She had received verification from the council I had not attended the course for the manual on 'Safer Food, Better Business,' which was compulsory, and she would be interested to see the system I had put in place.

I collected all the Risk Assessment Books, the manual, the charts, the logging sheets, and plonked it all down on the table in front of her.

'I'm so sorry I wasn't able to attend the course, but I have enforced the new system,' I said, smiling through gritted teeth.

'But how have you managed to do it without attending the course? I think I need to look closely at what you have done.'

Smiling sweetly, 'I do hope I have done everything right.'

She began by opening the training pages, scrutinising every one, then commented on how well I had filled in all the staff details. She then gradually inspected the rest of the manual, page by page, along with all the logging sheets and finally, she was smiling and suitably impressed.

She spent two hours in our restaurant, one hour, forty five minutes of that time was inspecting the paperwork and checking everything was satisfactory.

I was commended on the professionalism of doing the manual and my management skills; she agreed there was no need for me to go on the course after all. Hurrah.

After a lengthy interrogation regarding all aspects of health and hygiene, forms and more forms, and giving me a splitting headache, she put on her white coat, protective hat and gloves and went into the kitchen for what I thought was going to be a thorough inspection of every nook and cranny, and piece of equipment.

No – she spent less than fifteen minutes glancing round the kitchen, opened the fridge and freezer door, asked Daren the chef what he was cooking and how long had he worked for us, and that was that - wow, our kitchen must have been spotless.

We received four stars out of a possible five, and the only reason we didn't get five was because I didn't go on a course.

We were also dispatched a certificate to frame on the wall to display our stars to show the world what good operators of a business we were.

****

Congratulations to

Chris Gudgin - The Walnut Tree Shades

'The Best Bar Person'

Going Out Awards 2007

…representing The Best of the Best
in the Licensed Trade in Norwich & Norfolk

Craig McLaren
on behalf of the
NN LVA

Sophie Harrison
on behalf of the
Evening News

– the best of the best –

FINALIST

Congratulations to

The Walnut Tree Shades

The Best Bar

Going Out Awards 2007

…representing The Best of the Best
in the Licensed Trade in Norwich & Norfolk

Craig McLaren
on behalf of the
NN LVA

Sophie Harrison
on behalf of the
Evening News

– the best of the best –

in association with

Carlsberg

FURRY FRIENDS

The saga of Roland began one Thursday night. A live music band were about to play in the pub when it was discovered the P.A. system wasn't working adequately. Unable to resolve the situation that evening, the band still continued to play – although not very well as they were without any proper sound.

The electrician came the next day; he pulled the floor boards up and discovered some little teeth marks; some wires had been eaten.

'Oh shit, we've got mice.'

This is something you don't particularly want advertised to the general public when you are trying operate a restaurant. Chris rushed out and bought several mousetraps and poison.

Several days past, - nothing. Maybe they had packed their bags and gone.

The following week, the neon light tube in the kitchen broke - no problem, that could soon be replaced. However the new tube didn't work either.

OK. Lets ring Les the electrician again. He was there within the hour and pulled the wires down, and yes, they'd been eaten.

This time we didn't say,

'Oh shit'

We said,

'Oh fuck, they are still in the restaurant after all.'

All you can imagine is having a restaurant full of customers, when in runs the mouse or mice.

I can fanny my way out of a lot of things, but how would I talk my way out of that scenario?

Should I grab the remote control for the air conditioner, point it at the mouse and pretend it's a toy remote one, and haven't got the hang of using the controls yet?

Should I pretend it's our pet mouse escaped from his cage, then run after it up the restaurant, shouting, 'Come here Molly Mouse, you're not allowed down here, now get back to your cage?'

No, I think the best idea would be to run and hide.

The next morning, Nick the chef asked, 'Did you poke the ceiling near the fire exit door last night, because there was a little pile of dust on the floor when I arrived this morning?'

'No, oh shit, you know what that means?'

The following morning, not only was there a large pile of dust on the floor, but a big hole in the ceiling with teeth marks round the edge, along with bits of bread all over the kitchen floor.

Our little friend had got in the bread basket and had a tea party.

Right, first thing, off to the shops for more poison and traps. We'll get the little bastard.

That night, the traps were laid, the poison down and talc strewn over the floor so we could see where the footprints went.

Next morning, - nothing.

Following morning - nothing.

'Has he gone? Or maybe he is still stuffed with all the bread he consumed.'

Next morning, Nick arrived for work. A left over baked potato was on the floor, half eaten, and showing big teeth marks. Last night we forgot to put talc on the floor, so now we didn't know where he or his family lived.

After clearing up the mess, Nick began to clean the extraction hood. He had just taken all the metal spoons off the hooks making a fair amount of noise, when from under the oven, which is inches away from where he was standing, ran Roland our furry friend.

Nick rang us at home, 'I've just seen him, he's fucking huge, but he ran downstairs to the bar so I've shut the restaurant door so he can't get back in. I've gone all goose-pimply; he's massive, and it's not a fucking mouse, it's a big mother fucker rat. But now the rat's gone in the bar, the cleaner won't go down there anymore.'

'OK Nick, calm down, we're on our way.'

It was time to get in the man from the Pest Control.

He arrived with several rat size traps and big bowls of poison that were placed strategically all round the building in prominent places.

Another week went by and nothing.

Chris looked under the icemaker in the bar one lunchtime, as there appeared to be a smell wafting in that area. The bowl of poison under there was empty but he couldn't spot any bodies.

Great, he must have run off somewhere and died, that's why we haven't seen him.

Chris left for home; he'd only been indoors about ten minutes when Ali, our bar girl rang up,

'I've found Roland, he's by the icemaker, he's fucking huge.'

'Where are you now?'

'Down the fucking cellar'

'Well, is he dead?'

'I think so' said Ali,

'He's lying on his back with his feet in the air, but his eyes are wide open. I'll go and have another peek, keep on the phone.'

There was an almighty scream, she had caught sight of her own reflection on the icemaker door and thought it was the rat moving. She jumped in the air, making the customers in the pub wonder what the hell she was doing, but obviously couldn't tell anyone, so pretended she was dancing to the music.

'Don't touch it, I'll remove it when I get in at 6pm,' said Chris.

Poor Ali had to work for the next two hours with Roland the Rat seemingly winking at her throughout the afternoon.

When Chris discreetly removed it into the bin on his arrival at the pub, the staff were right, yes - it was fucking huge.

And that was the end of Roland.

After the episode of Roland the rat, we had no more repeat episodes of four legged furry animals obtaining free board and lodgings at the pub for several years, that was until the marketplace was being refurbished and disturbed the rats nests .

One Thursday evening, the band were preparing to play, and Chris was having problems with the CD player; it didn't seem to be working properly.

One of the speakers wasn't on, and attempts to change the music so the band amplifiers would work through our speakers just didn't seem to work. Eventually, after plenty of swearing from Chris, he managed to sort out most of the speakers so the show could go on.

The next morning Chris pulled all the stereo system out from the shelves to try and rectify the previous night's problems with the music, only to discover the wires had been eaten; a palpable observation, as there were several teeth marks in evidence.

It didn't take many seconds to realise that we had a rat problem again. We wasted no time in placing poison in strategic places behind the bar. After a thorough investigation of the restaurant, we didn't appear to have a problem upstairs; the lights were all on, no rat poo, and nothing eaten.

I spoke too soon - the next morning the little buggers had steered clear of the traps and poison in the bar, but enjoyed a feast in the kitchen on jacket potatoes left in a tray. Bread rolls had been munched and left strewn over the floor.

We had to clean every single plate, glass, bowl and work surface in case the rats had been running amok in the kitchen. We cleaned the poo dropped round the edges of the floor, until at last we were able to open the restaurant for service.

If only the customers knew what went on behind the scenes, although we were taking every precaution to prevent bacteria and vermin evidence being spread. This would be something to write about in my 'daily diary' for the environmental health officers!

When customers had left at the end of the following evening the traps and poison were put in place again and we just hoped that as we were closed on Sunday, we would come in on Monday morning to find dead rats.

I went into work early Monday morning before anybody else had arrived, and walked very warily in through the door. I looked in the traps - nothing, absolutely nothing, so I continued cautiously into the restaurant to discover more poo but no dead rats.

The exact same process of deep cleaning had to be done again, so I was feeling pretty pissed off as the problem was still not resolved.

On Monday evening the restaurant was closed and Chris was working by himself in the bar. There were a few customers drinking, and as he was serving someone their drinks, he spotted something out of the corner of his eye.

Running down the stairs from the restaurant to behind where Chris was standing, was a big fat rat who shot behind the bottle cooler and disappeared down a tiny hole in the floorboard.

Apart from the shock of seeing a rat running into the noisy bar he was relieved nobody else noticed, and just thought to himself, 'I hope the bastard stays where he is and doesn't appear while there are customers in the pub.'

We kept the restaurant door closed, so at least with the rat downstairs, it was nowhere near any food or the kitchen. Chris put four traps down with a piece of chocolate in each because, apparently, that's their favourite food.

The next day revealed what their favourite food was - and it wasn't chocolate! The traps were empty, the poison hadn't been touched, but they had munched their way through our spicy crisps. We had two racks on the wall with different flavoured crisps – the rat or rats had eaten seven packets of one particular flavour.

They must have climbed up the wall, opened the bags and eaten the crisps, still leaving the bags attached to the hook on the rack.

On Tuesday night the waitress telephoned me at home to tell me there were half a dozen rats outside in the car park running round and round in circles. There wasn't anything we could do, except give the staff instructions to keep the outer doors closed.

Rats enjoying a social gathering with each other, adjacent to the bar and restaurant isn't exactly the kind of advertising which is beneficial!

I know there is the saying: 'You are never more than ten feet away from a rat.'

That may be true, but they are normally out of sight, so that fact isn't something that crosses your mind every day.

Our rat saga continued for the next few days and so did the constant deep clean of every surface area and item used in the bar and restaurant. They still persisted in eating the crisps from the rack in the bar, although we had managed to keep them away from the restaurant, even though they had tried to tunnel their way through the corner of the door by scraping at the carpet, but to no avail.

At least they refrained from showing their faces or furry bodies during our opening hours, but it seemed as soon as the door was locked and everyone had gone home the rats would whistle to each other then shout, 'Come on boys, it's party time at the Walnut, there's plenty of food for everyone.'

Eventually, the rats got fed up eating crisps and finally emptied the bowls of poison, and I imagine scurried away to die. We never knew how many there were or where they died, because we never found any remains – or smelt any dead bodies.

****

BLOOD AND GORY BITS

One of our chefs was away on holiday, so during his absence I covered his shifts cooking in the kitchen.

On a Saturday lunchtime, it had been exceptionally busy from the moment we opened, until about 3pm. The evening chef was due to take over from me at 5pm, which gave me two hours to prep all the food for the night-time shift, stock the fridges up and give everywhere a good clean before his arrival.

Around 4pm, the preparation work was done and the work surfaces and floor were cleaned. I just had to give the outer rim of the fryer a wipe round to retrieve all the little bits of food which get left behind when the baskets are emptied of fried food.

J. cloth at the ready, I was carefully wiping round the edge, when my hand slipped on the basket and went the whole way into the fryer – which wouldn't have been a problem if it had been turned off. It was on, and the temperature was over 180 degrees.

I let out a scream and rushed through to the sink to run my hand under the cold tap. Jane, the waitress on duty that afternoon, came to see what had happened.

'I've burnt my hand, no problem; it will be alright in a minute.'

However, it wasn't alright in a minute. Every time I tried to take my hand away from the cold water, the pain was so excruciating I had to put it back under the tap.

Jane rushed downstairs to get some ice and a bucket to soak my hand in. In the meantime, all that running water meant I was bursting for a wee, so I went upstairs. In those few minutes the pain was unbearable; I was shaking with shock and crying but I thought the pain would disappear soon and then I would be able to continue cleaning the kitchen.

Jane had just finished attending a health and safety course, so insisted on being 'nurse Jane'. She looked at the size of the burn and said I must go to hospital, but in the interim she would wrap my whole hand in clingfilm to stop any blistering. (I had never heard of that before) but at that point I didn't really care, I just wanted the agonising pain to ease.

I telephoned Chris (who was still at home) to come back to the pub straight away as I needed him to drive me to hospital.

I still had my hand in a bowl of iced water when we arrived at Accident and Emergency, where they immediately gave me some strong painkillers.

After inspecting my burnt hand and praising me for having the prudence to wrap cling film around the injury (well done Jane,) they spread cream over my hand, which was, by now lacking a few layers of skin. The nurse put a huge plastic bag over it and told me not to take it off for five days, after which I had to return to hospital for a check up.

The pain, by now, wasn't quite so bad, but I felt exhausted, sick, and thoroughly miserable.

The next problem I had to encounter was being in the kitchen the following week as the chef was still away on holiday.

If only I was an employee, I could have had a week on the club, but there's no such luxury when you are the employer.

For the next five days before my return to the hospital I continued to work in the kitchen but with great difficulty. Not only was I wearing a large, cumbersome, rustling bag, restricting me from using my hand, but I was right handed, and so was my burnt hand.

Using my left hand to write, cut bread, cook burgers and steaks, and make the meals was not impossible, but extremely frustrating and every task took me twice as long to complete.

My writing looked like a three-year old's whenever I attempted to write the customer orders and do the paperwork.

But that was a minor inconvenience compared to every time I was standing close to the grill - the heat affected my burns and the pain increased significantly.

I was very cautious, and basically scared of using the fryer, but it was impossible not to when people ordered chips; so each time I picked up the basket, it was done very warily, I certainly didn't want another repetition of my previous experience.

On my return to outpatients, the bag was removed and the cream taken off, revealing a shrivelled, thinner hand through lack of some skin layers - but no blisters - and that was thanks to 'nurse Jane.'

I had to continue wearing a cloth glove for a further few weeks while the healing process continued. At least this glove had fingers, so I was able to gently use my hand again.

The hand eventually healed without a single scar. I was very lucky.

The moral to this story - don't clean the bloody fryer when it is boiling hot!

One very busy Friday night, Chris and Ingrid were firing on all cylinders as they worked behind the bar. When there were a few moments to spare and nobody required serving, Ingrid whizzed round the other side of the bar to collect dirty glasses.

Chris, in the meantime, went downstairs to the cellar in order to restock the bar with bottles of beer.

He went down the stone, winding cellar steps, quickly grabbed some bottles and headed back towards the stairs. He began his ascent, but tripped on one of the steps and fell forwards. Unfortunately as he fell, a bottle broke on the step and Chris' wrist went directly on top of the smashed glass, straight through an artery.

The blood spurted profusely, up the walls, over Chris and the cellar steps. He walked quickly behind the bar and grabbed a tea towel to wrap round his wrist, but not before the blood had squirted from his wrist all over the top of the bar, the shelves, the bottle cooler and the bar floor, already a bit wet from spilt beer and water splashed from the sink. The combination of blood, water and beer meant that the floor looked like a massacre had taken place!

Chris ran upstairs to grab my attention in the restaurant, tightly gripping the tea towel, strategically placed on his wrist,

'Quick, get me to the hospital.'

I shouted to one of our regular customers, who was drinking in the bar,

'Tell Ingrid we have gone to the hospital.'

He looked confused, but I didn't have time to explain, so without further ado, we were out of the door, speeding up the road towards Accident and Emergency.

Ingrid had still been collecting glasses, so was totally unaware we had left the pub and she had been left on her own. That was until she returned behind the bar.

'What the fuck's been going on, there's blood everywhere, where's Chris? Oh fuck.'

By now several customers were waiting to be served - and all wanting cocktails.

'You won't be getting any fucking cocktails, you can have beer or spirits, can't you see this bloodbath I'm trying to clear up.'

As the pub had completely filled up with customers, she had no option but continue working for the rest of the evening, surrounded by splatters of blood everywhere. But in her haste of serving beer, even more was getting spilt on the floor, consequently making the floor look like a slaughter house.

I drove Chris to the hospital like a woman possessed, travelling at break neck speed and jumping all the red lights. I screeched up to the accident and emergency ward and we hastily ran inside.

'You really need to see my husband quickly; he's lost an awful lot of blood.'

We had to remain in the waiting room for about half an hour before they came and took Chris into a cubicle.

After asking what the problem was, the nurse told him to take off the tea cloth, which Chris was still gripping with all his might. The cloth was removed, - it had stopped bleeding.

The doctor inspected his wrist, stating he had cut an artery. The nurse proceeded to clean his arm, hand and wrist and put on a small – plaster!

When Chris came out of the cubicle to join me in the waiting room, I just looked at him in amazement. I was predicting he would have had several stitches; his arm bound with gauze and maybe even a sling.

No, he had the tiniest plaster I have ever seen and two stitches.

Chris did ask the nurse if he could have a few more stitches and a much larger plaster or bandage to at least make the whole episode worthwhile. She didn't oblige.

On returning to the pub, Ingrid related her tale of working in a bloodbath and wondering what the fuck had been going on - especially when she saw Chris' plaster.

The same week Chris had his accident on the cellar steps, Charlie, a barman who worked for us, cut his finger badly on a knife whilst cutting lemons. He put on a couple of plasters but the cut was still bleeding profusely and did look quite nasty, so thought it may necessitate a stitch or two.

We made a visit to Accident and Emergency. After another long wait in the waiting room, and watching his cut drip onto the chair, he was eventually seen by a nurse. A stitch wasn't necessary - just a large bandage and he was told to keep his finger pointing in an upwards direction. – men will do anything to get out of work.

The following night, Chris W. our barman, was working, and obviously thought he didn't want to be left out from receiving an injury, so he cut his finger badly - this time on a broken glass.

He came upstairs to see 'nurse Jude' and get a plaster from the first aid box, which was by now dwindling in bandages after the week's events!

Any accidents in the work place had to be recorded with specific details in the Accident Book. At this rate the book would soon be full!

The plasters seeped with blood, Chris said, 'Jude, I think I ought to go to the hospital, it won't stop bleeding.'

'Oh, not again, that'll be three times in one week I've had to traipse up there.'

Off I went again to Accident and Emergency. This was beginning to get embarrassing, especially if anyone recognised me, or cottoned on that yet another member of staff from the Walnut Tree had been injured whilst working.

We sat in the waiting room, on the same chair Charlie had dripped blood on.

Chris was inspecting his cut finger,

'Jude look, it's stopped bleeding.'

He squeezed it, trying to make it bleed again but without any luck.

His name was called. The nurse beckoned to me to come as well – she probably thought I was his mother and would hold his hand. We entered the cubicle for the nurse to inspect his pathetic little cut.

Fortunately she was good humoured and laughed at his injury. She did clean the area on his finger and hand in case there was any glass, then finished off by putting a plaster on his finger (which had completely stopped bleeding).

After that episode I said that it was definitely the last time I was escorting a member of staff to hospital for cuts!

When a job entails standing on your feet day in and day out there are bound to be health repercussions. Legs get tired and start aching and then unsightly varicose veins appear.

I went to hospital first to have offending veins removed from both my legs. It was only an overnight stay and a simple procedure. The stipulations from the doctors were rest, then gentle exercise for a couple of weeks. This is easier said than done when you have a business to run.

It wasn't an operation caused by illness, needing convalescence it was basically an inconvenience as my mobility was limited and my legs ached constantly.

As I was not someone who could sit and do nothing all day, I used the time wisely and programmed a stock-check on the computer. It was extremely complicated as I had to work out the formulae, so that each column worked retrospectively with the others so as to achieve the end result of telling us our gross profit and percentage of each spirit, mineral and beer we sold. When the stock-check was finalised, it would mean we were able to produce our own monthly results without having to employ a stock-taker.

I returned to the physical side of work after about ten days, far too soon, as by the end of the evening it looked as if I had a bad back. I was walking so precariously - stiff and upright - slowly putting one leg in front of the other, as my legs were hurting so much.

However, progress was soon made, my legs were lovely (with no lumpy bits,) and I was soon running around as normal.

Chris' varicose veins were far more protruding than mine had ever been, so he decided to have his removed. In hospital, the surgeon came to see Chris before the operation to explain the procedure. Chris asked the doctor if he would put his varicose veins in a jar because he wanted to take them home.

The following morning the veins appeared in a glass jar, printed with his name and details of the contents. They looked revolting, immersed in sanitising liquid. There were little bits, long thin bits, and fat bits like squiggly looking worms; these were all Chris' varicose veins.

Chris was given the same stipulations from the hospital, to have a small amount of exercise and wear thick, white, hold-up supporting stockings for at least two weeks.

Women are used to wearing tights and stockings, but Chris had great difficulty in keeping his up as they kept rolling down and he was often seen at the bar, dropping his trousers so he could yank them up again.

When regular customers came into the bar and asked Chris how his legs were improving, he would have great delight in retrieving the jar of veins from the bar shelf and showing everybody.

'You're fucking disgusting Gudgin' was the usual comment made from people.

Showing customers the glass jar continued for several weeks, until eventually the veins started to deteriorate and shrivel up, so Chris reluctantly had to throw them away.

A male friend of ours popped in one day. He was walking very unsteadily into the restaurant and told us he had just had his varicose veins removed.

He revealed his secret of keeping his stockings secure without them falling down, and then proceeded to show us, by dropping his trousers and exposing his wife's suspender belt!

There was not a hope in hell of Chris being able to borrow my underwear to keep his stockings up!

A spot began to appear on the side of Chris' neck - it got bigger and bigger until it was so blown up that it definitely wasn't a spot; it looked more like a boil, and eventually was so painful that he made an appointment at the doctor's.

The doctor said it was a cyst and would need to be removed at the hospital in the day-procedure department. An appointment was soon made and off he went.

The cyst had to be cut out; consequently there was a hole left in the side of his neck which was packed with wadding. The nurse carrying out the procedure of dressing the wound was a lady we had known socially for a long time.

'I can't wait to do this for you Chris; I just need to collect the bandages and wadding.'

She packed the hole with the appropriate materials, then put the biggest, thickest wadding and bandage on his neck imaginable. It was probably about three times thicker and bigger than actually necessary. She was laughing and giggling the whole time she treated his neck wound; 'This serves you right for always undoing my bra and groping.'

She went on to tell him that he must not, under any circumstances, take the bandage off for a week until he returned for a change of dressing.

Chris had the piss taken out of him the whole week regarding his 'bandage' with people asking, 'Have you had the bolt taken out of your neck?'

The following week a different nurse was on duty – luckily for Chris - so this time he received a miniscule bandage, far more appropriate for his injury.

Late one morning, the dray boys arrived from the brewery with a delivery of beer. After the kegs of beer were lifted from the lorry they were rolled along the pathway to the entrance of the cellar where they were passed down a shoot.

Chris went downstairs to the cellar in preparation to off-load the beer barrels. Unfortunately, as he forcefully pushed up the cellar flap, thinking it felt heavier than usual, a member of the public happened to be walking directly over the cover at the precise moment Chris heaved the door open, forcing the guy up in the air, and then, consequently, flat on his face. The poor fellow, he must have thought the gates of hell were opening.

He wasn't hurt and didn't need any medical attention; although we were quite fortunate he didn't take any action against us and try to sue us for negligence.

Theoretically, we should have taken measures beforehand, by placing a rope round the cellar flap and putting out triangle signs to warn people of a hazard.

Even after that incident it was another little job we never seemed to get round to doing, but luckily for us, after having opened the cellar flap twice a week for 25-years, that was the only accident whichever occurred.

Nick worked as a chef at the Walnut for many years and gave us a scary moment when he was cooking at the chip fryer. The wire shorted and he received an electric shock from the equipment. It threw him back about three feet against the wall.

He didn't have long hair, but what he did have was standing upright. His whole body was shaking profusely and his face had gone a dreadful white/grey colour.

Chris put him in the car and drove like a lunatic to the hospital, jumping all the lights. On arrival, they gave Nick a scan to check his heart rate which was unsurprisingly higher than normal. Fortunately, this soon lowered to an acceptable rate.

He soon recovered, but did say he was more scared of Chris' driving to the Accident and Emergency department than the electric shock he had received.

****

WHOOPS – WE'VE BEEN TOLD OFF

We were reprimanded from various authorities a few times for contravening acts of law. Of course it was never done intentionally; we always went about our daily chores in the most professional manner, and ran the pub and restaurant to the best of our ability. Unfortunately, there were occasions when someone from a higher authority got a little upset and proceeded to send nasty letters to us.

Price increases were never the choice of the publican. These were forced upon us by the brewers, who increased the cost of barrels of beer yearly. On top of that, we had to contend with the annual budget from the Chancellor of the Exchequer who always imposed an increase of duty on beer, wine and spirits.

The breweries put their increases through the system first, but the majority of time we swallowed this cost and made our gross profit lower. But we knew the budget was always imminent, so rather than make customers miserable twice with two small price increases, it was always more sensible to have just one bigger one.

Customers never failed to moan and groan for a couple of weeks, blame us for putting too much money on and then gradually get used to the idea that their pint was an additional 10p. or more!

The tabloid press never had any hesitation publishing the budget results and saying that the cost of beer had gone up 1p. a pint!

What the budget and the press always failed to mention was that it was low alcohol strength beer that was increased by 1p; the higher the strength, the more the price went up, by as much as 5p. per pint! To achieve the correct margin of profit, increasing the cost of ale to the public had to go up by as much as 10p. a pint.

We were never concerned what other pubs were charging customers for beer and spirits. We knew establishments who sold alcohol cheaper than we could actually buy it for, but as far as the local pubs close to us were concerned, we all charged the prices we wanted to. We knew the gross profit we needed to create a profitable business, and if it meant being the most expensive pub in Norwich – well, so be it.

Occasionally publicans would ring each other when price increases were enforced, just out of curiosity, to ask how much you were putting your beer up by.

In 1990, not only had the cost of beer risen substantially, but there had been the introduction of the poll tax, and business rates had rocketed. All these increases combined to make a significant difference to our overheads. The only way to replenish the extra costs was to put the cost of alcohol up quite considerably.

Chris and I, along with three other publicans, had an informal chat regarding the increased price of liquor imposed upon us. We all decided to increase our charges by the same amount, while still selling alcohol at our own individual pricing structure.

A few weeks went by and we all received a letter from the Office of Fair Trading, stating we had been in breach of the Restrictive Trade Practice Act 1976. In other words we were price fixing.

We never found out who had complained to the authorities, but the implications were completely false. We informed a solicitor who replied to the Office of Fair Trading and stated: 'Our clients, along with other tenants and licensees in the city, did discuss together that, in the light of the recent increases of the sale of intoxicating liquor and the recent introduction of poll tax and new business rates, they did discuss informally between themselves what they considered would be a fair increase in the retail prices of intoxicating liquors within their premises - not only to enable them to cover their increased overheads, but also to give a reasonable price and service to their customers.

The meeting was purely informal, nothing was agreed in writing, various prices are being charged from the various licensed premises, which indeed vary considerably from public house to public house. In those circumstances our clients do not consider that there has been any breach whatsoever of the Restrictive Trade Practices Act 1976.'

The Office of Fair Trading were obviously satisfied with the response, and that was the last we heard from them.

Under the terms of our lease and agreement with Manns & Norwich Brewery, Norwich Brewery, Spring Inns, Phoenix, and Enterprise Inns, (or whoever we were owned by at the time) we were tied to buying all our kegs of beer, bottles of beer and bitters from the company.

We were fortunate that we weren't also tied for wines, spirits and minerals like several other pubs were, so weren't restricted in paying far in excess for them.

Being tied for beer meant paying up to £50 a barrel more than if we were allowed to buy it directly from a wholesalers, so making our gross profit considerably lower than if we were a free house. Consequently we had to charge more for a pint of beer than some other establishments.

If a case of bottled beer was bought from a supermarket, the cost was £10 including VAT. Under the terms of our lease, beer had to be bought through the brewery at their going rate at the time, and was anything in excess of £25 plus VAT, for the same case of beer.

There were distributors selling beer at exceptionally lower prices compared to the inflated prices charged by the brewery.

It made sense to buy a few cases of bottled beer and kegs of beer elsewhere. Our philosophy was that the brewery was already taking an extortionate rent from us and overcharging for beer. We were never greedy in buying out of the tie otherwise the alarm bells would ring at the brewery. So, each week, we bought an odd keg from a distributor and the rest from the brewery. As bottles of beer were so expensive, we only ordered one or two cases of each from the brewery; the rest came from a distributor.

We were happy with the situation, so were the brewing company because they still received a large order each week, and did not suspect anything untoward going on.

That was until we received an official letter in the mail from Manns & Norwich Brewery in 1990. 'It has come to our notice that you are in breach of the terms of your lease; you have purchased specified beers from someone other than otherselves.

We give you notice that, unless purchase of specified beer and non-beer drinks from sources other than ourselves ceases immediately, we will have no option but to take appropriate steps to forfeit your lease and recover possession of the premises.'

Were we concerned and worried after reading the letter? – No.

Did it change our buying concept in any shape or form and adhere to the legally binding agreement we had with Manns & Norwich Brewery? – No.

Did we relinquish any ties we had with the wholesale distributors who we purchased our 'specified' beer from? – No.

Nothing changed; we carried on with our business as if the letter had never been received.

During the late 80's and early 90's, before the recession all businesses, whether it retail or leisure, were taking vast amounts of money. Our pub was no exception and we were reaping the benefits.

We were constantly busy, but even this raised alarm bells with the brewery, who seemed to think that we were over-trading for the size of the pub, and selling kegs of beer to other premises, as we couldn't possibly be selling the volume of beer we were ordering.

Bloody breweries were never satisfied. First we received a bollocking because we were buying out of tie, now they were querying that we were buying too much!

When we were owned by Norwich Brewery, they occasionally organised events and invited a few of their best customers to enjoy an all-expenses paid trip.

We ascertained they actually liked us. OK, so we may have received a bollocking for selling unspecified beer, but we always paid our exorbitant rent on time and we were selling plenty of beer. Could they actually be of the opinion, at long last, that we were good operators?

The first invite we received from the brewery was an expenses-paid trip to London for the night.

We arrived at the hotel to be informed our room had been upgraded to the penthouse suite as the basic rooms were all full – that was fine by us, we didn't mind at all!

We had instructions to meet all the other publicans and managing directors in the bar at 6pm, where drinks would be supplied, before being taken by coach to a concert at the Albert Hall to see Eric Clapton. Seating had been arranged in a VIP box for special viewing, along with drinks and canapés. To finish off the evening, a slap-up meal in a top class restaurant was arranged.

After making ourselves comfortable and getting ready for the evening's events in our luxurious suite, we headed to the bar.

The managing directors didn't believe we had a penthouse suite when theirs' were the small basic rooms. That was, until we showed them proof of our 'special keys.' That went down extremely well with them. – Not, especially after we suggested they could visit our room for aperitifs, – they declined the offer.

The concert was brilliant and everyone really enjoyed it. During the interval the managing directors took us to one side for a chat.

'We know you are still buying beer from other suppliers, so stop doing it and for fuck's sake Gudge, just keep your mouth shut to everyone else about the beers you shouldn't be selling, but are.'

They were smiling through the entire comments; they were letting us know we were rumbled yet again, but didn't want us to inform the other publicans of our wrong doings.

We had consumed a few drinks by now, so were feeling quite good-humoured and not particularly perturbed by their comments. 'We're very sorry, we won't do it anymore.' (Thinking to ourselves, well not for a couple of weeks anyway).

It was a great trip, especially as it hadn't cost a penny. That was, until the next morning, when we were about to leave and discovered my purse containing £200, which had been left in the room whilst we were out, had been stolen. Although we informed the hotel, the culprit wasn't caught and the purse was never retrieved.

So the day turned out considerably more expensive than we had originally anticipated!

Other events we were fortunate in being invited to with the brewery were the races at Ascot, a concert at Wembly to see the Rolling Stones, and the last trip (a bit more downmarket) a visit to Great Yarmouth races! However, it was nice to receive some appreciation from the brewery for a change, and to spend some of their money (especially as they had collected enough from us over the past years).

The managing directors from the brewery would occasionally come to Norwich and spend a few days visiting the publicans in their leasehold properties. They came to the Walnut one Friday evening unannounced, with no prior warning - which meant Chris didn't get a chance to hide the bottles of beer we shouldn't have been selling.

On display in the glass fronted fridge were bottles of Budweiser, that couldn't possibly have been ordered from the brewery because they didn't even supply it at that point. If the directors noticed the beer, we were going to be in the shit.

The bar was busy when the directors came in. Unfortunately there were several customers already drinking Budweiser out of the bottle. Hoping the directors wouldn't notice, Chris shook their hands and asked what they would like to drink. They glanced at the pumps on the bar, the bottles in the fridge, and said, 'Two bottles of Bud please, but can you disguise them, and for fuck's sake don't mention to anyone what we've been drinking.'

Chris wrapped red serviettes round the labels of the bottles, passed them over, then proceeded to take a photograph of the directors, just at the point they were raising the bottles to their lips. They stayed in the Walnut the whole evening and consumed several more bottles of Budweiser.

They gave up bollocking us, as they knew we never took any notice, and eventually chose to ignore our misdemeanours, because at the end of the day, we were good operators. We always paid our rent on time and trade had increased considerably since we took over the pub, therefore it was a far better option for the brewery to have us as licensees than someone who might make a pig's ear of running our pub.

Every leased and tenanted pub was allocated a regional representative who was supposed to visit each premises once a month. Part of their job entailed checking the cellar to make sure there was no evidence of beer purchased outside the agreement. If we knew the rep was due to pay us a visit, we hid the 'bought in beers' from sight.

He would show us a graph showing the volume of beer sold the previous month – which had no consequence to us. We knew from our own figures how trade was fluctuating without him telling us.

Whenever a new representative from the brewery took over our area, they would eventually get round to visiting us at the pub and introduce themselves.

However, our preference was the reps that never bothered to visit, so we could subsequently carry on running our business in peace.

Then there were the reps freshly graduated from university who had never pulled a pint of beer, let alone run a pub, who would try and inform us how we could make improvements within our business and tell us what we should be charging for beers.

Those representatives were told in no uncertain terms that their ideas were a complete waste of time, that we knew our business, what selling price we needed to charge for beverages, and that we didn't need any assistance from them. It wasn't necessary for them to visit us on a regular basis; it would be more beneficial for them to concentrate on licensees who would appreciate their contributions on how to run a pub far more than we would.

That forthright approach generally worked and kept the representatives from annoying us for several months.

One day, the rep was walking towards the pub to pay us an unexpected visit. Unfortunately, the exact moment he arrived at the door, we had just received a delivery of beer from another wholesaler. Two kegs of beer had just been lifted from the lorry, along with several cases of beer. Whoops, we were rumbled – yet again.

The representative informed us that action would be taken and that we would be hearing from the brewery soon.

The last bollicking letter we received was in 2002. The correspondence we received this time was addressed from Unique Pub Co. (our new landlords).

'As you well know, purchasing for sale at the premises specified beers, supplied by third parties other than Supplyline is a breach of the agreement between us. Unique considers such breaches amongst the most serious of breaches of covenant and not to be tolerated in any case.

The purchasing obligations in your agreement are legally binding upon you. If you do not comply with them then it is this Company's policy to enforce them through the courts.

If you do not comply, the future of your agreement and possession of the premises may be sought.'

It went on to inform us of the court and solicitor costs, the claims and damages that could be awarded to them for the loss of business they had incurred by us for buying out of tie (which equated to a vast amount of money).

The letter finished off by giving us a document to sign and return to them confirming we would comply with our agreement and would not intend to breach it further. If we signed the letter they would not take any further action against us.

We signed the letter regrettably, and promised we would never misbehave again!

However, at a later date, Enterprise Inns made it compulsory for all their pubs to install a 'Bru-line' system which monitored through to their head office every drop of keg beer sold. Any beer bought from another distributor would show up on their readings.

Damn, so that put paid to any shenanigans as far as draught beer was concerned!

****

MONEY, MONEY, MONEY

There were one or two publicans who enjoyed telling other licensees about the amount of money they were taking over the bar and the quantity of kegs of beer they sold in a particular week or month.

I was always non-committal to the amount of cash going in our till, what our weekly takings were, or how much beer had been sold – in fact Chris didn't even know most of the time! As far as I was concerned, it was nobody's business except ours; we just listened to the figures they quoted then replied, 'That's an impressive amount, well done, and good for you. Yes, - we have been quite busy as well.' That was the only information they received from us.

A prime example of extreme exaggeration was during our first Christmas at the pub. A publican came in for a drink at about 3pm on Christmas Eve, and then proceeded to tell us how much money he had taken so far that day. 'Wow, that's amazing; you must have been exceptionally busy.'

That particular bar was much smaller than ours. We had been packed constantly since the moment the door was open in the morning, and hadn't taken anywhere near the amount the licensee was claiming to have achieved.

Later on, as an exercise, we worked out a few calculations, based on the number of bar staff this particular licensee had on duty, the amount allegedly taken in the till, and was it feasible?

No - the amount of money he was claiming was completely and utterly impossible, unless he was able to pour, serve, take the money and give change in less than twenty seconds per drink!

Businesses who employ people to work for them are undoubtedly going to suffer minor or sometimes major losses as some point or another. Although the majority of people are honest, there are still going to be situations when items go missing. An office environment may lose the odd pen, envelope or paper for personal use by staff.

A shop selling cosmetics may discover that the odd sample of cream or perfume finds its way into a staff handbag.

Staff employed in pubs and clubs may help themselves to a free drink, maybe discount a friend's drink, or not charge a friend at all.

Employees in restaurants will help themselves to something to eat or even take food home with them to consume later.

All these 'free' items are what an employee classes as perks. In their eyes it is acceptable, and there is absolutely nothing wrong with it.

From an employer's point of view, it is stealing; however, unless it gets out of control, the little perks are, some of the time, overlooked. Our business was certainly no exception to the rule; the majority of staff we employed were honest, but on the other hand, others enjoyed little perks if the opportunity arose.

Businesses also have to contend with break-ins, robberies or serious offences.

Over 25 years it does not bear thinking about, or even trying to hazard a guess, as to how much money and goods we actually lost through people stealing, or having perks; it would certainly be many thousands of pounds worth.

When the pub doors were closed at 2.30pm – in the days before all day opening commenced - Chris had already left for a meeting. Myself and Lucy, who was 9-years old at the time, were upstairs in the flat watching television.

A little later she asked if she could have a piece of chocolate fudge cake, so being the obliging mother that I was, I said I would go and get a piece for her from the restaurant.

I walked into the prep area section, and saw the fire escape door had not been closed properly. There were knives strewn on the work surface in the kitchen, and a pile of sugar sachets on the floor which must have fallen out of the box. However, the box was nowhere to be seen.

I thought it rather strange, and was annoyed that one of the staff had forgotten to shut the door securely, and that the chef hadn't put the knives away at the end of lunchtime.

I picked the sugar sachets up, put them in another container, and then cut a piece of cake from the fridge, finished off with a scoop of ice-cream. I returned upstairs to the flat and continued watching the television with Lucy.

Chris arrived home at 5pm and rushed upstairs to check that we were OK, before announcing we had been broken into.

The police were called and on investigation, the thieves had entered through the fire escape door, picked up a sugar box and knife, proceeded into the bar to prise the till open with the knife, and taken the notes from the till, along with £250 in bags of change, hence the need for the sugar box to put it all in.

They left the same way they had entered, - through the fire escape door.

The frightening concern was, the thieves were probably in the bar, knives in hand, whilst emptying the till, exactly the same time that I was in the restaurant getting Lucy's cake.

Had I gone down a few minutes earlier or later, I may have come face to face with the thieves. That is not something I would like to contemplate.

The thieves were never caught.

We were due to go on holiday in a few day's time, and in the meantime I had been very methodical in organising all the wages and banking, along with the paperwork, to make life easier for the person left in charge in our absence.

The safe was upstairs in the laundry room and the key kept on top of the door frame, so we never had to go hunting for the key and knew we wouldn't lose it if it was kept there.

Inside the safe were four large cloth money bags which I had labelled: one with 'wages' written on, another, 'banking,' another 'change.' and the last one 'holiday money,' which was our wad of money waiting to be exchanged for dollars.

The following day, Chris went to London by train, whilst I continued with the usual daily routine of running the pub. It was fairly busy but no problems occurred and everything was running smoothly, until the bar person asked for some pound coins as he had run out of change. I opened the safe only to find it empty – apart from the cloth bag with 'wages' written on.

My legs shook, I felt physically sick, and then cried.

I called the police, then telephoned Chris who was on his way home.

Whilst waiting for the police I had to continue working in the restaurant. I felt angry and upset, but tried to put on a brave face for the customers, when one of the bar staff came upstairs and told me someone had just taken the big surf board down from the bar (it was six ft. long and stood on top of the bar on the customers' side) and replaced it with a large lobster pot. He had walked out of the pub, along with the surf board tucked under his arm.

I was fuming to the point of rage; this was the last thing I needed tonight. I knew the guy who had stolen the surf board; he was pissed, and thought it a funny prank to play on us. Maybe in normal circumstances it may have been, but not that night. I rang him up and furiously told him, 'Bring the surf board back now, take the fucking lobster pot down, and put the board back where it belongs, and if you want to continue living, make sure you are back here immediately before Chris gets home.'

Ten minutes later he was back in the pub with the surf board, apologising profusely but saying it was only meant as a joke.

Shortly after that little saga the police arrived and asked if I had any idea who the culprit might be. We did have a niggling suspicion about someone, but then we thought, no, that person surely wouldn't steal from us and with no proof, I certainly didn't want to be in the situation of having everybody we employed being interviewed and accused of something they hadn't done. So we let the matter drop and decided we must be far more vigilant in our security.

There was £2,000 missing from the safe, so it was necessary to claim on our insurance to recuperate the lost money, and what a trauma that turned out to be.

I was interrogated for nearly an hour; they didn't want to replenish our holiday spending money because it was personal cash.

We showed our takings records and books as proof before they were convinced the money was taken out of the business as drawings.

They were also concerned why the wages had been left in the safe but everything else was stolen.

Well so were we, but maybe the thief was honourable and wanted to make sure all the staff received their wages.

They were eventually satisfied with my prognosis, and would reimburse us with the money, well, after deducting their £500 excess fee. By the time they had finished cross-examining me, I was the one who felt like the criminal.

The following day, Chris got one of our staff to help him move the safe into our lounge so we could keep the door locked at all times and hopefully avoid any more misdemeanours.

In the days when we were still living over the pub, I was upstairs in the flat, doing mundane paperwork at my desk in the lounge, when I sensed there was somebody close by. I couldn't hear anything, but rose quietly from the chair and peered out of the door. I suddenly spotted a man looking round the corner of the wall, at the end of the corridor.

I went chasing down the corridor after him,

'Oy, what the fuck do you think you're doing up here? It's private property.'

'Um, Um, I'm looking for the toilet.'

'Like fuck you are, you can piss off now.'

With that I frog marched him downstairs, into the restaurant, and out through the fire escape door which was apparently the way he had entered.

It wasn't until after he had gone that delayed shock set in, because from the moment I spotted him, adrenaline kicked in, and I was so angry that somebody unauthorised was upstairs in our living quarters, I never gave a second thought to the consequences which may have been forthcoming. Although from the tone and aggression of my voice I probably nearly scared him to death.

When dealing with cash on a daily basis, there are times when there are many fraudulent notes in circulation, so it was always necessary to check money from customers. We had an ultra violet light which glowed if a note wasn't real, however, on busy nights staff often forgot to use it.

If a forged note is taken to the bank, they instantly keep it, and do not reimburse the money, as it's not legal tender. Some fake notes were appalling and looked as if they had been photocopied, others seemed perfect and it was impossible to spot any differences between real and forged notes.

We received many fake notes over the years, but as we had obtained them from customers, it only seemed fair to give them back the counterfeit notes in their change. This was a relatively easy task if the phoney was a £5 note, as people generally paid with a larger denomination so would require a £5 note in their change. £20 forged notes were of course taken straight to the bank!

It was quite funny when the forged £5 notes were returned back to the bar again when customers bought another drink, then proceeded to pay with the fake we had already given them. We weren't able to tell them we couldn't accept the note because it was a forgery. The same forged note could end up going backwards and forwards all evening between the bar and the customer.

The biggest annual event to take place in Norwich every July is the Lord Mayor's procession, and it always attracts at least 25,000 people. There are floats travelling through the main streets, a funfair, live music, entertainment and fireworks set off from the top of the Castle Museum at the end of the evening.

This night (apart from Christmas Eve) was our busiest session of the year, and required extra staff to work. We used plastic glasses as there could be up to 200 people standing outside the pub drinking, so plastic avoided breakages and meant customers weren't walking off with our proper glasses.

Our pub was situated in a brilliant location for watching the £20,000 firework display at 10pm and so attracted huge numbers of customers who could drink and watch the spectacle at the same time.

The bar and restaurant had been packed with people all evening and we were taking loads of money. I thought it a good idea to take a pile of money from the bar till and put it upstairs out of the way.

I quickly counted the money, totalling £450, left it on the table in the lounge then rushed back downstairs to continue working.

It was about three hours later when I finished working downstairs and took the till containing the money upstairs to the flat to count. The money I had left on the table was gone. I was furious, mainly at myself for being incompetent for leaving it there in the first place and not putting it in the safe, and, secondly, that somebody had stolen it.

The culprit was never caught and we worked the busiest night of the year for a lot less money than we should have had.

Not long after we had taken over the pub we bought a champagne fountain for £100, I'm not sure why, but it seemed a good idea at the time. It may come in handy one day for a special occasion, be a centre piece on top of the bar and certainly a topic of conversation. It was in excess of three-foot tall, the most pretentious, over the top, obscene looking American type of object I had ever seen.

The fountain had a large silver bowl at the bottom where the champagne or any other drink was poured into. There was a large tube running through the centre of the bowl upwards to a smaller silver bowl which had tiny chains attached round the edge; when switched on, the tube shone a sickly pink colour.

Sitting on top was a silver vase to put flowers in. Once the fountain was erected and plugged in, the champagne would travel through the bowl on the top, trickle down the chains and into the larger bowl at the bottom.

We used it a couple of times in the bar, but it was so big, if you were standing behind the bar serving, it was difficult to see the customers on the other side of the fountain.

We decided to hire it out as it was an ideal centre piece for occasions such as a wedding. This started to prove quite successful, and we loaned it out a couple of times in quick succession.

The next person interested in hiring the fountain for his son's wedding was a major who lived in Lowestoft.

He arrived to pick it up during a busy lunchtime, Chris rushed upstairs to pack it safely in a box. The major was very impressed, said it was perfect for the wedding, and went on his way.

A week passed, the champagne fountain hadn't been returned. I told Chris we ought to ring the major and see when he anticipated bringing it back.

However, Chris had lost his telephone number, and not only that, he couldn't remember the guy's name either. To make matters even worse, he forgot to take a deposit for the champagne fountain.

That was the end of that, we never saw the champagne fountain again, although we have often wondered if one day it might suddenly appear on the Antiques Road Show – then we could say, 'That's our Champagne Fountain!'

Throughout our years in business we contributed quite generously towards various charities. There were certain causes we donated to regularly each year, and we were happy to do our little bit in aiding people less fortunate than ourselves.

Rupert the charity box always sat on the bar, in aid of Muscular Dystrophy, a charity close to our hearts, and this little box probably raised thousands of pounds from customers adding their spare change, and we would often top it up.

It was New Year's Eve 1984, and everyone was out having a good time and looking forward to the impending celebrations. However, our evening turned sour when we noticed some despicable person had stolen the charity box; we were so upset to think one of our customers had stooped that low.

We wanted to replenish the stolen money which we estimated was around £25. so decided to hold a sweepstake in the bar for the forthcoming Milk Cup Final.

Customers had to guess the name of the Norwich player to score the game's first goal, and time of scoring. We supplied a first and second prize for the winners.

Our efforts were published in the paper with the headlines:

'Bumper response to Theft,' printing details of our sweepstake and that we had managed to raise £65, far more than we anticipated was stolen.

Monday's was always the prime day for people to 'cold call' on the telephone, either to sell cleaning products at a discount rate, advertising, and charities asking for donations.

We also received many letters asking for money to send a sick child abroad for an operation.

I'm sure some 'cold calls' and letters are genuine, but sadly, the majority are scams.

People entered the pub selling various goods, usually cleaning products at a reasonable price.   We never bought any; especially after hearing other establishments had paid about £50 only to discover the containers were filled with coloured water.

People would telephone requesting money and bank details so they could set up a direct debit for a regular donation to be transferred to a particular charity. We were never gullible or fell into that trap, although we always told them to send all the details in the post and we would have a look before we committed ourselves. Of course nothing ever appeared.

Another scam we often encountered were people who rang to say we had very kindly donated to their charity the previous year and would we reiterate again by forwarding a cheque to them. No, we hadn't donated to that charity, and no we wouldn't be forwarding a cheque.

A number of fund raisers seemed to have the notion that raffling a teddy bear would encourage people to buy a ticket in the hope of winning, with proceeds subsequently forwarded to the specific charity.

The teddy bears were generally about six feet tall so, to begin with, we certainly did not have the space to have one and, secondly, our customers would have no interest in buying raffle tickets for a teddy bear, even if it was for a good cause, so we always gave that one a miss.

There were also the advertising scams who telephoned to ask if we would place an advert in the police magazine, or the fire station brochure which we had previously participated in and all proceeds would go to charity.

We had never advertised with them before, and the authorities had never even printed these particular magazines.

A guy came in the pub and showed us details of a map of Norwich he was producing for the benefit of tourists visiting for the first time. It was going to be circulated at the East Anglian Tourist Board, neighbouring hotels and shops, and would be free.

The brochure displayed a map in the centre along with adverts round the edge and directions how to get to each establishment. It appeared professional and an excellent concept which could possibly attract more clientele to our business. So we agreed to contribute to the brochure and gave him a £50 cheque for the deposit, signed the duplicate forms, and arranged for the remaining £100 to be paid on completion of the publication.

A few weeks passed and we didn't hear anything from the company producing the brochure. I retrieved the documents I had previously signed to salvage the phone number, and noticed the bottom of the duplicate page where my signature had been placed, was actually a direct debit form.

Alarm bells immediately rang, so a panic phone call was made to the bank. Fortunately no money had been taken from our account, and I stopped any future payments which may have taken place.

I telephoned a few businesses in Norwich who I knew had also placed an advert and warned them. Unfortunately, I wasn't quick enough because a couple of outlets had already been debited monies from their accounts up to the sum of £200.

I phoned the tourist board, who knew nothing about the publication, and a couple of hotels who had actually received a box containing the advertising brochure, but had no intention of displaying them, for the simple reason they wanted to promote their own restaurants and facilities, not neighbouring competition.

The end result could have been worse; at least we only lost £50 this time. Another lesson learnt, look at what you are signing and see if there is anything untoward lurking underneath.

We rented our fruit machine at the pub which was tucked in the corner. It was in view of the bar area but not placed obtrusively that customers who had no interest in gaming machines would be perturbed by its presence. However, on three separate occasions, it was a target for criminals.

The inside workings of many fruit machines are not particularly complex. They consist of two tubes containing £100 in denominations of £1 coins in each.

As people play the machine the coins automatically drop into the tube sections until such time that those are full, then the coins drop into a compartment at the back of the machine.

Criminals who target fruit machines obviously have knowledge on the inside mechanics because they know exactly how to retrieve the money.

Each time our gaming machine was targeted, it was during the quiet sessions in the afternoon and went completely unnoticed by the staff.

One time thieves drilled a hole in the side, inserted a screwdriver to release the lever, which consequently enabled the £200 from the tubes to drop into the tray. They must have put something soft down to catch the money and so avoiding the clanking sound of the coins pouring out.

Another time vandals forced the 'collect' button to pop out, then managed to flick the lever on the tubes to rescue the money, after which they glued the button back in the machine.

The criminal offence can pass completely unnoticed until an innocent customer is playing on the machine, has a win but receives no payout. It's not until after complaining to Chris, that the crime is discovered when Chris opens the door to the inside mechanics and sees the money has all gone.

We know for certain our fruit machine was targeted three times, but maybe it was more and we were none the wiser. As the years progressed, companies secured the machines far more making them virtually impossible to break into.

For a time I really thought senile dementia or Alzheimer's disease was setting in.

I would prepare all the wages for the staff and periodically one would go missing. I thought, Oh well, maybe I forgot to do that one, but I'm sure I did.

I paid some of our local suppliers with cash, and would have it all ready to give them, but then I couldn't find it. I would think to myself, 'Well did I do it? I'm sure I did. Oh, maybe not.'

I mislaid a purse which I thought had been left on the shelf in the restaurant. It had disappeared, maybe I had left it in Tesco, but I'm sure I didn't. This happened twice.

£200 float money just disappeared one morning, I'm damn sure it was there the previous evening.

Before we had the luxury of a till in the restaurant we kept the takings in a pot! – I know, not very secure, but this system had never been a problem in the past.

When my senile lapses were occurring sometimes I cashed up and discovered a shortage of money. I was the only waitress on duty and very methodical handling money, but I must have given a customer the wrong change, but was sure I hadn't, I was always so careful.

I thought I was really losing the plot and I had got to the point of doubting everything connected which involved handling money.

Whilst I'm on the subject of losing the plot; I had been working a busy evening in the restaurant and kept thinking how uncomfortable my footwear had been all night, especially as I was wearing my usual boots, I seemed to be walking with a limp, and one felt tighter than the other.

It wasn't until the end of the evening I actually looked down at my feet. In my haste of getting dressed at home I put on two different boots. They were both black, but one had a round toe, the other pointed, and one had a higher heal than the other. At least I had managed to put on a left and right shoe; otherwise I could have been walking round in circles all evening!

I could have kept quiet and not told anybody, but thought the staff would find it amusing. They did, but looked at me sympathetically, obviously thinking, 'Jude's lost the plot.'

Eventually my lapses of senile dementia made a remarkable recovery and strangely I never mislaid or lost anything else. I hadn't lost the plot after all, and I certainly made sure I was wearing identical boots before I left for work.

****

PARTIES

It had been a long cold winter; the celebrations of Christmas and New Year were well and truly over. By February, people were glum and fed up and summer seemed a long way off. We decided to hold an event to take place at the end of February, giving customers something to look forward to.

We settled on a fancy dress, rock and roll night, printed tickets to sell, put posters on the walls stating the evening's events, and offered prizes for the best dressed male and female. We organised a band to play good ole rock and roll music.

It was going to be a real fun night, staged on a Sunday when the pub was normally closed.

All we had to do was promote the evening to customers and sell tickets for the meagre amount of £2. Hopefully if we sold one hundred tickets, that would cover the cost of the band. Chris and I would both be working so we would only require one more bar tender.

Customers showed interest, but abstained from buying tickets saying they would pay at the door on the night. We sold four tickets but weren't too perturbed as we guessed people would just turn up on the evening.

Sunday arrived; Chris was dressed in a teddy boy jacket, Elvis wig, drainpipes and pink socks. I wore a bright yellow satin rock and roll dress, black belt and neckerchief, finished off with yellow socks and pumps. In fact our attire was the same clothes we wore for our 25th wedding anniversary when we renewed our vows in Vegas – with Elvis!

We went to the pub early to clean the bar area and stock the shelves with bottles. The band arrived and set up their equipment. Lynsay, the bar girl for the evening, made an effort with her attire and dressed in rock and roll gear, so all we had to do was wait for customers to come flocking in.

The four people arrived who had previously bought tickets, and weren't even in fancy dress costume, so the band decided to start playing to get the atmosphere going – what atmosphere, with four people!

A couple of our staff members turned up but that was it. Nobody else appeared all evening. With no work to do, we downed several vodka and tonics and beer, the band were really good fun so we danced the night away with Lynsay, as she certainly wasn't required to serve behind the bar either.

There was no necessity to present a prize to the best dressed customers because there weren't any.

An evening for the benefit of customers was an outstanding failure and we were out of pocket by several hundred pounds. Huh, last time we would do anything special for customers on our day off!

Chris' birthday fell on Christmas Eve, and every year he moaned and groaned like a broken record that he always had to work on his birthday. As it was going to be his 40th, I decided to organise something special for him - secretly.

I began the arrangements for his party in August. Terry, a friend of ours, owned a nightclub called Spencers, only five minutes' walk away from the pub, which would be ideal for the venue.

Christmas Eve fell on a Friday so, unfortunately, I couldn't hold a party then, as it was our busiest day of the year and Spencers would also be packed with customers that evening. I settled for the Sunday night, when our pub would be shut anyway, so it would be easy to get out and I wouldn't have the additional problem of employing extra staff to work.

It was my intention that the party wasn't going to be for customers who we had met since going in the pub. I wanted to invite only his friends from the 60's right through to present day. This involved a huge amount of research to find them all, as obviously over the years people had moved away or just lost touch. So I phoned John, a dear friend we had always stayed in contact with, and arranged to meet him for a secret cup of coffee.

If I nipped out of the pub in the mornings, Chris would always say, 'Where are you going?'

For the first time in our married life, I started lying to him, I couldn't tell him I was meeting John for coffee. So each time I snuck off to meet him, I had to give a cock and bull story as to where I was going. It was Tesco, or I wanted a new jumper, new pair of trousers, a skirt, I just had to remember to come back with an appropriate bag with some shopping inside.

John was able to trace many old friends from the 60's by ringing up various people who knew someone, who knew someone else which eventually gave me the information I needed.

I tried to find out from Chris the name of his first girlfriend so she could be invited, if she was traceable. But each time I started a conversation about the past and talked about previous girl and boy friends, he always said he couldn't remember her name.

Damn, so she wouldn't be invited, which meant I had to find a replacement.

I bought a blow up doll and dressed her up. Mind you, with her mouth wide open and her legs spread, she didn't look particularly attractive and hadn't worn well over the years, but she would have to do as Chris' first girlfriend and be presented to him on the night.

I drew up a list of people I knew Chris would love to see on his birthday, but it got longer and longer until I ended up with a list of nearly 250 people.

Another friend printed the invitations with the relevant details and, most importantly, that the event was top secret and Chris must not, on any account find out.

I started to compile a, 'This is your Life' book, which entailed finding old photographs, taking cuttings of headlines from newspapers relevant to the photo and then strategically placing them on the page as a title.

A couple of headlines: 'But why did chopper drop out' and 'It's not only tiny – it's a very awkward shape' were appropriate cuttings to a photo of Chris and a couple of mates standing having a pee.

Headline: 'You'll be sick, they said – and they were right!' was an ideal newspaper cutting for a photo of Chris on his stag night looking very pale and throwing up.

I had to make sure I destroyed the newspapers after mutilating them so Chris wouldn't question my actions. The staff were on alert and code red, when they knew I was upstairs sorting through pictures and headlines and so would quickly ring me on the internal phone if Chris was about to come upstairs. Then I could promptly hide everything and pretend to be doing paperwork.

The date was getting closer, a cake was ordered, the invitations sent, a band was organised and Harvey was sorting the music to be played by the DJ, and still Chris had no idea what lay ahead.

Friends who received an invitation were coming in the pub, giving me a smile and nod as a sign of acceptance. Some people were ringing to RSVP, which was fine if I answered the telephone, but if Chris got there first, they would either put the phone down immediately or pretend they had the wrong number.

After a couple of weeks, Chris remarked there seemed to be a lot phone calls and no one on the other end.

'Yes, very strange.'

Christmas Eve arrived, we worked our butts off as usual on this manic day, but it wasn't till later in the afternoon Chris remarked that none of his friends had been in for a drink to wish him Happy Birthday.

'They've been coming in to see me every year, and today when I'm 40, no one's here.'

He was a bit upset, but I couldn't tell him he would be seeing everyone in two days' time.

Upstairs in the restaurant, the chef and I managed to cook 200 sausage rolls and chicken drumsticks without Chris noticing. They were wrapped and put away in fridges. Unfortunately, Chris decided he wanted something to eat, so he went to open the fridge door, when Nick the chef jumped in front of him, nearly chopping his hand off to stop him opening the door and seeing all the party food.

'Fucking leave the fridge alone, tell me what you want and I'll get it'

Chris just thought the chef was having a grumpy moment, so asked if he could have a hot dog please.

Phew, that was a close shave.

The day of the party arrived so the next pre-organised plan of action was put in place.

Our friend Dave was in the process of taking over a restaurant. He rang in the morning to ask Chris if he would meet him as he would value his opinion on changes he wanted to make to his new premises. Chris wasn't particularly keen on turning out, but agreed to go and meet him.

As soon as he left, I ran down to the restaurant, hung a tea-towel out of the window as a code it was safe for people to arrive. I quickly prepared some more party food, by which time our friends were turning up to collect all the food and take it to the venue.

Chris returned two hours later - not happy.

'Fucking Dave, kept me talking and running on about the restaurant, I'm fucking frozen as I only took a thin jacket and it was fucking perishing in there.'

Chris knew we were going out for the evening, but thought we were going to a small drinks party at Terry's house. While Chris was having a nap in the afternoon I started to get ready. I told Lucy, who was 8-years old, about Daddy's party that night and she was sworn to secrecy.

I was feeling excited and nervous; after so much planning I just wanted the night to go well and for Chris to love it.

When Lucy and I were both dressed and dolled up, Chris looked me up and down,

'Why are you all tarted up, we're only going round Terry's house for a drink?'

'Well, it's Christmas, so thought I would make an effort and dress up for a change, as this is the first time we've been out for ages.'

'I'll put my DJ on shall I?'

'If you want to, but I think a suit will be fine.'

Chris got ready, picked up a bottle of champagne to take to Terry's then changed his mind,

'No fuck it; I'll drink his piss tonight.'

7pm on the dot, the phone rang; I waited for Chris to answer, as I knew the call was going to be from Terry.

Chris put the phone down,

'Change of plan, that was Terry on the phone, he wants us to meet him over at Spencers as he is sorting out some missing stock items, so he will give us a lift to his house rather than get a taxi.'

Norwich on a Sunday evening was generally like a ghost town, nobody walking and barely any traffic. We left the pub and started walking up the road towards Spencers. There were cars parked everywhere.

'Whatever's going on tonight with all these cars around?' said a bemused Chris.

'No idea.'

We opened the door of Spencers. It was very quiet and Terry was standing at the top of the steep flight of stairs by the reception desk. We walked to the top, looked over to the side where the bar and dance floor were located when Chris was greeted by 250 people singing 'Happy Birthday.'

He was speechless – for once. 'So that's why nobody came to see me on my birthday they're all here!'

'They didn't come in because they were too scared of letting the cat out of the bag.'

John and I did a short speech, then presented Chris with the 'This is Your Life Book' after which we announced the arrival of his first girlfriend – the blow-up doll.

It was such a great night, with people turning up from all over the country, some Chris hadn't seen for 20 years. Everyone had a really good time laughing, reminiscing about the good old days, dancing to 60's music and looking at numerous black and white photographs people had brought with them.

After all the preparation and organisation the evening was a blinding success and continued to be talked about by friends for months afterwards.

I told Chris the reason there were so many phone calls with no one on the other end; they were people ringing to say they would be attending the party.

I told him Dave didn't really need his opinions on the restaurant, it was a ploy to get him out of the pub while the food was been collected.

The times I nipped out supposedly shopping, was to meet John.

The fridge was full of party food, that's why the chef wouldn't let him inside.

Chris' first girlfriend – the blow-up doll, was not left discarded after the party. She came back to the pub and stayed upstairs, still blown up with legs spread and mouth open, waiting in anticipation for attention.

Dave drove to the pub one lunchtime and left his car outside whilst shopping in Norwich. As soon as he disappeared down the alleyway, Chris collected the blow up doll from upstairs and put her in the front seat of Dave's car with the seat belt on. She didn't look particularly comfortable as her legs wouldn't bend, and her mouth wouldn't close but she had the desired effect on the general public. Watching people's faces as they began to walk past the car, then suddenly double track on themselves in disbelief as to what they had just noticed.

When Dave returned from his shopping trip and got in the car, only to discover a companion beside him, he wasn't very happy. Especially when he had to undo the seat belt, remove the doll from the car, and walk her into the pub to hand her back to Chris in front of several other customers.

The doll often went abroad on holidays with friends having a boys' trip away. Unfortunately, the last time she embarked on a vacation, she never returned – the story we were told, the doll went down – on what or who she went down on, we never found out!

John had been my hairdresser for many years; he approached us to see if he and his twin sister could possibly hold their 30th birthday party at the pub on New Year's Eve.

That evening was generally a busy night anyway; however after giving it some thought, we decided to let him use the pub for a private function, especially as he said there would be in excess of 100 people attending.

He wanted to play his own acid house music instead of our usual blues and rock and the evening was to be themed as a black and white party.

The windows were all blacked out, the music blaring, and the place was so packed, people were even standing on the benches dancing. Because of the acid house music being played instead of our usual blues and rock, it didn't feel like being in the Walnut. But saying that, it was an excellent night and everyone really enjoyed it.

Very, very, occasionally over the years, we opened the pub on Sundays if people we knew wanted to hold their birthday parties at the Walnut. Each event was always a successful night and everyone had a good time. Sometimes they organised a band, which always enticed people to dance.

One girl at a party thought it a good idea to get on stage while the band was playing, lift her top and flash her boobs. John Langham, the lead guitarist was trying to continue playing whilst standing gawping with his mouth wide open.

Jason, the drummer stood up from his seat, still banging away at the drums, while desperately attempting to get a good look, but to no avail because he could only see her back. Lucas blissfully continued singing the number, totally oblivious to the girl parading in front of him.

When it was my 40th birthday, Chris organised a secret weekend away in Amsterdam. He gave me a couple of days' notice so I could sort out the restaurant and staff wages, and, of course, pack a few clothes.

The hotel was excellent and we had a lovely couple of days relaxing and eating good food. The down-side of the trip was the flight home, which was considerably delayed, so we didn't arrive back at the pub until about 10pm, only to discover balloons and banners everywhere. Several friends (who by now had consumed plenty of alcohol) were waiting for us, a band was playing 'Happy Birthday', and there was a cake with far too many candles. It was such a shame we were so late back, but we still managed to enjoy the rest of the evening with everyone.

When Chris' 50th birthday was looming, I again wanted to do a secret party, but certainly not on the large scale of his 40th bash.

I decided to hold a party at the pub on the evening of his actual birthday – Christmas Eve.

We had already made our minds up to close the pub in the evening, on the assumption that the manic day for drinkers would be Saturday instead.

To enable the staff to close the pub and get it ready for Chris' party I had to try to get Chris to go home in the afternoon instead of working until we closed.

The staff were happy to run the bar until closing time so Chris could go home and enjoy his birthday. Then later, Chris thought he was going to spend the evening at Harvey's house for drinks.

The bar was still packed when we eventually managed to get Chris to leave about 4pm. The staff called time at 5pm and stopped serving drinks, which didn't go down very well with the customers who wanted to prolong their drinking session.

When everybody had left the pub, the staff had just enough time to clean and stock the bar, and adorn the pub with banners, balloons and pictures of Chris when he was a boy.

A band was organised, so they cleared the stage area ready for them to play. I also had t-shirts printed with different photos of Chris as a child on the front for the staff to wear.

Just like Chris' 40th birthday party, he never had a clue about the forthcoming event. The evening approached and we were both ready to leave to go to Harvey's house so the next plan of action needed to be put in place.

As we drove along the road, I exclaimed, 'Oh shit, I've left Harvey's present at the pub, we will just have to swing by and pick it up.'

Chris glanced at me a little disapprovingly, but headed towards the pub, which of course he expected to be closed.

As soon as he drove up towards the pub, he knew something was going on. The lights were on and people still inside. He walked in and was greeted by many of our great friends who couldn't wait to see Chris' face, surprised yet again on his birthday, even if it was a decade later. It was another great night to be remembered.

However, I did promise Chris that would be the last surprise party I organised for him; I couldn't stand the deceit and lies involved keeping secrets from him anymore.

Although each year we gave the staff a Christmas gift, we occasionally had a staff party. It was out of the question to hold one during December as we were far too busy and knackered, so when we did organise a party it tended to be during the summer months.

Our first event was at the Wine Press, located just up the road from the pub; a meal was organised and we put money behind the bar for drinks.

The staff made full use of the free alcohol and everyone was extremely merry. Boobs were being flashed, bums were being mooned and a good time was had by all, including our daughter who was only 10-years old and managed to get drunk on sherry and red wine my mother-in-law was giving her.

Chris managed to consume copious amounts of wine, beer, and Jack Daniels until he announced to me, 'Take me home.'

I knew that was a bad sign, Chris has never, ever been an obnoxious, loud, bad mouthed drunk. He just giggles, gets touchy feely, goes quiet, and when he gets to the point of being unable to drink any more alcohol, he needs to go home – immediately.

I needed the assistance of my mother, who was at the party, to walk home a tipsy 10-year old daughter and a very drunk husband. With my mother holding one of Chris' arms, I had the other. Whilst also holding onto Lucy, we managed to walk, or should I say stagger back to the pub.

By the time we reached the alleyway Chris insisted he could walk without any aid from either me or my mother, so we watched him bounce from one wall to the opposite one, all the way down the alleyway until we reached the pub door.

As soon as we got inside Chris went down the rickety steps into the cellar. After several minutes of waiting, I said, 'What are you doing down there?'

'I'm talking to the tins of paint,' replied my drunken husband.

After he had finished his conversation with the 'paint', we somehow got Chris and Lucy upstairs. Chris was on his hands and knees scraping along the landing carpet. We steered him towards the bedroom, my mother laughing so much she nearly wet herself. We started undressing him and got him into bed – within minutes he was snoring like a train.

The staff working the following day shift were all very quiet, suffering with hangovers, but Chris was by far the worst and was incapable of doing anything constructive the whole day.

He was also somewhat bemused at how he managed to get carpet burns on his knees. 'Well, that could have been when you were grovelling along the landing on your hands and knees!'

Another birthday he decided to celebrate the night before Christmas Eve; forgetting the following day was the busiest of the year and the brewery were delivering at 7.30am. I heard him get out of bed and go into the bathroom – then silence. When the dray boys started banging on the door to be let in, I thought I had better go and investigate to see where Chris was; I found him fast asleep on the bathroom floor. 'What the fuck are you doing?'

'I don't feel very well, can you sort the brewery delivery out?'

I was thrilled at that prospect – not, but didn't have any other option.

Chris made his way back to bed, but when it got to 12pm, and the bar was packed and still no sign of Chris, I went storming up to the bedroom, 'Get your fucking arse downstairs – now.' That worked! But, ooh, he did look rough all day – serve him right!

We held another staff party in a country pub; a few regulars and friends were invited to join us, so we hired a coach to transport us there and back.

It was a beautiful summer's day, so after eating our Sunday roast we all went into the garden to consume more alcohol. There were a couple of joints being circulated, so at 30-years old I had my first puff of an illegal substance; that was all it took to give me the constant giggles, I continuously kept going um, um, um, um, in an attempt to sing.

The coach trip home was eventful with a few of the staff doing moonies out of the back window. Unfortunately, following the coach was a police car that was in full view of bare bums. Thank God they didn't stop us because if they had stepped inside the coach, they would have got high with the smell of fumes.

We held a staff party in a local restaurant by the river, where again plenty of alcohol was drunk, bums and boobs were flashed and everyone had a good time.

Gerry, one of my staff, had a little doze on the grass during the afternoon, so a great photo was taken of her laid out flat on her back, arms and legs spread out, surrounded by empty beer and wine bottles.

We held a couple of staff parties at our house. We organised a bouncy castle for the children, spent the whole of the previous day preparing the food and buying drink in readiness for 30 people to attend.

The beer and wine were all outside in a large bin full of ice for everyone to help themselves, and Chris and I spent the day cooking food and hosting the party.

They all had a great time; the children made full use of the bouncy castle, which gave the adults freedom to consume plenty of liquid refreshment before they proceeded to join in with the kids.

Just one minor mishap occurred when one of the children ran through the lounge into the conservatory. But instead of running out of the open door, he smacked straight into the closed window, with such force that he bounced back. The worst thing was, we could see him running and knew exactly what was about to occur, but couldn't stop him in time.

Several tears were shed and a big bump appeared, but apart from that, he was none the worse for his accident and our conservatory window remained intact.

Entertaining for large numbers entails a huge amount of work and effort as you always want people to enjoy the food and have a good time, so we always went out of our way to ensure that happened.

The next staff party we held at the house was also a successful day and everybody had a good time eating and drinking, although the following day when I asked one of the waitresses why she hadn't attended, her reply made me absolutely furious, 'I treasure my day off from work, and wanted to do what I wanted, and it wasn't spending the day with people I work with all week.'

'Yes, and I treasure my day off, but went to an awful amount of effort for the benefit of all the staff, to show our appreciation for all your hard work, and you couldn't be arsed to come. Well thanks.'

That was the last staff party I held at home on a large scale.

We held a party at the pub for all the customers and friends to celebrate our first year of trading. It was also a good excuse to have an extra busy night.

The chef made a special cake with a single candle; we put the silver champagne fountain on top of the bar. However, it wasn't filled with champagne. Instead Chris made a huge bowl of punch for people to help themselves.

Friends and customers brought us happy 1st birthday cards and were so generous with their kind thoughts and praises. It was a huge accolade for us to have achieved our first milestone and establish a good business and clientele and the evening was a roaring success.

Our next big celebration at the pub was for the 10th anniversary of being licensees at the pub. This time we organised a band to play in the car park outside.

We put several posters on the wall and spent a few weeks beforehand informing everyone about the forthcoming event and hoped plenty of friends and customers would turn up to celebrate the occasion with us.

We weren't disappointed; about 200 people were inside and spilling out onto the car park to listen to Worlds Apart rock the night away. In fact the band was so loud the music could be heard, not just in the alleyway, but several hundred metres away.

Lucy, who was 16-years old, unfortunately had to leave quite early because she had important exams at school the following day, so she went home in a taxi. (We had bought a house and were no longer living at the pub at this stage).

It was a great night; customers were more than generous supplying us with a constant stream of drinks, which is probably why Chris ended up drinking Jack Daniels and Coke from a pint glass.

We closed the bar for service and most customers had left but there were still a few regulars and staff who carried on consuming a few more drinks. There was singing and dancing and we were all pretty slaughtered.

Although I was fairly inebriated, I noticed Chris had gone missing.

'Anyone seen Chris?' Nobody had, so Chris W. (the bar person who was working that night) and myself went on the hunt for him.

It didn't take long to find him, or should I say, heard him, in the kitchen, bent over the sink being sick. He was absolutely plastered, and there was no way a taxi company would transport a drunken, sick man in their cab.

I was in a real predicament, because Lucy was at home, and I had to be there to take her to school for her exam the next morning, but I also worried about leaving Chris by himself in the pub for the night.

Chris W. came up with the ideal solution; he would sleep on the couch in the flat and baby-sit Chris for the night so I could go home to Lucy.

The following morning, I had the headache from hell and I'm sure was still a bit pissed when I drove Lucy to school. This was a dreadful thing to do but my brain wasn't functioning enough to have the intelligence to order her a cab.

Chris was no better; he couldn't remember being put to bed, and wondered why he had a grown man baby-sitting him for the night.

The next night, the local paper published an article along with a picture of the band standing with Chris, with the headline:

'Decade of blues at Walnut Tree Shades.'

It read: 'He never felt more like singing the blues ….. In fact Chris was in the pink as he celebrated a decade of the blues at the city centre's Walnut Tree Shades.

Chris and Jude were marking their tenth anniversary at the pub – and the sounds of Worlds Apart helped the occasion go with a swing.'

Approaching our 20th anniversary at the pub definitely deserved a special event. Throughout the years we had seen many pubs open and close in a short space of time. In fact there were very few pubs left in the city owned by individual licensees, as more and more were been taken over by large chains and adopting the same themes and boring minimal decoration.

Over 20 years we must have served thousands and thousands of people. Some had remained loyal and continued to come in the whole duration. Others had moved away and, of course, many had grown up, had children and settled down.

We decided to hold the party on a Sunday from 4pm onwards and hopefully attract past and present customers who would like to come and celebrate with us.

We booked two bands. Starting the proceedings would be 'Barry Homan Band' and later on in the evening, 'Keno Kings' with a few guest appearances from musicians joining in.

I sent letters to our numerous suppliers, friends and colleagues to try and persuade them to dig into their pockets to donate a prize for the raffle we were going to run, in aid of Motor Neurone Disease.

Everybody was so generous, and we received forty fantastic prizes ranging from meal vouchers in various restaurants, a suede jacket, a BBQ, champagne, a ghost tour, Paul Smith clothes, hair cuts and highlights, a DVD and CD player, to name just a few.

Posters were designed and placed on the walls and windows and raffle tickets were on sale. I printed some flyers to hand out to customers and friends about the events going to take place on the night in question and a few memoirs about our twenty years at the pub. The final paragraph went like this:

'We were considering selling drinks at the price they were twenty years ago, but changed our minds on account of Chris' heart condition! However, he did agree to pay the staff the same wages as 1984, which is why we have no chefs available to cook food, so make sure you've already eaten.'

We received extensive publicity in the local newspapers regarding celebrating twenty years as licensees in the same pub and so were in no doubt a huge turnout was imminent.

We were right, there must have been well in excess of 200 people standing outside listening and dancing to the music. Fortunately it was a beautiful hot summer's day and evening, - the amount of people who turned up would never have been able to squeeze inside the pub. There were so many faces from the past and present, and numerous friends who all came to see us and rock the night away.

On this occasion we didn't get drunk, it was so busy we never got a chance to have a drink, so at least we didn't suffer the following morning with a hangover!

The raffle was a huge success and we managed to raise £1,275 for Motor Neurone Disease.

****

No 35 February 2008
The Gig Guide

EASTERN   FREE

The
WALNUT TREE

Tel 01603 620166   **SHADES**   OLD P. O. COURT

NORWICH
RESTAURANT & BAR
DINING THE *AMERICAN* WAY
PRIME STEAKS, RIBS, BURGERS, FISH, COCKTAILS.
COLD BEER & *HOT* MUSIC

LIVE MUSIC IN FEBRUARY

Thurs   7th THE DAVE THOMAS BAND
Thurs 14th THE KENO KINGS
Thurs 21st BEYOND DUPLICATION
Thurs 28th PAUL TINKLERS BLUES BAND
Thurs   6th RAMON GOOSE

FREE ENTRY FOR PRICELESS MUSIC
THE BEST INTERNATIONAL BLUES BAR IN EAST
ANGLIA
HASTA LA VISTA! (You'll Be Back)
(Voted Best Bar, Best landlord, Best dressed man, Best all round Mr nice guy etc etc)

NEWSPAPER ARTICLES

Newspapers writing an article about your business is the best form of advertising and doesn't cost a penny – that is, as long as the article is complimentary; bad press can ruin your good reputation over night.

In 1986 the headlines for an article about tourism was: 'WE'RE NOT MISERIES'

Britain was being slammed as an ill-mannered place and a real turn off for foreign visitors. Waitressess and waiters were accused of being surly, bar staff were miserable and clock watching, and British staff were making tourists feel uncomfortable.

The press interviewed Chris and the bar staff to get their opinion about this and took photographs of Chris, our bar girl and me – all smiling and happy looking.

I'm not sure why the press came to talk to Chris, because he was always renowned for being a grumpy, obnoxious old git, who didn't appear to smile much. However, we were happy to oblige; it was all free advertising and would certainly give the customers ammunition to take the piss out of Chris.

The comments on the above statement which were printed in the paper from Chris were:

'The Walnut Tree is the happiest, most welcoming pub in Norwich; there's never any tension or bad vibes here'.

Chris did get the piss ripped out of him for weeks afterwards by regular customers who kept waiting in anticipation for the welcoming greeting as they walked in for a drink – they waited a long time.

In 1987 The Walnut Tree was the first pub to sell American Budweiser lager on tap in Norfolk. To begin with, the beer was run for a trial period through Norwich Brewery, who were eager to test the reactions from customers on the lager being supplied on draught, as well as sold in a bottle. It was sold for £1.20 a pint, which in 1987 was expensive. The final price we sold it at in 2007 was £3.20 a pint!

The article regarding the Budweiser was titled: 'GOOD BUDDY' with a picture of Chris and I, along with a staff member and an American yellow cab, straight from the streets of New York, which used to ferry people to feasts celebrating Thanksgiving where they drank plenty of Budweiser.

The cab was parked outside the Walnut to mark the Norwich Brewery Company's official launch of draught Budweiser in East Anglia.

The article pointed out that, although the lager had only just been promoted in the last couple of weeks, we were already selling 600 pints a week. We were the biggest outlet for Budweiser in East Anglia!

In1988 there was an article on how to get rid of a hangover: 'THE HAIR OF THE DOG'

'The drinker's dilemma, the boozer's burden or the nocturnal nightmare, call it what you will, the hangover is never quite as much fun as the night before.

Chris Gudgin, at the Walnut Tree Shades, said the best thing to cure a hangover was to jump in the shower (cold) with a Bloody Mary. If you don't have anyone called Mary, this could be a problem.'

In 1991 we employed an Australian barman who we nicknamed Skippy. The tabloid press thought it a good idea to take a picture of me pretending to pour a pint of beer over Skippy (holding a boomerang) as England were playing Australia in the rugby finals at Twickenham.

The headline: 'RUGBY FEVER HITS CITY'

Skippy remarked that: 'The Poms will come out hard, but I think we'll win in the end.'

The article went on to say how city pubs and clubs were busy stocking up on Australian beer, as fans head down to their local in time for the England v Australia kick off.

We certainly weren't stocking up with extra supplies of beer. We knew nothing about rugby, or football, in fact we weren't even interested in it. So we were definitely not one of the pubs people would come flocking into in the hope of watching any sport on our miniscule television.

However, we didn't mind having the article printed, after all, it did help to promote the pub.

Skippy was right – England lost the game.

In 1992 there was a whole page promoting our new restaurant menu and mentioning the different meals we had on offer. Positioned around the article were adverts from many of our suppliers, wishing us every success for the future, and saying how pleased they were to be associated with us.

Philip Browne (a friend of ours who owned a men's outfitters in Norwich) also published an advert on the page. However, his announcement read: 'Loads of alcohol and abusive language from Chris Gudgin.'

In 1995 two pictures of Chris appeared in the press; one with him shaking a cocktail, the other with him holding a shooter.

The headline read: 'MEET THE COCKTAIL CONJURER'

'While people associate cocktails with blissful holiday evenings, there remains a steady demand for the tasty mixtures and concoctions back home. Chris Gudgin has been mixing cocktails for more than 20 years and is a self-styled specialist at the art. Today, around 100 are listed on the pub's menu. He is also doing a new line in shooters, test tube concoctions where the drinks are layered rather than mixed. It's a delicate operation and can be prone to disaster.'

In 1997 a half page article in the paper mentioning several restaurants who catered for vegetarians and the quality of food served. Um, we didn't cater for vegetarians much as you will be able to tell as you read on.

The headline read: 'WHERE CAN YOU EAT OUT IF YOU ARE VEGETARIAN?'

'The Walnut Tree Shades, a great place for cocktails, but with very little choice as far as vegetarian food goes. For £2.90 you can have a veggie burger, which is quite reasonable, but is 50p more than a meat burger, which isn't fair, or veggie nachos which isn't the most exciting alternative. All in all the Walnut Tree boasts a fun Tex Mex atmosphere, but is pretty hopeless if you're not into great hunks of charred meat.'

In 1998 a half page spread in the paper showed an unusual picture of Chris – he was smiling!

The headline: 'GIVE THE CUP A RED CARD!'

'The World Cup has already hit fever pitch and it has not even started yet. But what happens if you are not soccer-crazy – how can you score a football-free summer?'

It went on to say:

'The world does not have to revolve around football this summer. For five solid weeks most people you know will remain slumped in front of the TV in their World Cup strips. Some pubs in Norwich are declaring themselves football-free zones. The Walnut Tree is avoiding TV screenings. 'I don't like football' said Chris Gudgin, 'so I'm going on holiday.'

Not the best bit of media attention published about the pub, or Chris' views about football not being shown in the Walnut. The philosophy behind his comments were that we may attract a lot of women or people disinterested in football during the World Cup.

Wrong - when the World Cup was televised it was the worst four weeks trade we ever encountered during all our years at the Walnut – serve us right!

In 1998 the headline read: 'WE ARE NUDGING OUT THE CRIMINALS'

The tabloid press featured the problems caused by amusement arcades and the war against thieves stealing thousands of pounds from fruit machines every year.

The article mentioned that our machine in the pub had also been targeted three times and then went on to say how security had been increased at the amusement arcades, and that the mechanics of fruit machines been made more secure to deter the criminals.

There was also a picture of a fruit machine and another one of Chris – unfortunately, you could see, and read very easily, a sign pinned on the wall behind his head, which said,

'Arrive stoned'. – Not the best picture to print when you have been discussing criminals.

In 2004 Chris had a double spread in the local paper on 'His Life' saying that landlord reveals his true passions in life!

It started by saying that, although other city pubs may have changed beyond all recognition over the last two decades, the Walnut Tree Shades had not.

'This week Chris Gudgin celebrates 20 years at the pub. He answered questions after mentioning that he had still hung on to his marbles for 20 years.'

Q. List five words that describe you.
A. Unkempt, scruffy, haven't grown up.

Q. What is your earliest memory?
A. Wearing woollen swimming trunks that went all baggy when I came out of the sea.
Q. What was your favourite childhood toy?
A. My teddy bear, and his name is 'Teddy.'

Q. When did you last lose your temper?
A. I don't lose my temper, believe it or not. When I throw people out of the pub I do it nicely.
Q. What is the best piece of advice you've ever been given?
A Don't get a pub if you want to maintain your sanity. I ignored it.

In 2004 another two page spread was published, one week after Chris' Life Story had been printed. The regular customers were moaning that every time they opened the paper there was a picture of Chris' ugly face looking at them,

'For God's sake, you're in the bloody paper again, haven't they got anything more interesting to write about, other than you? Is the name of the newspaper going to change soon to 'Gudgins News?'

The editorial mentioned the city's pub scene had changed beyond all recognition since Chris and Jude Gudgin took over at the Walnut Tree.

It mentioned the pub history, memorabilia on the walls, the restaurant, the food and drinks we promoted and our life before and since taking the pub over.

It went on to say how Norwich had changed over the past two decades with new developments and pedestrianisation on many streets.

It referred to the celebrations taking place for our anniversary and the fliers I had printed which mentioned we were considering selling drinks at the price they were 20 years ago, but changed our minds.

The headline: 'STANDING THE TEST OF TIME IN AN OLD CITY PUB. PUBLICANS CELEBRATE TWO DECADES IN SAME PREMISES.'

It went on to say:

'I'm the grumpy old git behind the bar. Jude's the skinny bird in the restaurant. I think back to when I was young and used to go into pubs. There was always an old geezer behind the bar – now I'm the old geezer, and people have been known to call me the miserable old sod behind the bar; they can call me what they like, just as long as they give me their money.'

Chris and Jude's marriage has also survived 20 years of working together. 'We pass each other on the stairs a lot. We don't row, because I'm always right', says Jude.

In 2004 just to make the customers even more pissed off with reading about us and our life at the Walnut Tree, the paper did yet another full page article, just a few weeks after the previous two.

This time it concentrated on the restaurant, although it again mentioned the history and concept of the pub and our 20 years of being landlords, – just in case someone may have missed reading about it several times before.

The headline: 'TWO DECADES AND STILL GOING STRONG'

And of course it had to portray the fact that: 'Chris is still the grumpy old git behind the bar and Jude is still the skinny bird in the restaurant.

In 2005 a few months had elapsed before the Evening News decided to do another page article on the pub along with a few pictures.

This was entitled: 'A PROPER HONEST BOOZER.'

This article portrayed the different types of pubs:

The 'Chavs' favourites were run-down dens and sold drinks cheaper than their undesirable clientele.

At the other end of the spectrum was the yuppies' choice; these were the latest bars in town that had had thousands of pounds spent on them, and had as much natural character as the pretentious drinkers that resided in them.

In that environment the average person was often left wandering around town looking for an oasis of charm in a characterless desert. One such oasis was the Walnut Tree Shades.

'OK- it may be a little rough round the edges but it hasn't just got character – it's got soul! A plaque on the wall proclaims 'unattended children will be kidnapped and sold into slavery' and this seems to sum up the landlords dry humour. Don't expect polished service here either.'

There's a genuine take it or leave attitude and this makes a refreshing change from the sickeningly artificial bar staff that you often get.

The Walnut is a great choice for anyone who prefers the character of a genuine pub to the gloss of a trendy bar and is in danger of spontaneously combusting if they hear one more cheesy track from today's fickle charts!'

The 2007 headline was: 'THIS GEM IS A FIRM FAVOURITE'

The local paper seemed to enjoy repeating everything written about us many times before, - but with a different headline, which was perfectly acceptable as far as we were concerned.

If we paid for an advertisement printed in the newspaper it would cost several hundreds of pounds. So we were more than happy for them to write about us for nothing and publish photographs of the pub.

Although the article was gracious throughout, it finished by saying:

'They have an extensive cocktail list, but don't expect sleek, sophisticated modernity. This has a battered, old lived-in feel, and its fans wouldn't have it any different.'

In 2007 there had been an excessive amount of controversy about burgers and how they were cooked. The paper published an article with the heading: 'DEADLY BACTERIA ALERT ON RESTAURANT BURGERS'

It mentioned E-coli and various other potentially deadly bacteria which had been found in burgers in restaurants across Norwich in alarmingly high numbers, prompting officials to warn owners not to serve them rare.

The Council would not name the restaurants where dangerous burgers were found but advised customers to be extra vigilant if they wished to continue eating burgers in eating establishments.

This was definitely not an article we were happy to see published, especially as our top selling product was burgers. We were one of the many restaurants who had had their burgers tested, but results were conclusive. Absolutely no evidence of bacteria was found from the samples they took from us.

Neither the press nor the Council were prepared to name and shame the restaurants that had an issue, which was so unfair from our point of view. However, it didn't seem to put people off eating burgers – luckily.

And as the old saying goes: 'This week's news is next week's fish and chip shop paper.' (An old saying because fish and chip shops can't use newspaper to wrap the food up anymore.)

In 2007 here we go again – another full page in the paper. We had been at the pub for 23 years, the history remains the same, the memorabilia hasn't changed and neither has the ambience but the tabloid felt the need to publish it all again.

The headline: 'I'M STUCK IN A TIMEWARP'

'Gastro pubs seem to be taking over the city's entertainment scene but there is one traditional boozer which has successfully remained the same for 23 years and whose landlord would never want it any different.'

The tabloid asked Chris a few personal questions about how he enjoyed his free time and where his favourite beach was. His reply: 'Brancaster Beach.'

When I read the article, I said, 'Where on earth is Brancaster Beach? We've never been there.'

It was the first thing that came into his head whilst being interviewed, so I made him promise we must visit 'his favourite beach' as soon as we had time.

In 2007 'Eating out Reviews' published in the local paper gave us another page spread, with the headline: 'A TRIED AND TESTED FORMULA'

'A 'Big Mac' has got nothing on the burgers at this Norwich institution. They are the type of burger you need hands the size of shovels to pick up in one piece. Culinary fashions may come and go, but here nothing changes. There's something reassuring about that. Why change a winning formula?

We ate a hickory burger with added cheese, bbq sauce and a mass of sweet grilled onions, which we tried to pick up, but when it spilled everywhere, had to opt for knives and forks – bet they won't resort to such namby pamby things on Route 66.

It was all flavoursome, tasty and most of all filling. You know what you're going to get and cannot argue with it. Yet I couldn't get too excited by it either.'

On Tuesday May 13th 2008 was the final editorial the Norwich Evening News ever wrote about the memorabilia and history of the pub before we retired from the business and left the Walnut forever.

The article showed a picture of Chris – nearly smiling - while he was leaning on the jukebox with the headline: 'LANDLORD CALLS TIME ON HIS CAREER BEHIND THE BAR'

'A city centre pub will never be the same again for many punters when a popular landlord calls it quits, after more than 30 years in the business.

Asked why he was quitting, with tongue firmly in cheek, Mr. Gudgin said,

'Because I'm old, knackered, worn out and don't like people anymore. My one ambition when I retire is to go to sleep on the same day I wake up.'

His wife Jude, who runs the pub with him, is looking forward to spending hot summer days in the garden.

'We will miss the Thursday band nights. Some of our customers are upset, some are traumatised, and some are even seeing counsellors.'

Apart from the press releases we received, there were also many articles written about the pub and restaurant in various magazines, books and brochures supplied to tourists and locals.

The East Anglian Tourist Board: 'The Walnut Tree Shades is well worth seeking out because it is a pub that is a bit different. Chris and Jude Gudgin are the cheerful landlords whose keen sense of humour is much appreciated by the regulars.

The pub is famous for potato skins all served with dips; ribs and large portions of steak are very much in evidence.

It is fun to eat and drink here and it will not hurt your pocket.

The staff are very welcoming and helpful and all in all it is a well run successful operation.'

A magazine called 'Out and About' wrote: 'Infamous proprietor, Chris Gudgin is, without a shadow of doubt a unique character, and has managed to take a little piece of America and drop it in Norwich. Upstairs is one of the finest American Style restaurants I have visited. I would highly recommend a visit at any time.'

****

The Lonely Planet Guide: 'The best kept secret in Norwich, selling an excellent steak diane and well worth a visit.'

****

We received many, many reviews posted on the internet, complimenting the food, drink, and ambience; there were also some funny ones and some less flattering comments.

****

'This place serves the best burgers in the whole of Norwich! The service is friendly, funny and fast and leaves you not wanting to leave.'

****

'Considered by some drinkers to be a 'hidden' jewel in the heart of Norwich, its ambience helps attract a good clientele and conversely creates a formidable force field that effortlessly repels the occasional gangs of witless wankspurts who wander through Norwich city centre. It is a complete muppet-free zone.'

****

'The Walnut is great as you will never be eating alone. Once when I went, the pub provided some company for me, unfortunately I had already started eating my lettuce. And rather than leaving me its telephone number, it left a trail of slime across the table. Aren't blind dates the best. I know that I'm not really that picky, but I don't date slugs.'

Someone replied to this posting on the internet:

'I'm in no position to turn down a slug….. Did you get it's number?'

****

'There is not a whiff of the forced crappiness that sometimes affects pubs which try to conjure up character by ramming every available space with visual bollocks, as clearly the Shades has been put together with some style and a large dollop of care. Hence, it is more likely you'll pause to examine each separate hanging and sign, rather than walk to the landlord and ask him whether his pub was furnished by a car boot sale or a skip.

There is a joyful ambience – helped by flawlessly polite staff which undoubtedly helps attract a good clientele.'

****

'One of my favourite pubs in Norwich – great atmosphere and music (although sometimes turned up so loud you can't actually hear each other) and the food upstairs is nice too, only other problem is the grumpy barman but don't let him put you off.'

****

Several local Norfolk bands produced a newsletter where we invariably received a mention; also the gig guides advertising the month's events often made a few comments.

'Worlds Apart' sent a newsletter out to their followers once a month and we often received a mention if they had played at the pub or were about to.

'We had our debut gig at the Walnut and thanks to the brilliant crowd, managed to take the roof off the place! Three encores later.'

One of their newsletters showed a section 'spot the difference' (which consisted of pictures of Chris and the band) for people to find the alterations and send in five reasons why you think Chris Gudgin is a jolly nice chap, but don't worry if you can only think of one – it'll probably be more than anyone else can!)

****

There were occasionally articles published in the press from different musicians on their likes and dislikes in the music industry.

Ron Sayer, a musician who often played with his band in the pub, was asked, 'Where do you most love playing?'

'We play a lot of places locally and I like them all, but we love the Walnut best (possibly because of the landlord's amenable nature and sunny disposition hah!')

****

An article about a London based band called Texas Thunder said, 'Landlord Chris Gudgin's been flying the flag for the blues for many years, and if I didn't live 50 miles away, I'm sure it would become one of my locals! Not the biggest bar in the world but has a great atmosphere.'

****

A newsletter written by a local band '4D Jones' who often played at the pub was circulated to their fans, always giving us a mention when they were due to play.

'Always a pleasure, seldom a chore. One of the last decent pubs in the city; this may be the last time we play here before it is sold. With Chris at the 'controls', Gawd help us if he ever flew a plane.'

****

Keno Kings were another excellent local band who produced a newsletter and loved to make comments about Chris before and after their gig at the pub.

'Another great evening at the pub, that is if being man-groped from behind by Chris Gudgin can truly be regarded as great!'

****

'Very pleased to report much less man groping from the Gudge last night. And what a great night of in-yer-face R&B it was. Enthusiastic crowd support, with the Keno Kings sweet rendition of 'Happy Birthday for Jude' was beyond compare.'

****

'The Keno Kings notched up their 500th show at the Walnut Tree which enjoys a reputation as Norwich's premier R&B pub venue, where bands and audiences – and legendary landlord Chris Gudgin – combine to create the best atmosphere in town.'

****

Evening News Music Notes: 'This week it is farewell to Chris Gudgin at the Walnut Tree Shades.

It's rare these days to find someone who has supported the Norwich music scene for an entire business life. He deserves a medal surely for that alone.

He is one of Norwich's characters, a larger than life personality, a friendly smiling face, well most of the time.'

****

HOW TO MAKE
SHOOTERS

*These are short, potent drinks that are mixed with a
combination of spirits and liqueurs, served
in a shot glass.*

*Pouring and floating the liquid is done by using the back of a spoon to gently
float the ingredients already in the glass.
Remember: Apply the theory of specific gravity! heavy spirits sink, and lighter
liquid rises – so don't layer them in the wrong order.*

MONKEY'S LUNCH

*½oz Kahlua or Tia Maria
½oz Crème de Banana
½oz Baileys*

*Pour Kahlua into a shot glass.
Float the Crème de Banana on top.
Float the Baileys on top of second layer.*

B.52

*½oz Kahlua
½oz Baileys
½oz Grand Marnier or Cointreau*

*Pour Kahlua in a shot glass.
Float Baileys on top.
Float Grand Marnier on top of second layer.*

AWARDS

The first award we received was in 1992 for runner up in the Innkeeper of the Year competition, organised through Norwich Brewery. In later years we won another award for the best music venue, even though there was only one other music venue in that category of the competition.

One day in 2007 we received some junk mail, which was usually slung straight in the rubbish bin. However this particular day a few lines in a magazine caught our eye announcing the Eastern Evening News and the Norfolk and Norwich Licensed Victuallers Association (NNLVA) were showcasing the public's favourite services and venues competition for 'The Best of the Best' going out awards for 2007. It was the first of its kind and the result of collaboration between the NNLVA and the Evening News to recognise the 'best of the best' in the licensed trade.

They had selected different categories in the leisure industry based in Norwich and Norfolk, ranging from the best loo to best restaurant, best taxi company, best lunchtime menu, best DJ, best door supervisor, best manager, best customer service, best bar, best nightclub, best bar person, best community service, best family venue and best live music venue.

Voting was in two stages, the first being nominations from the general public. Then the venues with the most votes would be put through to the finals.

The closing date for the first stage of the competition was in a week's time, so if we were going to enter there was only a minimum amount of time left.

This started as a joke, especially as time was not on our side. To have any chance of winning through nominations let alone getting to the final stage, we had to move fast, as they announced a vast number of votes had already been cast.

I printed off some strips of paper on the computer, with the website details for people to vote on, and the categories we would like to be nominated for, or any other categories people may think we were worthy of (except the best loo!)

Our toilets could win the worst toilets, but certainly not the best. Let me just point out that they were always clean. That's it - they were clean - and nothing else.

The hand-dryer blew out warm air capable of drying your hands in about two hours if you were lucky. There was a container which said hand wash on the label, but when empty it was replaced with washing up liquid, diluted with water.

Sometimes there was toilet paper, but only when someone was brave enough to tell Chris there wasn't any left. He may give them a tissue or tell them to drip dry. You were in big trouble if you needed a poo, especially the men's toilet which only had half a door.

Anyway, that's enough toilet talk and the reason why we didn't stand a cat in hell's in chance of winning that category.

We spent the following week telling people, or should I say threatening them, to go on the internet and vote or text for us. We gave out our slips of paper for people to pass round their offices at work.

To be honest, with only a week for people to vote we really did not think we had a chance of coming anywhere, but it was a bit of fun.

A couple of weeks after the closing date, a letter dropped on the doorstep.

'Congratulations' you are in the finals for:- The best bar, The best live music venue and Chris for The best bar person.

Well, laugh, we couldn't stop. We were in the finals for three categories. It was actually quite ironic as we hadn't even noticed the 'best bar person' category, so hadn't threatened people to vote for that one.

It wasn't until we began telling everyone about Chris being in the finals, that it emerged that many of the customers who had voted for him did so only because he was such an obnoxious, grumpy old git; after so many years of working behind a bar they felt he did deserve some recognition.

The next stage of the competition was attending an event to meet the rest of the finalists. We were greeted with champagne and met our competitors who thought it hilarious we had managed to get into three categories, especially the one for Chris in the Best Bar Person group.

We were up against three other bars in the 'Best Bar Category' which were completely different in every aspect from the Walnut. The first was Rocco's - a large venue, the second was Indulge - a fashionable bar, and the third was the Lawyer, which had been opened for two years after a major refit.

All were very modern with a contemporary feel, unlike the Walnut which was dark, dingy, rough round the edges and had not been decorated for years.

We didn't feel we had the slightest chance of winning the 'Best Live Music Venue' as the other finalists we were up against were the University of East Anglia, the Norwich Arts Centre and the Waterfront, the three principal music venues in and around Norwich who all played different kinds of music every night, and had the capacity of admitting several hundred people at any one time. Our little bar held 100 people and we put on live music once a week.

It certainly didn't seem a very fair contest from our point of view; if we'd been up against other pubs doing live music, we may have had a chance.

Chris being nominated for the Best Bar Person was definitely a different kettle of fish, he was competing against someone young from the Eagle Pub, a young girl from the Lawyer, and another youngster from Rocco's.

Chris was 61 years old, and had been working behind a bar since before the other finalists were even born. So yes, he deserved to win that category.

Nick, who owned the Lawyer Pub, told Chris he should win and would vote for him, even though one of his staff was in the final. He continued by saying to Chris,

'Well, at least look happy about it you miserable bastard.'

The organisers of the event explained the final stage of the competition which entailed further voting from customers by sending a text message or going online.

After a few speeches, they tried to encourage everyone to buy printed cards to give out to customers, to print banners, do mailshots and mass emailing and printed special tee shirts - in fact all conceivable ways for us to spend money in publicising the event and gaining votes.

The prize for the winners in each category was – nothing, but you did receive an award to display in your bar.

A holiday for two would have been nice. Oh well; hopefully the publicity would be beneficial whether we won or not.

The final award ceremony was to be held at Mercy nightclub with an awards party in Roccos in January. Consequently there was a month in which to get people voting.

December being our busiest month of the year meant I unquestionably had no time whatsoever to spend coming up with ideas for voting strategies, let alone for organising printed cards and banners to display, unlike some of the finalists, who obviously spent quite a lot of money and time promoting and marketing their pub for voting, by getting the staff to wear tee-shirts such as 'Vote for the Lawyer,' and posh printed cards handed out to every customer.

Oh well, whatever!! Other finalists were really pulling out the stops to win.

I quickly typed the internet details, and text details on scraps of paper and put those in all my Christmas Cards to send and hand out to customers. I made a couple of crappy posters for the walls and that was that.

At the beginning we weren't particularly bothered if we won or not, but on reflection felt it would be nice to receive some appreciation and recognition after being licensees at the pub for the previous 23 years.

The staff all entered into the spirit of the competition by trying to get people to vote. When regulars came in the pub, they were immediately asked by Chris and/or bar staff if they had voted yet. If those same customers continued to the restaurant for a meal and would be asked again by my waitress on duty or myself if they had voted for us yet?

'Yes, how many more times are we going to be asked?'

'Loads', would be the reply, 'and make sure you tell everyone you know to vote.'

It did get to a point when people would come in the pub and before they were even spoken to by Chris, would say, 'Before you ask, yes I have voted for you, because we want the grumpy old bastard to win, then maybe it will put a smile on your face.'

By the end of December customers were beginning to get a bit pissed off with us for constantly asking, or should I say, telling them to vote.

New Year's Eve was the last day of voting, and our evening in the Walnut comprised of a ticket-only event with live music played by Egypt to rock us into 2008.

We came up with a plan for a last purge of voting from customers. At 10pm when the majority of customers had consumed several drinks, Chris announced over the microphone that everyone must take their mobile phones out of their pockets or bags.

Everyone conformed but weren't sure why, until Chris proceeded to give exact instructions on which buttons to press and hey presto, the last votes were in.

All we had to do now was wait until the Awards Ceremony to determine the outcome.

We bought tickets for the staff and a few of the regular customers to attend the event and all wore our best bibs and tuckers. So, even if we didn't win anything, at least we were dressed for the part.

On arrival it felt like the Baftas, with the red carpet, except there weren't any famous stars or photographers at the entrance. This was very disappointing as I had been practicing the celebrity pose - you know, the one where you look over your shoulder, lips pouting, and tits out. One slight problem, I don't have any boobs, but the pout I could do!

The finalists had the seating area at the front, everyone else stood near the bar, which pleased our staff and friends.

The evening began with some entertainment before the awards were announced. They had received over 20,000 votes for the categories.

After listening to other categories and winners being announced – not involving the Walnut, especially the pub who won 'Best Toilet.'

Our first category was announced for - the Best Bar Person.

The presenter read out the nominations before broadcasting that the person who had won this category made the best Bloody Marys in town. We knew it had to be Chris.

The noise was unbelievable – mainly from our staff and friends who went wild. It was fantastic to see people standing, cheering and clapping; I felt so proud and happy for him, and I genuinely think that everybody there felt Chris deserved to win - and he did.

He got up on stage, collected his award, waved it in the air gave the 'YES'.

He was a bit peeved they wouldn't let him make a speech, but were probably scared as to what he might say.

After a short break to consume a few drinks and to discover that most of the staff were well oiled with alcohol by now, we told them to continue shouting and cheering as loud as they liked, especially as someone had already asked us if we had bought along rent-a-mob.

After a few more awards were handed out, our name came up for the Best Live Music Venue. Although the cheers were excessively loud when the Walnut's name was mentioned, we didn't win that one.

In retrospect we shouldn't have won it: the other venues were so large and diverse in the music they put on, and we were just a little back street pub with music been played once a week.

The next category announced was for the Best Bar and the nominations were read. As soon as the Walnut Tree Shades' name was mentioned, the announcer could barely be heard above the shouting and screaming from our staff 'Walnut, Walnut, Walnut'.

We won. Chris and I were jumping up and down with excitement, we must have looked so stupid, but who cared - we certainly didn't. We went on stage to collect the award and have press photographs taken.

The atmosphere was great; people were standing, clapping, kissing and congratulating us. It was a tremendous feeling on both our parts. After all the years of hard slog and labour, we had been given appreciation and recognition from all the people who had supported and obviously voted for us.

With all the awards out of the way, the evening continued by consuming more alcohol, and enjoying the celebrations.

The two awards were proudly placed on a shelf in the bar for the customers to see, although it did mean each time somebody picked them up to have a closer look, Chris would polish them afterwards to keep them free of fingerprints. I had never seen him do so much cleaning.

Numerous customers enjoyed taking the piss out of Chris' achievement and hoped he wouldn't be so grumpy in the future, that maybe he would dress smarter, and live up to the accolade of being the Best Bar Person.

'Will I fuck? That's why you all voted for me in the first place, because I am an obnoxious old git!'

****

A SECTION FROM
THE WALNUT COCKTAIL LIST
IN THE 2000's

LOTSA COLADAS
Puerto Rico's most famous drink, blended long, smooth and creamy

PINA COLADA
Large Bacardi Gold, pineapple juice & coconut cream — **£4.30**

BANANA COLADA Large Banana liqueur, Bacardi Gold, pineapple juice, & coconut cream — **£5.80**

CHERRY COLADA Large Cherry liqueur, Bacardi Gold, pineapple juice, & coconut cream — **£5.80**

MELON COLADA Large Melon liqueur, Bacardi Gold, pineapple juice, & coconut cream — **£5.80**

COMFORT COLADA Large Southern Comfort, pineapple juice, & coconut cream — **£4.30**

MARGARITA'S Mexico's favourite cocktail

MARGARITA
Large Tequila, Triple Sec, and sweet & sour mix — **£4.70**

MARGARITA ROYALE Large Gold Tequila, Orange Curacao, and sweet & sour mix — **£5.00**

FROZEN MARGARITA Large Tequila, Triple Sec, and sweet & sour mix, blended with ice — **£4.70**

MARGARITA BLUES
Large Tequila, Blue Curacao, and sweet & sour mix — **£4.70**

MELON MARGARITA
Large Tequila, Melon liqueur, and sweet & sour mix — **£4.70**

MAI-TAI Light Rum, Dark Rum, Orange Curacao, lime juice, grenadine & Orgeat — **£5.30**

MUDSLIDE Vodka, Kahlua, & Baileys — **£5.00**

OLD FASHIONED Wild Turkey, Sugar, Angorsturas & Soda — **£2.20**

POLYNESIAN SLING
Gin, Blackberry liqueur, lemon juice, & sprite — **£4.00**

PLANTERS PUNCH Bacardi, Dark Rum, lemon juice, grenadine, pineapple & orange j. — **£3.90**

SELLING

Slowly recovering from ME, which knocked me for six for quite a long period of time, I began to think about our future in the pub. After 21 years and still working anything up to 70 hours a week, we were tired, enthusiasm was waning, and we didn't seem to have the energy and drive required to run a cut-throat business anymore.

After enduring yet another exhausting Christmas working our butts off while everybody else was enjoying themselves, I kept going over and over in my mind, did I really want to keep doing this?

I know there are always times you don't feel like going to work or aren't enjoying it, but each week seemed to be getting more of a struggle to appear enthusiastic.

Being an employee, there is a choice, if you hate the job – then leave. An employer has no means of escape; you persevere and have to get over any bad feelings and just get on with the job.

Daily tasks and pressures were increasingly harder with new regulations and red tape. The administrative requirements were escalating, and resolving any minor problems on a daily basis was becoming a major issue, and, in a way, was being blown out of proportion.

A particular crisis which may have occurred a few years ago and been easily resolved and rectified without a second thought now seemed to be far more difficult to sort out, making it twice as stressful.

I approached Chris on how much longer he intended to carry on at the pub and I did really feel, initially, he was quite content to continue for some time. Well, that is, until he began to give the matter serious thought.

Spending over 20 years working virtually 24/7, living and breathing the Walnut, feeling knackered all the time, not having the motivation to move the business forward or the energy to put any ideas in motion, we felt that we needed a life for us and not one for the customers.

Of course, there had been some really good times with many memories to treasure, but it was time for us to have quality life together; to enjoy our home and garden, socialise with friends, travel more; to have an evening at home with our feet up, or even do the mundane tasks of decorating and shopping.

After waying up the pros and cons of leaving the Walnut, the decision was made; The Walnut was going on the market.

Ironically, a couple of days later, someone came in the bar before we had even seen an agent or told a soul about our decision. He mentioned he had heard a rumour the pub was on the market for £165,000.

The first local agent had knowledge of the pub and area and was confident he wouldn't have any problem selling our successful business.

He priced it at £165,000 including fixtures and fittings, (exactly the same figure as the rumour! - spooky) after his fees and solicitors' costs, we should end up with about £145,000.

The glossy brochure was printed, describing every aspect of the pub in great detail, with some very impressive photos. In fact, it looked so good I would have been tempted to buy it myself. The pub was ready to be advertised to the general public.

It suddenly felt very scary and worrying and emotions ran high,

Was this the right thing to do? Did we really want to leave our life at the pub?

Before the selling process became common knowledge it was essential to inform the staff so they were completely aware of the situation. Quite a daunting prospect; What would they say? Would they all leave before it was sold?

The first person I told was Julia, a long serving member of staff. As soon as the words came out of my mouth that the pub was going on the market to sell, I burst into tears.

It now seemed so final, it was out in the open and there was no going back. She was absolutely fine, as were all the staff when we told them. Whether some made different comments behind our backs we will never know, but it seemed on the surface they all understood our reasons. We had worked hard for years and needed our own quality time, so they didn't blame us for making the decision.

We assured them their jobs were safe, as new owners were obligated to take on existing staff.

The staff may have approved of our decision, but the customers certainly didn't.

'You can't leave; it will never be the same.'

'Whoever buys it might rip it apart and turn it into a wine bar.'

'Who's going to replace Chris? There's no one on this earth who could be as obnoxious, rude and grumpy as he is.'

Hearing customers genuinely upset that we were selling was a great accolade, but we did try and convince them the pub and restaurant might be even better if the right people took over.

The pub was advertised at the end of May 2005, so our thoughts were if someone came along within the next couple of months, an ideal time to leave would be October and we wouldn't have to do that mad Christmas season. Although the takings are good, as it was our busiest time of the year, we decided our sanity was more important; so yes, October would be perfect.

October arrived, the Christmas bookings were starting to come in. We were very busy and were beginning to feel a little pissed off. That's it for this year, another bloody Christmas to do. Ho fucking Ho.

Six months later, at the end of December, we had heard nothing and seen nobody. The general analysis from the agent for the lack of interest was that nobody local would buy the pub as they didn't feel trade could be increased anymore, nor changes made to the original concept. And finally, we were too hard an act to follow.

Unlike selling a home and having the advantage of using several agents to sell your property, with commercial premises you have to give exclusivity to one agent at a time for a minimum period of six months.

We changed agents to one of the biggest and most nationally known for selling public houses. Their fees were expensive but they assured us they would have no problem selling our business priced at the same valuation as the previous agents.

Another glossy brochure was produced and they began to market our property.

Three weeks later we received our first viewing. A family arrived, - mother, father, daughter and boyfriend, who all appeared very pleasant. We showed them round the building answering questions; it soon became apparent the father wanted to buy a business for his daughter to run. They eventually left, saying they would be in touch soon.

They telephoned a couple of weeks later with a few more questions. Unfortunately, it was a Sunday whilst we were at home and had just consumed two bottles of wine and eaten a large roast dinner, so weren't been particularly professional with our replies.

We told them what hard work it was, a total commitment was vital, and of course we would help out during the transition period. But no, we would not be prepared to continue working alongside them for six months after the sale had gone through.

They didn't buy our pub because, after doing some research, felt we were too hard an act to follow with the reputation and the fact that we were so well known in Norwich, and felt they wouldn't have been able to put their own stamp on the pub or make any changes.

They may not have bought our pub but they did purchase a local bar in Norwich which proved to be very successful.

Maybe they were correct in their logic and we had made a rod for our own backs by making the Walnut too personal. It had always been known as Chris and Jude's place, 'a family run business.'

However, it was inevitable that various emotions go through your mind, yes we did want to sell, but we wanted it to go to a good operator - someone we thought would carry on in the same tradition we had started all those years ago.

This was definitely not the correct attitude to adopt when trying to sell a business. It shouldn't matter who buys the bloody place, just give us the cheque, then we are out of there.

That was how we should have been thinking.

In fact, numerous customers were commenting on the fact that friends, acquaintances and regulars came in especially to see us, because they knew we would always be there.

We had created an institution, where so many customers have heaps of recollections of the Walnut and, in a way, we were part of their memories.

If anyone else took the pub over, the place would never be the same; business would go downhill and toll the death knell of the Walnut.

Shortly after the family viewing we received another. A guy on his own, who seemed to know what he was talking about with regards to the leisure industry. He had plenty of experience working with big companies, and wanted to branch out on his own.

He asked all the right questions regarding sales figures, staff costing and potential for the business. We liked his professionalism and personality and thought he could actually make a go of it.

This time we tried to make sure we gave the answers he would want to hear, as opposed to being slightly negative. However, our replies obviously weren't good enough, as that was the last we heard from him.

Things were looking up - we had another viewing. A guy on his own, looked about 12-years old, but assured us he was 30, and presently working as a manager in a chain pub.

He had as much personality as a wet rag, but keen, really keen and asked lots of questions which were answered enthusiastically by us. He said he would be in touch.

About two weeks later he rang the agent requesting balance sheets and weekly overheads; of course we eagerly obliged.

Another couple of weeks went by and he started drinking in the pub which, of course, was the correct procedure. Potential buyers need to see when the pub is busy and to ascertain what type of clientele were frequenting the pub at different times.

Then the bombshell came. He asked for a quiet word with us, and proceeded to tell us how interested he was in purchasing but didn't have enough capital.

He had tried interested investors and securing loans without any success, so wondered if we would loan him the money.

Well, let's get to the crunch, 'How much is your shortfall?'

'£70,000'. The answer didn't require much thought.

We didn't even know this guy, and he wanted us to lend him nearly half the total purchase price of the business. It was bye-bye to him.

After that episode everything went quiet from the agent. We later found out that they had been inundated with a batch of 500 pubs to dispose of, so it looked as if we had been put at the bottom of the pile.

After six months we chose another big national company, who valued the property at £159,500. They were recommended to us by someone who told us what an excellent job they had done in selling their business. I'm so pleased for them, because we didn't receive a single viewing in six months, even though they told us they had plenty of individuals on their books looking for our kind of business. Their contract was terminated.

When Christmas descended upon us for the second time since the pub had been on the market, it was time to put the Christmas decorations up.

However, when I had put them away the previous year, instead of folding them up neatly and placing them gently in the box, I just slung them in, never visualising I would be the person taking them out of the box a year later to decorate the bar and restaurant. Unfortunately I was, and ended up spending £50 replacing the creased up, broken scraps of tired looking tinsel and streamers that greeted me when I opened the Christmas box.

When the yuletide was over I tidily folded the decorations and put them neatly back in their plastic bags. Good, because the following year, 2007, I was still at the pub to open the Christmas box again!

Three agents had given us unfulfilled promises of selling our pub, so we were feeling very disillusioned with all of them. However, without an agent we wouldn't sell. So I had to have yet another go.

This time, it was going to be on my rules. I didn't want to hear any waffle from the agents, any promises, what businesses they had sold the previous week, or how quick they could sell ours. I had heard it all before, with no conclusive results.

I rang up three more agents, stressing to each one that I wanted a quick unbiased opinion of our business, valuation and summary of their fees, and no waffle. I made appointments for all of them to come in on the same day, at different times.

What a stressful day that turned out to be! The first agent paid no heed to my instructions and consequently started the conversation by relaying the businesses he had sold lately. He showed me his folder containing pie graphs of sales from his company, pictures of other pubs sold and then proceeded to tell me where he had been for lunch the previous day and what he had eaten.

'I am not interested in looking at graphs, hearing about other pubs you have sold, let alone what you ate for lunch; I just want to discuss my business.'

He continued to waffle on until he eventually gave us a valuation, the same as the other agents. I said I would be in touch, but thought to myself, it would be in another life.

The next agent arrived, he was worse than the first one. I couldn't get any straight answers from him and was left with the impression he was more interested in his commission than working for the client. Bye bye.

The third agent arrived, this time a lady. She sat down, introduced herself and stated she wouldn't beat around the bush, would tell us exactly what she thought of the premises and give us a valuation. Hooray, at last, someone on my level.

After a tour of the building she looked at the accounts, and valued the business at £120,000, and said she couldn't promise, even at that price that she would get a quick sale. At least she was honest, and after two hours of listening to crap from other agents, I had had enough. They were to be our next agent.

A few weeks went by, and it began to feel like history was repeating itself; no contact; no viewings.

After a couple of months, a prospective buyer came for a viewing. Our hopes rose, maybe this could be the one. Wrong – a foreign lady breezed in, whizzed round the place in the space of ten minutes, then left.

Another month went by and we had another viewing. A guy came in the pub and ordered a drink, then proceeded to question the staff, how busy was the bar? What type of clientele frequented the bar? What type of bands played live at the pub?

Very unprofessional behaviour, as selling a business is often a confidential matter without outsiders or staff being aware of the situation.

He eventually introduced himself, and was escorted round the bar and restaurant about which he showed no interest whatsoever.

He seemed to place more significance on the flat roof outside our living accommodation, stating he would put some Astroturf down so he could go outside and sunbathe in the summer.

Oh what an excellent idea, as if you are going to have any time basking in the sun. He left and that was the last we heard from him.

Two years had gone by, and nothing, absolutely nothing. Four agents had been unable to sell our business; desperate action was required. I wondered if I could market the pub without the use of an agent.

After scouring the internet, I found a couple of sites to advertise our business. I subsequently typed information about the interior of the pub and restaurant, which was relatively easy, as I used all the best bits of detail compiled on our selling brochures which the four previous agents had produced.

I assembled further information about future potential for the business, including utility figures, gross profit and takings for the past three years. Job done.

We decided to market the property at £120,000. The property was dropping in value due to the economic climate, national property prices falling and the amount of years left on our lease.

It was only a few days before we began to receive enquiries for more details from prospective buyers.

Many enquiries were time-wasters, or people just nosy to see how much turnover we achieved per year. But our first viewing was a couple of guys who were genuinely interested and already knew the pub from drinking there regularly.

They remained in contact for a few weeks, asking various questions regarding the business. Unfortunately, it later emerged that they were unable to collate enough funds for the purchase. That was the end of them.

Questions and many rumours were escalating around Norwich regarding our future.

What were we going to do when we eventually did sell?

Where were we going to live?

Apparently, we were moving to France – no we weren't.

Apparently, we were moving to America – no we weren't.

Apparently, we had bought a hotel in Spain and were moving there – no we weren't.

Apparently, we had bought a Bed and Breakfast establishment in France and moving there – no we weren't.

How rumours start or where they come from has never ceased to amaze me. All I can say is, had they all been true, retirement, when it eventually came, would be extremely busy!

A national newspaper published an article regarding celebrity chefs who, apart from owning several restaurants of their own, also presented cookery shows on television. It went on to say a couple of them were purchasing more pubs and restaurants in the UK – um, very interesting.

Gordon Ramsay – renowned for his attitude, rudeness and bad language in the kitchen was sent a tongue in cheek email informing him that our pub and restaurant was on the market. I pointed out that Norwich needed Gordon, and the Walnut was an ideal proposition for him to consider.

To be honest, I didn't expect even to receive a reply, but he kindly emailed to say that unfortunately he wasn't purchasing any more properties at the present time.

Strange, as shortly afterwards I read in the papers he had just purchased a restaurant in New York for two million pounds. He lied to me! Well, it was worth a try.

I emailed Anthony Worrall-Thompson who had previously owned a pub in rural Norfolk, thinking that maybe he would like a property in Norwich.

I received a very nice personal reply from him – he was only concentrating on purchasing pubs around the London area. OK, so he didn't want the Walnut either.

We completed our third Christmas since going on the market; we were knackered and quite frankly had had enough.

Pub purchase prices were decreasing nationally, potential buyers were finding financial support and funding impossible through the banks. Businesses were of the opinion that a recession was forthcoming, as trade overall was declining, although we seemed to be holding our own at present.

We felt the only option left open, if we really wanted to sell the pub, was to drastically lower the price – again, but with no negotiation from any interested parties.

A few more inconsequential viewings took place, so at least there had been more interest from potential buyers, and we had shown more people round the pub since I began marketing on the internet, than the four previous agents had done collectively.

A couple of guys from Great Yarmouth were interested and spent a considerable amount of time preparing business plans and discussing future ideas for the pub. We began to think our retirement was imminent.

Unfortunately they were unable to raise enough funds to buy the pub and asked if we could lend them £40,000.

A quick reply – No.

They were pleasant, enthusiastic guys who I feel would have been ideal tenants, but we were not prepared to loan them our retirement fund.

If we had received £1 from each customer who came in the pub and said they would love to buy the Walnut, we wouldn't need to sell, it but would have gained enough money to enable us to give it away.

A very smart guy in his 50's, walking with the aid of a stick, arrived for a viewing. Our hearts' sank - another hopeless waste of time – but we went through the spiel, showed him round, although somewhat apathetically and certainly not passionately, or with our usual enthusiasm that is, until he said he was very interested and wished to return with his wife and business partner.

He explained that he was waiting for an operation on his knee, hence the walking stick, and already ran a pub in North Norfolk but would rather be in the centre of Norwich. Now our eagerness rose and we were instantly keen to answer any questions.

They returned a few days later, the business partner didn't say much, glanced round the building, but looked approving. The wife got very excited when she saw the kitchen, especially the chargrill – we were not sure why – it was just a grill.

Finishing the tour, I gave them details of turnover and costs to peruse if they were interested; they left and said they would be in touch.

We thought that would be the last we saw of them, so were very surprised to receive a phone call soon after their viewing, requesting a meeting as they were interested in our business and wished to see us.

Still dubious, and I suppose somewhat disheartened at the whole process of trying to sell the business without any luck, I didn't imagine for one minute they would buy it.

The business partner, husband and wife arrived at our home, asked a few questions, and announced they would like to purchase the Walnut. My legs were shaking; I tried to contain my excitement by restraining myself from jumping up and down and cheering. I still had to appear professional; I didn't want them to suddenly change their minds.

On Chris' arrival at home shortly afterwards, I couldn't wait to say to him,

'Meet the new landlords of the Walnut.'

He looked dumbstruck, as if he hadn't quite heard correctly.

After three years of being on the market, although we may have at long last found a buyer for our lease, we still didn't allow ourselves to get too over-excited at the prospect that our retirement might be forthcoming.

In our heart-of-hearts did we really think they were the right people to take over the Walnut from us?

It didn't matter what our thoughts or opinions were on their suitability. The ultimate decision came from Enterprise Inns, the owners of the building.

The potential buyers would have to attend a gruelling interview before they were accepted and we could all commence the selling process with solicitors.

The meeting went well and Enterprise Inns were happy with the prospective buyers' credibility and future concepts for the pub; consequently they were accepted to become the new landlords of the Walnut Tree Shades!

****

THE SELLING PROCESS

During our third year of attempting to sell the Walnut, our friend Jack, had sold his pub and was going through the selling process with the solicitors. However, his stress levels had escalated and he just constantly moaned and groaned about everything and everybody. I just couldn't understand why; he had a buyer for his pub; it was all going through and he should be thrilled that he would soon be out of the pub industry. Whatever was wrong with him?

Oh boy, we soon found out why he was so grumpy. I really thought our last couple of months at the pub would engender a feeling of euphoria; the end was in sight, there would be a few forms to sign at the solicitors, we would work alongside the new tenants through the transitional period, and then finally organise a leaving party for staff and customers. Then retirement, here we come.

When we bought the pub 25 years previously from Norwich Brewery, a price was agreed from the previous tenant, a meeting was organised with the solicitors to sign on the dotted line, money was transferred and, basically, that was that. I guessed it would probably be a bit more involved after all those years, but never visualised what lay ahead.

To re-assign the lease we required a solicitor; the buyers obviously needed one, and finally Enterprise Inns used a solicitor which we had to pay for.

Under the terms of our agreement and as part of the selling process, certificates for gas, electricity and fire had to be rechecked and new certificates issued.

An asbestos check on the building was necessary, even though the pub was over 100 years old. The cost was £200 for two men to walk round the building rapping their knuckles on the walls in various places for twenty minutes in order to tell us, 'No; we did not have any asbestos.' That was one certificate completed.

A PAT test was obligatory; another £200 for somebody to check every plug used for electric appliances in the building, placing a dated sticker on each one. We received another certificate to say the work was completed satisfactorily and was thus able to pass this on to the solicitor.

The gas appliances in the kitchen had to be checked; no unforeseen problems arose as our equipment had always been looked after and well-maintained over the years.

We used the regular company who normally carried out maintenance checks and issued gas certificates for our equipment. The man serviced the chargrill – fine; he serviced the oven – fine. But then decided, after lots of tutting and oohs and ahs, that he was unable to issue a certificate, as the oven wasn't underneath the extractor fan. Chris' reaction to that remark was, 'Well, it's been there for over 20 years, what's the fucking difference now?'

'With all the new health and safety rules and regulations everything is changing, so what was fine last year was completely unacceptable now.'

He left.

The following day the governor from the company, whom we had known for 30 years came to see what the problem was.

To move the oven would be an impossible task as there physically wasn't anyway else it could go. To change the extractor canopy would cost thousands of pounds and we certainly were not prepared to do that so close to retirement. It was decided, after all, it would be satisfactory under the health and safety regulations, because to swap the oven and fryers over would be more dangerous and as the oven was 90% under the extractor, a certificate would be forthcoming.

The next day another guy came in towards the end of the lunchtime session in the restaurant and started to service the oven – again.

'Why do you need to service the oven again when yesterday it was satisfactory?' I asked.

'Because someone else did it yesterday, and it is my name on the bottom of the certificate, so therefore I have to do the service.'

Great, that's more money!

We left him to it and went home at 3pm.

At 4pm, Neil, who was working in the bar, rang us at home,

'You're not going to be happy, the guy servicing the cooker wants a word with you.'

Neil was dead right, we weren't happy – the cooker had been disconnected. The service engineer had detected a gas leak, but couldn't find the location of the leakage. Therefore the cooker was unsafe to use.

This occurred on a Thursday when the restaurant is always busy in the evening, and now we didn't have a cooker.

Chris got in his car, and with an upturn of shingle in the drive, disappeared at great speed to buy a cooker from the company we always used.

'I need a fucking cooker – now,' said Chris in his politest tone - good thing the guys knew him well.

The prices were anything from £1,200 upwards. They suddenly remembered there was a brand new one in the backyard which had been lent out on loan. Unfortunately, it was in a disgusting dirty state, but we could have it for £750.

'That'll do, but I need it now.'

'Oh no, it's LPG gas, so needs to be converted. No problem, we can sort that out quickly.'

Two of the boys kindly said they would deliver the oven to the pub, but needed a pulley lift. The only way it would get in the kitchen, located on the first floor, was through the window.

Chris rushed back to the pub, by which time it was 5.30 pm. The next problem, would the cooker fit through the window and slot into the already narrow section in the kitchen? The tape measure came out and there was about half an inch to spare, - but only if the window and frame were removed.

The only way the old oven could be removed to enable the new one to be installed was to take every piece of equipment out of the kitchen first. The grill, fryers, griddle and stainless steel table were lifted into the restaurant.

Even with the window and frame removed, the dilapidated cooker still wouldn't fit through and so had to be pushed through the kitchen, passed through the dry store area, onto the fire escape, over the banister and sent crashing to the ground - that was the end of the cooker.

The new oven arrived, was hoisted up to the first floor kitchen window where it just squeezed through. The rest of the kitchen equipment was placed back in its usual position, and we were ready for service.

The saga of the cooker problem began at 4pm, and was resolved with business back to normal by 7.30pm – Phew. Did we need that hassle when it was only a couple of weeks before the changeover date?

Gaining the issue of a new electricity certificate turned out to be an absolute nightmare. The electricians arrived during opening hours and were constantly in the way behind the bar pulling out wires, checking plugs, and turning the music system on and off several times.

In the restaurant, equipment was turned on, then off; one minute we could serve food, and then we couldn't. The fuse box with circuits and trip switches was checked and rechecked. It turned out to be an extremely frustrating day.

Before they would issue a certificate, we needed some electrical work doing to bring our system up to the present regulations of Health and Safety – God, we were getting really pissed off, hearing those words health and safety and new regulations. Nothing was broken, everything was working fine; God, no wonder we had had enough of pub life.

The electricians worked in the pub for three days, pulled wires about and added a few more plugs and hooray, we received a certificate - £1,800 later!

We received a visit from the fire inspector, who was keen to see my paperwork and risk assessment. Were all the log sheets up to date? Did we have a regular routine fire evacuation? Were all the staff trained? Did we regularly check the fire alarm?

Yes, to all questions, of course we did! We received our final certificate, and didn't even have to pay for it. Thank God for that as, due to the amount of money we had already shelled out for certificates and a new cooker, our retirement fund was rapidly diminishing.

There was an unbelievable amount of administration work involved before changeover. Dealing with three solicitors was not an easy task. They kept requiring more documentation, had a constant stream of questions and issues to be resolved, and an endless amount of paperwork to sign. The problems and queries never seemed to cease.

Eventually, after signing on the dotted line, a date was set for the changeover 6th May 2008.

It was really happening, and we would soon be starting our new life together. Now we could organise our farewell party.

****

PRICE COMPARISON DURING OUR
25 YEARS AT THE WALNUT TREE

	1984	1994	2008
Bottled Beer	.85p	£2.00	£3.20
Draught lager (pint)	.90p	£2.00	£3.20
Draught Bitter (pint)	.75p	£1.80	£2.80
Gin and Tonic	.85p	£1.65	£2.80
6oz Cheese Burger and Fries	£2.10	£5.50	£7.65
Rent	£6,200	£28,000	£35,500
Rates	£1,800	£4,319	£11,588
Fuel and Water	£3,188	£9,912	£12,508
Wages	£11,681	£37,328	£56,646

FAREWELL

Our retirement was imminent; we were excited for the future, but looking forward to our farewell party, which would enable us to say good-bye to all our loyal customers who had supported us throughout our 25 years.

I printed flyers and posters which adorned the pub, although word had already escalated around Norwich and beyond, that we were about to leave the Walnut.

Customers were sad,

'You can't go.'

'Gudge you're a legend, no one can replicate you, you grumpy old bastard.'

'It will be the end of an era.'

'The Walnut is an institution.'

People who dined in the restaurant were saying,

'We've come in for the last supper.'

'We won't eat here anymore after you've gone.'

We felt very touched by their comments and were in two minds whether we should start counselling sessions for customers to help them survive the trauma of the Walnut without us there – we decided against it!

Strangely enough, we didn't see much of the new owners during the transitional period before the changeover of the lease and our subsequent departure.

I know, if I was taking over a business, I would want to spend as much time as possible meeting regular customers and being shown how the business was operated but, then again, everyone's different in their approach.

I had always been methodical with administration and organisation of the business and, just because we were leaving, my approach to work didn't diminish. In fact, I went way beyond the call of duty, subsequently spending many hours compiling information regarding every aspect of the daily running of our business to assist the new owners.

The 'farewell gig' was due to take place on Sunday 4th May. We needed plenty of staff to work behind the bar, to allow us to circulate amongst the customers and say our good-byes.

Obviously, all the staff wanted to join in the festivities and not work the entire day and evening. We came up with a plan of action; staff were to work in two-hour shifts, enabling them to enjoy the occasion.

We also managed to get hold of several staff we had previously employed who were happy to come and work behind the bar for a short spell and only for the cost of a couple of drinks – sorted.

The 'farewell gig' would take place in the car park, kicking off with live music from The Keno Kings in the afternoon, then Egypt playing throughout the evening.

I had accumulated many photographs of customers in the pub over the years, and so I placed them on large sheets of paper to pin on the walls of the pub both inside and outside so people could reminisce and see how much they had changed over the years.

I bought a couple of books for people to write comments in that they felt were apt for our departure. Everything was organised, and only a week to go!

We received a dreaded phone call. The new owner had been in hospital and there were a few minor hiccups with the selling process; therefore the date of our departure would have to be changed.

'Shit.'

So close to retirement, but so far away. We were both suddenly very despondent, even at this late stage, the whole selling process could still fall through.

Problems were resolved and the buyer's health improved. Although the date for changeover was now May 8th, instead of May 6th – no worries, it was only a few more extra days of work.

Two days before our 'farewell gig' there was another phone call, to say certain documents were waiting to be signed and forwarded, therefore the date of leaving would have to be changed again.

'Shit, Shit.'

This time we weren't downhearted, we were pissed off; it could all still go horribly wrong.

Our solicitor was doing everything possible to rectify matters so the next, and hopefully final date, was fixed for 22nd May.

There was no time to change the leaving party for a later date, so we decided to continue with the festivities. But we thought to ourselves, at this rate, with problems constantly arising, if the worst comes to the worst, we may possibly be holding a Walnut opening night with us as the new licensees in a couple of weeks' time.

May 4th arrived and the weather was beautiful – at least something was going our way and meant the live music could be played outside in the car park. We arrived at the pub early to ensure the bar was stocked full to capacity with alcohol before we opened at 4pm.

Friends and customers had previously told us they wouldn't miss the event for anything. The local paper had also published an article about our departure and farewell gig.

We knew we were in for a busy day, but it wasn't until we received a phone call in the morning from a friend in Thailand wishing us luck for the future and he was sorry he was unable to be with us that we knew it wasn't going to be 'just busy.' If word of our departure had reached Thailand, we realised we had created a monster of a party.

I cannot lie, but I'm afraid my recollections of the 'farewell gig' are very limited and therefore reflected in my anecdote. No, I wasn't drunk and nor was Chris. The whole seven hours when we were open for business was surreal and, in a strange way, seemed a complete haze.

The bar had only been open for fifteen minutes and already the Walnut was packed with customers. They were appearing in droves, from both ends of the alleyway and by 5pm, there were already about 200 people inside and outside the building.

So much for spending the day circulating with friends and customers; instead we spent the whole time working. Although I did manage to take a small amount of video of people enjoying themselves, – a good job too, as at a later date after watching it, we couldn't even remember seeing many of the people there, let alone talk to them.

The Walnut had always been renowned for good service – but not that day. Although there were plenty of staff on duty working their butts off, the pub had never, ever, been that busy; consequently some people were waiting over half an hour for a drink. Some regulars, who got fed up queuing, went behind the bar, helped themselves, then chucked some money in the till.

I can't imagine how many people passed through the pub during the course of the day but there were several hundred.

Many friends and customers wrote messages in the comment books. There were numerous poignant notes from people wishing us luck in the future, saying that we would be sadly missed at the pub; thanking us for memories they would treasure, and wishing us a well deserved retirement.

There were also plenty of cheeky remarks - most of them directed towards Chris.

'Thanks for being such a grumpy old git.'

'Bollocks to you, you cantankerous bastard, and thanks for undoing our bras and nipping our arses for the past 20 years.'

'You are quite possibly the most miserable, tight, mother-fucker I have ever met – congratulations.'

'I only came in the pub for the abuse.'

'I wish you all the best for the future, but feel sorry for poor Jude who will have to put up with you every day at home.'

'Happy retirement to the most miserable bloke ever to grace a bar, and to the skinniest bird ever to serve fat food.'

Everybody enjoyed the entire proceedings and copious amounts of alcohol were drunk by customers. But as the day turned into evening the staff had also managed to consume several drinks and so were finding it increasingly difficult to work behind the bar.

Even my future son-in-law attempted to serve customers, but was so drunk I sent him on glass collecting duties, along with our daughter who I think probably drank my share of alcohol as well.

We were left with no alternative but to close the pub at 11pm for one reason, and one reason only. For the first time in the history of our years spent in the Walnut, we ran out of everything. There wasn't even a single bottle of beer in the place.

What a night,

Wow.

Did that really happen?

Unbelievable.

It was undeniable that our 'farewell gig' at the Walnut was a resounding success, enjoyed by everybody and was a huge tribute. Many people came to see us; regular customers who had drank in the pub ever since we opened, customers we hadn't seen for years and friends and colleagues, – maybe they were all glad to see the back of us, although from the comments we heard, I don't think so.

Last Orders at The Walnut Tree Shades

Tim, Wendy and Digby, a lovely family, who had been supportive and loyal to us ever since we opened the Walnut, wrote us a poem which I was so touched to receive and I think effectively sums up the feelings of our customers.

Chris, Jude and the Shades
With love from Tim, Wendy and Digby xxxx

The Gudgins aren't here,
Its not very clever.
A Norwich Institution
Now gone forever.

The Shades' not the same,
Our lives are bereft
Chris and Jude have retired.
They've packed up and left.

The building's still here,
The same bricks and mortor,
But will we see Lucy,
Their slim, gorgeous daughter?

And what about Joel?
That clone of old Chris?
His bright little face
Will be sadly missed.

We've watched Chris at work -
The best barman in Norwich.
He'd throw out the idiots.
He never lacked courage!

He'd sometimes be grumpy,
But always was steady.
He'd often be rude,
But he had my wine ready.

New women were shocked -
He'd grope and then kiss!
But still they all loved him.
His skill will be missed.

He'd walk in the bar.
We knew he'd arrived -
Music volume was painful,
Our patience was tried.

Farewell

His cocktails were legendary,
His style was unique!
We enjoyed his company,
We came every week!

And then, lovely Jude!
Her smile, that figure!
We loved all her stories
Will her perfume still linger?

She'd walk in, all glamorous,
Could it be that she's Bowie!
She'd always be funny,
We laughed very loudly.

She controlled the accounts.
Her scrapbooks are good.
She hired all the staff,
And then, there's the food!

Upstairs – her domain.
She made up the dishes:
'Half a pound New Yorker, chilli hot dog, ceasar salad?' –
She knew all our wishes.

We knew it was Christmas.
Out came the same things -
Holly napkins, gold deccies,
Cheap crackers, coloured strings.

If you wanted a party,
Jude knew what to do -
Banners, balloons, funny photos,
Lots of tape, pins and glue.

Its been important to Digby
He first ever came here.
He's grown with the place
Known it, year after year.

Chris and Jude need their freedom,
But we feel very sad.
We've some wonderful memories
But for us, its quite bad.

We'll still eat the burgers,

And drink all the beer -
But it can't be the same ….
Chris and Jude aren't here.

****

We had less than two weeks to go before we really were retired from the pub, so in the meantime carried on our daily routine as usual. Although it did seem a strange scenario - we had just laid on a 'farewell gig,' customers had said good-bye and wished us the best of luck but, we were still at the pub working.

May 22nd, the morning of the changeover had, at long last, arrived. We were at the pub by 8.30am – the earliest we had been there for years!

I had already counted and priced all the stock left in the restaurant. An independent stock-taker was in the process of pricing the remaining minerals, beer, wine and spirits in the bar.

We were expecting to hear from the solicitors by lunchtime at the latest that monies had been transferred and the changeover was complete.

We sat with the new buyers who had already paid us for the stock left in the pub and waited to hear from the solicitors, and waited, and waited. It was 5pm and still no word.

Theoretically, we still owned the lease, but the new buyers had bought the stock, so if it didn't go through at this late stage who was entitled to the day's takings?

At 6pm the buyer's solicitor said they wouldn't exchange contracts as she had discovered a problem when we had extended our lease way back in 1989. It transpired we hadn't paid the stamp duty.

'What stamp duty?'

We were totally unaware that any stamp duty was due and definitely had never been told otherwise.

'So how much is it?'

'£5,000 which must be paid before I can exchange contracts.'

'Shit, Shit, Shit, Oh well, we've shelled out enough money lately; we may as well continue to do so.

By 7pm the Walnut was no longer ours and we handed over the keys to the new owners.

****

AND FINALLY

The Walnut Tree Shades has been our life. When we took over, we were both young with loads of energy – now we are old and knackered.

Maybe we were naughty on occasions and didn't do everything by the book; but who does? It's called, 'Survival!'

Yes, of course, we will genuinely miss the life of the pub. We will miss the customers who had such loyalty towards the pub and made it their own local.

We will miss the staff who were so vital to us.

However, we are looking forward to a new chapter in our lives; when our life is our own, to do what we want to, when we want to.

If that means waking up one morning and saying,

'I don't feel like doing anything today.'

Then great, we don't have to do anything.

We have 25 years of memories from the Walnut which will be treasured forever, so a big thanks to all those people who have contributed.

We have been through recessions, licensing reforms, smoking bans, all day opening.

We've seen trendy places open, then close down, fashions and vogues change, and above all, Norwich has grown considerably, with new developments springing up which have attracted more tourists and shoppers to the area.

The only place that remained in a time warp was the Walnut Tree. It has been an institution that hasn't changed, apart from the occasional bit of decorating and an odd new picture on the wall.

Our life at the Walnut was over – or was it?

No, not quite.

We had only been retired for two weeks when a few problems arose at the Walnut – so being the kind hearted people we were, Chris ended up working behind the bar for a week, and I continued working there for a further six weeks.

We hope the Walnut continues to be a thriving success for future landlords, but for us it's definite; retirement has really commenced, and there is no going back – ever.

****

ACKNOWLEDGEMENTS

First and foremost, I would like to thank all my staff for putting up with us, because without you we wouldn't have been able to operate a successful business, and each and every one of you contributed towards making the Walnut Tree a success – so a huge thank you.

Thank you to Harvey, because he made it possible for us in the beginning with his financial backing and faith in us to run the Walnut Tree Shades.

Thank you to all our loyal customers who supported us and spent lots of money in the pub. Without you we wouldn't have the memories, but more importantly we wouldn't have had a business. So a huge thank you to everybody.

Thank you to our local suppliers: Archer's for top quality meat, Burgers Plus for our renowned burgers and Easters for all our vegetables and salad. A big thank you, because the quality of your food enhanced our restaurant business.

Thank you to all our tradesmen who often helped us out of muddles at a moments notice.

Thank you to all the musicians' who played over the years and gave us such a good reputation for live music.

Thank you to Simon Nicolls (the best solicitor in Norwich) who was the first person to read this book in its rough form, giving me valuable advice and persuading me that I should get it published.

A massive, massive thank you to Wendy, who painstakingly took on the mammoth task of going through my book correcting all my grammar and punctuation errors – and trust me, there were plenty!

Thank you to Richard, Phill and all the staff at Barnwell Print Ltd for their patience on my frequent visits to see them, whilst they tirelessly helped me through the whole production process.

Although nothing to do with acknowledgements for the book, I just want to say thank you to Lucy for being a wonderful daughter and best friend. Love you. xxx

Finally, thank you Chris for doing most of the cooking whilst I spent hours upon hours, months upon months, typing this book. And I don't care what anyone else says - you're not really grumpy! Love you. xxx

****